BARRON'S
POCK
VOCA

Fourth Edition

Sharon Weiner Green

Former Instructor in English
Merritt College, Oakland, California

Samuel C. Brownstein

Former Chairman, Science Department
George W. Wingate High School, Brooklyn, New York

Mitchel Weiner

Former Member, Department of English
James Madison High School, Brooklyn, New York

All inquiries should be addressed to:
Barron's Educational Series, Inc.
250 Wireless Boulevard
Hauppauge, New York 11788
www.barronseduc.com

International Standard Book No. 0-7641-2694-6

Library of Congress Catalog Card No. 2004041036

Library of Congress Cataloging-in-Publication Data
Green, Sharon, 1939–
    A pocket guide to vocabulary / Sharon Weiner Green,
Samuel C. Brownstein, Mitchel Weiner. — 4th ed.
        p. cm. — (Barron's pocket guides)
    ISBN 0-7641-2694-6
    1. Vocabulary. I. Title: Title appears on item as: Barron's a
pocket guide to vocabulary. II. Brownstein, Samuel C., 1909–
III. Weiner, Mitchel, 1907–1985 . IV. Title. V. Series.
PE1449.G66   2004
428.1—dc22   2004041036

PRINTED IN CHINA
9 8 7 6 5 4 3 2

Contents

Acknowledgments

Special acknowledgment is made to the following organization for allowing us to reprint copyrighted or previously published material.

The system of indicating pronunciation is used by permission. From *Merriam-Webster's Collegiate® Dictionary,* Tenth Edition, © 2001 by Merriam-Webster, Inc.

Preface

This book is designed to serve as a handy reference to the spelling, syllabication, pronunciation, part of speech, and meaning of over 3,000 words that appear most frequently on standardized exams like the SAT, PSAT, GMAT, and GRE. It is intended for use by students, executives, secretaries, proofreaders, writers, or anyone else in need of a quick, easy-to-use word reference book.

The plan of *A Pocket Guide to Vocabulary* is straightforward. Designed in dictionary format, each entry contains the word broken into syllables, its preferred pronunciation based on *Merriam-Webster's Collegiate® Dictionary,* Tenth Edition, its part of speech, its meaning, and a sentence illustrating its use. Some entries contain other forms of the word as well.

A detailed explanation of the pronunciation symbols precedes the full list of words; a concise pronunciation key appears at the bottom of each page of the list.

A Pocket Guide to Vocabulary is a power tool. Based on computer analysis of actual published standardized tests, this book enables its users to reach their goal: a strong working vocabulary of college-level words.

Pronunciation Symbols

ə ... banana, collide, abut

'ə, ˌə ... humdrum, abut

ᵊ ... immediately preceding \l\, \n\, \m\, \ŋ\, as in battle, mitten, eaten, and sometimes open \'ōp-ᵊn\, lock and key \-ᵊŋ-\; immediately following \l\, \m\, \r\, as often in French table, prisme, titre

ər ... further, merger, bird

'ər- } ... as in two different pronunciations of hurry
'ə-r } ... \'hər-ē, 'hə-rē\

a ... mat, map, mad, gag, snap, patch

ā ... day, fade, date, aorta, drape, cape

ä ... bother, cot, and, with most American speakers, father, cart

à ... father as pronounced by speakers who do not rhyme it with *bother*

aù ... now, loud, out

b ... baby, rib

ch ... chin, nature \'nā-chər\ (actually, this sound is \t\ + \sh\)

d ... did, adder

e ... bet, bed, peck

'ē, ˌē ... beat, nosebleed, evenly, easy

ē ... easy, mealy

f ... fifty, cuff

g ... go, big, gift

h ... hat, ahead

hw ... whale as pronounced by those who do not have the same pronunciation for both *whale* and *wail*

i ... tip, banish, active

ī ... site, side, buy, tripe (actually, this sound is \ä\ + \i\, or \a\ + \i\)

j ... job, gem, edge, join, judge (actually, this sound is \d\ + \zh\)

k ... kin, cook, ache

k̠ ... German ich, Buch; one pronunciation of loch

l ... lily, pool

m ... murmur, dim, nymph

n ... no, own

ⁿ ... indicates that a preceding vowel or diphthong is pronounced with the nasal passages open, as in French *un bon vin blanc* \œⁿ-bōⁿ-vaⁿ-bläⁿ\

ŋ ... sing \'siŋ\, singer \'siŋ-ər\, finger \'fiŋ-gər\, ink, \'iŋk\

ō ... bone, know, beau

ȯ ... saw, all, gnaw, caught

œ ... French boeuf, German Hölle

œ̄ ... French feu, German Höhle

ȯi ... coin, destroy

p ... pepper, lip

r ... red, car, rarity

s ... source, less

sh ... as in shy, mission, machine, special (actually, this is a single sound, not two); with a hyphen between two sounds as in *grasshopper* \'gras-ˌhäp-ər\

t ... tie, attack, late, later, latter

th ... as in thin, ether (actually, this is a single sound, not two); with a hyphen between, two sounds as in *knighthood* \'nīt-ˌhůd\

th̠ ... then, either, this (actually, this is a single sound, not two)

ü ... rule, youth, union \'yün-yən\, few \'fyü\

ů ... pull, wood, book, curable \'kyůr-ə-bəl\, fury \'fyů(ə)r-ē\

ue ... German füllen, hübsch

ūe ... French rue, German fühlen

vii

v . . . vi**v**id, gi**v**e

w . . . **w**e, a**w**ay; in some words having final \\₍ᵢ₎ō\\, \\₍ᵢ₎yü\\, or \\₍ᵢ₎ü\\ a variant \\ə-w\\ occurs before vowels, as in \\ˈfäl-ə-wiŋ\\, covered by the variant \\ə(-w)\\ or \\yə(-w)\\ at the entry word

y . . . **y**ard, **y**oung, cue \\ˈkyü\\, mute \\ˈmyüt\\, union \\ˈyün-yən\\

ʸ . . . indicates that during the articulation of the sound represented by the preceding character the front of the tongue has substantially the position it has for the articulation of the first sound of *yard,* as in French *digne* \\dēnʸ\\

z . . . **z**one, rai**s**e

zh . . . as in vi**s**ion, a**z**ure \\ˈazh-ər\\ (actually, this is a single sound, not two); with a hyphen between, two sounds as in *hogshead* \\ˈhȯgz-ˌhed, ˈhägz-\\

\\ . . . slant line used in pairs to mark the beginning and end of a transcription: \\pen\\

ˈ . . . mark preceding a syllable with primary (strongest) stress: \\ˈpen-mən-ˌship\\

ˌ . . . mark preceding a syllable with secondary (medium) stress: \\ˈpen-mən-ˌship\\

- . . . mark of syllable division

( ) . . . indicate that what is symbolized between is present in some utterances but not in others: *factory* \\ˈfak-t(ə-)rē\\

÷ . . . indicates that many regard as unacceptable the pronunciation variant immediately following: *cupola* \\ˈkyü-pə-lə, ÷-ˌlō\\

A

a-base \ə-'bās\ (v) lower; humiliate. Defeated, Queen Zenobia was forced to *abase* herself before the conquering Romans, who made her march in chains before the Emperor in the procession celebrating his triumph.

a-bash \ə-'bash\ (v) embarrass. He was not at all *abashed* by her open admiration.

a-bate \ə-'bāt\ (v) subside; decrease, lessen. Rather than leaving immediately, they waited for the storm to *abate*. abate-ment \ə-'bāt-mənt\ (n)

ab-bre-vi-ate \ə-'brē-vē-ˌāt\ (v) shorten. Because we were running out of time, the lecturer had to *abbreviate* her speech.

ab-di-cate \'ab-di-ˌkāt\ (v) renounce; give up. When Edward VIII *abdicated* the British throne, he surprised the entire world.

ab-er-ra-tion \ˌab-ə-'rā-shən\ (n) deviation from the expected or normal; mental irregularity or disorder. Survivors of a major catastrophe are likely to exhibit *aberrations* of behavior because of the trauma they have experienced. ab-er-rant \a-'ber-ənt\ (*adj* and *n*)

a-bet \ə-'bet\ (v) aid, usually in doing something wrong; encourage. She was unwilling to *abet* him in the swindle he had planned.

a-bey-ance \ə-'bā-ən(t)s\ (n) suspended action. The deal was held in *abeyance* until his arrival.

ab-hor \ab-'hȯ(ə)r\ (v) detest; hate. He *abhorred* all forms of bigotry. ab-hor-rence \əb-'hȯr-ən(t)s\ (n)

ab-jure \ab-'ju̇(ə)r\ (v) renounce upon oath. The traitor *abjured* his allegiance to the king. ab-ju-ra-tion \ˌab-jə'rā-shən\ (n)

ab-lu-tion \ə-'blü-shən\ (n) washing. His daily *ablutions* were accompanied by loud noises that he humorously labeled "Opera in the Bath."

\ə\ abut \ᵊ\ kitten, F table \ər\ **further** \a\ ash \ā\ **ace** \ä\ cot, cart \au̇\ **out** \ch\ **chin** \e\ bet \ē\ **easy** \g\ **go** \i\ hit \ī\ ice \j\ **job** \ŋ\ **sing** \ō\ **go** \ȯ\ **law** \ȯi\ **boy** \th\ **thin** \th̲\ **the** \ü\ **loot** \u̇\ **foot** \y\ **yet** \zh\ **vision** \à, k̲, ⁿ, œ, œ̄, ᵫ, ᵫ̄, ʸ\ *see* Pronunciation Symbols

ab-ne-ga-tion \ˌab-ni-'gā-shən\ (*n*) renunciation; self-sacrifice. Though Rudolph and Duchess Flavia loved one another, their love was doomed, for she had to marry the king; their act of *abnegation* was necessary to preserve the kingdom.

a-bol-ish \ə-'bäl-ish\ (*v*) cancel; put an end to. The president of the college refused to *abolish* the physical education requirement. ab-o-li-tion \ˌab-ə-'lish-ən\ (*n*)

a-bom-i-na-ble \ə-'bäm-ə-ˌnə-bəl\ (*adj*) detestable; extremely unpleasant; very bad. Mary liked John until she learned he was dating Susan; then she called him an *abominable* young man, with *abominable* taste in women.

ab-o-rig-i-nal \ˌab-ə-'rij-nəl\ (*adj, n*) being the first of its kind in a region; primitive; native. His studies of the primitive art forms of the *aboriginal* Indians were widely reported in the scientific journals. ab-o-rig-i-ne \ˌab-ə-'rij-ə(ˌ)nē\ (*n*)

a-bor-tive \ə-'bort-iv\ (*adj*) unsuccessful; fruitless. Attacked by armed troops, the Chinese students had to abandon their *abortive* attempt to democratize Beijing peacefully.

a-brade \ə-'brād\ (*v*) wear away by friction; erode. Because the sharp rocks had *abraded* the skin on her legs, she dabbed iodine on the scrapes and *abrasions*. a-bra-sion \ə-'brā-zhən\ (*n*)

a-bridge \ə-'brij\ (*v*) condense or shorten. Because the publishers felt the public wanted a shorter version of *War and Peace,* they proceeded to *abridge* the novel.

ab-ro-gate \'ab-rə-ˌgāt\ (*v*) abolish. He intended to *abrogate* the decree issued by his predecessor.

ab-scond \ab-'skänd\ (*v*) depart secretly and hide. The teller who *absconded* with the bonds went uncaptured until someone recognized him from his photograph on *America's Most Wanted.*

\ə\ **abut** \ᵊ\ **kitten,** F **table** \ər\ **further** \a\ **ash** \ā\ **ace** \ä\ **cot, cart**
\au̇\ **out** \ch\ **chin** \e\ **bet** \ē\ **easy** \g\ **go** \i\ **hit** \ī\ **ice** \j\ **job**

ab-solve \əb-'zälv\ (*v*) pardon (an offense). The father confessor *absolved* him of his sins. ab-so-lu-tion \ˌab-sə-'lü-shən\ (*n*)

ab-ste-mi-ous \ab-'stē-mē-əs\ (*adj*) temperate; sparing in drink, etc. Concerned whether her vegan son's *abstemious* diet provided him with sufficient protein, the worried mother pressed food on him.

ab-sti-nence \'ab-stə-nən(t)s\ (*n*) restraint from eating or drinking. The doctor recommended total *abstinence* from salted foods. ab-stain \əb-'stān\ (*v*)

ab-stract \ab-'strakt\ (*adj*) theoretical; not concrete; non-representational. To him, hunger was an *abstract* concept; he had never missed a meal.

ab-struse \əb-'strüs\ (*adj*) obscure; profound; difficult to understand. Baffled by the *abstruse* philosophical texts assigned in class, Dave asked Lexy to explain Kant's *Critique of Pure Reason*.

a-bu-sive \ə-'byü-siv\ (*adj*) coarsely insulting; physically harmful. An *abusive* parent damages a child both mentally and physically.

a-but \ə-'bət\ (*v*) border upon; adjoin. Where our estates *abut*, we must build a fence.

a-byss \ə-'bis\ (*n*) enormous chasm; vast bottomless pit. Darth Vader seized the evil emperor and hurled him down into the *abyss*.

ac-cede \ak-'sēd\ (*v*) agree. If I *accede* to this demand for blackmail, I am afraid that I will be the victim of future demands.

ac-cel-er-ate \ik-'sel-ə-rāt\ (*v*) move faster. In our science class, we learn how falling bodies *accelerate*.

ac-ces-si-ble \ik-'ses-a-bal\ (*adj*) easy to approach; obtainable. We asked our guide whether the ruins were *accessible* on foot.

ac-ces-so-ry \ik-'ses-(ə-)rē\ (*n*) additional object; useful but not essential thing. The *accessories* she bought cost more than the dress. also (*adj*).

\ŋ\ sing \ō\ go \ò\ law \òi\ boy \th\ thin \t͟h\ the \ü\ loot \u̇\ foot
\y\ yet \zh\ vision \à, k̲, ⁿ, œ, œ̄, ue, ūe, ʸ\ *see* Pronunciation Symbols

ac-claim \ə-ˈklām\ (*v*) applaud; announce with great approval. The NBC sportscasters *acclaimed* every American victory in the Olympics and decried every American defeat. also (*adj*).

ac-cli-mate \ˈak-lə-ˌmāt\ (*v*) adjust to climate. One difficulty of our present air age is the need of travelers to *acclimate* themselves to new and often strange environments.

ac-cliv-i-ty \ə-ˈkliv-ət-ē\ (*n*) sharp upslope of a hill. The car could not go up the *acclivity* in high gear.

ac-co-lade \ˈak-ə-ˌlād\ (*n*) award of merit. In Hollywood, an "Oscar" is the highest *accolade*.

ac-com-plice \ə-ˈkäm-pləs\ (*n*) partner in crime. Because he had provided the criminal with the lethal weapon, he was arrested as an *accomplice* in the murder.

ac-cord \ə-ˈkȯ(ə)rd\ (*n*) agreement. He was in complete *accord* with the verdict.

ac-cost \ə-ˈkȯst\ (*v*) approach and speak first to a person. When the two young men *accosted* me, I was frightened because I thought they were going to attack me.

ac-cou-tre \ə-ˈküt-ər\ (*v*) equip. The fisherman was *accoutred* with the best that the sporting goods store could supply. ac-cou-tre-ment \ə-ˈkü-trə-mənt\ (*n*)

ac-cre-tion \ə-ˈkrē-shən\ (*n*) growth; increase. Over the years, Bob put on weight; because of this *accretion* of flesh, he went from size M to size XXL.

ac-crue \ə-ˈkrü\ (*v*) come about by addition. You must pay the interest that has *accrued* on your debt as well as the principal sum. ac-cru-al \ə-ˈkrü-əl\ (*n*)

a-cer-bi-ty \ə-ˈsər-bət-ē\ (*n*) bitterness of speech and temper. The meeting of the United Nations Assembly was marked with such *acerbity* that little hope of reaching any useful settlement of the problem could be held.

a-ce-tic \ə-ˈsēt-ik\ (*adj*) vinegary. The salad had an exceedingly *acetic* flavor.

\ə\ **abut** \ᵊ\ **kitten**, F **table** \ər\ **further** \a\ **ash** \ā\ **ace** \ä\ **cot, cart** \au̇\ **out** \ch\ **chin** \e\ **bet** \ē\ **easy** \g\ **go** \i\ **hit** \ī\ **ice** \j\ **job**

a·cid·u·lous \ə-'sij-ə-ləs\ (*adj*) slightly sour; sharp, caustic. James was unpopular because of his sarcastic and *acidulous* remarks.

ac·knowl·edge \ik-'näl-ij\ (*v*) recognize; admit. Although Iris *acknowledged* that the Beatles' tunes sounded pretty dated nowadays, she still preferred them to the hiphop songs her brothers played.

ac·me \'ak-mē\ (*n*) peak; pinnacle; highest point. Welles's success in *Citizen Kane* marked the *acme* of his career as an actor; never again did he achieve such public acclaim.

a·cous·tic \ə-'kü-stik\ (*n*) science of sound; quality that makes a room easy or hard to hear in. Disney Hall is liked by music lovers because of its fine *acoustics*.

ac·qui·esce \,ak-wē-'es\ (*v*) assent; agree passively. Although she appeared to *acquiesce* to her employer's suggestions, I could tell she had reservations about the changes he wanted made. ac·qui·es·cence \ak-wē-'es-ᵊn(t)s\ (*n*); ac·qui·es·cent \ak-wē-'es-ᵊnt\ (*adj*)

ac·quit·tal \ə-'kwit-ᵊl\ (*n*) deliverance from a charge. His *acquittal* by the jury surprised those who had thought him guilty. ac·quit \ə-'kwit\ (*v*)

ac·rid \'ak-rəd\ (*adj*) sharp; bitterly pungent. The *acrid* odor of burnt gunpowder filled the room after the pistol had been fired.

ac·ri·mo·ni·ous \,ak-rə-'mō-nē-əs\ (*adj*) bitter in words or manner. The candidate attacked his opponent in highly *acrimonious* terms. ac·ri·mo·ny \'ak-rə-,mō-nē\ (*n*)

ac·tu·ar·i·al \,ak-chə-'wer-ē-əl\ (*adj*) calculating; pertaining to insurance statistics. According to recent *actuarial* tables, life expectancy is greater today than it was a century ago.

ac·tu·ate \'ak-chə-,wāt\ (*v*) motivate. I fail to understand what *actuated* you to reply to this letter so nastily.

\ŋ\ sing   \ō\ go   \ȯ\ law   \ȯi\ boy   \th\ thin   \th̲\ the   \ü\ loot   \u̇\ foot
\y\ yet   \zh\ vision   \à, k̲, ⁿ, œ, œ̄, ᵫ, ᵫ̄, ʸ\ *see* Pronunciation Symbols

a-cu-ity \ə-'kyü-ət-ē\ (*n*) sharpness. In time his youthful *acuity* of vision failed him, and he needed glasses.

a-cu-men \ə-'kyü-mən\ (*n*) mental keenness. His business *acumen* helped him to succeed where others had failed.

ad-age \'ad-ij\ (*n*) wise saying; proverb. There is much truth in the old *adage* about fools and their money.

ad-a-mant \'ad-ə-mənt\ (*adj*) hard; inflexible. Bronson played the part of a revenge-driven man, *adamant* in his determination to punish the criminals who destroyed his family. ad-a-man-tine \'ad-ə-,man-'tēn\ (*adj*)

a-dapt \ə-'dapt\ (*v*) alter; modify. Some species of animals have become extinct because they could not *adapt* to a changing environment.

ad-dic-tion \ə-'dik-shən\ (*n*) compulsive, habitual need. His *addiction* to drugs caused his friends much grief.

ad-dle \'ad -əl\ (*v*) muddle; drive crazy; become rotten. This idiotic plan is confusing enough to *addle* anyone.

a-dept \ə-'dept\ (*adj*) expert at. He was *adept* at the fine art of irritating people. ad-ept \'ad-,ept\ (*n*)

ad-here \ad-'hi(ə)r\ (*v*) stick fast to. I will *adhere* to this opinion until proof that I am wrong is presented. ad-he-sion \ ad-,hē-zhən\ (*n*)

ad-i-pose \'ad-ə-,pōs\ (*adj*) fatty. Excess *adipose* tissue should be avoided by middle-aged people.

ad-junct \'aj-,əŋ(k)t\ (*n*) something added on or attached (generally nonessential or inferior). Although I don't absolutely need a second computer, I plan to buy a lap-top to serve as an *adjunct* to my desktop model.

ad-ju-ra-tion \,aj-ə-'rā-shən\ (*n*) solemn urging. His *adjuration* to tell the truth did not change the witnesses' testimony.

ad-jure \ə-'jü(ə)r\ (*v*) request solemnly. I must *adjure* you to consider this important matter carefully.

ad-mon-ish \ad-'män-ish\ (*v*) warn; reprove. The preacher *admonished* his listeners to change their wicked ways.

\ə\ **abut** \ᵊ\ **kitten, F table** \ər\ **further** \a\ **ash** \ā\ **ace** \ä\ **cot, cart**
\aú\ **out**   \ch\ **chin**   \e\ **bet**   \ē\ **easy**   \g\ **go**   \i\ **hit**   \ī\ **ice**   \j\ **job**

ad-mo-ni-tion \\,ad-mə-'nish-ən\ (*n*) warning. After the student protesters repeatedly rejected the dean's *admonitions,* the administration issued an ultimatum: either the students would end the demonstration at once or the campus police would arrest the demonstrators.

a-dorn \ə-'dȯ(ə)rn\ (*v*) decorate. Wall paintings and carved statues *adorned* the temple. adorn-ment \ə-'dȯ(ə)rn-mant\ (*n*)

a-droit \ə-'drȯit\ (*adj*) skillful. Her *adroit* handling of the delicate situation pleased her employers.

ad-u-la-tion \\,aj-ə-'lā-shən\ (*n*) flattery; admiration. The rock star thrived on the *adulation* of his groupies and yes-men.

a-dul-ter-ate \ə-'dəl-tə-,rāt\ (*v*) make impure by mixing with baser substances. It is a crime to *adulterate* foods without informing the buyer. also (*adj*).

ad-vent \'ad-,vent\ (*n*) arrival. Most Americans were unaware of the *advent* of the Nuclear Age until the news of Hiroshima reached them.

ad-ven-ti-tious \\,ad-vən-'tish-əs\ (*adj*) accidental; casual. He found this *adventitious* meeting with his friend extremely fortunate.

ad-verse \ad-'vərs\ (*adj*) unfavorable; hostile. The recession had a highly *adverse* effect on Father's investment portfolio: he lost so much money that he could no longer afford the butler and the upstairs maid.

ad-ver-si-ty \ad-'vər-sət-ē\ (*n*) poverty; misfortune. We must learn to meet *adversity* gracefully.

ad-vo-cate \'ad-və-,kāt\ (*v*) urge; plead for. The abolitionists *advocated* freedom for the slaves. also (*n*).

ae-gis \'ē-jəs\ (*n*) shield; defense. Under the *aegis* of the Bill of Rights, we enjoy our most treasured freedoms.

ae-on \'ē-ən\ (*n*) long period of time; an age. It has taken *aeons* for our civilization to develop.

\ŋ\ **sing** \ō\ **go** \ȯ\ **law** \ȯi\ **boy** \th\ **thin** \<u>th</u>\ **the** \ü\ **loot** \u̇\ **foot**
\y\ **yet** \zh\ **vision** \à, <u>k</u>, ⁿ, œ, œ̄, ue, ūe, ʸ\ *see* Pronunciation Symbols

aes-thet-ic \es-'thet-ik\ (*adj*) artistic, dealing with or capable of appreciation of the beautiful. The beauty of Tiffany's stained glass appealed to Esther's *aesthetic* sense. aes-thete \'es-ˌthēt\ (*n*)

af-fa-ble \'af-ə-bəl\ (*adj*) courteous; cordial; approachable. Accustomed to cold, aloof supervisors, Nicholas was amazed by how *affable* his new employer was.

af-fect-ed \ə-'fek-təd\ (*adj*) artificial; pretended; assumed in order to impress. His *affected* mannerisms—his "Harvard" accent, air of boredom, use of obscure foreign words—annoyed us: he acted as if he thought he was too good for his old high school friends. af-fec-ta-tion \ˌaf-ˌek-'tā-shən\ (*n*)

af-fi-da-vit \ˌaf-ə-'dā-vət\ (*n*) written statement made under oath. The court refused to accept his statement unless he presented it in the form of an *affidavit*.

af-fil-i-a-tion \ə-'fil-ē-ā-shən\ (*n*) joining; associating with. His *affiliation* with the political party was of short duration for he soon disagreed with his colleagues. affil-i-ate \ə-'fil-ē-ˌāt\ (*v*)

af-fin-i-ty \ə-'fin-ət-ē\ (*n*) kinship. He felt an *affinity* with all who suffered; their pains were his pains.

af-fir-ma-tion \ˌaf-ər-'mā-shən\ (*n*) positive assertion; confirmation; solemn pledge by one who refuses to take an oath. Despite Tom's *affirmations* of innocence, Aunt Polly still suspected he had eaten the pie.

af-flu-ence \'af-ˌlü-ən(t)s\ (*n*) abundance; wealth. Foreigners are amazed by the *affluence* and luxury of the American way of life.

af-fray \ə-'frā\ (*n*) public brawl. He was badly mauled by the fighters in the *affray*.

a-gape \ə-'gāp\ (*adj*) openmouthed. He stared, *agape,* at the many strange animals in the zoo.

a-gen-da \ə-'jen-də\ (*n*) items of business at a meeting. We had so much difficulty agreeing upon an *agenda* that there was very little time for the meeting.

ag-glom-er-a-tion \ə-ˌgläm-ə-'rā-shən\ (*n*) collection; heap. It took weeks to assort the *agglomeration* of miscellaneous items he had collected on his trip.

ag-gran-dize \ə-'gran-ˌdīz\ (*v*) increase or intensify. The history of the past quarter century illustrates how a president may *aggrandize* his power to act aggressively in international affairs without considering the wishes of Congress.

ag-gre-gate \'ag-ri-gāt\ (*v*) gather; accumulate. Before the Wall Street scandals, dealers in so-called junk bonds managed to *aggregate* great wealth in short periods of time. also (*adj*).

a-ghast \ə-'gast\ (*adj*) horrified. He was *aghast* at the nerve of the speaker who had insulted his host.

a-gil-i-ty \ə-'jil-ət-ē\ (*n*) nimbleness. The *agility* of the acrobat amazed and thrilled the audience.

ag-i-tate \'aj-ə-ˌtāt\ (*v*) stir up; disturb. His fiery remarks *agitated* the already angry mob. ag-i-ta-tion \ˌaj-ə-'tā-shən\ (*n*).

ag-nos-tic \ag-'näs-tik\ (*n*) one who is skeptical of the existence or knowability of a god or any ultimate reality. *Agnostics* say we can neither prove nor disprove the existence of god; we simply just can't know. also (*adj*).

a-grar-i-an \ə-'grer-ē-ən\ (*adj*) pertaining to land or its cultivation. Because its recent industrialization has transformed farmhands into factory workers, the country is gradually losing its *agrarian* traditions. also (*n*).

a-lac-ri-ty \ə-'lak-rət-ē\ (*n*) cheerful promptness. Eager to get away to the mountains, Phil and Dave packed up their ski gear and climbed into the van with *alacrity*.

al-che-my \'al-kə-mē\ (*n*) medieval chemistry. The changing of baser metals into gold was the goal of the students of *alchemy*. al-che-mist \'al-kə-məst\ (*n*)

a-li-as \'ā-lē-əs\ (*n*) an assumed name. John Smith's *alias* was Bob Jones. also (*adv*).

\ŋ\ si**ng**   \ō\ go   \ȯ\ law   \ȯi\ boy   \th\ thin   \t̲h̲\ the   \ü\ loot   \u̇\ foot
\y\ yet   \zh\ vision   \ə, k̲, ⁿ, œ, œ̄, ue, ūe, ʸ\ *see* Pronunciation Symbols

al·ien·ate \\'al-yə-ˌnāt\ (*v*) make hostile; separate. His attempts to *alienate* the two friends failed because they had complete faith.

al·i·men·ta·ry \ˌal-ə-'ment-ə-rē\ (*adj*) supplying nourishment. When asked for the name of the digestive tract, Sherlock Holmes replied, "*Alimentary,* my dear Watson."

al·i·mo·ny \\'al-ə-ˌmō-nē\ (*n*) payments made to an ex-spouse after divorce. Because Tony had supported Tina through medical school, on their divorce he asked the court to award him $500 a month in *alimony*.

al·lay \ə-'lā\ (*v*) calm; pacify. The crew tried to *allay* the fears of the passengers by announcing that the fire had been controlled.

al·lege \ə-'lej\ (*v*) state without proof. Although it is *alleged* that she has worked for the enemy, she denies the *allegation* and, legally, we can take no action against her without proof. **al·le·ga·tion** \ˌal-i'gā-shən\ (*n*)

al·le·go·ry \\'al-ə-ˌgōr-ē\ (*n*) story in which characters are used as symbols; fable. *Pilgrim's Progress* is an *allegory* of the temptations and victories of man's soul. **al·le·gor·i·cal** \ˌal-ə-'gȯr-i-kəl\ (*adj*)

al·le·vi·ate \ə-'lē-vē-ˌāt\ (*v*) relieve. This should *alleviate* the pain; if it does not, we shall have to use stronger drugs.

al·lit·er·a·tion \ə-ˌlit-ə-'rā-shən\ (*n*) repetition of beginning sound in poetry. "The furrow followed free" is an example of *alliteration*.

al·lo·cate \\'al-ə-ˌkāt\ (*v*) assign. Even though the Red Cross had *allocated* a large sum for the relief of the sufferers of the disaster, many people perished.

al·loy \\'al-ˌȯi\ (*n*) a mixture as of metals. *Alloys* of gold are used more frequently than the pure metal. **al·loy** \ə-'lȯi\ (*v*)

\ə\ **abut** \ᵊ\ **kitten, F table** \ər\ **further** \a\ **ash** \ā\ **ace** \ä\ **cot, cart**
\au̇\ **out** \ch\ **chin** \e\ **bet** \ē\ **easy** \g\ **go** \i\ **hit** \ī\ **ice** \j\ **job**

al-lude \ə-'lüd\ (*v*) refer indirectly. Try not to mention divorce in Jack's presence because he will think you are *alluding* to his marital problems with Jill.

al-lu-sion \ə-'lü-zhən\ (*n*) indirect reference. When Amanda said to the ticket scalper, "Three hundred bucks? What do you want, a pound of flesh?" she was making an *allusion* to Shakespeare's *Merchant of Venice.*

al-lu-vi-al \ə-'lü-vē-əl\ (*adj*) pertaining to soil deposits left by rivers, etc. The farmers found the *alluvial* deposits at the mouth of the river very fertile.

a-loft \ə-'lȯft\ (*adv*) upward. To get into a loft bed, you have to climb *aloft.*

a-loof \ə-'lüf\ (*adj*) apart; reserved. He remained *aloof* while all the rest conversed.

al-ter-ca-tion \ȯl-tər-'kā-shən\ (*n*) wordy quarrel. In that hot-tempered household, no meal ever came to a peaceful conclusion; the inevitable *altercation* sometimes even ended in blows.

al-tru-ism \'al-trü-ˌiz-əm\ (*n*) unselfish aid to others; generosity. Even at Christmas time, Scrooge refused to give alms to the poor: he was not noted for his *altruism.* al-tru-is-tic \ˌal-trü-'is-tik\ (*adj*)

a-mal-gam-ate \ə-mal-gə-ˌmāt\ (*v*) combine; unite in one body. The unions will attempt to *amalgamate* their groups into one national body.

a-mass \ə-'mas\ (*v*) collect. The miser's aim is to *amass* and hoard as much gold as possible.

am-a-zon \'am-ə-ˌzän\ (*n*) female warrior. Venus and Serena Williams, modern *amazons,* clash with their foes on tennis courts, not battlefields.

am-bi-dex-trous \ˌam-bi-'dek-strəs\ (*adj*) capable of using either hand with equal ease. A switch-hitter in baseball should be naturally *ambidextrous.*

\ŋ\ **sing**　\ō\ **go**　\ȯ\ **law**　\ȯi\ **boy**　\th\ **thin**　\<u>th</u>\ **the**　\ü\ **loot**　\u̇\ **foot**
\y\ **yet**　\zh\ **vision**　\à, <u>k</u>, ⁿ, œ, œ̄, ᴜe, ᴜ̅e, ʸ\ *see* Pronunciation Symbols

am-bi-ence \'am-bē-ən(t)s\ (*n*) environment; atmosphere. She went to the restaurant not for the food but for the *ambience*.

am-big-u-ous \am-'big-yə-wəs\ (*adj*) doubtful in meaning. His *ambiguous* direction misled us; we did not know which road to take. am-bi-gu-i-ty \‚am-bə-'gyü-ət-ē\ (*n*)

am-biv-a-lence \am-'biv-ə-lən(t)s\ (*n*) the state of having contradictory or conflicting emotional attitudes. Torn between loving her parents one minute and hating them the next, she was confused by the *ambivalence* of her feelings. am-biv-a-lent \am-'biv-ə-lənt\ (*adj*)

am-ble \'am-bəl\ (*n*) moving at an easy pace. When she first mounted the horse, she was afraid to urge the animal to go faster than a gentle *amble*. also (*v*).

am-bro-sia \am-'brō-zh(ē-)ə\ (*n*) food of the gods. *Ambrosia* was supposed to give immortality to any human who ate it.

am-bu-la-tor-y \'am-byə-lə-‚tōr-ē\ (*adj*) able to walk. Calvin was a highly *ambulatory* patient; not only did he refuse to be confined to bed, but he also insisted on riding his skateboard up and down the halls.

a-me-lio-rate \ə-'mēl-yə-‚rāt\ (*v*) improve. Many social workers have attempted to *ameliorate* the conditions of people living in the slums.

a-me-na-ble \ə-'mē-nə-bəl\ (*adj*) readily managed; willing to be led. Although the ambassador was usually *amenable* to friendly suggestions, he balked when we hinted that he should pay his parking tickets.

a-mend \ə-'mend\ (*v*) correct; change, generally for the better. Hoping to *amend* his condition, he left Vietnam for the United States.

a-me-ni-ties \ə-'men-ət-ēz\ (*n*) convenient features; courtesies. In addition to the customary *amenities* for the business traveler—fax machines, modems, a health

---

\ə\ **abut** \ᵊ\ **kitten,** F **table** \ər\ f**urther** \a\ **ash** \ā\ **ace** \ä\ **cot, cart**
\aù\ **out** \ch\ **chin** \e\ **bet** \ē\ **easy** \g\ **go** \i\ **hit** \ī\ **ice** \j\ **job**

club—the hotel offers the services of a butler versed in the social *amenities*.

a-mi-a-ble \ˈā-mē-ə-bəl\ (*adj*) agreeable; lovable. In *Little Women,* Beth is the *amiable* daughter whose loving disposition endears her to all who know her.

am-i-ca-ble \ˈam-i-kə-bəl\ (*adj*) politely friendly; not quarrelsome. Beth's sister Jo is the hot-tempered tomboy who has a hard time maintaining *amicable* relations with those around her. Jo's quarrel with her friend Laurie finally reaches an *amicable* settlement, but not because Jo turns amiable overnight.

a-miss \ə-ˈmis\ (*adj*) wrong; faulty. Seeing her frown, he wondered if anything were *amiss*. also (*adv*).

am-i-ty \ˈam-ət-ē\ (*n*) friendship. Student exchange programs such as the Experiment in International Living were established to promote international *amity*.

am-ne-sia \am-ˈnē-zhə\ (*n*) loss of memory. Because she was suffering from *amnesia,* the police could not get the young girl to identify herself.

am-nes-ty \ˈam-nə-stē\ (*n*) pardon. When his first child was born, the king granted *amnesty* to all in prison.

a-mor-al \ˈⁿā-ˈmòr-əl\ (*adj*) nonmoral. An *amoral* individual lacks a code of ethics; he cannot tell right from wrong. An immoral person can tell right from wrong; he simply chooses to do something he knows is wrong.

a-mor-phous \ə-ˈmor-fəs\ (*adj*) formless; lacking shape or definition. As soon as we have decided on our itinerary, we shall send you a copy; right now, our plans are still *amorphous*.

am-phib-i-an \am-ˈfib-ē-ən\ (*adj*) able to live both on land and in water. Frogs are classified as *amphibian*. also (*n*).

am-phi-the-ater \ˈam(p)-fə-ˌthē-ət-ər\ (*n*) oval building with tiers of seats. The spectators in the *amphitheater* cheered the gladiators.

\ŋ\ **sing**   \ō\ **go**   \ò\ **law**   \òi\ **boy**   \th\ **thin**   \t͟h\ **the**   \ü\ **loot**   \ù\ **foot**
\y\ **yet**   \zh\ **vision**   \à, k̲, ⁿ, œ, œ̄, ue, ūe, ʸ\ *see* Pronunciation Symbols

am-ple \'am-pəl\ (*adj*) abundant. Bond had *ample* opportunity to escape. Why did he let us catch him when he had plenty of chances to get away?

am-pli-fy \'am-plə-ˌfī\ (*v*) broaden or clarify by expanding; intensify; make stronger. Charlie Brown tried to *amplify* his remarks, but he was drowned out by jeers from the audience. Lucy was smarter: she used a loudspeaker to *amplify* her voice.

am-pu-tate \'am-pyə-ˌtāt\ (*v*) cut off part of body; prune. Though the doctors had to *amputate* his leg to prevent the spread of cancer, the young man refused to let the loss of his leg keep him from participating in sports.

a-muck \ə-'mək\ (*adv*) in a state of rage. The police had to be called in to restrain him after he ran *amuck* in the department store.

am-u-let \'am-yə-lət\ (*n*) charm; talisman. Around his neck he wore the *amulet* that the witch doctor had given him.

a-nach-ro-nism \ə-'nak-rə-ˌniz-əm\ (*n*) an error involving time in a story. The reference to clocks in *Julius Caesar* is an *anachronism*: clocks did not exist in Caesar's time.

an-al-ge-sic \ˌan-ᵊl-'jē-zik\ (*adj*) causing insensitivity to pain. The *analgesic* qualities of this lotion will provide temporary relief. **an-al-ge-sia** \ˌan-ᵊl-jē-zha\ (*n*)

a-nal-o-gous \ə-'nal-ə-gəs\ (*adj*) comparable. He called our attention to the things that had been done in an *analogous* situation and recommended that we do the same.

a-nal-o-gy \ə-'nal-ə-jē\ (*n*) similarity; parallelism. A well-known *analogy* compares the body's immune system with an army whose defending troops are the lymphocytes or white blood cells.

an-ar-chist \'an-ər-kəst\ (*n*) person who rebels against the established order. Denying she was an *anarchist,* Katya maintained she wished only to make changes in our government, not to destroy it entirely.

\ə\ **abut** \ᵊ\ **kitten**, F **table** \ər\ **further** \a\ **ash** \ā\ **ace** \ä\ **cot**, **cart**
\au̇\ **out** \ch\ **chin** \e\ **bet** \ē\ **easy** \g\ **go** \i\ **hit** \ī\ **ice** \j\ **job**

an-ar-chy \'an-ər-kē\ (*n*) absence of governing body; state of disorder. The assassination of the leaders led to a period of *anarchy*.

a-nath-e-ma \ə-'nath-ə-mə\ (*n*) solemn curse. The Ayatolla Khomeini heaped *anathema* upon "the Great Satan," that is, the United States. To the Ayatolla, America and the West were *anathema*; he loathed the democratic nations, cursing them in his dying words.

an-chor \'aŋ-kər\ (*v*) secure or fasten firmly; be fixed in place. We set the post in concrete to *anchor* it in place. an-chor-age \'aŋ-k(ə-)rij\ (*n*)

an-cil-lar-y \'an(t)-sə-ˌler-ē\ (*adj*) serving as an aid or accessory; auxiliary. In an *ancillary* capacity, Doctor Watson was helpful; however, Holmes could not trust the good doctor to solve a perplexing case on his own. also (*n*).

a-ne-mi-a \ə-'nē-mē-ə\ (*n*) condition in which blood lacks red corpuscles. The doctor ascribes his tiredness to *anemia*. a-ne-mic \ə-nē-mik\ (*adj*).

an-es-thet-ic \ˌan-əs-'thet-ik\ (*n*) substance that removes sensation with or without loss of consciousness. His monotonous voice acted like an *anesthetic;* his audience was soon asleep. an-es-the-sia \an-əs-'thē-zhə\ (*n*)

an-gu-lar \'an-gyə-lər\ (*adj*) sharp and stiff in character. Mr. Spock's features, though *angular,* were curiously attractive, in a Vulcan way.

an-i-mad-ver-sion \ˌan-ə-ˌmad-'vər-zhən\ (*n*) critical remark. He resented the *animadversions* of his critics, particularly because he realized they were true.

an-i-mat-ed \'an-ə-ˌmāt-əd\ (*adj*) lively. Jim Carrey's facial expressions are amazingly *animated*: when he played Ace Ventura, he looked practically rubber-faced.

an-i-mos-i-ty \ˌan-ə-'mäs-ət-ē\ (*n*) active enmity. He incurred the *animosity* of the ruling class because he advocated limiting their power.

\ŋ\ **sing** \ō\ **go** \o\̇ **law** \oi\̇ **boy** \th\ **thin** \t̲h̲\ **the** \ü\ **loot** \u\̇ **foot**
\y\ **yet** \zh\ **vision** \à, k̲, ⁿ, œ, œ̄, ue, üe, ʸ\ *see* Pronunciation Symbols

an-i-mus \\'an-ə-məs\ (*n*) hostile feeling or intent. The speaker's sarcastic comments about liberal do-gooders and elitist snobs revealed his deep-seated *animus* against his opponent.

an-nals \\'an-əlz\ (*n*) records; history. "In this year our good King Richard died," wrote the chronicler in the kingdom's *annals*.

an-neal \ə-'nē(ə)l\ (*v*) reduce brittleness and improve toughness by heating and cooling. After the glass is *annealed*, it will be less subject to chipping and cracking.

an-ni-hi-late \ə-'nī-ə-ˌlāt\ (*v*) destroy. The enemy in its revenge tried to *annihilate* the entire population.

an-no-tate \\'an-ə-ˌtāt\ (*v*) comment; make explanatory notes. In explanatory notes following each poem, the editor carefully *annotated* the poet's more esoteric references.

an-nu-i-ty \ə-'n(y)ü-ət-ē\ (*n*) yearly allowance. The *annuity* he set up with the insurance company supplements his social security benefits so that he can live very comfortably without working.

an-nul \ə-'nəl\ (*v*) make void. The parents of the runaway couple tried to *annul* the marriage.

a-noint \ə-'nöint\ (*v*) consecrate. The prophet Samuel *anointed* David with oil, crowning him king of Israel.

a-nom-a-lous \ə-'näm-ə-ləs\ (*adj*) abnormal; irregular. He was placed in the *anomalous* position of seeming to approve procedures he despised.

a-nom-a-ly \ə-'näm-ə-lē\ (*n*) irregularity. A bird that cannot fly is an *anomaly*.

a-non-y-mous \ə-'nän-ə-məs\ (*adj*) having no name. He tried to ascertain the identity of the writer of the *anonymous* letter.

an-tag-o-nism \an-'tag-ə-niz-əm\ (*n*) active resistance. Barry showed his *antagonism* toward his new stepmother by ignoring her whenever she tried talking to him.

\ə\ abut \ᵊ\ kitten, F table \ər\ further \a\ ash \ā\ ace \ä\ cot, cart
\au̇\ out \ch\ chin \e\ bet \ē\ easy \g\ go \i\ hit \ī\ ice \j\ job

an-te-cede \ant-ə-'sēd\ (*v*) precede. The invention of the radiotelegraph *anteceded* the development of television by a quarter of a century.

an-te-di-lu-vi-an \ant-i-də-'lü-vē-ən\ (*adj*) antiquated; ancient. Looking at his great-aunt's old-fashioned furniture, which must have been cluttering up her attic since the time of Noah's flood, the young heir exclaimed, "Heavens! How positively *antediluvian!*"

an-thro-poid \'an(t)-thrə-,pȯid\ (*adj*) manlike. The gorilla is the strongest of the *anthropoid* animals. also (*n*).

an-thro-pol-o-gist \an(t)-thrə-'päl-ə-jəst\ (*n*) a student of the history and science of mankind. *Anthropologists* have discovered several relics of prehistoric man in this area.

an-thro-po-mor-phic \an(t)-thrə-pə-'mȯr-fik\ (*adj*) having human form or characteristics. Primitive religions often have dieties with *anthropomorphic* characteristics.

an-ti-cli-max \ant-i-'klī-,maks\ (*n*) letdown in thought or emotion. After the fine performance in the first act, the rest of the play was an *anticlimax*. **an-ti-cli-mac-tic** \ant-i-'klī-,mak-tik\ (*adj*)

an-tip-a-thy \an-'tip-ə-thē\ (*n*) aversion; dislike. Tom's extreme *antipathy* to disputes keeps him from getting into arguments with his hot-tempered wife.

an-ti-sep-tic \ant-ə-'sep-tik\ (*n*) substance that prevents infection. It is advisable to apply an *antiseptic* to any wound, no matter how slight or insignificant. also (*adj*).

an-tith-e-sis \an-'tith-ə-səs\ (*n*) contrast; direct opposite of or to. This tyranny was the *antithesis* of all that he had hoped for, and he fought it with all his strength.

ap-a-thy \'ap-ə-thē\ (*n*) lack of caring; indifference. A firm believer in democratic government, she could not understand the *apathy* of people who never bothered to vote. **ap-a-thet-ic** \àp-ə-'thet-ik\ (*adj*)

---

ape \āp\ (*v*) imitate or mimic. He was suspended for a week because he had *aped* the principal in front of the whole school.

ap·er·ture \'ap-ə(r)-ˌchu̇(ə)r\ (*n*) opening; hole. He discovered a small *aperture* in the wall, through which the insects had entered the room.

a·pex \'ā-ˌpeks\ (*n*) tip; summit; climax. At the *apex* of his career, the star was deluged with offers of leading roles; two years later, he was reduced to acting in mouthwash ads.

a·pha·sia \a-'fā-zh(ē-)ə\ (*n*) loss of speech due to injury. After the automobile accident, the victim had periods of *aphasia* when he could not speak at all or could only mumble incoherently.

aph·o·rism \'af-ə-ˌriz-əm\ (*n*) pithy maxim. An *aphorism* is usually philosophic or scientific; an adage is usually more homely and concrete. For example, "The proper study of mankind is man" is an *aphorism*; "There's no smoke without a fire," however, is an adage. aph·o·ris·tic \af-ə-'ris-tik\ (*adj*)

a·pi·ar·y \'ā-pē-ˌer-ē\ (*n*) a place where bees are kept. Although he spent many hours daily in the *apiary,* he was very seldom stung by a bee.

a·plomb \ə-'pläm\ (*n*) poise. Gwen's *aplomb* in handling potentially embarrassing moments was legendary around the office; when one of her clients broke a piece of her best crystal, she coolly picked up her own glass and hurled it at the wall.

a·poc·a·lyp·tic \ə-ˌpäk-ə-'lip-tik\ (*adj*) prophetic; pertaining to revelations. The crowd jeered at the street preacher's *apocalyptic* predictions of doom. The *Apocalypse* or *Book of Revelations* of Saint John prophesies the end of the world as we know it and foretells marvels and prodigies that signal the coming doom.

---

a·poc·ry·phal \ə-'päk-rə-fəl\ (*adj*) not genuine; sham. To impress his friends, Tom invented *apocryphal* tales of his adventures in the big city.

ap·o·gee \'ap-ə-⁽ˈ⁾jē\ (*n*) highest point. When the moon in its orbit is furthest away from the earth, it is at its *apogee.*

a·pos·tate \ə-'päs-ˌtat\ (*n*) one who abandons his or her religious faith or political beliefs. Because he switched from one party to another, his former friends shunned him as an *apostate.*

a·poth·e·cary \ə-'päth-ə-ˌker-ē\ (*n*) druggist. In Holland, *apothecaries* still sell spices as well as the customary ointments and pills.

ap·o·thegm \'ap-ə-ˌthem\ (*n*) pithy, compact saying. Proverbs are *apothegms* that have become familiar sayings.

a·po·the·o·sis \ə-ˌpäth-ē-'ō-səs\ (*n*) deification; glorification; elevation to godhead; an ideal example of something. The *apotheosis* of Emperor Augustus was designed to insure his eternal greatness: Romans would worship at his altar forever.

ap·pall \ə-'pȯl\ (*v*) dismay; shock. We were *appalled* by the horrifying conditions in the city's jails.

ap·pa·ri·tion \ˌap-ə-'rish-ən\ (*n*) ghost; phantom. On the castle battlements, an *apparition* materialized and spoke to Hamlet, warning him of his uncle's treachery. In *Ghostbusters,* hordes of *apparitions* materialized, only to be dematerialized by the specialized apparatus wielded by Bill Murray.

ap·pease \ə-'pēz\ (*v*) pacify; soothe; relieve. Tom and Jody tried to *appease* their crying baby by offering him a rubber pacifier. However, he would not calm down until they *appeased* his hunger by giving him a bottle.

ap·pel·la·tion \ˌap-ə-'lā-shən\ (*n*) name; title. Macbeth was startled when the witches greeted him with an incorrect *appellation.* Why did they call him Thane of

---

\ŋ\ **sing**   \ō\ **go**   \ȯ\ **law**   \ȯi\ **boy**   \th\ **thin**   \t̲h̲\ **the**   \ü\ **loot**   \u̇\ **foot**
\y\ **yet**   \zh\ **vision**   \à, k̲, ⁿ, œ, œ̄, ue, ūe, ʸ\ *see* Pronunciation Symbols

Cawdor, he wondered, when the holder of that title still lived?

ap-pend \ə-'pend\ (*v*) attach. When you *append* a bibliography to a text, you have just created an *appendix*.

ap-po-site \'ap-ə-zət\ (*adj*) appropriate; fitting. He was always able to find the *apposite* phrase, the correct expression for every occasion.

ap-praise \ə-'prāz\ (*v*) estimate value of. It is difficult to *appraise* the value of old paintings; it is easier to call them priceless. ap-prais-al \ə-'prā-zəl\ (*n*)

ap-pre-hend \ˌap-ri-'hend\ (*v*) arrest (a criminal); dread; perceive. The police will *apprehend* the culprit and convict him before long.

ap-pre-hen-sive \ap-ri-'hen(t)-siv\ (*adj*) fearful; discerning. His *apprehensive* glances at the people who were walking in the street revealed his nervousness.

ap-prise \ə-'prīz\ (*v*) inform. When he was *apprised* of the dangerous weather conditions, he decided to postpone his trip.

ap-pro-ba-tion \ˌap-rə-'bā-shən\ (*n*) approval. She looked for some sign of *approbation* from her parents.

ap-pro-pri-ate \ə-'prō-prē-ˌāt\ (*v*) acquire; take possession of for one's own use. The ranch owners *appropriated* the lands that had originally been set aside for the Indians' use.

ap-pur-te-nance \ə-'pərt-nən(t)s\ (*n*) subordinate possession. He bought the estate and all its *appurtenances*.

ap-ro-pos \ˌap-rə-'pō\ (*prep*) with reference to; properly. I find your remarks *apropos* of the present situation timely and pertinent. also (*adj* and *adv*).

ap-ti-tude \'ap-tə-ˌt(y)üd\ (*n*) fitness; talent. The counselor gave him an *aptitude* test before advising him about the career he should follow.

aq-ui-line \'ak-wə-ˌlīn\ (*adj*) curved, hooked. Cartoonists exaggerated the senator's *aquiline* nose, curving it until it looked like the beak of an eagle.

\ə\ **abut** \ᵊ\ **kitten**, F **table** \ər\ **further** \a\ **ash** \ā\ **ace** \ä\ **cot, cart** \au̇\ **out** \ch\ **chin** \e\ **bet** \ē\ **easy** \g\ **go** \i\ **hit** \ī\ **ice** \j\ **job**

ar-a-ble \'ar-ə-bəl\ (*adj*) fit for growing crops. The first settlers wrote home glowing reports of the New World, praising its vast acres of *arable* land ready for the plow.

ar-bi-ter \'är-bət-ər\ (*n*) a person with power to decide a dispute; judge. As an *arbiter* in labor disputes, he has won the confidence of the workers and the employers.

ar-bi-trar-y \'är-bə-ˌtrer-ē\ (*adj*) unreasonable or capricious; randomly chosen; tyrannical. The coach claimed the team lost because the umpire made some *arbitrary* calls.

ar-cade \är-'kād\ (*n*) a covered passageway, usually lined with shops. The *arcade* was popular with shoppers because it gave them protection from the summer sun and the winter rain.

ar-cane \är-'kān\ (*adj*) secret; mysterious; known only to the initiated. Secret brotherhoods surround themselves with *arcane* rituals and trappings to mystify outsiders. So do doctors. Consider the *arcane* terminology they use and the impression they try to give that what is *arcane* to us is obvious to them.

ar-chae-ol-o-gy \ˌär-kē-'äl-əjē\ (*n*) study of artifacts and relics of early mankind. The professor of *archaeology* headed an expedition to the Gobi Desert in search of ancient ruins.

ar-cha-ic \är-'kā-ik\ (*adj*) antiquated. "Methinks," "thee," and "thou" are *archaic* words that are no longer part of our normal vocabulary.

ar-che-type \'är -ki-ˌtīp\ (*n*) prototype; primitive pattern. The Brooklyn Bridge was the *archetype* of the many spans that now connect Manhattan with Long Island and New Jersey.

ar-chi-pel-a-go \ˌär-kə-'pel-ə-gō\ (*n*) group of closely located islands. When he looked at the map and saw the *archipelagoes* in the South Seas, he longed to visit them.

\ŋ\ sing \ō\ go \ò\ law \òi\ boy \th\ thin \th\ the \ü\ loot \ů\ foot
\y\ yet \zh\ vision \à, k̲, ⁿ, œ, œ̄, ue, ūe, ʸ\ *see* Pronunciation Symbols

ar-chive \'är-ˌkīv\ (*n*) public records; place where public records are kept. These documents should be part of the *archives* so that historians may be able to evaluate them in the future.

ar-dor \'ärd-ər\ (*n*) heat; passion; zeal. His *ardor* for the cause was contagious; converts eagerly flocked to him.

ar-du-ous \'ärj-(ə-)was\ (*adj*) hard; strenuous. His *arduous* efforts had sapped his energy.

ar-got \'är-gət\ (*n*) slang. In the *argot* of the underworld, he "was taken for a ride."

a-ri-a \'är-ē-ə\ (*n*) operatic solo. At her Metropolitan Opera audition, Marian Anderson sang an *aria* from *Norma.*

ar-id \'ar-əd\ (*adj*) dry; barren. The cactus has adapted to survive in an *arid* environment.

ar-ma-da \är-'mäd-ə\ (*n*) fleet of warships. Queen Elizabeth's navy defeated the mighty *armada* that threatened the English coast.

ar-o-mat-ic \ˌar-ə-'mat-ik\ (*adj*) fragrant. Medieval sailing vessels brought *aromatic* herbs from China to Europe. also (*n*).

ar-raign \ə-'rān\ (*v*) charge in court; indict. After his indictment by the Grand Jury, the accused man was *arraigned* in the County Criminal Court.

ar-ray \ə-'rā\ (*v*) marshal; place in proper or desired order. His actions were bound to *array* public sentiment against him. also (*n*).

ar-ray \ə-'rā\ (*v*) clothe; adorn. She liked to watch her mother *array* herself in her finest clothes before going out for the evening. also (*n*).

ar-rears \ə-'ri(ə)rz\ (*n*) being in debt. He was in *arrears* with his payments on the car.

ar-ro-gance \'ar-ə-gən(t)s\ (*n*) haughtiness. Convinced that Emma thought she was better than anyone else in the class, Ed rebuked her for her *arrogance*. ar-rogant \'ar-ə-gənt\ (*adj*)

\ə\ abut \ᵊ\ kitten, F table \ər\ further \a\ ash \ā\ ace \ä\ cot, cart
\au̇\ out \ch\ chin \e\ bet \ē\ easy \g\ go \i\ hit \ī\ ice \j\ job

ar-roy-o \ə-'rȯi-ə\ (*n*) gully. Until the heavy rains of the past spring, this *arroyo* had been a dry bed.

ar-tic-u-late \är-'tik-yə-lət\ (*adj*) effective; distinct. Her *articulate* presentation of the advertising campaign impressed her employers. also (*v*).

ar-tic-u-late \är-'tik-yə-ˌlāt\ (*v*) to utter distinctly. The singer *articulated* every consonant.

ar-ti-fact \'ärt-ə-ˌfakt\ (*n*) product of primitive culture. Archaeologists endlessly debated the significance of the *artifacts* discovered in the ruins of Asia Minor.

ar-ti-fice \'ärt-ə-fəs\ (*n*) deception, trickery. Their victory in the Trojan War convinced the Greeks that cunning and *artifice* were often more effective than military might.

ar-ti-san \'ärt-ə-zən\ (*n*) a manually skilled worker. Artists and *artisans* both are necessary to the development of a culture.

as-cen-dan-cy \ə-'sen-dən-sē\ (*n*) controlling influence. President Marcos failed to maintain his *ascendancy* over the Philippines.

as-cer-tain \ˌas-ər-'tān\ (*v*) find out for certain. Please *ascertain* his present address.

as-cet-ic \ə-'set-ik\ (*adj*) practicing self-denial; austere. The wealthy, self-indulgent young man felt oddly drawn to the strict, *ascetic* life led by the sober monks. also (*n*).

as-cribe \ə-'skrīb\ (*v*) refer; attribute; assign. I can *ascribe* no motive for his acts.

a-sep-tic \ˌ(ˌ)ā-'sep-tik\ (*adj*) preventing putrefaction or blood poisoning by killing bacteria. Hospitals succeeded in lowering the mortality rate as soon as they introduced *aseptic* conditions.

ash-en \'ash-ən\ (*adj*) ash-colored. His face was *ashen* with fear.

as-i-nine \'as-ᵊn-ˌīn\ (*adj*) stupid. "What an *asinine* comment!" said Bob contemptuously. "I've never heard such a stupid remark."

a-skance \ə-'skan(t)s\ (*adv*) with a sideways or indirect look. Looking *askance* at her questioner, she displayed her scorn.

a-skew \ə-'skyü\ (*adv*) crookedly; slanted; at an angle. Judy constantly straightened the doilies on her furniture: she couldn't stand seeing them *askew.*

as-per-i-ty \a-'sper-ət-ē\ (*n*) sharpness (of temper). These remarks, spoken with *asperity,* stung the boys to whom they had been directed.

as-per-sion \ə-'spər-zhən\ (*n*) slanderous remark. Unscrupulous politicians practice character assassination as a political tool, casting *aspersions* on their rivals.

as-pi-rant \'as-p(ə-)rənt\ (*n*) seeker after position or status. Although I am an *aspirant* for public office, I refuse to accept the dictates of the party bosses. also (*adj*).

as-pi-ra-tion \,as-pə-'rā-shən\ (*n*) noble ambition. One's *aspirations* should be as lofty as the stars.

as-sail \ə-'sā(ə)l\ (*v*) assault. He was *assailed* with questions after his lecture.

as-say \a-'sā\ (*v*) analyze; evaluate. When they *assayed* the ore, they found that they had discovered a very rich vein. as-say \'as-ˌā\ (*n*)

as-sess-ment \ə-'ses-mənt\ (*n*) appraisal; estimation. Your high school record plays an important part in the admission committee's *assessment* of you as an applicant.

as-sid-u-ous \ə-'sij-(ə-)wəs\ (*adj*) diligent. He worked *assiduously* at this task for weeks before he felt satisfied with his results. as-si-du-i-ty \,as-ə-'d(y)ü-ət-ē\ (*n*)

as-sim-i-late \ə-'sim-ə-ˌlāt\ (*v*) absorb; cause to become homogeneous. The manner in which the United States was able to *assimilate* the hordes of immigrants during the nineteenth and the early part of the twentieth centuries will always be a source of pride.

\ə\ **abut** \ᵊ\ **kitten**, F **table** \ər\ **further** \a\ **ash** \ā\ **ace** \ä\ **cot, cart**
\au̇\ **out** \ch\ **chin** \e\ **bet** \ē\ **easy** \g\ **go** \i\ **hit** \ī\ **ice** \j\ **job**

as-suage \ə-'swāj\ (*v*) ease or lessen (pain); satisfy (hunger); soothe (anger). Jilted by Jane, Dick tried to *assuage* his heartache by indulging in ice cream. One gallon later, he had *assuaged* his appetite but not his grief. as-suage-ment \ə-'swāj-mənt\ (*n*)

as-sumed \ə-'sümd\ (*adj*) pretended; feigned, fictitious. The forger used an *assumed* name when passing bad checks.

as-sump-tion \ə-'səm(p)-shən\ (*n*) something taken for granted; taking over or taking possession of. The young princess made the foolish *assumption* that the regent would not object to her *assumption* of power. Clearly, she *assumed* too much.

as-ter-oid \'as-tə-ˌrȯid\ (*n*) small planet. Most *asteroids* are found in the region of space located between Mars and Venus, commonly known as the *Asteroid* Belt.

a-stig-ma-tism \ə-'stig-mə-ˌtiz-əm\ (*n*) eye defect that prevents proper focus. As soon as his parents discovered that the boy suffered from *astigmatism,* they took him to the optometrist for corrective glasses.

as-tral \'as-trəl\ (*adj*) relating to the stars. He was amazed at the number of *astral* bodies the new telescope revealed.

as-trin-gent \ə-'strin-jənt\ (*adj*) binding; causing contraction. The *astringent* quality of the unsweetened lemon juice made swallowing difficult. also (*n*).

as-tro-nom-i-cal \ˌas-trə-'näm-i-kəl\ (*adj*) enormously large or extensive. The government seems willing to spend *astronomical* sums on weapons development.

as-tute \ə-'st(y)üt\ (*adj*) wise; shrewd. John Jabob Astor made *astute* investments in land, shrewdly purchasing valuable plots throughout New York City.

a-sy-lum \ə-'sī-ləm\ (*n*) place of refuge or shelter; protection. The refugees sought *asylum* from religious persecution in a new land.

---

at-a-vism \\'at-ə-ˌviz-əm\\ (*n*) reversion to an earlier type; throwback. In his love for gardening, Martin seemed an *atavism* to his Tuscan forebears who lavished great care on their small plots of soil.

a-te-lier \\at-ᵊl-'yā\\ (*n*) workshop; studio. Stories of Bohemian life in Paris are full of tales of artists' starving or freezing in their *ateliers*.

a-the-is-tic \\ā-thē-'is-tik\\ (*adj*) denying the existence of God. His *atheistic* remarks shocked his religious neighbors. a-the-ist \\ā-thē-əst\\ (*n*)

a-troc-i-ty \\ə-'träs-ət-ē\\ (*n*) brutal deed. In time of war, many *atrocities* are committed by invading armies.

at-ro-phy \\'a-trə-fē\\ (*v*) waste away. After three months in a cast, your calf muscles are bound to *atrophy*; you'll need physical therapy to get back in shape.

at-ten-u-ate \\ə-'ten-yə-ˌwāt\\ (*v*) make thin; weaken. By withdrawing their forces, the generals hoped to *attenuate* the enemy lines.

at-test \\ə-'test\\ (*v*) testify, bear witness. Having served as a member of the Grand Jury, I can *attest* that our system of indicting individuals is in need of improvement.

at-tri-bute \\'a-trə-ˌbyüt\\ (*n*) essential quality. His outstanding *attribute* was his kindness.

at-tri-bute \\a-'trib-yət, -yüt\\ (*v*) ascribe; explain. I *attribute* her success in science to the encouragement she received from her parents.

at-tri-tion \\ə-'trish-ən\\ (*n*) gradual decrease in numbers; reduction in the work force without firing employees; wearing away of opposition by means of harassment. In the 1960s urban churches suffered from *attrition* as members moved from the cities to the suburbs. Rather than fire staff members, church leaders followed a policy of *attrition,* allowing elderly workers to retire without replacing them.

\\ə\\ abut \\ᵊ\\ kitten, F table \\ər\\ further \\a\\ ash \\ā\\ ace \\ä\\ cot, cart
\\aů\\ out \\ch\\ chin \\e\\ bet \\ē\\ easy \\g\\ go \\i\\ hit \\ī\\ ice \\j\\ job

a·typ·i·cal \\(ₗ)ā-'tip-i-kəl\ *(adj)* not normal. The child psychiatrist reassured Mrs. Keaton that playing doctor was not *atypical* behavior for a child of young Alex's age. "Yes," she replied, "but not charging for house calls!"

au·dac·i·ty \ȯ-'das-ət-ē\ *(n)* boldness. His *audacity* in this critical moment encouraged us.

au·dit \'ȯd-ət\ *(n)* examination of accounts. When the bank examiners arrived to hold their annual *audit,* they discovered the embezzlements of the chief cashier. also *(v)*.

aug·ment \ȯg-'ment\ *(v)* increase; add to. Armies *augment* their forces by calling up reinforcements; teachers *augment* their salaries by taking second jobs.

au·gu·ry \'ȯ-gyə-rē\ *(n)* omen; prophecy. He interpreted the departure of the birds as an *augury* of evil. au·gur \'ȯ-gər\ *(v, n)*

aus·pi·cious \ȯ-'spish-əs\ *(adj)* favoring success. With favorable weather conditions, it was an *auspicious* moment to set sail.

aus·tere \ȯ-'sti(ə)r\ *(adj)* forbiddingly stern; severely simple and unornamented. The headmaster's *austere* demeanor tended to scare off the more timid students, who never visited his study willingly. The room reflected the man, as *austere* and bare as a monk's cell, with no touches of luxury to moderate its *austerity*.

au·then·ti·cate \ə-'thent-i₋kāt\ *(v)* prove genuine. After a thorough chemical analysis of the pigments and canvas, the experts were prepared to *authenticate* the painting as an original Rembrandt.

au·thor·i·ta·tive \ə-'thär-ə-₋tāt-iv\ *(adj)* having the weight of authority; dictatorial. Impressed by the young researcher's well-documented presentation, we accepted her analysis of the experiment as *authoritative*.

au·to·crat \'ȯt-ə-₋krat\ *(n)* one having absolute, unchecked power; dictator. Someone accustomed to exercising

---

\ŋ\ sing   \ō\ go   \ȯ\ law   \ȯi\ boy   \th\ thin   \th̲\ the   \ü\ loot   \u̇\ foot
\y\ yet   \zh\ vision   \ȧ, k̲, ⁿ, œ, œ̄, ue, ūe, ʸ\ *see* Pronunciation Symbols

authority may turn into an *autocrat* if his power is unchecked. Dictators by definition are *autocrats.* Bosses who dictate behavior as well as letters can be *autocrats* too. au-toc-ra-cy \ò-'täk-rə-sē\ (*n*)

au-tom-a-ton \ò-'täm-ət-ən\ (*n*) robot; person performing a task mechanically. The assembly line job called for no initiative or intelligence on Homer's part; on automatic pilot, he pushed button after button like an *automaton.*

au-ton-o-mous \ò-'tän-ə-məs\ (*adj*) self-governing. Although the University of California at Berkeley is just one part of the state university system, in many ways Cal Berkeley is *autonomous,* for it runs several programs that are not subject to outside control. au-ton-o-my\ò-'tän-ə-mē\ (*n*)

au-top-sy \'ò-ˌtäp-sē\ (*n*) examination of a dead body; post mortem. The medical examiner ordered an *autopsy* to determine the cause of death. also (*v*).

aux-il-ia-ry \òg-'zil-yə-rē\ (*adj*) helper, additional or subsidiary. To prepare for the emergency, they built an *auxiliary* power station. also (*n*).

av-a-rice \'av-(ə-)rəs\ (*n*) greediness for wealth. King Midas is a perfect example of *avarice*: he was so greedy that he wished everything he touched would turn to gold. av-a-ri-cious \ˌav-ə-'rish-əs\ (*adj*)

a-ver \ə-'vər\ (*v*) state confidently. Despite overwhelming popular skepticism about his voyage, Columbus *averred* he would succeed in finding a direct sea route to the Far East.

a-verse \ə-'vərs\ (*adj*) reluctant. The reporter was *averse* to revealing the sources of his information.

a-ver-sion \ə-'vər-zhən\ (*n*) firm dislike. Their mutual *aversion* was so great that they refused to speak to one another.

a-vert \ə-'vərt\ (*v*) prevent; turn away. She *averted* her eyes from the dead cat on the highway.

\ə\ abut \ᵊ\ kitten, F table \ər\ further \a\ ash \ā\ ace \ä\ cot, cart
\aú\ out \ch\ chin \e\ bet \ē\ easy \g\ go \i\ hit \ī\ ice \j\ job

av·id \'av-əd\ (*adj*) greedy; eager for. *Avid* for pleasure, Abner partied with great *avidity*. a·vid·i·ty \ə-vid ət-ē\ (*n*).

av·o·ca·tion \ˌav-ə-'kā-shən\ (*n*) secondary or minor occupation. His hobby proved to be so fascinating and profitable that gradually he abandoned his regular job to concentrate on his *avocation.*

a·vow \ə-'vaů\ (*v*) declare openly. Lana *avowed* that she never meant to steal Debbie's boyfriend, but no one believed her *avowal* of innocence.

a·vun·cu·lar \ə-'vəŋ-kyə-lər\ (*adj*) like an uncle. *Avuncular* pride did not prevent him from noticing his nephew's shortcomings.

awe \'ȯ\ (*n*) solemn wonder. The tourists gazed with *awe* at the tremendous expanse of the Grand Canyon.

a·wry \ə-'rī\ (*adv*) crooked; wrong; amiss. Noticing that the groom's tie was slightly *awry,* the bride reached over to set it straight. A careful organizer, she hated to have anything go *awry* with her plans. also (*adj*).

ax·i·om \'ak-sē-əm\ (*n*) self-evident truth requiring no proof. Before a student can begin to think along the lines of Euclidean geometry, he must accept certain principles or *axioms.*

az·ure \'azh-ər\ (*adj*) sky blue. *Azure* skies are indicative of good weather.

B

bab·ble \'bab-əl\ (*v*) chatter idly. The little girl *babbled* about her doll. also (*n*).

bad·ger \'baj-ər\ (*v*) pester; annoy. She was forced to change her telephone number because she was *badgered* by obscene phone calls.

ba·di·nage \ˌbad-ᵊn-'äzh\ (*n*) teasing conversation. Her friends at work greeted the news of her engagement with cheerful *badinage*.

baf·fle \'baf-əl\ (*v*) frustrate; perplex. The new code *baffled* the enemy agents. also (*n*).

bait \'bāt\ (*v*) harass; tease. The school bully *baited* the smaller children, taunting them.

bale·ful \'bā(ə)l-fəl\ (*adj*) having a malign influence; ominous. The fortune-teller made *baleful* predictions of terrible things to come.

balk \'bȯk\ (*v*) foil or thwart; stop short; refuse to go on. When the warden learned that several inmates were planning to escape, he took steps to *balk* their attempt. However, he *balked* at punishing them by shackling them to the walls of their cells.

bal·last \'bal-əst\ (*n*) heavy substance used to add stability or weight. The ship was listing badly to one side; it was necessary to shift the *ballast* in the hold to get it back on an even keel. also (*v*).

balm \'bä(l)m\ (*n*) something that relieves pain. Friendship is the finest *balm* for the pangs of disappointed love.

balm·y \'bäm-ē\ (*adj*) mild; fragrant. A *balmy* breeze refreshed us after the sultry blast.

ba·nal \bə-'näl\ (*adj*) hackneyed; commonplace; trite. His frequent use of clichés made his essay seem *banal*. ba·nal·i·ty \bə-'nal-ət-ē\ (*n*)

ban·dy \'ban-dē\ (*v*) discuss lightly; exchange blows or words. The president refused to *bandy* words with the reporters at the press conference.

\ə\ abut \ᵊ\ kitten, F table \ər\ further \a\ ash \ā\ ace \ä\ cot, cart
\au̇\ out \ch\ chin \e\ bet \ē\ easy \g\ go \i\ hit \ī\ ice \j\ job

bane \'bān\ (*n*) curse. Lucy's little brother was the *bane* of her existence: he made her life so miserable that she was ready to poison him with ratsbane for having such a *baneful* effect. bane-ful \'bān-fəl\ (*adj*)

ban-ter \'bant-ər\ (*n*) good-natured ridiculing. They resented his *banter* because they thought he was being sarcastic. also (*v*).

barb \'bärb\ (*n*) cutting remark; sharp projection from fishhook, etc. Who can blame the President if he's happier fishing than back in the capitol listening to his critics' verbal *barbs*? The *barb* from the fishhook caught in his finger as he grabbed the fish. also (*v*).

ba-roque \bə-'rōk\ (*adj*) highly ornate. Accustomed to the severe lines of contemporary buildings, the architecture students found the flamboyance of *baroque* architecture amusing.

bar-rage \bə-'räzh\ (*n*) barrier laid down by artillery fire. The company was forced to retreat through the *barrage* of heavy cannons. also (*v*).

bar-ris-ter \'bar-ə-stər\ (*n*) counselor-at-law. Galsworthy started as a *barrister*, but when he found the practice of law boring, turned to writing.

bar-ter-er \'bärt-ər-ər\ (*n*) trader. The *barterer* exchanged trinkets for the natives' furs. It's sometimes smarter to *barter* than to pay cash. bar-ter \'bärt-ər\ (*v*)

bask \'bask\ (*v*) luxuriate; take pleasure in warmth. *Basking* on the beach, she relaxed so completely that she fell asleep.

bas-tion \'bas-chən\ (*n*) fortress; defense. The villagers fortified the town hall, hoping this improvised *bastion* could protect them from the guerrillas' raids.

bate \'bāt\ (*v*) let down; restrain. Until it was time to open the presents, the children had to *bate* their curiosity.

bau-ble \'bȯ-bəl\ (*n*) trinket; trifle. The child was delighted with the *bauble* she had won in the grab bag.

---

bawdy \'bȯd-ē\ (*adj*) indecent; obscene. She took offense at his *bawdy* remarks.

be·a·ti·fic \ˌbē-ə-'tif-ik\ (*adj*) giving bliss; blissful. The *beatific* smile on the child's face made us very happy.

be·at·i·tude \bē-'at-ə-ˌt(y)üd\ (*n*) blessedness; state of bliss. Growing closer to God each day, the mystic achieved a state of indescribable *beatitude*.

be·di·zen \bi-'dīz -ᵊn\ (*v*) dress with vulgar finery. The witch doctors were *bedizened* in all their gaudiest costumes.

be·drag·gle \bi-'drag-əl\ (*v*) wet thoroughly. We were so *bedraggled* by the severe storm that we had to change into dry clothing. **be·drag·gled** \bi-'drag-əld\ (*adj*)

be·guile \bi-'gī(ə)l \ (*v*) mislead or delude; cheat; pass time. With flattery and big talk of easy money, the con men *beguiled* Cal into betting his allowance on the shell game. Broke, he *beguiled* himself for hours playing solitaire.

be·he·moth \bi-'hē-məth\ (*n*) huge creature; something of monstrous size or power. Sportscasters nicknamed the linebacker "The *Behemoth.*"

be·hold·en \bi-'hōl-dən\ (*adj*) obligated; indebted. Since I do not wish to be *beholden* to anyone, I cannot accept this favor.

be·hoove \bi-'hüv\ (*v*) suited to; incumbent upon. In an emergency, it *behooves* all of us to remain calm and await instructions from the authorities.

be·la·bor \bi-'lā-bər\ (*v*) beat soundly; assail verbally; harp on. The police officer was *belaboring* the rioter, battering him with his nightstick.

be·lat·ed \bi-'lāt-əd\ (*adj*) delayed. He apologized for his *belated* note of condolence to the widow of his friend and explained that he had just learned of her husband's untimely death.

be·lea·guer \bi-'lē-gər\ (*v*) besiege or attack; harass. The baby-sitter was surrounded by a crowd of unmanageable brats who relentlessly *beleaguered* her.

\ə\ abut \ᵊ\ kitten, F table \ər\ further \a\ ash \ā\ ace \ä\ cot, cart
\au̇\ out \ch\ chin \e\ bet \ē\ easy \g\ go \i\ hit \ī\ ice \j\ job

be·lie \bi-ˈlī\ (*v*) contradict; give a false impression. His coarse, hard-bitten exterior *belied* his inner sensitivity.

be·lit·tle \bi-ˈlit-ᵊl\ (*v*) disparage; deprecate. Barry was a put-down artist: he was a genius at *belittling* people and making them feel small.

bel·li·cose \ˈbel-i-ˌkōs\ (*adj*) warlike. His *bellicose* disposition led him to reject the enemy's proposal of a truce.

bel·lig·er·ent \bə-ˈlij(ə)-rənt\ (*adj*) quarrelsome. Whenever he had too much to drink, he became *belligerent* and tried to pick fights with strangers.

ben·e·dic·tion \ˌben-ə-ˈdik-shən\ (*n*) blessing. The appearance of the sun after the many rainy days was like a *benediction.*

ben·e·fac·tor \ˈben-ə-ˌfak-tər\ (*n*) gift-giver; patron. Scrooge later became Tiny Tim's *benefactor.*

ben·e·fi·ci·ary \ˌben-ə-ˈfish-ē-er-ē\ (*n*) person entitled to benefits or proceeds of an insurance policy or will. In Scrooge's will, he made Tiny Tim his *beneficiary*: everything he left would go to young Tim. also (*adj*).

be·nev·o·lent \bə-ˈnev(-ə)-lənt\ (*adj*) generous; charitable. Mr. Fezziwig was a *benevolent* employer, who wished to make Christmas merrier for young Scrooge and his other employees.

be·nign \bi-ˈnīn\ (*adj*) kindly; favorable; not malignant. Though her *benign* smile and gentle bearing made Miss Marple seem a sweet little old lady, in reality she was a tough-minded, shrewd observer of human nature.

be·rate \bi-ˈrāt\ (*v*) scold strongly. He feared she would *berate* him for his forgetfulness.

be·reave·ment \bi-ˈrēv-mənt\ (*n*) state of being deprived of something valuable or beloved. His friends gathered to console him upon his sudden *bereavement.*

be·reft \bi-ˈreft\ (*adj*) deprived of; lacking. The foolish gambler soon found himself *bereft* of funds.

\ŋ\ **sing** \ō\ **go** \ȯ\ **law** \ȯi\ **boy** \th\ **thin** \t͟h\ **the** \ü\ **loot** \ u̇ \ **foot**
\y\ **yet** \zh\ **vision** \à, k̲, ⁿ, œ, œ̄, ue, ūe, ʸ\ *see* Pronunciation Symbols

ber-serk \bə(r)-'sərk\ (*adv*) frenzied. Angered, he went *berserk* and began to wreck the room. also (*n*).

be-smirch \bi-'smərch\ (*v*) soil, defile. The scandalous remarks in the newspaper gossip columns *besmirch* the reputations of respectable members of society.

bes-tial \'bes(h)-chəl\ (*adj*) beastlike; brutal. According to legend, the werewolf was able to abandon its human shape and take on a *bestial* form.

be-stow \bi-'stō\ (*v*) confer. King Hrothgar wished to *bestow* great honors upon the hero.

be-troth \bi-'träth\ (*v*) become engaged to marry. The announcement that they had become *betrothed* surprised their friends who had not suspected any romance. **be-troth-al** \bi-'trōth-əl\ (*n*)

be-vy \'bev-ē\ (*n*) large group. The movie actor was surrounded by a *bevy* of starlets.

bi-cam-er-al \(ˌ)bī-'kam-(ə-)rəl\ (*adj*) two-chambered, as a legislative body. The United States Congress is a *bicameral* body.

bick-er \'bik-ər\ (*v*) quarrel. The children *bickered* morning, noon, and night, exasperating their parents.

bi-en-ni-al \(ˌ)bī-'en-ē-əl\ (*adj*) every two years. Seeing no need to meet more frequently, the group held *biennial* meetings instead of annual ones. Plants that bear flowers *biennially* are known as *biennials*. also (*n*)

bi-fur-cate \(ˌ)bi-'fər-kət\ (*adj*) divided into two branches; forked. With a *bifurcate* branch and a piece of elastic rubber, he made a crude but effective slingshot.

big-ot-ry \'big-ə-trē\ (*n*) stubborn intolerance. Brought up in a tolerant home, the student was shocked by the *bigotry* and prejudice expressed by several of his classmates.

bil-ious \'bil-yəs\ (*adj*) suffering from indigestion; irritable. His *bilious* temperament was apparent to anyone who heard him rant about his difficulties.

\ə\ abut \ə\ kitten, F table \ər\ further \a\ ash \ā\ ace \ä\ cot, cart
\au̇\ out \ch\ chin \e\ bet \ē\ easy \g\ go \i\ hit \ī\ ice \j\ job

bilk \'bilk\ (*v*) swindle; cheat. The con man specialized in *bilking* insurance companies.

bi-zarre \bə-'zär\ (*adj*) fantastic; violently contrasting. The plot of the novel was too *bizarre* to be believed.

blanch \'blanch\ (*v*) bleach; whiten. Although age had *blanched* his hair, he was still vigorous and energetic.

bland \'bland\ (*adj*) soothing; mild. She used a *bland* ointment for her sunburn.

blan-dish-ment \'blan-dish-mənt\ (*n*) flattery. Despite the salesperson's *blandishments,* the customer did not buy the outfit.

bla-sé \blä-'zā\ (*adj*) bored with pleasure or dissipation. Although Beth was as thrilled with the idea of a trip to Paris as her classmates were, she tried to act super cool and *blasé*, as if she'd been abroad hundreds of times.

blas-phe-mous \'blas-fə-məs\ (*adj*) profane; impious. In my father's house, the Dodgers were the holiest of holies; to cheer for another team was to be *blasphemous*.

bla-tant \'blāt-ᵊnt\ (*adj*) flagrant; conspicuously obvious; loudly offensive. To the unemployed youth from Dublin, the "No Irish Need Apply" placard in the shop window was a *blatant* mark of prejudice. bla-tan-cy \'blāt-ᵊn-sē\ (*n*)

bla-zon \'blāz-ᵊn\ (*v*) decorate with an heraldic coat of arms. *Blazoned* on his shield were the two lambs and the lion, the traditional coat of arms of his family. also (*n*).

bleak \'blēk\ (*adj*) cold or cheerless; unlikely to be favorable. The frigid, inhospitable Aleutian Islands are *bleak* military outposts. It's no wonder that soldiers assigned there have a *bleak* attitude toward their posting.

blight-ed \'blīt-əd\ (*adj*) suffering from a disease; destroyed. The extent of the *blighted* areas could be seen only when viewed from the air. blight \'blīt\ (*n*)

blithe \'blith\ (*adj*) gay; joyous; carefree. Without a care in the world, Beth went her *blithe*, lighthearted way.

bloat-ed \'blōt-əd\ (*adj*) swollen or puffed as with water or air. The *bloated* corpse was taken from the river. bloat \'blōt\ (*n, v*)

blud-geon \'bləj-ən\ (*n*) club; heavy-headed weapon. Attacked by Dr. Moriarty, Holmes used his walking stick as a *bludgeon* to defend himself. also (*v*).

blun-der \'blən-dər\ (*n*) error. The criminal's fatal *blunder* led to his capture. also (*v*).

blurt \'blərt\ (*v*) utter impulsively. Before she could stop him, he *blurted* out the news.

bode \'bōd\ (*v*) foreshadow; portend. The gloomy skies and the sulphurous odors from the mineral springs seemed to *bode* evil to those who settled in the area.

bo-gus \'bō-gəs\ (*adj*) counterfeit; not authentic. The police quickly found the distributors of the *bogus* twenty-dollar bills.

bois-ter-ous \'bȯi-st(ə-)rəs\ (*adj*) violent; rough; noisy. The unruly crowd became even more *boisterous* when he tried to quiet them.

bol-ster \'bōl-stər\ (*v*) support; prop up. The debaters amassed file boxes full of evidence to *bolster* their arguments. also (*n*).

bom-bas-tic \bäm-'bas-tik\ (*adj*) pompous; using inflated language. Puffed up with conceit, the orator spoke in such a *bombastic* manner that we longed to deflate him. bom-bast \'bäm-ˌbast\ (*n*)

boor-ish \'bu̇(ə)r-ish\ (*adj*) rude; insensitive. Though Mr. Collins constantly interrupted his wife, she ignored his *boorish* behavior, for she had lost hope of teaching him courtesy.

boun-ti-ful \'bȧunt-i-fəl\ (*adj*) abundant; graciously generous. Thanks to the good harvest, we had a *bountiful* supply of food and we could be as *bountiful* as we liked in distributing food to the needy.

\ə\ **abut** \ᵊ\ **kitten**, F **table** \ər\ **further** \a\ **ash** \ā\ **ace** \ä\ **cot, cart**
\au̇\ **out** \ch\ **chin** \e\ **bet** \ē\ **easy** \g\ **go** \i\ **hit** \ī\ **ice** \j\ **job**

bour-geois \'bu̇(ə)rzh-ˌwä\ (*adj*) middle class; selfishly materialistic; dully conventional. Technically, anyone who belongs to the middle class is *bourgeois*, but, given the word's connotations, most people resent it if you call them that.

brack-ish \'brak-ish\ (*adj*) somewhat saline. He found the only wells in the area were *brackish;* drinking the water nauseated him.

bra-va-do \brə-'väd-₍ₗ₎ō\ (*n*) swagger; assumed air of defiance. The *bravado* of the young criminal disappeared when he was confronted by the victims of his brutal attack.

bra-zen \'brāz-ᵊn\ (*adj*) insolent. Her *brazen* contempt for authority angered the officials. also (*v*).

breach \'brēch\ (*n*) breaking of contract or duty; fissure; gap. Jill sued Jack for *breach* of promise, claiming he had broken his promise to marry her. They found a *breach* in the enemy's fortifications and penetrated their lines. also (*v*).

breadth \'bretth\ (*n*) width; extent. We were impressed by the *breadth* of her knowledge.

brev-i-ty \'brev-ət-ē\ (*n*) conciseness. *Brevity* is essential when you send a telegram or cablegram; you are charged for every word.

bris-tling \'bris-(ə-)liŋ\ (*adj*) rising like bristles, showing irritation. The dog stood there, *bristling* with anger. bris-tle \'bris-əl\ (*n, v*)

broach \'brōch\ (*v*) open up. Jack did not even try to *broach* the subject of religion with his in-laws. If you *broach* a touchy subject, it may cause a breach.

bro-chure \brō-'shu̇(ə)r\ (*n*) pamphlet. This *brochure* on farming was issued by the Department of Agriculture.

brusque \'brəsk\ (*adj*) blunt; abrupt. She was offended by his *brusque* reply.

\ŋ\ sing \ō\ go \ȯ\ law \ȯi\ boy \th\ thin \t͟h\ the \ü\ loot \u̇\ foot
\y\ yet \zh\ vision \à, k̲, ⁿ, œ, œ̄, ᴜe, ᴜ̄e, ʸ\ *see* Pronunciation Symbols

bu·col·ic \byü-'käl-ik\ *(adj)* rustic; pastoral. Filled with browsing cows and bleating sheep, the meadow was a charmingly *bucolic* sight.

buf·foon·er·y \(ᵒ)bə-'fün-(ə-)rē\ *(n)* clowning. Jim Carrey's *buffoonery* was hilarious.

bul·lion \'bul-yən\ *(n)* gold and silver in the form of bars. Much *bullion* is stored in the vaults at Fort Knox.

bul·wark \'bul-(ᵒ)wərk\ *(n)* earthwork or other strong defense; person who defends. The navy is our principal *bulwark* against invasion.

bun·gle \'bəŋ-gəl\ *(v)* mismanage; blunder. Don't botch this assignment, Bumstead; if you *bungle* the job, you're fired!

bu·reau·cra·cy \'byu-'räk-rə-sē\ *(n)* overregulated administrative system marked by red tape. The Internal Revenue Service is the ultimate *bureaucracy*: taxpayers wasted so much paper filling out IRS forms that the IRS *bureaucrats* printed up a new set of rules requiring taxpayers to comply with the Paperwork Reduction Act.

bur·geon \'bər-jən\ *(v)* grow forth; send out buds. In the spring, the plants that *burgeon* are a promise of the beauty that is to come.

bur·lesque \(ᵒ)bər-'lesk\ *(v)* give an imitation that ridicules. In *Spaceballs*, Rick Moranis *burlesques* Darth Vader of *Star Wars*, outrageously parodying Vader's stiff walk and hollow voice. also *(n)*.

bur·ly \'bər-lē\ *(adj)* husky; muscular. The *burly* mover lifted the packing crate with ease.

bur·nish \'bər-nish\ *(v)* make shiny by rubbing; polish. The *burnished* metal reflected the lamplight. also *(n)*.

but·tress \'bə-trəs\ *(n)* support or prop. The huge cathedral walls were supported by flying *buttresses*. also *(v)*.

bux·om \'bək-səm\ *(adj)* plump; vigorous; jolly. Fashion models are usually slim and willowy rather than *buxom*.

\ə\ **abut** \ᵊ\ **kitten**, F **table** \ər\ **further** \a\ **ash** \ā\ **ace** \ä\ **cot**, c**art**
\aů\ **out** \ch\ **chin** \e\ **bet** \ē\ **easy** \g\ **go** \i\ **hit** \ī\ **ice** \j\ **job**

C

ca·bal \kə-'bal\ (*n*) small group of persons secretly united to promote their own interests. The *cabal* was defeated when their scheme was discovered. also (*v*).

cache \'kash\ (*n*) hiding place. The detectives followed the suspect until he led them to the *cache* where he had stored his loot. also (*v*).

ca·coph·o·ny \ka-'käf-ə-nē\ (*n*) discord. Some people seem to enjoy the *cacophony* of an orchestra that is tuning up.

ca·dav·er \kə-'dav-ər\ (*n*) corpse. In some states, it is illegal to dissect *cadavers*.

ca·dav·er·ous \kə-'dav-(ə-)rəs\ (*adj*) like a corpse; pale. From his *cadaverous* appearance, we could see how the disease had ravaged him.

ca·jole \kə-'jōl\ (*v*) coax; wheedle. Cher tried to *cajole* her father into letting her drive the family car.

cal·i·ber \'kal-ə-bər\ (*n*) ability; capacity. The scholarship committee searched for students of high *caliber*, ones with the intelligence and ability to be a credit to the school.

cal·lig·ra·phy \kə-'lig-rə-fē\ (*n*) beautiful writing; excellent penmanship. As we examine ancient manuscripts, we become impressed with the *calligraphy* of the scribes.

cal·lous \'kal-əs\ (*adj*) hardened; unfeeling. He had worked in the hospital for so many years that he was *callous* to the suffering in the wards. cal·lus \'kal-əs\ (*n*)

cal·low \'kal-ˌō\ (*adj*) youthful; immature; inexperienced. As a freshman, Jack was sure he was a man of the world; as a sophomore, he made fun of freshmen as *callow* youths.

cal·o·rif·ic \kal-ə-'rif-ik\ (*adj*) heat-producing. Coal is much more *calorific* than green wood.

cal-um-ny \'kal-əm-nē\ (*n*) malicious misrepresentation; slander. He could endure his financial failure, but he could not bear the *calumny* that his foes heaped upon him.

cam-e-o \'kam-ē-,ō\ (*n*) shell or jewel carved in relief; star's special appearance in a minor role in a film. Don't buy *cameos* from the street peddlers in Rome: the workmanship is wretched. Did you catch Bill Murray's *cameo* in *Little Shop of Horrors*? He was onscreen so briefly that if you blinked you missed him.

can-dor \'kan-dər\ (*n*) frankness. Jack can carry *candor* too far: when he told Jill his honest opinion of her, she nearly slapped his face. **can-did** \'kan-dəd\ (*adj*)

ca-nine \'kā-,nīn\ (*adj*) related to dogs; doglike. Some days the *canine* population of Berkeley seems almost to outnumber the human population.

can-ny \'kan-ē\ (*adj*) shrewd; thrifty. The *canny* Scotsman was more than a match for the swindlers.

cant \'kant\ (*n*) insincere expressions of piety; jargon of thieves. Shocked by news of the minister's extramarital affairs, the worshippers dismissed his talk about the sacredness of marriage as mere *cant*.

can-tan-ker-ous \kan-'tan-k(ə)rəs\ (*adj*) ill humored; irritable. Constantly complaining about his treatment and refusing to cooperate with the hospital staff, he was a *cantankerous* patient.

can-ter \'kant-ər\ (*n*) slow gallop. Because the racehorse had outdistanced its competition so easily, the reporter wrote that the race was won in a *canter*. also (*v*).

can-vass \'kan-vəs\ (*v*) determine votes, etc. After *canvassing* the sentiments of his constituents, the congressman was confident that he represented the majority opinion of his district. also (*n*).

\ə\ **abut** \ʰ\ **kitten**, F **table** \ər\ **further** \a\ **ash** \ā\ **ace** \ä\ **cot, cart**
\au̇\ **out** \ch\ **chin** \e\ **bet** \ē\ **easy** \g\ **go** \i\ **hit** \ī\ **ice** \j\ **job**

ca-pa-cious \ kə-'pā-shəs\ (*adj*) spacious. In the *capacious* areas of the railroad terminal, thousands of travelers lingered while waiting for their train.

ca-par-i-son \ kə-'par-ə-sən\ (*n*) showy harness or ornamentation for a horse. The audience admired the *caparison* of the horses as they made their entrance into the circus ring. also (*v*).

cap-il-lar-y \ 'kap-ə-ˌler-ē\ (*adj*) having a very fine bore. The changes in surface tension of liquids in *capillary* vessels is of special interest to physicists. also (*n*).

ca-pit-u-late \ kə-'pich-ə-ˌlāt\ (*v*) surrender. The enemy was warned to *capitulate* or face annihilation.

ca-pri-cious \ kə-'prish-əs\ (*adj*) fickle; incalculable. The storm was *capricious*: it changed course constantly. Jill was *capricious*, too: she changed boyfriends almost as often as she changed clothes. ca-price \ kə-'prēs\ (*n*)

cap-tion \ 'kap-shən\ (*n*) title; chapter heading; text under illustration. The *captions* that accompany *The Far Side* cartoons are almost as funny as the pictures. also (*v*).

cap-tious \ 'kap-shəs\ (*adj*) faultfinding. His criticisms were always *captious* and frivolous, never offering constructive suggestions.

ca-rafe \ kə-'raf\ (*n*) glass water bottle; decanter. With each dinner, the patron receives a *carafe* of red or white wine.

car-at \ 'kar-ət\ (*n*) unit of weight for precious stones; measure of fineness of gold. He gave her a three-*carat* diamond mounted in an eighteen-*carat* gold band.

car-cin-o-gen-ic \ kär-sin-ə-'jen-ik\ (*adj*) causing cancer. Many supposedly harmless substances have been revealed to be *carcinogenic*.

car-di-nal \ 'kärd-nəl\ (*adj*) chief. If you want to increase your word power, the *cardinal* rule of vocabulary-building is to read.

---

ca-reen \kə-'rēn\ (*v*) lurch; sway from side to side. The taxicab *careened* wildly as it rounded the corner.

car-i-ca-ture \'kar-i-kə-ˌchu̇(ə)r\ (*n*) exaggerated picture or description; distortion. The cartoonist's *caricature* of President Bush grossly exaggerated the size of the president's ears. also (*v*).

car-nage \'kär-nij\ (*n*) destruction of life. The film *The Killing Fields* vividly depicts the bloody *carnage* wreaked by Pol Pot's followers in Cambodia.

car-nal \'kärn-ᵊl\ (*adj*) fleshly. Are people more interested in *carnal* pleasures than in spiritual matters? Compare the number of people who read *Playboy* daily to the number of those who read the Bible or Koran every day.

car-niv-o-rous \kär-'niv-(ə-)rəs\ (*adj*) meat-eating. The lion's a *carnivorous* beast. A hunk of meat makes up his feast. A cow is not a *carnivore*. She likes the taste of grain, not gore. car-ni-vore \'kär-nə-ˌvō(ə)r\ (*n*)

ca-rous-al \kə-'rau̇-zəl\ (*n*) drunken revel. The party degenerated into an ugly *carousal*.

carp-ing \'kär-piŋ\ (*adj*) finding fault. A *carping* critic is a nitpicker: he loves to point out flaws. If you dislike this definition, feel free to *carp*.

car-ri-on \'kar-ē-ən\ (*n*) rotting flesh of a dead body. Buzzards are nature's scavengers; they eat the *carrion* left behind by other predators.

car-tog-ra-pher \kär-'täg-rə-fər\ (*n*) maker of maps or charts. *Cartographers* are unable to provide accurate maps of legal boundaries in the Near East because of the unsettled political situation in that part of the world following the recent military actions.

cas-cade \⁽ⁱ⁾kas-'kād\ (*n*) small waterfall. On such a hot day, the hikers felt refreshed by the spray from the series of *cascades* pouring down the cliffside. also (*v*).

---

caste \ˈkast\ (*n*) one of the hereditary classes in Hindu society. The differences created by the *caste* system in India must be eradicated if true democracy is to prevail in that country.

cas-ti-gate \ˈkas-tə-ˌgāt\ (*v*) criticize severely; punish. When the teacher threatened that she would *castigate* the mischievous boys if they didn't behave, they shaped up in a hurry.

ca-su-al-ty \ˈkazh-əl-tē\ (*n*) serious or fatal accident. The number of *casualties* on this holiday weekend was high.

cat-a-clysm \ˈkat-ə-ˌkliz-əm\ (*n*) violent upheaval; deluge. The Russian Revolution was a political and social *cataclysm* that overturned czarist society. **cat-a-clys-mic** \ˈkat-ə-ˌkliz-mik\ (*adj*)

cat-a-lyst \ˈkat-ᵊl-əst\ (*n*) agent that brings about a chemical change while it remains unaffected and unchanged. Many chemical reactions cannot take place without the presence of a *catalyst.*

cat-a-pult \ˈkat-ə-ˌpəlt\ (*n*) slingshot; a hurling machine. Airplanes are sometimes launched from battleships by *catapults.* also (*v*).

cat-a-ract \ˈkat-ə-ˌrakt\ (*n*) great waterfall; eye abnormality. She gazed with awe at the mighty *cataract* known as Niagara Falls.

ca-tas-tro-phe \kə-ˈtas-trə-ˌfē\ (*n*) calamity. The 1906 San Francisco earthquake was a *catastrophe* that destroyed most of the city.

cat-e-chism \ˈkat-ə-ˌkiz-əm\ (*n*) book for religious instruction; instruction by question and answer. He taught by engaging his pupils in a *catechism* until they gave him the correct answer.

ca-thar-sis \ka-ˈthär-səs\ (*n*) purging or cleansing of any passage of the body. Aristotle maintained that tragedy created a *catharsis* by purging the soul of base concepts.

\ŋ\ sing \ō\ go \ò\ law \òi\ boy \th\ thin \th̲\ the \ü\ loot \u̇\ foot
\y\ yet \zh\ vision \à, k̲, ⁿ, œ, œ̄, ue, œ̄, ʸ\ *see* Pronunciation Symbols

ca-thar-tic \kə-'thärt-ik\ (*n*) purgative. Some drugs act as laxatives when taken in small doses but act as *cathartics* when taken in much larger doses. also (*adj*).

cath-o-lic \ˌkath-(ə-)lik\ (*adj*) broadly sympathetic; liberal. He was extremely *catholic* in his reading tastes and read everything he could find in the school library.

cau-cus \'kȯ-kəs\ (*n*) private meeting of members of a party to select officers or determine policy. At the opening of Congress, the members of the Democratic Party held a *caucus* to elect the Majority Leader of the House and the Party Whip. also (*v*).

caus-tic \'kȯ-stik\ (*adj*) burning; sarcastically biting. The critic's *caustic* remarks angered the actors, who resented his cutting remarks.

cav-al-cade \'kav-əl-ˌkād\ (*n*) procession; parade. As described by Chaucer, the *cavalcade* of Canterbury pilgrims was a motley group.

cav-il \'kav-əl\ (*v*) make frivolous objections. I respect your sensible criticisms, but I dislike the way you *cavil* about unimportant details. also (*n*).

cede \'sēd\ (*v*) transfer; yield title to. Eventually the descendants of England's Henry II were forced to *cede* their French territories to the King of France.

ce-ler-i-ty \sə-'ler-ət-ē\ (*n*) speed; rapidity. Hamlet resented his mother's *celerity* in remarrying within a month after his father's death.

ce-les-tial \sə-'les(h)-chəl\ (*adj*) heavenly; relating to the sky. Pointing his primitive telescope at the heavens, Galileo explored the *celestial* mysteries.

cel-i-bate \'sel-ə-bət\ (*adj*) unmarried; abstaining from sexual intercourse. Though Havelock Ellis wrote extensively about sexual practices, recent studies maintain he was *celibate* throughout his life. cel-i-ba-cy \'sel-ə-bə-sē\ (*n*)

\ə\ abut \ᵊ\ kitten, F table \ər\ **further** \a\ ash \ā\ ace \ä\ cot, cart
\au̇\ **out** \ch\ **chin** \e\ bet \ē\ **easy** \g\ go \i\ hit \ī\ ice \j\ **job**

cen·sor \'sen(t)-sər\ (*n*) overseer of morals; person who studies material to eliminate inappropriate remarks. Soldiers dislike having their mail read by a *censor* but understand the need for this precaution. also (*v*).

cen·so·ri·ous \sen-'sȯr-ē-əs\ (*adj*) critical. *Censorious* people delight in casting blame.

cen·sure \'sen-chər\ (*v*) blame; criticize. He was *censured* for his ill-advised act. also (*n*).

cen·ti·grade \'sent-ə-ˌgrād\ (*adj*) measure of temperature used widely in Europe. On the *centigrade* themometer, the freezing point of water is zero degrees.

cen·trif·u·gal \sen-'trif-yə-gəl\ (*adj*) radiating; departing from the center. Many automatic drying machines remove excess moisture from clothing by *centrifugal* force. also (*n*).

cen·trip·e·tal \sen-'trip-ət-ᵊl\ (*adj*) tending toward the center. Does *centripetal* force or the force of gravity bring orbiting bodies to the earth's surface?

ce·re·bral \sə-'rē-brəl\ (*adj*) pertaining to the brain or intellect. The heroes of *Dumb and Dumber* were poorly equipped for *cerebral* pursuits.

cer·e·bra·tion \ˌser-ə-'brā-shən\ (*n*) thought. Mathematics problems sometimes require much *cerebration*. **cer·e·brate** \'ser-ə-ˌbrāt\ (*v*)

ces·sa·tion \se-'sā-shən)\ (*n*) stopping. The workers threatened a *cessation* of all activities if their demands were not met. **cease** \'sēs\ (*v*)

ces·sion \'sesh-ən\ (*n*) yielding to another; ceding. The *cession* of Alaska to the United States is discussed in this chapter.

chafe \'chāf\ (*v*) warm by rubbing; make sore by rubbing. Chilled, he *chafed* his hands before the fire. The collar *chafed* his neck. also (*n*).

\ŋ\ **sing**　\ō\ **go**　\ȯ\ **law**　\ȯi\ **boy**　\th\ **thin**　\t͟h\ **the**　\ü\ **loot**　\u̇\ **foot**
\y\ **yet**　\zh\ **vision**　\à, k̲, ⁿ, œ, œ̄, ue, ue̅, ʸ\ *see* Pronunciation Symbols

chaff \'chaf\ (*n*) worthless products of an endeavor. When you separate the wheat from the *chaff,* be sure you throw out the *chaff.*

chaff-ing \'chaf-iŋ\ (*adj*) bantering; joking. Sometimes his flippant and *chaffing* remarks annoy us.

cha-grin \sha-'grin\ (*n*) vexation (caused by humiliation or injured pride); disappointment. Embarrassed by his parents' shabby, working-class appearance, Doug felt their visit to his school would bring him nothing but *chagrin.* also (*v*).

chal-ice \'chal-əs\ (*n*) goblet; consecrated cup. In a small room adjoining the cathedral, many ornately decorated *chalices* made by the most famous European gold-smiths were on display.

cha-me-leon \kə-'mēl-yən\ (*n*) lizard that changes color in different situations. Like the *chameleon,* he assumed the political thinking of every group he met.

cham-pi-on \'cham-pē-ən\ (*v*) support militantly. Martin Luther King, Jr., won the Nobel Peace Prize because he *championed* the oppressed in their struggle for equality.

cha-ot-ic \kā-ät-ik\ (*adj*) in utter disorder. He tried to bring order into the *chaotic* state of affairs. cha-os \'kā-,äs\ (*n*)

char-ac-ter-ize \'kar-ik-tə-,rīz\ (*v*) describe; distinguish. Heavy use of garlic and tomatoes *characterizes* the food of Provence. char-ac-ter-is-tic \,kar-ik-tə-'ris-tik\ (*adj*)

cha-ris-ma \kə-'riz-mə\ (*n*) divine gift; great popular charm or appeal of a political leader. Political commentators have deplored the importance of a candidate's *charisma* in these days of television campaigning.

char-la-tan \'shär-lə-tən\ (*n*) quack; pretender to knowledge. When they realized that the Wizard didn't know how to get them back to Kansas, Dorothy and her companions were indignant that they'd been duped by a *charlatan.*

\ə\ **abut** \ᵊ\ **kitten, F table** \ər\ **further** \a\ **ash** \ā\ **ace** \ä\ **cot, cart**
\aů\ **out** \ch\ **chin** \e\ **bet** \ē\ **easy** \g\ **go** \i\ **hit** \ī\ **ice** \j\ **job**

char-y \'cha(ə)r-ē\ (*adj*) cautious; sparing or restrained about giving. A prudent, thrifty New Englander, DeWitt was as *chary* of investing money in junk bonds as he was *chary* of paying people unnecessary compliments.

chasm \'kaz-əm\ (*n*) abyss. Looking down from the Cliffs of Doom, Frodo and his companions could not see the bottom of the *chasm*.

chas-sis \'shas-ē\ (*n*) framework and working parts of an automobile. Examining the car after the accident, the owner discovered that the body had been ruined but that the *chassis* was unharmed.

chaste \'chāst\ (*adj*) pure; virginal; modest. To ensure that his bride would stay *chaste* while he was off to the wars, the crusader had her fitted out with a *chastity* belt. chas-ti-ty \'chas-tət-ē\ (*n*)

chas-tise \⁽ˡ⁾chas-'tīz\ (*v*) punish. "Spare the rod and spoil the child" was Miss Watson's motto: she relished whipping Huck with a birch rod to *chastise* him.

chat-tel \'chat'-əl\ (*n*) personal property. When he bought his furniture on the installment plan, he signed a *chattel* mortgage.

chau-vin-ist \'shō-və-nəst\ (*n*) blindly devoted patriot. A *chauvinist* cannot recognize any faults in his country, no matter how flagrant they may be. Likewise, a male *chauvinist* cannot recognize how biased he is in favor of his own sex, no matter how flagrant his bias may be.

check-ered \'chek-ərd\ (*adj*) marked by changes in fortune. During his *checkered* career, he had lived in palatial mansions and dreary boardinghouses.

che-ru-bic \chə-'rü-bik\ (*adj*) angelic; innocent-looking. With her cheerful smile and rosy cheeks, she was a particularly *cherubic* child.

chi-ca-ner-y \skik-'ān-(ə-)rē\ (*n*) trickery. Those sneaky lawyers misrepresented what occurred, made up all

---

\ŋ\ **sing** \ō\ **go** \ȯ\ **law** \ȯi\ **boy** \th\ **thin** \t̲h̲\ **the** \ü\ **loot** \u̇\ **foot**
\y\ **yet** \zh\ **vision** \à, k̲, ⁿ, œ, ɶ, ɷe, ɷ, ʲ\ *see* Pronunciation Symbols

sorts of implausible alternative scenarios to confuse the jurors, and in general depended on *chicanery* to win the case.

chide \'chīd\ (*v*) scold. Grandma began to *chide* Steven for his lying.

chi-me-ri-cal \kī-'mer-i-kəl\ (*adj*) fantastically improbable; highly unrealistic; imaginative. As everyone expected, Ted's *chimerical* scheme to make a fortune by raising ermines in his backyard proved a dismal failure. **chi-me-ra** \kī-'mir-ə\ (*n*)

cho-ler-ic \'käl-ə-rik\ (*adj*) hot-tempered. His flushed, angry face indicated a *choleric* nature.

cho-re-og-ra-phy \ˌkȯr-ē-'äg-rə-fē\ (*n*) art of representing dances in written symbols; arrangement of dances. Merce Cunningham uses a computer in designing *choreography*: a software program allows him to compose sequences of possible moves and immediately view them onscreen.

chron-ic \'krän-ik\ (*adj*) long established as a disease. The doctors were able finally to attribute his *chronic* headaches and nausea to traces of formaldehyde gas in his apartment.

churl-ish \'chər-lish\ (*adj*) boorish; rude. Dismayed by his *churlish* manners at the party, the girls vowed never to invite him again.

cir-cu-i-tous \ˌsər-'kyü-ət-əs\ (*adj*) roundabout. Because of the traffic congestion on the main highways, he took a *circuitous* route. **cir-cuit** \'sər-kət\ (*n, v*)

cir-cum-lo-cu-tion \ˌsər-kəm-lō-'kyü-shən\ (*n*) indirect or roundabout expression. He was afraid to call a spade a spade and resorted to *circumlocution* to avoid direct reference to his subject.

cir-cum-scribe \'sər-kəm-ˌskrīb\ (*v*) limit; confine. School regulations *circumscribed* Elle's social life: she hated having to follow rules that limited her activities.

\ə\ abut \ᵊ\ kitten, F table \ər\ further \a\ ash \ā\ ace \ä\ cot, cart
\au̇\ out \ch\ chin \e\ bet \ē\ easy \g\ go \i\ hit \ī\ ice \j\ job

cir-cum-spect \'sər-kəm-ˌspekt\ (*adj*) prudent; cautious. Investigating before acting, he tried always to be *circumspect.*

cir-cum-vent \ˌsər-kəm-'vent\ (*v*) outwit; baffle. In order to *circumvent* the enemy, we will make two preliminary attacks in other sections before starting our major campaign.

cit-a-del \'sit-əd-ᵊl\ (*n*) fortress. The *citadel* overlooked the city like a protecting angel.

cite \'sīt\ (*v*) quote; commend. He could *cite* passages in the Bible from memory. ci-ta-tion \sī-'tā-shən\ (*n*)

clair-voy-ant \kla(ə)r-'vȯi-ənt\ (*adj*) having foresight. Cassandra's *clairvoyant* warning was not heeded by the Trojans. also (*n*). clair-voy-ance \kla(ə)r-'vȯi-ən(t)s\ (*n*)

clam-ber \'klam-(b)ər\ (*v*) climb by crawling. He *clambered* over the wall.

clan-des-tine \klan-'des-tən\ (*adj*) secret. After avoiding Juliet's chaperone, the lovers had a *clandestine* meeting.

clar-i-on \'klar-ē-ən\ (*adj*) shrill trumpetlike sound. We woke to the *clarion* call of the bugle. also (*n*).

claus-tro-pho-bi-a \ˌklȯ-strə-'fō-bē-ə\ (*n*) fear of being shut in. His classmates laughed at his *claustrophobia* and threatened to lock him in a closet.

clav-i-cle \'klav-i-kəl\ (*n*) collarbone. Even though he wore shoulder pads, the football player broke his *clavicle* during a practice scrimmage.

cleave \'klēv\ (*v*) split asunder. The lightning *cleaves* the tree in two. cleav-age \'klē-vij\ (*n*)

cleft \'kleft\ (*n*) split. There was a *cleft* in the huge boulder. also (*adj*).

clem-en-cy \'klem-ən-sē\ (*n*) disposition to be lenient; mildness, as of the weather. The lawyer was pleased when the case was sent to Judge Smith's chambers because Smith was noted for his *clemency* toward first offenders.

\ŋ\ sing \ō\ go \ȯ\ law \ȯi\ boy \th\ thin \t͟h\ the \ü\ loot \u̇\ foot
\y\ yet \zh\ vision \à, k̲, ⁿ, œ, œ̄, ᵫ, œ, ᵊ\ *see* Pronunciation Symbols

cli-ché \kli-'shā\ (*n*) phrase dulled in meaning by repetition. High school compositions are often marred by such *clichés* as "strong as an ox."

cli-mac-tic \klī-'mak-tik\ (*adj*) relating to the highest point. When he reached the *climactic* portions of the book, he could not stop reading. cli-max \'klī-,maks\ (*n*)

clime \'klīm\ (*n*) region; climate. His doctor advised him to move to a milder *clime.*

clique \'klēk\ (*n*) small exclusive group. Fitzgerald wished that he belonged to the *clique* of popular athletes and big men on campus who seemed to run Princeton's social life.

clois-ter \'kloi-stər\ (*n*) monastery or convent. The nuns lived in the *cloister.* also (*v*).

clo-ven \'klō-vən\ (*adj*) split. Popular legends maintain that the devil has *cloven* hooves like a goat.

co-a-lesce \,kō-ə-'les\ (*v*) combine; fuse. The brooks *coalesce* into one large river.

cod-dle \'käd-ᵊl\ (*v*) treat gently; pamper. Don't *coddle* the children so much; they need a taste of discipline.

cod-i-cil \'käd-ə-səl\ (*n*) supplement to the body of a will. This *codicil* was drawn up five years after the writing of the original will.

co-erce \kō-ərs\ (*v*) force; repress. The inquisitors *coerced* Joan of Arc both physically and psychologically, hoping to force her to deny that her visions were sent by God. co-er-cion \kō-'ər-zhən\ (*n*)

co-eval \kō-'ē-vəl\ (*adj*) living at the same time as; contemporary. *Coeval* with the dinosaur, the pterodactyl flourished during the Mesozoic era.

cog \'käg\ (*n*) tooth projecting from a wheel. On steep slopes, *cog* railways are frequently used to prevent slipping.

co-gent \'kō-jənt\ (*adj*) convincing. Katya used such *cogent* arguments in presenting her case that she quickly convinced the jury to decide in favor of her client.

\ə\ **abut** \ᵊ\ **kitten,** F **table** \ər\ **further** \a\ **ash** \ā\ **ace** \ä\ **cot, cart**
\aú\ **out** \ch\ **chin** \e\ **bet** \ē\ **easy** \g\ **go** \i\ **hit** \ī\ **ice** \j\ **job**

cog-i-tate \\'käj-ə-ˌtāt\\ (*v*) think over. *Cogitate* on this problem; the solution will come.

cog-nate \\'käg-ˌnāt\\ (*adj*) related linguistically: allied by blood: similar or akin in nature. The English word "mother" is *cognate* to the Latin word "mater," whose influence is visible in the words "maternal" and "maternity." also (*n*).

cog-ni-zance \\'käg-nə-zən(t)s\\ (*n*) knowledge. During the election campaign, the two candidates were kept in full *cognizance* of the international situation.

co-here \\kō-ˌhi(ə)r\\ (*v*) stick together. Solids have a greater tendency to *cohere* than liquids.

co-he-sion \\kō-'hē-zhən\\ (*n*) tendency to keep together. A firm believer in the maxim "Divide and conquer," the evil emperor sought to disrupt the *cohesion* of the federation of free nations.

co-hort \\'kō-ˌhȯ(ə)rt\\ (*n*) armed band. Caesar and his Roman *cohorts* conquered almost all of the known world.

col-lab-o-rate \\kə-'lab-ə-ˌrāt\\ (*v*) work together. Two writers *collaborated* in preparing this book.

col-late \\kə-'lāt\\ (*v*) examine in order to verify authenticity; arrange in order. They *collated* the newly found manuscripts to determine their age.

col-lat-er-al \\kə-'lat-ə-rəl\\ (*n*) security given for loan. The sum you wish to borrow is so large that it must be secured by *collateral*.

col-la-tion \\kə-'lā-shən\\ (*n*) a light meal. Tea sandwiches and cookies were offered at the *collation*.

col-lier \\'käl-yər\\ (*n*) worker in coal mine; ship carrying coal. The extended cold spell has prevented the *colliers* from delivering the coal to the docks as scheduled.

col-lo-qui-al \\kə-'lō-kwē-əl\\ (*adj*) pertaining to conversational or common speech. Some of the new, less formal reading passages on SAT I have a *colloquial* tone that is intended to make them more appealing to students.

\\ŋ\\ si**ng** \\ō\\ g**o** \\ȯ\\ l**aw** \\ȯi\\ b**oy** \\th\\ **th**in \\th\\ **th**e \\ü\\ l**oo**t \\u̇\\ f**oo**t
\\y\\ **y**et \\zh\\ vi**si**on \\à, <u>k</u>, ⁿ, œ, œ̄, ue, œ̄, ʸ\\ *see* Pronunciation Symbols

col·lo·quy \\'käl-ə-kwē\\ (*n*) informal discussion. While a colloquium often is a formal seminar or conference, a *colloquy* traditionally is merely a conversational exchange.

col·lu·sion \\ kə-'lü-zhən\\ (*n*) conspiring in a fraudulent scheme. The swindlers were found guilty of *collusion.*

co·los·sal \\ kə-'läs-əl\\ (*adj*) huge. Radio City Music Hall has a *colossal* stage.

co·ma·tose \\'kō-mə-ˌtōs\\ (*adj*) in a coma; extremely sleepy. The long-winded orator soon had his audience in a *comatose* state.

com·bus·ti·ble \\ kəm-'bəs-tə-bəl\\ (*adj*) easily burned. After the recent outbreak of fires in private homes, the fire commissioner ordered that all *combustible* materials be kept in safe containers. also (*n*).

come·ly \\'kəm-lē\\ (*adj*) attractive; agreeable. I would rather have a *comely* wife than a rich one.

co·mes·ti·ble \\ kə-'mes-tə-bəl\\ (*n*) something fit to be eaten. The roast turkey and other *comestibles,* the wines, and the excellent service made this Thanksgiving dinner particularly memorable.

co·mi·ty \\'käm-ət-ē\\ (*n*) courtesy; civility. A spirit of *comity* should exist among nations.

com·man·deer \\ ˌkäm-ən-'di(ə)r\\ (*v*) to draft for military purposes; to take for public use. The policeman *commandeered* the first car that approached and ordered the driver to go to the nearest hospital.

com·men·su·rate \\ kə-'men(t)s(-ə)-rət\\ (*adj*) equal in extent. Your reward will be *commensurate* with your effort.

com·mis·er·ate \\ kə-'miz-ə-ˌrāt\\ (*v*) feel or express pity or sympathy for. Her friends *commiserated* with the widow.

com·mo·di·ous \\ kə-'mōd-ē-əs\\ (*adj*) spacious and comfortable. After sleeping in small roadside cabins, they found their hotel suite *commodious.*

\\ə\\ **abut** \\ᵊ\\ **kitten**, F **table** \\ər\\ **further** \\a\\ **ash** \\ā\\ **ace** \\ä\\ **cot, cart**
\\aú\\ **out** \\ch\\ **chin** \\e\\ **bet** \\ē\\ **easy** \\g\\ **go** \\i\\ **hit** \\ī\\ **ice** \\j\\ **job**

com-mu-nal \kə-'myün-ᵊl\ (*adj*) held in common; of a group of people. When they were divorced, they had trouble dividing their *communal* property.

com-pact \'käm-ˌpakt\ (*n*) agreement; contract. The signers of the Mayflower *Compact* were establishing a form of government. com-pact \kəm-'pakt\ (*v, adj*)

com-pat-i-ble \kəm-'pat-ə-bəl\ (*adj*) harmonious; in harmony with. They were *compatible* neighbors, never quarreling over unimportant matters.

com-pen-di-um \kəm-'pen-dē-əm\ (*n*) brief comprehensive summary. This text can serve as a *compendium* of the tremendous amount of new material being developed in this field.

com-pen-sa-tory \kəm-'pen(t)-sə-ˌtōr-ē\ (*adj*) making up for; repaying. Can a *compensatory* education program make up for inadequate schooling received in earlier years?

com-pi-la-tion \ˌkäm-pə-'lā-shən\ (*n*) listing of statistical information in tabular or book form. The *compilation* of available scholarships serves a very valuable purpose.

com-pla-cent \kəm-'plās-ᵊnt\ (*adj*) self-satisfied. Feeling *complacent* about his latest victories, he looked smugly at the row of trophies on his mantelpiece. com-pla-cen-cy \kəm-'plās-ᵊn-sē\ (*n*)

com-plai-sant \kəm-'plās-ᵊnt\ (*adj*) trying to please; obliging. Always ready to accede to his noble patron's wishes, Mr. Collins was a *complaisant*, even obsequious, character.

com-ple-ment \'käm-plə-mənt\ (*v*) complete; consummate; make perfect. The waiter recommended a glass of port to *complement* the cheese. also (*n*).

com-pli-ant \kəm-'plī-ənt\ (*adj*) yielding. Because Joel usually gave in and went along with whatever his friends desired, his mother worried that he might be too *compliant*.

\ŋ\ sing \ō\ go \ȯ\ law \ȯi\ boy \th\ thin \<u>th</u>\ the \ü\ loot \u̇\ foot
\y\ yet \zh\ vision \à, <u>k</u>, ⁿ, œ, œ̄, ue, œ̄, ʸ\ *see* Pronunciation Symbols

com·plic·i·ty \kəm-'plis-ət-ē\ (*n*) participation; involvement. You cannot keep your *complicity* in this affair secret very long; you would be wise to admit your involvement immediately.

com·port \kəm-'pō(ə)rt\ (*v*) bear one's self; behave. He *comported* himself with great dignity.

com·po·sure \kəm-'pō-zhər\ (*n*) mental calmness. Even the latest work crisis failed to shake her *composure*.

com·pre·hen·sive \ˌkäm-pri-'hen(t)-siv\ (*adj*) thorough; inclusive. This book provides a *comprehensive* review of verbal and math skills for the SAT.

com·press \kəm-'pres\ (*v*) squeeze; contract. She *compressed* the package under her arm. com·pres·sion \kəm-'presh-ən\ (*n*)

com·pro·mise \'käm-prə-ˌmīz\ (*v*) adjust or settle by making mutual concessions; endanger the interests or reputation of. Sometimes the presence of a neutral third party can help adversaries *compromise* their differences. Unfortunately, you're not neutral. Therefore, your presence here *compromises* our chances of reaching an agreement. also (*n*).

com·punc·tion \kəm-'pəŋ(k)-shən\ (*n*) remorse. The judge was especially severe in his sentencing because he felt that the criminal had shown no *compunction* for his heinous crime.

com·pute \kəm-'pyüt\ (*v*) reckon; calculate. He failed to *compute* the interest.

con·cave \kän-'kāv\ (*adj*) hollow. The backpackers found partial shelter from the storm by huddling against the *concave* wall of the cliff.

con·cen·tra·tion \'kän(t)-sən-ˌtrā-shən\ (*n*) close attention or focus; density or clustering. The children's playground was closed because of the high *concentration* of toxic chemicals in the soil.

\ə\ **abut** \ᵊ\ **kitten, F table** \ər\ **further** \a\ **ash** \ā\ **ace** \ä\ **cot, cart** \au̇\ **out** \ch\ **chin** \e\ **bet** \ē\ **easy** \g\ **go** \i\ **hit** \ī\ **ice** \j\ **job**

con-cen-tric \kən-'sen-trik\ (*adj*) having a common center. The target was made of *concentric* circles.

con-cep-tion \kən-'sep-shən\ (*n*) beginning; forming of an idea. At the first *conception* of the work, he was consulted. con-ceive \kən-'sēv\ (*v*)

con-ces-sion \kən-'sesh-ən\ (*n*) an act of yielding. Before they could reach an agreement, both sides had to make certain *concessions.*

con-cil-i-ate \kən-'sil-ē-ˌāt\ (*v*) pacify; win over. She tried to *conciliate* me with a gift. con-cil-ia-to-ry \kən-'sil-yə-ˌtōr-ē\ (*adj*)

con-cise \kən-'sīs\ (*adj*) brief and compact. When you define a new word, be *concise*: the shorter the definition, the easier it is to remember.

con-clave \'kän-ˌklāv\ (*n*) private meeting. He was present at all their *conclaves* as a sort of unofficial observer.

con-coct \kən-'käkt\ (*v*) prepare by combining; make up in concert. How did you ever *concoct* such a strange dish? con-coc-tion \kən-'käk-shən\ (*n*)

con-com-i-tant \kən-'käm-ət-ənt\ (*n*) that which accompanies. Culture is not always a *concomitant* of wealth; you can be rich and a philistine. also (*adj*).

con-cor-dat \kən-'kȯr-ˌdat\ (*n*) agreement, usually between the papal authority and the secular. One of the most famous of the agreements between a pope and an emperor was the *Concordat* of Worms in 1122.

con-crete \'kän-ˌkrēt\ (*adj*) real or substantial. Being busy is no excuse; you must have a more *concrete* reason for postponing taking your exam.

con-cur-rent \kən-'kər-ənt\ (*adj*) happening at the same time. In America, the colonists were resisting the demands of the mother country; at the *concurrent* moment in France, the middle class was sowing the seeds of rebellion.

---

con-de-scend \ˌkän-di-'send\ (*v*) act conscious of descending to a lower level; patronize. Though Jill had been a star softball player in college, when she played a pickup game at the park she never *condescended* to her less experienced teammates. **con-de-scen-sion** \ˌkän-di-'sen-chən\ (*n*)

con-di-ment \'kän-də-mənt\ (*n*) seasoning; spice. Spanish food is full of *condiments.*

con-dole \kən-'dōl\ (*v*) express sympathetic sorrow. His friends gathered to *condole* with him over his loss. **con-do-lence** \kən-'dō-lən(t)s\ (*n*)

con-done \kən-'dōn\ (*v*) overlook; forgive. Unlike Widow Douglass, who *condoned* Huck's minor offenses, Miss Watson did nothing but scold the lad.

con-duit \'kän-ˌd(y)ü-ət\ (*n*) aqueduct; passageway for fluids. Water came to the army in the desert via an improvised *conduit* from the adjoining mountain.

con-fer \kən-'fər\ (*v*) discuss or compare ideas; grant or bestow. The members of the committee *conferred* before reaching a final decision.

con-fi-dant \'kän-fə-ˌdant\ (*n*) a person to whom one can tell secrets. When my best friend moved, I lost my only *confidant.*

con-fis-cate \'kän-fə-ˌskāt\ (*v*) seize; commandeer. The army *confiscated* all available supplies of uranium. also (*adj*).

con-fla-gra-tion \ˌkän-flə-'grā-shən\ (*n*) great fire. In the *conflagration* that followed the 1906 earthquake, much of San Francisco was destroyed.

con-for-mi-ty \kən-'for-mət-ē\ (*n*) harmony; agreement. In *conformity* with our rules and regulations, I am calling a meeting of our organization.

con-geal \kən-'jē(ə)l\ (*v*) freeze, coagulate. His blood *congealed* in his veins as he saw the dread monster rush toward him.

\ə\ abut \ᵊ\ kitten, F table \ər\ further \a\ ash \ā\ ace \ä\ cot, cart
\au̇\ out \ch\ chin \e\ bet \ē\ easy \g\ go \i\ hit \ī\ ice \j\ job

con-gen-i-tal \ kän-'jen-ə-tᵊl\ (*adj*) existing at birth. Doctors are able to cure some *congenital* deformities such as cleft palates by performing operations on infants.

con-glom-er-a-tion \ kən-ˌgläm-ə-'rā-shən\ (*n*) mass of material sticking together. In such a *conglomeration* of miscellaneous statistics, it was impossible to find a single area of analysis.

con-gre-ga-tion \ˌkäŋ-gri-'gā-shən\ (*n*) a gathering or assembly. There was a great *congregation* of protesters outside the courthouse after the verdict was read.

con-gru-ence \kən-'grü-ən(t)s\ (*n*) correspondence of parts; harmonious relationship. The student demonstrated the *congruence* of the two triangles by using the hypotenuse-arm theorem.

co-ni-fer \'kän-ə-fər\ (*n*) pine tree; cone-bearing tree. According to geologists, *conifers* were the first plants to bear flowers.

con-jec-ture \kən-'jek-chər\ (*n*) surmise; guess. Although there was no official count, the organizers *conjectured* that over 10,000 marchers took part in the March for Peace.

con-ju-gal \'kän-ji-gəl\ (*adj*) pertaining to marriage. Their dreams of *conjugal* bliss were shattered as soon as their temperaments clashed.

con-jure \'kän-jər\ (*v*) summon a devil; practice magic; imagine; invent. Sorcerers *conjure* devils to appear. Magicians *conjure* white rabbits out of hats. Political candidates *conjure* up images of reformed cities and a world at peace.

con-niv-ance \kə-'nī-vən(t)s\ (*n*) pretense of ignorance of something wrong; assistance; permission to offend. With the *connivance* of his friends, he plotted to embarrass the teacher. con-nive \kə-'nīv\ (*v*)

\ŋ\ si**ng**   \ō\ g**o**   \ȯ\ l**aw**   \ȯi\ b**oy**   \th\ **th**in   \t̲h̲\ **the**   \ü\ l**oo**t   \u̇\ f**oo**t
\y\ **y**et   \zh\ vi**s**ion   \à, k̲, ⁿ, œ, œ̄, ue, œ̄, ʸ\ *see* Pronunciation Symbols

con-nois-seur \ˌkän-ə-'sər\ (*n*) person competent to act as a judge of art, etc.; a lover of art. He had developed into a *connoisseur* of fine china.

con-no-ta-tion \ˌkän-ə-'tā-shən\ (*n*) suggested or implied meaning of an expression. Foreigners frequently are unaware of the *connotations* of the words they use.

con-nu-bi-al \kə-'n(y)ü-bē-əl\ (*adj*) pertaining to marriage or the matrimonial state. In his telegram, he wished the newlyweds a lifetime of *connubial* bliss.

con-sci-en-tious \ˌkän-chē-'en-chəs\ (*adj*) scrupulous; careful. A *conscientious* editor, she checked every definition for its accuracy.

con-se-crate \'kän(t)-sə-ˌkrāt\ (*v*) dedicate; sanctify. We shall *consecrate* our lives to this noble purpose. also (*adj*).

con-sen-sus \kən-'sen(t)-səs\ (*n*) general agreement. Every time the garden club members had nearly reached a *consensus* about what to plant, Mistress Mary, quite contrary, disagreed.

con-se-quen-tial \ˌkän(t)-sə-'kwen-chəl\ (*adj*) following as an effect; important; self-important. Convinced of his own importance, the actor strutted about the dressing room with a *consequential* air. con-se-quence \'kän(t)sə-'kwen(t)s\ (*n*); con-se-quent \'kän(t)-sə-kwent\ (*adj*)

con-so-nance \'kän(t)-s(ə-)nən(t)s\ (*n*) harmony; agreement. Her agitation seemed out of *consonance* with her usual calm.

con-sort \kən-'sȯ(ə)rt\ (*v*) associate with. We frequently judge people by the company with whom they *consort*. con-sort \'kän-ˌsȯ(ə)rt\ (*n*)

con-spic-u-ous \kən-'spik-yə-wəs\ (*adj*) easily seen; noticeable; striking. Janet was *conspicuous* both for her red hair and for her height.

\ə\ **abut** \ᵊ\ **kitten**, F **table** \ər\ **further** \a\ **ash** \ā\ **ace** \ä\ **cot, cart** \au̇\ **out** \ch\ **chin** \e\ **bet** \ē\ **easy** \g\ **go** \i\ **hit** \ī\ **ice** \j\ **job**

con-spir-a-cy \kən-'spir-ə-sē\ (*n*) treacherous plot. Brutus and Cassius joined in the *conspiracy* to kill Julius Caesar.

con-stit-u-ent \kən-'stich-(ə-)wənt\ (*n*) supporter. The congressman received hundreds of letters from angry *constituents* after the Equal Rights Amendment failed to pass.

con-straint \kən-'strānt\ (*n*) compulsion; repression of feelings. There was a feeling of *constraint* in the room because no one dared to criticize the speaker. con-strain \kən-'strān\ (*v*)

con-strue \kən-'strü\ (*v*) explain; interpret. If I *construe* your remarks correctly, you disagree with the theory already advanced.

con-sum-mate \kən-'səm-ət\ (*adj*) complete. I have never seen anyone who makes as many stupid errors as you do; what a *consummate* idiot you are! con-sum-mate \'kän(t)-sə-ˌmāt\ (*v*)

con-tam-i-nate \kən-'tam-ə-ˌnāt\ (*v*) pollute. The sewage system of the city so *contaminated* the water that swimming was forbidden.

con-ten-tious \kən-'ten-chəs\ (*adj*) quarrelsome. Disagreeing violently with the referees' ruling, the coach became so *contentious* that they threw him out of the game.

con-text \'kän-ˌtekst\ (*n*) writings preceding and following the passage quoted. Because these lines are taken out of *context,* they do not convey the message the author intended.

con-tig-u-ous \kən-'tig-yə-wəs\ (*adj*) adjacent to; touching upon. The two countries are *contiguous* for a few miles; then they are separated by the gulf.

con-ti-nence \'känt-ᵊn-ən(t)s\ (*n*) self-restraint; sexual chastity. At the convent, Connie vowed to lead a life of *continence.* The question was, could Connie be content with always being *continent*? con-ti-nent \känt-ᵊn-ᵊnt\ (*adj*)

con-tin-gent \kən-'tin-jənt\ (*adj*) dependent on; conditional. Cher's father informed her that any raise in her allowance was *contingent* on the quality of her final grades. con-tin-gen-cy \kən-'tin-jən-sē\ (*n*)

con-tor-tion \kən-'tȯr-shən\ (*n*) twisting; distortion. As the effects of the opiate wore away, the *contortions* of the patient became more violent and demonstrated how much pain he was enduring. con-tort \kən-'tȯ(ə)rt\ (*v*)

con-tra-band \'kän-trə-ˌband\ (*adj*) illegal trade; smuggling. The Coast Guard tries to prevent traffic in *contraband* goods. also (*n*).

con-tract \ˌkän-'trakt\ (*v*) to compress or shrink; to enter into a binding agreement. The application of electric current can cause muscles to *contract*.

con-tra-vene \ˌkän-trə-'vēn\ (*v*) contradict; oppose; infringe on or transgress. Mr. Barrett did not expect his frail daughter Elizabeth to *contravene* his will by eloping with Robert Browning.

con-trite \'kän-ˌtrīt\ (*adj*) penitent. Her *contrite* tears did not influence the judge when he imposed sentence. con-tri-tion \kən-'trish-ən\ (*n*)

con-tro-vert \'kän-trə-ˌvərt\ (*v*) oppose with arguments; attempt to refute; contradict. The witness's testimony was so clear and her reputation for honesty so well established that the defense attorney decided it was wiser to make no attempt to *controvert* what she said.

con-tu-ma-cious \ˌkän-t(y)ə-'mā-shəs\ (*adj*) disobedient; resisting authority. The *contumacious* mob shouted defiantly at the police. con-tu-ma-cy \kən-'t(y)ü-mə-sē\ (*n*)

con-tu-sion \kən-'t(y)ü-zhən\ (*n*) bruise. Black and blue after her fall, Sue was treated for *contusions* and abrasions.

\ə\ **abut** \ᵊ\ **kitten**, F **table** \ər\ **further** \a\ **ash** \ā\ **ace** \ä\ **cot, cart**
\aú\ **out** \ch\ **chin** \e\ **bet** \ē\ **easy** \g\ **go** \i\ **hit** \ī\ **ice** \j\ **job**

co·nun·drum \kə-'nən-drəm\ (*n*) riddle; difficult problem. During the long car ride, she invented *conundrums* to entertain the children.

con·vene \kən-'vēn\ (*v*) assemble. Because much needed legislation had to be enacted, the governor ordered the legislature to *convene* in special session by January 15.

con·ven·tion·al \kən-'vench-nəl, -'ven-chən-ᵊl\ (*adj*) ordinary or typical. His *conventional* upbringing left him wholly unprepared for his wife's eccentric family.

con·ver·sant \kən-'vərs-ᵊnt\ (*adj*) familiar with. The lawyer is *conversant* with all the evidence.

con·vey·ance \kən-'vā-ən(t)s\ (*n*) vehicle; transfer. During the transit strike, commuters used various kinds of *conveyances*.

con·vic·tion \kən-'vik-shən\ (*n*) judgment that someone is guilty of a crime; strongly held belief. Even her *conviction* for murder did not shake Peter's *conviction* that Harriet was innocent of the crime.

con·viv·ial \kən-'viv-yəl\ (*adj*) festive; gay; characterized by joviality. The *convivial* celebrators of the victory sang their college songs.

con·voke \kən-'vōk\ (*v*) call together. Congress was *convoked* at the outbreak of the emergency. con·vo·ca·tion \ˌkän-və-'kā-shən\ (*n*)

con·vo·lut·ed \'kän-və-ˌlüt-əd\ (*adj*) coiled around; involved; intricate. The new tax regulations are so *convoluted* that even accountants have trouble following their twists and turns.

co·pi·ous \'kō-pē-əs\ (*adj*) plentiful. He had *copious* reasons for rejecting the proposal.

co·quette \kō-'ket\ (*n*) flirt. Because she refused to give him any answer to his proposal of marriage, he called her a *coquette*. also (*v*).

cor·dial \'kȯr-jəl\ (*adj*) gracious; heartfelt. Our hosts greeted us at the airport with a *cordial* welcome and a hearty hug.

\ŋ\ **sing** \ō\ **go** \ȯ\ **law** \ȯi\ **boy** \th\ **thin** \t̲h̲\ **the** \ü\ **loot** \u̇\ **foot**
\y\ **yet** \zh\ **vision** \à, k̲, ⁿ, œ, œ̄, ᵫ, œ, ᵉ\ *see* Pronunciation Symbols

cor-don \'kȯrd-ᵊn\ (*n*) extended line of men or fortifications to prevent access or egress. The police *cordon* was so tight that the criminals could not leave the area. also (*v*).

cor-ol-lar-y \'kȯr-ə-ˌler-ē\ (*n*) consequence; accompaniment. Brotherly love is a complex emotion, with sibling rivalry its natural *corollary.*

cor-po-re-al \kȯr-'pōr-ē-əl\ (*adj*) bodily; material. The doctor had no patience with spiritual matters: his job was to attend to his patients' *corporeal* problems, not to minister to their souls.

cor-pu-lent \'kȯr-pyə-1ənt\ (*adj*) very fat. The *corpulent* man resolved to reduce. **cor-pu-lence** \'kȯr-pyə-lən(t)s\ (*n*)

cor-re-la-tion \ˌkȯr-ə-lā-shən\ (*n*) mutual relationship. He sought to determine the *correlation* that existed between ability in algebra and ability to interpret reading exercises.

cor-rob-o-rate \kə-'räb-ə-ˌrāt\ (*v*) confirm. Though Huck was quite willing to *corroborate* Tom's story, Aunt Polly knew better than to believe either of them.

cor-ro-sive \kə-'rō-siv\ (*adj*) eating away by chemicals or disease. Stainless steel is able to withstand the effects of *corrosive* chemicals.

cor-ru-gat-ed \'kȯr-ə-ˌgāt-əd\ (*adj*) wrinkled; ridged. She wished she could smooth away the wrinkles from his *corrugated* brow.

cor-tege \kȯr-'tezh\ (*n*) procession. The funeral *cortege* proceeded slowly down the avenue.

cos-mic \'käz-mik\ (*adj*) pertaining to the universe; vast. *Cosmic* rays derive their name from the fact that they bombard the earth's atmosphere from outer space. **cos-mos** \'käz-məs\ (*n*)

co-te-rie \'kōt-ə-ˌ₍₎rē\ (*n*) group that meets socially; select circle. After his book had been published, he was invit-

---

\ə\ **abut** \ᵊ\ **kitten, F table** \ər\ **further** \a\ **ash** \ā\ **ace** \ä\ **cot, cart**
\aú\ **out** \ch\ **chin** \e\ **bet** \ē\ **easy** \g\ **go** \i\ **hit** \ī\ **ice** \j\ **job**

ed to join the literary *coterie* that lunched daily at the hotel.

coun-te-nance \'kaůnt-ᵊn-ən(t)s\ (*v*) approve; tolerate. Miss Manners refused to *countenance* such rude behavior on their part.

coun-ter-mand \'kaůnt-ər-ˌmand\ (*v*) cancel; revoke. The general *countermanded* the orders issued in his absence. also (*n*).

coun-ter-part \'kaůnt-ər-ˌpärt\ (*n*) a thing that completes another; things very much alike. Night and day are *counterparts*, complementing one another.

coup \'kü\ (*n*) highly successful action or sudden attack. As the news of his *coup* spread throughout Wall Street, his fellow brokers dropped by to congratulate him.

cou-ple \'kəp-əl\ (*v*) join; unite. The Flying Karamazovs *couple* expert juggling and amateur joking in their nightclub act.

cou-ri-er \'kůr-ē-ər\ (*n*) messenger. The publisher sent a special *courier* to pick up the manuscript.

cov-e-nant \'kəv-(ə-)nənt\ (*n*) agreement. We must comply with the terms of the *convenant.* also (*v*).

co-vert \'kō-ˌvərt\ (*adj*) secret; hidden; implied. Investigations of the Central Intelligence Agency and other secret service networks reveal that such *covert* operations can get out of control.

cov-et-ous \'kəv-ət-əs\ (*adj*) avaricious; eagerly desirous of. The child was *covetous* by nature and wanted to take the toys belonging to his classmates. **cov-et** \'kəv-ət\ (*v*)

cow-er \'kaů(-ə)r\ (*v*) shrink quivering, as from fear. The frightened child *cowered* in the corner of the room.

coy \'kȯi\ (*adj*) shy; coquettish. Reluctant to commit herself so early in the game, Cora was *coy* in her answer to Ken's offer.

coz-en \'kəz-ᵊn\ (*v*) cheat; hoodwink; swindle. He was the kind of individual who would *cozen* his friends in a cheap card game but remain eminently ethical in all his business dealings.

crab-bed \'krab-əd\ (*adj*) sour; peevish. The children avoided the *crabbed* old man because he scolded them when they made noise.

crass \'kras\ (*adj*) very unrefined; grossly insensible. The film critic deplored the *crass* commercialism of moviemakers who abandon artistic standards in order to make a quick buck.

cra-ven \'krā-vən\ (*adj*) cowardly. Lillian's *craven* refusal to join the protest was criticized by her comrades, who had expected her to be brave enough to stand up for her beliefs.

cre-dence \'krēd-ᵊn(t)s\ (*n*) belief. Do not place any *credence* in his promises.

cred-i-bil-i-ty \ˌkred-ə-'bil-ət-ē\ (*n*) believability. The defense attorney tried to destroy the *credibility* of the witness for the prosecution.

cre-do \'krēd-ˌō\ (*n*) creed. I believe we may best describe his *credo* by saying that it approximates the Golden Rule.

cre-du-li-ty \kri-'d(y)ü-lət-ē\ (*n*) belief on slight evidence; gullibility; naivete. Con artists take advantage of the *credulity* of inexperienced investors to swindle them out of their savings. cred-u-lous \'krej-ə-ləs\ (*adj*)

creed \'krēd\ (*n*) system of religious or ethical beliefs. Any loyal American's *creed* must emphasize love of democracy.

cre-scen-do \krə-'shen-ˌdō\ (*n*) increase in the volume or intensity, as in a musical passage; climax. The music suddenly shifted its mood, dramatically switching from a muted, contemplative passage to a *crescendo* with blaring trumpets and clashing cymbals.

crest-fall-en \'krest-ˌfȯ-lən\ (*adj*) dejected; dispirited. We were surprised at his reaction to the failure of his pro-

---

ject; instead of being *crestfallen,* he was busily engaged in planning new activities.

crev-ice \\'krev-əs\\ (*n*) crack; fissure. The mountain climbers found footholds in the tiny *crevices* in the mountainside.

cringe \\'krinj\\ (*v*) shrink back, as if in fear. The dog *cringed,* expecting a blow.

cri-te-ri-on \\krī-'tir-ē-ən\\ (*n*) standard used in judging. What *criterion* did you use when you selected this essay as the prizewinner?

crone \\'krōn\\ (*n*) hag. The toothless *crone* frightened us when she smiled.

crotch-et-y \\'kräch-ət-ē\\ (*adj*) eccentric; whimsical. Although he was reputed to be a *crotchety* old gentleman, I found his ideas substantially sound and sensible.

crux \\'krəks\\ (*n*) essential or main point. This is the *crux* of the entire problem: everything centers on its being resolved.

crypt \\'kript\\ (*n*) secret recess or vault, usually used for burial. Until recently, only bodies of rulers and leading statesmen were interred in this *crypt.*

cryp-tic \\'krip-tik\\ (*adj*) mysterious; hidden; secret. Thoroughly baffled by Holmes's *cryptic* remarks, Watson wondered whether Holmes was intentionally concealing his thoughts about the crime.

cu-bi-cle \\'kyü-bi-kəl\\ (*n*) small compartment partitioned off; small bedchamber. Hoping to personalize their workspace, the staff members decorated their tiny identical *cubicles* in markedly individual ways.

cui-sine \\kwi-'zēn\\ (*n*) style of cooking. French *cuisine is* noted for its use of sauces and wines.

cul-de-sac \\'kəl-di-ˌsak\\ (*n*) blind alley; trap. The soldiers were unaware that they were marching into a *cul-de-sac* when they entered the canyon.

\\ŋ\\ **sing** \\ō\\ **go** \\ȯ\\ **law** \\ȯi\\ **boy** \\th\\ **thin** \\th̲\\ **the** \\ü\\ **loot** \\u̇\\ **foot**
\\y\\ **yet** \\zh\\ **vision** \\à, k̲, ⁿ, œ, œ̄, ue, œ̄, ˀ\\ *see* Pronunciation Symbols

cu·li·nar·y \'kel-ə-ˌner-ē\ (*adj*) relating to cooking. Many chefs attribute their *culinary* skill to the wise use of spices.

cull \'kəl\ (*v*) pick out; reject. Every month the farmer *culls* the nonlaying hens from his flock and sells them to the local butcher. also (*n*).

cul·mi·na·tion \ˌkəl-mə-'nā-shən\ (*n*) attainment of highest point. His inauguration as President of the United States marked the *culmination* of his political career.

cul·pa·ble \'kəl-pə-bəl\ (*adj*) deserving blame. Corrupt politicians who condone the illegal activities of gamblers are equally *culpable*.

cul·vert \'kəl-vərt\ (*n*) artificial channel for water. If we build a *culvert* under the road at this point, we will reduce the possibility of the road's being flooded during the rainy season.

cum·ber·some \'kəm-bər-səm\ (*adj*) heavy; hard to manage. He was burdened down with *cumbersome* parcels.

cu·pid·i·ty \kyu̇-'pid-ət-ē\ (*n*) greed. The defeated people could not satisfy the *cupidity* of the conquerors, who demanded excessive tribute.

cu·ra·tor \'kyu̇(ə)r-ˌāt-ər\ (*n*) superintendent; manager. The members of the board of trustees of the museum expected the new *curator* to plan events and exhibitions that would make the museum more popular.

cur·mud·geon \ˌ(ˌ)kər-'məj-ən\ (*n*) churlish, miserly individual. Although many regarded him as a *curmudgeon,* a few of us were aware of the many kindnesses and acts of charity he secretly performed.

cur·ry \'kər-ē\ (*v*) seek favor; groom a horse. The courtier *curried* favor with the king.

cur·sive \'kər-siv\ (*adj*) flowing, running. In normal writing we run our letters together in *cursive* form; in printing, we separate the letters. also (*n*).

\ə\ **abut** \ᵊ\ **kitten,** F **table** \ər\ **further** \a\ **ash** \ā\ **ace** \ä\ **cot, cart**
\au̇\ **out** \ch\ **chin** \e\ **bet** \ē\ **easy** \g\ **go** \i\ **hit** \ī\ **ice** \j\ **job**

cur-so-ry \'kərs-(ə-)rē\ (*adj*) casual; hastily done. Because a *cursory* examination of the ruins indicates the possibility of arson, we recommend that the insurance agency undertake a more extensive investigation of the fire's cause.

cur-tail \₍ᵢ₎kər-'tā(ə)l\ (*v*) shorten; reduce. When Elton asked Cher for a date, she said she was really sorry she couldn't go out with him, but her dad had ordered her to *curtail* her social life.

cyn-ic \'sin-ik\ (*n*) one who is skeptical or distrustful of human motives. A *cynic* from birth, Cynthia was suspicious whenever anyone gave her a gift "with no strings attached." cyn-i-cal \'sin-i-kəl\ (*adj*)

cy-no-sure \'sī-nə-ˌshu̇(ə)r\ (*n*) the object of general attention. As soon as the movie star entered the room, she became the *cynosure* of all eyes.

D

da-is \\dā-əs\\ (*n*) raised platform for guests of honor. When he approached the *dais,* he was greeted by cheers from the people who had come to honor him.

dal-ly \\dal-ē\\ (*v*) trifle with; procrastinate. Laertes told Ophelia that Hamlet could not marry her but could only *dally* with her affections.

dank \\daŋk\\ (*adj*) damp. The walls of the dungeon were *dank* and slimy.

dap-pled \\dap-əld\\ (*adj*) spotted. The sunlight filtering through the screens created a *dappled* effect on the wall.

daub \\dȯb\\ (*v*) smear (as with paint). From the way he *daubed* his paint on the canvas, I could tell he knew nothing of oils. also (*n*).

daunt \\dȯnt\\ (*v*) intimidate. Your threats cannot *daunt* me.

daunt-less \\dȯnt-ləs\\ (*adj*) bold. Despite the dangerous nature of the undertaking, the *dauntless* soldier volunteered for the assignment.

daw-dle \\dȯd-ᵊl\\ (*v*) loiter; waste time. We have to meet a deadline. Don't *dawdle*; just get down to work.

dead-lock \\ded-ˌläk\\ (*n*) standstill; stalemate. Because negotiations had reached a *deadlock*, some of the delegates had begun to mutter about breaking off the talks. also (*v*).

dead-pan \\ded-ˌpan\\ (*adj*) wooden; impassive. We wanted to see how long he could maintain his *deadpan* expression.

dearth \\dərth\\ (*n*) scarcity. The *dearth* of skilled labor compelled the employers to open trade schools.

de-ba-cle \\di-'bäk-əl\\ (*n*) sudden downfall; complete disaster. In the *Airplane* movies, every flight turns into a *debacle*, with passengers and crew members collapsing, engines falling apart, and carry-on baggage popping out of the overhead bins.

\\ə\\ **abut** \\ᵊ\\ **kitten,** F **table** \\ər\\ **further** \\a\\ **ash** \\ā\\ **ace** \\ä\\ **cot, cart**
\\au̇\\ **out** \\ch\\ **chin** \\e\\ **bet** \\ē\\ **easy** \\g\\ **go** \\i\\ **hit** \\ī\\ **ice** \\j\\ **job**

de-base \di-'bās\ (*v*) reduce in quality or value; lower in esteem; degrade. In *The King and I*, Anna refuses to kneel down and prostrate herself before the king, for she feels that to do so would *debase* her position.

de-bauch \di-'bȯch\ (*v*) corrupt; seduce from virtue. Did Socrates' teachings lead the young men of Athens to be virtuous citizens, or did they *debauch* the young men, causing them to question the customs of their fathers? **de-bauch-er-y** \‚di-'bȯch-(ə-)-rē\ (*n*)

de-bil-i-tate \di-'bil-ə-‚tāt\ (*v*) weaken; enfeeble. Michael's severe bout of the flu *debilitated* him so much that he was too tired to go to work for a week.

deb-o-nair \‚deb-ə-'na(ə)r\ (*adj*) friendly; aiming to please. Everyone liked the *debonair* youth because of his cheerful and obliging manner.

deb-u-tante \'deb-yü-‚tänt\ (*n*) young woman making formal entrance into society. As a *debutante*, she was often mentioned in the society columns of the newspapers.

dec-a-dence \'dek-əd-ən(t)s\ (*n*) decay. The moral *decadence* of the people was reflected in the lewd literature of the period.

de-cap-i-tate \di-'kap-ə-‚tāt\ (*v*) behead. "Off with her head!" cried the Duchess, eager to *decapitate* poor Alice.

de-cid-u-ous \di-'sij-ə-wəs\ (*adj*) falling off as of leaves. The oak is a *deciduous* tree, losing its leaves in autumn.

dec-i-mate \'des-ə-‚māt\ (*v*) kill, usually one out of ten. We do more to *decimate* our population in automobile accidents than we do in war.

de-ci-pher \di-'sī-fər\ (*v*) decode. I could not *decipher* the doctor's handwriting.

de-cliv-i-ty \di-'kliv-ət-ē\ (*n*) downward slope. The children loved to ski down the *declivity.*

de-com-po-si-tion \‚(‚)dē-‚käm-pə-'zish-ən\ (*n*) decay. Despite the body's advanced state of *decomposition,* the police were able to identify the murdered man. **de-com-pose** \‚dē-kəm-'pōz\ (*v*)

---

dec·o·rous \\'dek-ə-rəs\\ (*adj*) proper. Her *decorous* behavior was praised by her teachers. de·co·rum \\di-'kōr-əm\\ (*n*)

de·coy \\'de-ˌkȯi\\ (*n*) lure or bait. The wild ducks were not fooled by the *decoy.* de·coy \\di-'kȯi \\ (*v*)

de·crep·it \\di-'krep-ət\\ (*adj*) worn out by age. The *decrepit* car blocked traffic on the highway.

de·crep·i·tude \\di-'krep-ə-t(y)üd\\ (*n*) state of collapse caused by illness or old age. I was unprepared for the state of *decrepitude* in which I had found my old friend; he seemed to have aged twenty years in six months.

de·cry \\di-'krī\\ (*v*) express strong disapproval of; disparage. The founder of the Children's Defense Fund, Marian Wright Edelman, strongly *decries* the lack of financial and moral support for children in America today.

de·duc·i·ble \\di-'d(y)ü-sə-bəl\\ (*adj*) derived by reasoning. If we accept your premise, your conclusions are easily *deducible.*

def·a·ma·tion \\ˌdef-ə-mā-shən\\ (*n*) harming a person's reputation. Such *defamation* of character may result in a slander suit.

de·fault \\di-'fȯlt\\ (*n*) failure to act. When the visiting team failed to show up for the big game, they lost the game by *default.* also (*v*).

de·feat·ist \\di-'fēt-əst\\ (*adj*) attitude of one who is ready to accept defeat as a natural outcome. If you maintain your *defeatist* attitude, you will never succeed. also (*n*).

de·fec·tion \\di-'fek-shən\\ (*n*) desertion. The children, who had made him an idol, were hurt most by his *defection* from our cause.

def·er·ence \\'def-(ə-)rən(t)s\\ (*n*) courteous regard for another's wish. In *deference* to the minister's request, please do not take photographs during the wedding service.

de·file \\di-'fī(ə)l\\ (*v*) pollute; profane. The hoodlums *defiled* the church with their scurrilous writing.

\\ə\\ **abut** \\ᵊ\\ **kitten**, F **table** \\ər\\ **further** \\a\\ **ash** \\ā\\ **ace** \\ä\\ **cot, cart**
\\au̇\\ **out** \\ch\\ **chin** \\e\\ **bet** \\ē\\ **easy** \\g\\ **go** \\i\\ **hit** \\ī\\ **ice** \\j\\ **job**

de-fin-i-tive \di-'fin-ət-iv\ (*adj*) final; complete. Carl Sandburg's *Abraham Lincoln* may be regarded as the *definitive* work on the life of the Great Emancipator.

de-flect \di-'flekt\ (*v*) turn aside. His life was saved when his cigarette case *deflected* the bullet.

de-fray \di-'frā\ (*v*) pay the costs of. Her employer offered to *defray* the costs of her postgraduate education.

deft \'deft\ (*adj*) neat; skillful. The *deft* waiter uncorked the champagne without spilling a drop.

de-funct \di-'fən(k)t\ (*adj*) dead; no longer in use or existence. The lawyers sought to examine the books of the *defunct* corporation.

de-grad-ed \di-'grād-əd\ (*adj*) humiliated; debased. Some secretaries object to fetching their boss a cup of coffee because they feel *degraded* by being made to do such lowly tasks.

de-i-fy \'dē-ə-ˌfī\ (*v*) turn into a god; idolize. Admire the rock star all you want; just don't *deify* him.

deign \'dān\ (*v*) condescend. The celebrated fashion designer would not *deign* to speak to a mere seamstress.

de-lec-ta-ble \di-'lek-tə-bəl\ (*adj*) delightful; delicious. We thanked our host for a most *delectable* meal.

de-lete \di-'lēt\ (*v*) erase, strike out. If you *delete* this paragraph, the composition will have more appeal.

del-e-te-ri-ous \ˌdel-ə-'tir-ē-əs\ (*adj*) harmful. If you believe that smoking is *deleterious* to your health (and the Surgeon General certainly does), then quit!

de-lib-er-ate \di-'lib-ə-ˌrāt\ (*v*) consider; ponder. The judge took time to *deliberate* before reaching her decision.

de-lin-e-a-tion \di-ˌlin-ē-'ā-shən\ (*n*) portrayal. Austen's *delineation* of character is masterful: using only a few descriptive phrases, she depicts him so well that we can predict his every move.

de-lir-i-um \di-'lir-ē-əm\ (*n*) mental disorder marked by confusion. In his *delirium*, the drunkard saw pink panthers and talking pigs.

\ŋ\ sing   \ō\ go   \ȯ\ law   \ȯi\ boy   \th\ thin   \th\ the   \ü\ loot   \u̇\ foot
\y\ yet   \zh\ vision   \à, k̲, ⁿ, œ, œ, ue, œ, ᵊ\ *see* Pronunciation Symbols

de-lude \di-'lüd\ (*v*) deceive. Marilyn Monroe may have *deluded* herself into believing that JFK would leave Jackie and marry her.

de-lu-sion \di-'lü-zhən\ (*n*) false belief; hallucination. Don suffers from *delusions* of grandeur: he thinks he's a world-famous author when he's published just one paperback book.

de-lu-sive \di-'lü-siv\ (*adj*) deceptive; raising vain hopes. Do not raise your hopes on the basis of his *delusive* promises.

dem-a-gogue \'dem-ə-ˌgäg\ (*n*) person who appeals to people's prejudice; false leader of people. He was accused of being a *demagogue* because he made promises that aroused futile hopes in his listeners.

de-mean \di-'mēn\ (*v*) degrade; humiliate. Standing on his dignity, he refused to *demean* himself by replying to the offensive letter.

de-mean-or \di-'mē-nər\ (*n*) behavior; bearing. His sober *demeanor* quieted the noisy revelers.

de-ment-ed \di-'ment-əd\ (*adj*) insane. Doctor Demento was a lunatic radio personality who acted as if he were truly *demented*.

de-mise \di-'mīz\ (*n*) death. Upon the *demise* of the dictator, a bitter dispute about succession to power developed. also (*v*).

de-mo-li-tion \ˌdem-ə-'lish-ən\ (*n*) destruction. One of the major aims of the air force was the complete *demolition* of all means of transportation by bombing of rail lines and terminals.

de-mo-ni-ac \di-'mō-nē-ˌak\ (*adj*) fiendish. The Spanish Inquisition devised many *demoniac* means of torture. de-mon \'dē-mən\ (*n*)

de-mur \di-'mər\ (*v*) object (because of doubts, scruples); hesitate. When asked to serve on the board, David *demurred*: he had scruples about taking on one more job because he had too many other duties. also (*n*).

\ə\ **abut** \ᵊ\ **kitten**, F **table** \ər\ **further** \a\ **ash** \ā\ **ace** \ä\ **cot, cart**
\aú\ **out** \ch\ **chin** \e\ **bet** \ē\ **easy** \g\ **go** \i\ **hit** \ī\ **ice** \j\ **job**

de-mure \di-'myù(ə)r\ (*adj*) grave; serious; coy. She was *demure* and reserved, a modest girl whom any young man would be proud to take home to his mother.

den-i-grate \'den-i-,grāt\ (*v*) blacken. All attempts to *denigrate* the character of our late president have failed; the people still love him and cherish his memory.

den-i-zen \'den-ə-zən\ (*n*) inhabitant or resident; regular visitor. In *The Untouchables*, Eliot Ness fights Al Capone and the other *denizens* of Chicago's underworld.

de-no-ta-tion \,dē-nō-'tā-shən\ (*n*) meaning; distinguishing by name. A dictionary will always give us the *denotation* of a word; frequently, it will also give us its connotation.

de-noue-ment \,dā-,nü-'mäⁿ\ (*n*) outcome; final development of the plot of a play. The play was childishly written; the *denouement* was obvious to sophisticated theatergoers as early as the middle of the first act.

de-pict \di-'pikt\ (*v*) portray. In this sensational exposé, the author *depicts* Beatle John Lennon as a drug-crazed neurotic.

de-plete \di-'plēt\ (*v*) reduce; exhaust. We must wait until we *deplete* our present inventory before we order replacements.

de-ploy \di-'plói\ (*v*) spread out [troops] in an extended though shallow battle line. The general ordered the battalion to *deploy* in order to meet the offensive of the enemy.

de-pose \di-'pōz\ (*v*) dethrone; remove from office. The army attempted to *depose* the king and set up a military government.

de-po-si-tion \,dep-ə-'zish-ən\ (*n*) testimony under oath. She made her *deposition* in the judge's chamber.

de-prav-i-ty \di-'prav-ət-ē\ (*n*) corruption, wickedness. The *depravity* of Caligula's behavior came to sicken

---

\ŋ\ sing \ō\ go \ò\ law \òi\ boy \th\ thin \th\ the \ü\ loot \ù\ foot
\y\ yet \zh\ vision \à, k̲, ⁿ, œ, œ̄, ue, œ̄, ʸ\ *see* Pronunciation Symbols

even those who had willingly participated in his earlier, comparatively innocent orgies.

dep-re-cate \\'dep-ri-ˌkāt\\ (*v*) disapprove regretfully. A firm believer in old-fashioned courtesy, Miss Post *deprecated* the modern tendency to address new acquaintances by their first names.

de-pre-ci-ate \\di-'prē-shē-ˌāt\\ (*v*) lessen in value. If you neglect this property, it will *depreciate*.

dep-re-da-tion \\ˌdep-rə-'dā-shən\\ (*n*) plundering. After the *depredations* of the invaders, the people were penniless.

de-range \\di-'rānj\\ (*v*) make insane. Hamlet's cruel rejection *deranged* poor Ophelia; in her madness, she drowned herself.

der-e-lict \\'der-ə-ˌlikt\\ (*adj*) abandoned. The *derelict* craft was a menace to navigation. also (*n*).

de-ride \\di-'rīd\\ (*v*) make fun of; ridicule. The critics *derided* his play for its simple-minded sentimentality. Despite their *derision*, however, people flocked to the play, cheering its unabashedly romantic ending. de-ri-sion \\di-'rizh-ən\\ (*n*)

de-riv-a-tive \\di-'riv-ət-iv\\ (*adj*) unoriginal; derived from another source. Although her early poetry was clearly *derivative* in nature, the critics thought she had promise and eventually would find her own voice.

der-ma-tol-o-gist \\ˌder-mə-'täl-ə-jəst\\ (*n*) one who studies the skin and its disease. I advise you to consult a *dermatologist* about your acne.

de-rog-a-to-ry \\di-'räg-ə-ˌtōr-ē\\ (*adj*) expressing a low opinion. I resent your *derogatory* remarks.

des-cant \\'des-ˌkant\\ (*v*) discuss fully. He was willing to *descant* upon any topic, even when he knew very little about the subject under discussion. also (*n*).

de-scry \\di-'skrī\\ (*v*) catch sight of. In the distance, we could barely *descry* the enemy vessels.

---

des-e-crate \'des-i-ˌkrāt\ (v) profane; violate the sanctity of. Shattering the altar and trampling the holy objects underfoot, the invaders *desecrated* the sanctuary.

des-ic-cate \'des-i-ˌkāt\ (v) dry up. A tour of this smokehouse will give you an idea of how the pioneers used to *desiccate* food in order to preserve it.

de-spise \di-'spīz\ (v) look on with scorn; regard as worthless or distasteful. Mr. Bond, I *despise* spies; I look down on them as mean, *despicable*, honorless men, whom I would wipe from the face of the earth with as little concern as I would scrape dog droppings from the bottom of my shoe. **de-spi-ca-ble** \ di-'spik-ə-bəl\ (*adj*)

de-spoil \di-'spȯi(ə)l\ (v) strip of valuables; rob. Seeking plunder, the raiders *despoiled* the village, carrying off any valuables they found.

de-spon-dent \di-'spän-dənt\ (*adj*) depressed, gloomy. To the dismay of his parents, William became seriously *despondent* after he broke up with Jan. **de-spon-den-cy** \di-'spän-dən-sē\ (*n*)

des-po-tism \'des-pə-ˌtiz-əm\ (*n*) tyranny. The people rebelled against the *despotism* of the king.

des-ti-tute \'des-tə-ˌt(y)üt\ (*adj*) extremely poor. Because they lacked health insurance, the father's costly illness left the family *destitute*.

des-ul-to-ry \'des-el-ˌtōr-ē\ (*adj*) aimless; haphazard; digressing at random. In prison Malcolm X set himself the task of reading straight through the dictionary; to him, reading was purposeful, not *desultory*.

de-tached \di-'tacht\ (*adj*) emotionally removed; calm and objective; indifferent. Psychoanalysts must remain *detached* and stay uninvolved in their patients' personal lives.

de-ter-gent \di-'tər-jənt\ (*n*) cleansing agent. Many new *detergents* have replaced soap.

---

de-ter-mi-nate \di-'tərm-(ə-)nət\ *(adj)* having a fixed order of procedure; invariable. At the royal wedding, the procession of the nobles followed a *determinate* order of precedence.

det-o-na-tion \ˌdet-ᵊn-'ā-shən\ *(n)* initiation of an explosion. The *detonation* could be heard miles away.

de-trac-tion \di-'trak-shən\ *(n)* slandering; aspersion. He is offended by your frequent *detractions* of his ability as a leader.

det-ri-ment \'de-trə-mənt\ *(n)* harm; damage. The candidate's acceptance of major financial contributions from a well-known racist ultimately proved a *detriment* to his campaign, for he lost the backing of many of his early grassroots supporters.

de-vi-ate \'dē-vē-ˌāt\ *(v)* turn away from (a principle, norm); depart; diverge. Richard never *deviated* from his daily routine: every day he set off for work at eight o'clock, had his sack lunch at noon, and headed home at the stroke of five. **de-vi-ate** \dē-vē-ət\ *(adj)*

de-vi-ous \'dē-vē-əs\ *(adj)* roundabout; erratic; not straightforward. The Joker's plan was so *devious* that it was only with great difficulty we could follow its shifts and dodges.

de-void \di-'vóid\ *(adj)* lacking. You may think Cher's mind is a total void, but she's actually not *devoid* of intelligence.

de-volve \di-'välv\ *(v)* deputize; pass to others. It *devolved* upon us, the survivors, to arrange peace terms with the enemy.

de-vout \di-'vaút\ *(adj)* pious. The *devout* man prayed daily.

dex-ter-ous \'dek-st(ə-)rəs\ *(adj)* skillful. The magician was so *dexterous* that we could not follow him as he performed his tricks.

di-a-bol-i-cal \ˌdī-ə-'bäl-i-kəl\ *(adj)* devilish. "What a fiend I am, to devise such a *diabolical* scheme to destroy Gotham City," chortled the Joker gleefully.

---

di-a-lec-tic \ˌdī-ə-'lek-tik\ (*n*) art of debate. *Dialectic*, or the art of logical argumentation, involves examining opinions for their truth.

di-aph-a-nous \dī-'af-ə-nəs\ (*adj*) sheer; transparent. Through the *diaphanous* curtains, the burglar could clearly see the large jewelry box on the dressing table.

di-a-tribe \'dī-ə-ˌtrīb\ (*n*) bitter scolding; invective. During the lengthy *diatribe* delivered by his opponent he remained calm and self-controlled.

di-chot-o-my \dī-'kät-ə-mē\ (*n*) split; branching into two parts (especially contradictory ones). Willie didn't know how to resolve the *dichotomy* between his ambition to go to college and his childhood longing to run away and join the circus.

dic-tum \'dik-təm\ (*n*) authoritative and weighty statement; saying; maxim. University administrations still follow the old *dictum* of "Publish or perish": a teacher who doesn't publish enough papers is soon out of a job.

di-dac-tic \dī-'dak-tik\ (*adj*) teaching; instructional. Pope's lengthy poem *An Essay on Man* is too *didactic* for my taste: I dislike it when poets turn preachy and moralize.

dif-fi-dence \'dif-əd-ən(t)s\ (*n*) shyness. You must overcome your *diffidence* if you intend to become a salesperson.

dif-fu-sion \dif-'yü-zhən\ (*n*) wordiness; spreading in all directions like a gas. Your composition suffers from *diffusion*: try to be more concise. dif-fuse \dif-'yüs\ (*adj*); \dif-'yüz\ (*v*)

di-gres-sive \dī-'gres-iv\ (*adj*) wandering away from the subject. If you cut out all the off-topic, *digressive* passages in this essay, you'd have barely two pages left.

di-lap-i-da-tion \də-ˌlap-ə-'dā-shən\ (*n*) ruin because of neglect. The old building was in such a state of *dilapidation* that we wondered whether it was worth remodeling.

---

di-late \dī-'lāt\ (v) expand. In the dark, the pupils of your eyes *dilate.*

dil-a-to-ry \'dil-ə-ˌtōr-ē\ (adj) delaying. If you are *dilatory* in paying bills, your credit rating may suffer.

di-lem-ma \də-'lem-ə\ (n) problem; choice of two unsatisfactory alternatives. In this *dilemma,* he knew no one to whom he could turn for advice.

dil-et-tante \'dil-ə-tänt\ (n) aimless follower of the arts; amateur; dabbler. He was not serious in his painting; he was rather a *dilettante.*

dim-i-nu-tion \ˌdim-ə-'n(y)ü-shən\ (n) lessening; reduction in size. Old Jack was as sharp at eighty as he had been at fifty; increasing age led to no *diminution* of his mental acuity.

dint \'dint\ (n) means; effort. By *dint* of much hard work, the volunteers were able to place the raging forest fire under control. also (v).

dip-so-ma-ni-ac \ˌdip-sə-'mā-nē-ˌak\ (n) one who has a strong craving for intoxicating liquor. The movie *The Lost Weekend* was an excellent portrayal of the struggles of the *dipsomaniac.*

dire \'dī(ə)r\ (adj) disastrous. People ignored his *dire* predictions of an approaching depression.

dirge \'dərj\ (n) lament with music. The funeral *dirge* moved us to tears.

dis-a-buse \ˌdis-ə-'byüz\ (v) correct a false impression; undeceive. I will attempt to *disabuse* you of your impression of my client's guilt; I know he is innocent.

dis-ar-ray \ˌdis-ə-'rā\ (n) a disorderly or untidy state. After the New Year's party, the once orderly house was in total *disarray.*

dis-a-vow-al \ˌdis-ə-'vau̇(-ə)l\ (n) denial; disclaiming. The jury doubted his *disavowal* of his part in the conspiracy.

dis-burse \dis-'bərs\ (v) pay out. When you *disburse* money on the company's behalf, be sure to get a receipt.

---

dis·cern·i·ble \dis-'ər-nə-bəl\ (*adj*) distinguishable; perceivable. The ships in the harbor were barely *discernible* in the fog.

dis·cern·ing \dis-'ər-niŋ\ (*adj*) mentally quick and observant; having insight. Because he was considered the most *discerning* member of the firm, he was assigned the most difficult cases.

dis·claim \dis-'klām\ (*v*) disown; renounce claim to. If I grant you this privilege, will you *disclaim* all other rights?

dis·close \dis-'klōz\ (*v*) reveal. Although competitors offered him bribes, he refused to *disclose* any information about his company's forthcoming product. dis·clo·sure \dis-'klō-zhər\ (*n*)

dis·com·fit \dis-'kəm(p)-fət\ (*v*) put to rout; defeat; disconcert. This ruse will *discomfit* the enemy. dis·com·fi·ture \dis-'kəm(p)-fə-,chu̇(ə)r\ (*n*)

dis·con·cert \,dis-kən-'sərt\ (*v*) confuse; upset; embarrass. The lawyer was *disconcerted* by the evidence produced by his adversary.

dis·con·so·late \dis-'kän(t)-s(ə-)lət\ (*adj*) sad. The death of his wife left him *disconsolate*.

dis·cor·dant \dis-'kȯrd-ᵊnt\ (*adj*) inharmonious; conflicting. Nothing is quite so *discordant* as the sound of a junior high school orchestra tuning up.

dis·count \'dis-,kau̇nt\ (*v*) disregard. Be prepared to *discount* what he has to say about his ex-wife. (secondary meaning)

dis·cred·it \⁽ʼ⁾dis-'kred-ət\ (*v*) defame; destroy confidence in; disbelieve. The campaign was highly negative in tone; each candidate tried to *discredit* the other.

dis·crep·an·cy \dis-'krep-ən-sē\ (*n*) lack of consistency; difference. The police noticed some *discrepancies* in his description of the crime and did not believe him.

---

dis-crete \dis-'krēt\ (*adj*) separate; unconnected. The universe is composed of *discrete* bodies.

dis-cre-tion \dis-'kresh-ən\ (*n*) prudence; ability to adjust actions to circumstances. Use your *discretion* in this matter. In other words, please be *discreet*!

dis-crim-i-nat-ing \dis-'krim-ə-nāt-iŋ\ (*adj*) able to see differences. A superb interpreter of Picasso, she was sufficiently *discriminating* to judge the most complex works of modern art. (secondary meaning) dis-crim-i-na-tion \dis-ˌkrim-ə-'nā-shən\ (*n*); dis-crim-i-nate \dis-'krim-ə-nāt\ (*v*)

dis-cur-sive \dis-'kər-siv\ (*adj*) digressing; rambling. As the lecturer wandered from topic to topic, we wondered what point there was to his *discursive* remarks.

dis-dain \dis-'dān\ (*v*) view with scorn or contempt. In the film *Funny Face*, the bookish heroine *disdained* fashion models for their lack of intellectual interests. also (*n*).

dis-grun-tle \dis-'grənt-ᵊl\ (*v*) make discontented. The passengers were *disgruntled* by the numerous delays.

dis-heart-ened \⁽ᵗ⁾dis-'härt-ᵊnd\ (*adj*) lacking courage and hope. His failure to pass the bar exam *disheartened* him.

di-shev-eled \dish-'ev-əld\ (*adj*) untidy. Your *disheveled* appearance will hurt your chances in this interview.

dis-in-gen-u-ous \ˌdis-ᵊn-'jen-yə-wəs\ (*adj*) lacking genuine candor; insincere. Now that we know that the mayor and his wife are engaged in a bitter divorce fight, we find their earlier remarks regretting their lack of time together remarkably *disingenuous*.

dis-in-ter-est-ed \⁽ᵗ⁾dis-'in-trəst-əd\ (*adj*) unprejudiced. Given the judge's political ambitions and the lawyers' financial interest in the case, the only *disinterested* person in the courtroom may have been the court reporter.

dis-joint-ed \⁽ᵗ⁾dis-'jȯint-əd\ (*adj*) disconnected. His remarks were so *disjointed* that we could not follow his reasoning.

dis-mem-ber \⁽ⁱ⁾dis-ˈmem-bər\ (*v*) cut into small parts. When the Austrian Empire was *dismembered,* several new countries were established.

dis-par-age \dis-ˈpar-ij\ (*v*) belittle. A doting mother, Emma was more likely to praise her son's crude attempts at art than to *disparage* them.

dis-pa-rate \dis-ˈpar-ət\ (*adj*) basically different; unrelated. Unfortunately, Tony and Tina have *disparate* notions of marriage: Tony sees it as a carefree extended love affair, while Tina sees it as a solemn commitment to build a family and a home.

dis-par-i-ty \dis-ˈpar-ət-ē\ (*n*) difference; condition of inequality. Their *disparity* in rank made no difference at all to the prince and Cinderella.

dis-pas-sion-ate \⁽ⁱ⁾dis-ˈpash-(ə-)nət\ (*adj*) calm; impartial. In a *dispassionate* analysis of the problem, he carefully examined the causes of the conflict and proceeded to suggest suitable remedies.

dis-per-sion \dis-ˈpər-zhən\ (*n*) scattering. To promote literacy and the *dispersion* of knowledge, Andrew Carnegie founded public libraries throughout the English-speaking world.

dis-pir-it-ed \⁽ⁱ⁾dis-ˈpir-ət-əd\ (*adj*) lacking in spirit. The coach used all the tricks at his command to buoy up the enthusiasm of his team, which had become *dispirited* at the loss of the star player.

dis-pu-ta-tious \ˌdis-pyə-ˈtā-shəs\ (*adj*) argumentative; fond of argument. Convinced he knew more than his lawyers, Tony was a *disputatious* client, ready to argue about the best way to conduct the case.

dis-qui-si-tion \ˌdis-kwə-ˈzish-ən\ (*n*) a formal systematic inquiry; an explanation of the results of a formal inquiry. In his *disquisition,* he outlined the steps he had taken in reaching his conclusions.

\ŋ\ **sing** \ō\ **go** \ȯ\ **law** \ȯi\ **boy** \th\ **thin** \t͟h\ **the** \ü\ **loot** \u̇\ **foot**
\y\ **yet** \zh\ **vision** \à, k̲, ⁿ, œ, œ̄, ue, œ̄, ʸ\ *see* Pronunciation Symbols

dis-sec-tion \dis-'ek-shən\ (*n*) analysis; cutting apart in order to examine. The *dissection* of frogs in the laboratory is particularly unpleasant to some students.

dis-sem-ble \dis-'em-bəl\ (*v*) disguise; pretend. Even though John tried to *dissemble* his motive for taking modern dance, we all knew he was there not to dance but to meet girls.

dis-sem-i-nate \dis-'em-ə-ˌnāt\ (*v*) distribute; spread; scatter (like seeds). By using the Internet, propagandists have been able to *disseminate* their pet doctrines to new audiences around the globe.

dis-sent \dis-'ent\ (*v*) disagree. In the recent Supreme Court decision, Justice O'Connor *dissented* from the majority opinion. also (*n*).

dis-ser-ta-tion \ˌdis-ər-'tā-shən\ (*n*) formal essay. In order to earn a graduate degree from many of our universities, a candidate is frequently required to prepare a *dissertation* on some scholarly subject.

dis-sim-u-late \ˌ(ˌ)dis-'im-yə-ˌlāt\ (*v*) pretend; conceal by feigning. Although the governor tried to *dissimulate* his feelings about the opposition candidate, we all knew he hated his rival's guts.

dis-si-pate \'dis-ə-ˌpāt\ (*v*) squander; waste; scatter. He is a fine artist, but I fear he may *dissipate* his gifts if he keeps wasting his time playing Trivial Pursuit.

dis-so-nance \'dis-ə-nən(t)s\ (*n*) discord. Composer Charles Ives often used *dissonance*—clashing or unresolved chords—for special effects in his musical works.

dis-suade \dis-'wād\ (*v*) advise against; persuade not to do; discourage. Since Tom could not *dissuade* Huck from running away from home, he decided to run away with his friend.

\ə\ **abut** \ᵊ\ **kitten, F table** \ər\ **further** \a\ **ash** \ā\ **ace** \ä\ **cot, cart**
\aú\ **out** \ch\ **chin** \e\ **bet** \ē\ **easy** \g\ **go** \i\ **hit** \ī\ **ice** \j\ **job**

dis-tend \dis-'tend\ (*v*) expand; swell out. I can tell when he is under stress by the way the veins *distend* on his forehead.

dis-tinct \dis-'tiŋ(k)t\ (*adj*) separate; clear or plain. No one could fail to notice the *distinct* odor of skunk while driving down that country road.

dis-tor-tion \dis-'tor-shən\ (*n*) twisting out of shape. It is difficult to believe the newspaper accounts of the riots because of the reporters' *distortions* and exaggerations.

dis-traught \dis-'trot\ (*adj*) upset; distracted by anxiety. The *distraught* parents searched the ravine for their lost child.

di-ur-nal \dī-'ərn-əl\ (*adj*) daily. A farmer cannot neglect his *diurnal* tasks at any time; cows, for example, must be milked every day.

di-va \'dē-və\ (*n*) operatic singer; prima donna. Although world famous as a *diva*, she did not indulge in fits of temperament.

di-verge \də-'vərj\ (*v*) vary; go in different directions from the same point. The spokes of the wheel *diverge* from the hub.

di-verse \dī-'vərs\ (*adj*) differing in some characteristics; various. The professor suggested *diverse* ways of approaching the assignment and recommended that we choose one of them. di-ver-si-ty \də-'vər-sət-ē\ (*n*)

di-vest \dī-'vest\ (*v*) strip; deprive. He was *divested* of his power to act.

div-i-na-tion \,div-ə-'nā-shən\ (*n*) foreseeing the future with aid of magic. Aunt Polly's ability to recognize when Tom was telling the truth seemed magic to the boy, who credited her with great powers of *divination*.

di-vulge \də-'vəlj\ (*v*) reveal. No lover of gossip, Charlotte would never *divulge* anything that a friend told her in confidence.

\ŋ\ sing \ō\ go \o\ law \oi\ boy \th\ thin \th\ the \ü\ loot \u\ foot
\y\ yet \zh\ vision \à, k̲, ⁿ, œ, œ̄, ue, œ, ᵞ\ *see* Pronunciation Symbols

doc-ile \\'däs-əl\\ (*adj*) obedient; easily managed. As *docile* as he seems today, that old lion was once a ferocious, snarling beast.

dock-et \\'däk-ət\\ (*n*) program as for trial; book where such entries are made. The case of Smith vs. Jones was entered in the *docket* for July 15. also (*v*).

doc-u-ment \\'däk-yə-ˌment\\ (*v*) provide written evidence. She kept all the receipts from her business trip in order to *document* her expenses for the firm. also (*n*).

dod-der-ing \\'däd-(ə-)riŋ\\ (*adj*) shaky; infirm from old age. Playing for laughs, the actor portrayed the aged king not as a tragic figure but as a *doddering* old fool.

doff \\'däf\\ (*v*) take off. He *doffed* his hat to the lady.

dog-ger-el \\'dȯg-(ə-)rəl\\ (*n*) poor verse. Although we find occasional snatches of genuine poetry in his work, most of his writing is mere *doggerel*.

dog-mat-ic \\dȯg-'mat-ik\\ (*adj*) opinionated; arbitrary; doctrinal. We tried to discourage Doug from being so *dogmatic*, but never could convince him that his opinions might be wrong.

dol-drums \\'dōl-drəmz\\ (*n*) blues; listlessness; slack period. Once the excitement of meeting her deadline was over, she found herself in the *doldrums*.

do-lor-ous \\'dō-lə-rəs\\ (*adj*) sorrowful. At the funeral, the organist played a *dolorous* melody that left many mourners in tears.

dolt \\'dōlt\\ (*n*) stupid person. The heroes of *Dumb and Dumber* are, as the title suggests, a classic pair of *dolts*.

do-mi-cile \\'däm-ə-ˌsīl\\ (*n*) home. Although his legal *domicile* was in New York City, his work kept him away from his residence for many years. also (*v*).

dor-mant \\'dȯr-mənt\\ (*adj*) sleeping; lethargic; latent. At fifty her long-*dormant* ambition to write flared up once

---

\\ə\\ **abut** \\ᵊ\\ **kitten**, F **table** \\ər\\ **further** \\a\\ **ash** \\ā\\ **ace** \\ä\\ **cot, cart**
\\au̇\\ **out** \\ch\\ **chin** \\e\\ **bet** \\ē\\ **easy** \\g\\ **go** \\i\\ **hit** \\ī\\ **ice** \\j\\ **job**

more; within a year she had completed the first of her great historical novels. **dor·man·cy** \\'dȯr-mən-sē\ (*n*)

dor·sal \\'dȯr-səl\ (*adj*) relating to the back of an animal. A shark may be identified by its *dorsal* fin, which projects above the surface of the ocean. also (*n*).

dot·age \\'dōt-ij\ (*n*) senility. In his *dotage*, the old man bored us with long tales of events in his childhood.

dough·ty \\'daut-ē\ (*adj*) courageous. Many folk tales have sprung up about this *doughty* pioneer who opened up the New World for his followers.

dour \\'dau̇(ə)r\ (*adj*) sullen; stubborn. The man was *dour* and taciturn.

douse \\'daus\ (*v*) plunge into water; drench; extinguish. They *doused* each other with hoses and water balloons.

dowdy \\'daud-ē\ (*adj*) slovenly; untidy. She tried to change her *dowdy* image by buying a new fashionable wardrobe.

dreg \\'dreg\ (*n*) sediment; worthless residue. David poured the wine carefully to avoid stirring up the *dregs*.

droll \\'drōl\ (*adj*) queer and amusing. He was a popular guest because his *droll* anecdotes were always amusing.

drone \\'drōn\ (*n*) idle person; male bee. Content to let his wife support him, the would-be writer was in reality nothing but a *drone?*

drone \\'drōn\ (*v*) talk dully; buzz or murmur like a bee. On a gorgeous day, who wants to be stuck in a classroom listening to the teacher *drone*?

dross \\'dräs\ (*n*) waste matter; worthless impurities. Many methods have been devised to separate the valuable metal from the *dross*.

drudg·ery \\'drəj-(ə-)rē\ (*n*) menial work. Cinderella's fairy godmother rescued her from a life of *drudgery*.

du·bi·ous \\'d(y)ü-bē-əs\ (*adj*) questionable; filled with doubt. Many critics of SAT I contend the test is of *dubious* worth. Tony claimed he could get a perfect 1600 on

SAT I, but Tina was *dubious*: she knew he hadn't cracked a book in three years.

du-en-na \d(y)ü-'en-ə\ (*n*) attendant of young female; chaperone. Their romance could not flourish because of the presence of her *duenna.*

dul-cet \'dəl-sət\ (*adj*) sweet sounding. The *dulcet* sounds of the birds at dawn were soon drowned out by the roar of traffic passing our motel.

du-plic-i-ty \d(y)ü-'plis-ət-ē\ (*n*) double-dealing; hypocrisy. When Tanya learned that Mark had been two-timing her, she was furious at his *duplicity.*

du-ress \d(y)ü-'res\ (*n*) forcible restraint, especially unlawfully. The hostages were held under *duress* until the prisoners' demands were met.

dwin-dle \'dwin-dᵊl\ (*v*) shrink; reduce. They spent so much money that their funds *dwindled* to nothing.

dy-nam-ic \dī-'nam-ik\ (*adj*) energetic; vigorously active. The *dynamic* aerobics instructor kept her students on the run; she was a little *dynamo.* dy-nam-o \dī-'nam-ō\ (*n*)

dys-pep-tic \dis-'pep-tik\ (*adj*) suffering from indigestion. All the talk about rich food made him feel *dyspeptic.* dys-pep-sia \dis-'pep-shə\ (*n*)

E

earth-y \'ər-thē\ (*adj*) unrefined; coarse. His *earthy* remarks often embarrassed the women in his audience.

e-bul-lient \i-'bùl-yənt\ (*adj*) showing excitement; overflowing with enthusiasm. Amy's *ebullient* nature could not be repressed; she was always bubbling over with excitement. **e-bul-lience** \i-'bùl-yən(t)s\ (*n*)

ec-cen-tric-i-ty \ˌek-ˌsen-'tris-ət-ē\ (*n*) oddity; idiosyncrasy. Some of his friends tried to account for his rudeness to strangers as the *eccentricity* of genius. **ec-cen-tric** \ik-sen-trik\ (*adj, n*)

ec-cle-si-as-tic \ik-ˌlē-zē-'as-tik\ (*adj*) pertaining to the church. The minister donned his *ecclesiastic* garb and walked to the pulpit. also (*n*).

e-clec-ti-cism \e-'klek-tə-ˌsiz-əm\ (*n*) selection of elements drawn from disparate sources. The designer's decor was noted for its *eclecticism*: Danish modern furniture, medieval tapestries, Japanese pillows, the occasional Indian rug.

eclipse \i-'klips\ (*v*) darken; extinguish; surpass. The new stock market high *eclipsed* the previous record set in 1989.

ec-sta-sy \'ek-stə-sē\ (*n*) rapture; joy; any overpowering emotion. When Allison received her long-hoped-for letter of acceptance from Yale, she was in *ecstasy*.

ed-i-fy \'ed-ə-ˌfī\ (*v*) instruct; correct morally. Although his purpose was to *edify* and not to entertain his audience, many of his listeners were amused and not enlightened.

ee-rie \'i(ə)r-ē\ (*adj*) weird. In that *eerie* setting, it was easy to believe in ghosts and other supernatural beings.

ef-face \i-'fās\ (*v*) rub out. The coin had been handled so many times that its date had been *effaced*.

ef-fec-tu-al \i-'fek-chə(-wə)l\ (*adj*) able to produce a desired effect; valid. Medical researchers are concerned because of the development of drug-resistant strains of

---

bacteria; many once useful antibiotics are no longer *effectual* in curing bacterial infections.

ef-fem-i-nate \ə-'fem-ə-nət\ *(adj)* having womanly traits. His voice was high-pitched and *effeminate.* also *(n).*

ef-fer-vesce \ˌef-ər-'ves\ *(v)* bubble over; show excitement. Soda that ceases to *effervesce* goes flat. Bubbly, cheerful cheerleaders by definition *effervesce*; doomsayers and brooders don't.

ef-fete \e-'fēt\ *(adj)* worn out; exhausted; barren. Is the Democratic Party still a vital political force, or is it an *effete*, powerless faction, wedded to outmoded liberal policies?

ef-fi-ca-cy \'ef-i-kə-sē\ *(n)* power to produce desired effect. The *efficacy* of this drug depends on the regularity of the dosage.

ef-fi-gy \'ef-ə-jē\ *(n)* dummy. The mob showed its irritation by hanging the judge in *effigy.*

ef-flu-vi-um \e-'flü-vē-əm\ *(n)* noxious smell. Air pollution has become a serious problem in our major cities; the *effluvium* and the poisons in the air are hazards to life.

ef-fron-ter-y \i-'frənt-ə-rē\ *(n)* shameless boldness. He had the *effrontery* to insult the guest.

ef-fu-sion \i-'fyü-zhən\ *(n)* pouring forth. The critics objected to his literary *effusion* because it was too flowery.

ef-fu-sive \i-'fyü-siv\ *(adj)* pouring forth; gushing. Her *effusive* manner of greeting her friends finally began to irritate them.

e-go-ism \'e-gə-ˌwiz-əm\ *(n)* excessive interest in one's self; belief that one should be interested in one's self rather than in others. His *egoism* prevented him from seeing the needs of his colleagues.

e-go-tism \'ē-gə-ˌtiz-əm\ *(n)* conceit; vanity. Classic *egotism*: "But enough of this chitchat about you and your problems. Let's talk about what's really important: *Me!*"

\ə\ **abut** \ə\ **kitten, F table** \ər\ **further** \a\ **ash** \ā\ **ace** \ä\ **cot, cart**
\aü\ **out** \ch\ **chin** \e\ **bet** \ē\ **easy** \g\ **go** \i\ **hit** \ī\ **ice** \j\ **job**

e·gre·gious \i-'grē-jəs\ *(adj)* gross; shocking. She was an *egregious* liar; everyone knew better than to believe a word she said.

e·gress \'ē-ˌgres\ *(n)* exit. Barnum's sign "To the *Egress*" fooled many people who thought they were going to see an animal and instead found themselves in the street. **e·gress** \ē-'gres\ *(v)*

e·jac·u·la·tion \i-jak-yə-'lā-shən\ *(n)* exclamation. He could not repress an *ejaculation* of surprise when he heard the news.

e·lab·o·ra·tion \i-ˌlab-ə-'rā-shən\ *(n)* addition of details; intricacy. Tell what happened simply, without any *elaboration.* **e·lab·o·rate** \i-'lab-ə-ˌrāt\ *(v)*

e·la·tion \i-'lā-shən\ *(n)* a rise in spirits; exaltation. Grinning from ear to ear, Bonnie Blair clearly showed her *elation* at winning her fifth Olympic gold medal.

el·e·gi·a·cal \ˌel-ə-'jī-ə-kəl\ *(adj)* like an elegy; mournful. On the death of Edward King, Milton composed his great *elegiacal* poem "Lycidas." **el·e·gy** \'el-ə-jē\ *(n)*

e·lic·it \i-'lis-ət\ *(v)* draw out by discussion. The detectives tried to *elicit* where he had hidden his loot.

e·lix·ir \i-'lik-sər\ *(n)* cure-all; something invigorating. The news of her chance to go abroad acted on her like an *elixir.*

el·o·quence \'el-ə-kwən(t)s\ *(n)* expressiveness; persuasive speech. The crowds were stirred by Martin Luther King's *eloquence.*

e·lu·ci·date \i-'lü-sə-ˌdāt\ *(v)* explain; enlighten. He was called upon to *elucidate* the disputed points in his article.

e·lu·sive \ē-'lü-siv\ *(adj)* evasive; baffling; hard to grasp. Trying to pin down exactly when the contractors would be done remodeling the house, Nancy was frustrated by their *elusive* replies.

\ŋ\ **sing**   \ō\ **go**   \ȯ\ **law**   \ȯi\ **boy**   \th\ **thin**   \t͟h\ **the**   \ü\ **loot**   \u̇\ **foot**
\y\ **yet**   \zh\ **vision**   \à, k̲, ⁿ, œ, œ̄, ᵫe, ᵫē, ʸ\ *see* Pronunciation Symbols

e·ly·sian \i-'lizh-ən\ (*adj*) relating to paradise; blissful. An afternoon sail on the bay was for her an *elysian* journey.

e·ma·ci·ate \i-'mā-shē-ˌāt\ (*v*) to make thin and wasted. Many severe illnesses *emaciate* their victims, who must gain back their lost weight before making a full recovery.

em·a·nate \'em-ə-ˌnāt\ (*v*) issue forth. A strong odor of sulphur *emanated* from the spring.

e·man·ci·pate \i-'man(t)-sə-ˌpāt\ (*v*) set free. At first, the attempts of the Abolitionists to *emancipate* the slaves were unpopular in New England as well as in the South.

em·bark \im-'bärk\ (*v*) commence; go on a boat or airplane; begin a journey. In devoting herself to the study of gorillas, Dian Fossey *embarked* on a course of action that was to cost her her life.

em·bed \im-'bed\ (*v*) enclose; place in something. Tales of actual historical figures like King Alfred have become *embedded* in legends.

em·bel·lish \im-'bel-ish\ (*v*) adorn. His handwriting was *embellished* with flourishes.

em·bez·zle·ment \im-'bez-əl-mənt\ (*n*) stealing. The bank teller confessed his *embezzlement* of the funds.

em·bla·zon \im-'blāz-ən\ (*v*) deck in brilliant colors. *Emblazoned* on his shield was his family coat of arms.

em·broil \im-'brȯi(ə)l\ (*v*) throw into confusion; involve in strife; entangle. He became *embroiled* in the heated discussion when he tried to arbitrate the dispute.

em·bry·on·ic \ˌem-brē-'än-ik\ (*adj*) undeveloped; rudimentary. The CEO reminisced about the good old days when the new computer industry was still in its *embryonic* stage and startup companies were founded in family garages.

e·mend \ē-'mend\ (*v*) correct; correct by a critic. The critic *emended* the book by selecting the passages that he thought most appropriate to the text.

---

e-men-da-tion \ˌē-ˌmen-ˈdā-shən\ (*n*) correction of errors; improvement. Please initial all the *emendations* you have made in this contract.

e-mer-i-tus \i-ˈmer-ət-əs\ (*adj*) retired but retained in an honorary capacity. As professor *emeritus,* he retained all his honors without having to meet the obligations of daily assignments. also (*n*).

em-i-nent \ˈem-ə-nənt\ (*adj*) high; lofty. After her appointment to this *eminent* position, she seldom had time for her former friends.

em-is-sary \ˈem-ə-ˌser-ē\ (*n*) agent; messenger. The secretary of state was sent as the president's special *emissary* to the conference on disarmament.

e-mol-lient \i-ˈmäl-yənt\ (*n*) soothing or softening remedy. The nurse applied an *emollient* to the inflamed area. also (*adj*).

em-pir-i-cal \im-ˈpir-i-kəl\ (*adj*) based on experience. He distrusted hunches and intuitive flashes; he placed his reliance entirely on *empirical* data.

em-u-late \ˈem-yə-ˌlāt\ (*v*) rival; imitate. In a brief essay, describe a person you admire, someone whose virtues you would like to *emulate*.

en-am-or \in-ˈam-ər\ (*v*) overwhelmed by love. Narcissus was *enamored* of his own beauty.

en-clave \ˈen-ˌklāv\ (*n*) territory enclosed within an alien land. The Vatican is an independent *enclave* in Italy.

en-co-mi-um \en-ˈkō-mē-əm\ (*n*) praise; eulogy. Uneasy with the *encomiums* expressed by his supporters, Tolkien felt unworthy of such high praise.

en-com-pass \in-ˈkəm-pəs\ (*v*) surround. A moat, or deep water-filled trench, *encompassed* the castle, defending it from attack.

en-coun-ter \in-ˈkau̇nt-ər\ (*n*) meeting. Native Americans suffered from new diseases after their first *encounters* with Europeans. also (*v*).

\ŋ\ **sing**   \ō\ **go**   \ȯ\ **law**   \ȯi\ **boy**   \th\ **thin**   \t̲h̲\ **the**   \ü\ **loot**   \u̇\ **foot**
\y\ **yet**   \zh\ **vision**   \à, k̲, ⁿ, œ, œ̄, ue, ūe, ʸ\ *see* Pronunciation Symbols

en-croach-ment \in-'krōch-mənt\ (*n*) gradual intrusion. The *encroachment* of the factories upon the neighborhood lowered the value of the real estate.

en-cum-ber \in-'kəm-bər\ (*v*) burden. Some people *encumber* themselves with too much luggage when they take short trips.

en-dear-ment \in-'di(ə)r-mənt\ (*n*) fond statement. Your gifts and *endearments* cannot make me forget your earlier insolence.

en-dem-ic \en-'dem-ik\ (*adj*) prevailing among a specific group of people or in a specific area or country. This disease is *endemic* in this part of the world; more than 80 percent of the population are at one time or another affected by it.

en-dorse \in-'dȯ(ə)rs\ (*v*) approve; support. Everyone waited to see which one of the rival candidates for the city council the mayor would *endorse*. (secondary meaning) en-dorse-ment \in-'dȯr-smənt\ (*n*)

en-er-gize \'en-ər-ˌjīz\ (*v*) invigorate; make forceful and active. Rather than exhausting Maggie, dancing *energized* her.

e-ner-vate \'en-ər-ˌvāt\ (*v*) weaken. She was slow to recover from her illness; even a short walk to the window *enervated* her. e-ner-vate \i-'nər-vət\ (*adj*)

en-gen-der \in-'jen-dər\ (*v*) cause; produce. To receive praise for real accomplishments *engenders* self-confidence in a child.

en-grossed \in-'grōst\ (*adj*) occupied fully. John was so *engrossed* in his studies that he did not hear his mother call. en-gross \in-'grōs\ (*v*)

en-hance \in-'han(t)s\ (*v*) advance; improve. You can *enhance* your chances of being admitted to the college of your choice by learning to write well; an excellent essay can *enhance* any application.

\ə\ **abut** \ᵊ\ **kitten**, F **table** \ər\ **further** \a\ **ash** \ā\ **ace** \ä\ **cot, cart**
\aù\ **out** \ch\ **chin** \e\ **bet** \ē\ **easy** \g\ **go** \i\ **hit** \ī\ **ice** \j\ **job**

e-nig-ma \i-'nig-mə\ (*n*) puzzle. "What *do* women want?" asked Dr. Sigmund Freud. Their behavior was an *enigma* to him.

e-nig-mat-ic \,en-(ı)ig-'mat-ik\ (*adj*) obscure; puzzling. Many have sought to fathom the *enigmatic* smile of the *Mona Lisa.*

en-join \in-'jȯin\ (*v*) command; order; forbid. The owners of the company asked the court to *enjoin* the union from picketing the plant.

en-mi-ty \'en-mət-ē\ (*n*) ill will; hatred. At Camp David, President Carter labored to bring an end to the *enmity* that prevented the peaceful coexistence of Egypt and Israel.

en-nui \'än-'wē\ (*n*) boredom. The monotonous routine of hospital life induced a feeling of *ennui* that made him moody and irritable.

e-nor-mi-ty \i-'nȯr-mət-ē\ (*n*) hugeness (in a bad sense). He did not realize the *enormity* of his crime until he saw what suffering he had caused.

en-rap-ture \in-'rap-chər\ (*v*) please intensely. The audience was *enraptured* by the freshness of the voices and the excellent orchestration.

en-sconce \in-'skän(t)s\ (*v*) settle comfortably. Now that their children were *ensconced* safely in the private school, the jet-setting parents decided to leave for Europe.

en-sue \in-'sü\ (*v*) follow. In *The Taming of the Shrew*, when Kate meets Petruchio, a battle of wits and wills *ensues.*

en-thrall \in-'thrȯl\ (*v*) capture; enslave. From the moment he saw her picture, he was *enthralled* by her beauty.

en-tice \in-'tīs\ (*v*) lure; attract; tempt. She always tried to *entice* her baby brother into mischief.

en-ti-ty \'en(t)-ət-ē\ (*n*) real being. As soon as the Charter was adopted, the United Nations became an *entity* that had to be considered as a factor in world diplomacy.

en-to-mol-o-gy \ˌent-ə-'mäl-ə-jē\ (*n*) study of insects. I found *entomology* the least interesting part of my course in biology; studying insects bored me.

en-trance \in-'tran(t)s\ (*v*) put under a spell; carry away with emotion. Shafts of sunlight on a wall could *entrance* her and leave her spellbound.

en-treat \in-'trēt\ (*v*) plead; ask earnestly. She *entreated* her father to let her stay out till midnight.

en-trée \'än-ˌtrā\ (*n*) entrance. Because of his wealth and social position, he had *entrée* into the most exclusive circles.

en-tre-pre-neur \ˌänⁿ-trə-p(r)ə-'nər\ (*n*) businessman; contractor. Opponents of our present tax program argue that it discourages *entrepreneurs* from trying new fields of business activity.

e-phem-er-al \i-'fem(-ə)-rəl\ (*adj*) short-lived; fleeting. The mayfly is an *ephemeral* creature: its adult life lasts little more than a day. also (*n*).

ep-ic \'ep-ik\ (*n*) long heroic poem, novel, or similar work of art. Kurosawa's film *Seven Samurai* is an *epic* portraying the struggle of seven warriors to destroy a band of robbers.

ep-ic \'ep-ik\ (*adj*) unusually great in size or extent; heroic; impressive. The task of renovating the decrepit subway system was one of truly *epic* dimensions; it would cost millions of dollars and involve thousands of laborers working night and day.

ep-i-cure \'ep-i-ˌkyu̇(ə)r\ (*n*) connoisseur of food and drink. *Epicures* frequent this restaurant because it features exotic wines and dishes.

ep-i-cu-re-an \ˌep-i-kyu̇-'rē-ən\ (*n*) person who devotes himself to pleasures of the senses, especially to food. This restaurant is famous for its menu, which can cater to the most exotic whim of the *epicurean*. also (*adj*).

\ə\ **abut** \ə\ **kitten**, F **table** \ər\ **further** \a\ **ash** \ā\ **ace** \ä\ **cot, cart**
\au̇\ **out** \ch\ **chin** \e\ **bet** \ē\ **easy** \g\ **go** \i\ **hit** \ī\ **ice** \j\ **job**

ep-i-gram \\'ep-ə-ˌgram\ (*n*) witty thought or saying, usually short. Poor Richard's *epigrams* made Benjamin Franklin famous.

ep-i-logue \\'ep-ə-ˌlȯg\ (*n*) short speech at conclusion of dramatic work. The audience was so disappointed in the play that many did not remain to hear the *epilogue.*

ep-i-taph \\'ep-ə-ˌtaf\ (*n*) inscription in memory of a dead person. In his will, he dictated the *epitaph* he wanted carved on his tombstone.

ep-i-thet \\'ep-ə-ˌthet\ (*n*) descriptive word or phrase. So many kings of France were named Charles that you could tell them apart only by the *epithets*: Charles the Wise was someone far different from Charles the Fat.

e-pit-o-me \i-'pit-ə-mē\ (*n*) perfect example or embodiment. Singing "I am the very model of a modern Major-General," in *The Pirates of Penzance*, Major-General Stanley proclaimed himself the *epitome* of an officer and a gentleman. **e-pit-o-mize** \i-'pit-ə-ˌmīz\ (*v*)

ep-och \\'ep-ək\ (*n*) period of time. The glacial *epoch* lasted for thousands of years.

eq-ua-ble \\'ek-wə-bəl\ (*adj*) tranquil; steady; uniform. After the hot summers and cold winters of New England, he found the climate of the West Indies *equable* and pleasant.

e-qua-nim-i-ty \ˌē-kwə-'nim-ət-ē\ (*n*) calmness of temperament; composure. Even the inevitable strains of caring for an ailing mother did not disturb Bea's *equanimity.*

e-ques-tri-an \i-'kwes-trē-ən\ (*n*) rider on horseback. These paths in the park are reserved for *equestrians* and their steeds. also (*adj*).

e-qui-lib-ri-um \ˌē-kwə-'lib-rē-əm\ (*n*) balance. After the divorce, he needed some time to regain his *equilibrium.*

---

e-qui-nox \\'e-kwə-ˌnäks\ (*n*) period of equal days and nights; the beginning of spring and autumn. The vernal *equinox* is usually marked by heavy rainstorms.

eq-ui-ta-ble \\'ek-wət-ə-bəl\ (*adj*) fair; impartial. I am seeking an *equitable* solution to this dispute, one that will be fair and acceptable to both sides.

eq-ui-ty \\'ek-wət-ē\ (*n*) fairness; justice. Our courts guarantee *equity* to all.

e-quiv-o-cal \i-'kwiv-ə-kəl\ (*adj*) ambiguous; intentionally misleading. Rejecting the candidate's *equivocal* comments on tax reform, the reporters pressed him to state clearly where he stood on the issue.

e-quiv-o-cate \i-'kwiv-ə-ˌkāt\ (*v*) lie; mislead; attempt to conceal the truth. No matter how bad the news is, give it to us straight. Above all, don't *equivocate*.

e-rode \i-'rōd\ (*v*) eat away. The limestone was *eroded* by the dripping water until only a thin shell remained.

e-rot-ic \i-'rät-ik\ (*adj*) arousing sexual desire; pertaining to sexual love. Films with significant *erotic* content are rated R; pornographic films are rated X.

er-rat-ic \ir-'at-ik\ (*adj*) odd; unpredictable. Investors become anxious when the stock market appears *erratic*.

er-ro-ne-ous \ir-'ō-nē-əs\ (*adj*) mistaken; wrong. I thought my answer was correct, but it was *erroneous*.

er-u-dite \\'er-(y)ə-ˌdīt\ (*adj*) learned; scholarly. Readers found his *erudite* writing challenging because he made many obscure allusions.

er-u-di-tion \ˌer-(y)ə-'dish-ən\ (*n*) high degree of knowledge and learning. Though his fellow students respected his *erudition*, Paul knew he would have to spend many years in serious study before he could consider himself a scholar.

es-ca-pade \\'es-kə-ˌpād\ (*n*) prank; flighty conduct. The headmaster could not regard this latest *escapade* as a boyish joke and expelled the young man.

\ə\ abut \ᵊ\ kitten, F table \ər\ further \a\ ash \ā\ ace \ä\ cot, cart
\au̇\ out \ch\ chin \e\ bet \ē\ easy \g\ go \i\ hit \ī\ ice \j\ job

es-chew \is(h)-'chü\ (*v*) avoid. Hoping to present himself to his girlfriend as a totally reformed character, he tried to *eschew* all the vices, especially chewing tobacco and drinking bathtub gin.

es-o-ter-ic \ˌes-ə-'ter-ik\ (*adj*) hard to understand; known only to the chosen few. *New Yorker* short stories often include *esoteric* allusions to obscure people and events. The implication is, if you are in the in-crowd, you'll get the reference; if you come from Cleveland, you won't.

es-pi-o-nage \'es-pē-ə-ˌnäzh\ (*n*) spying. In order to maintain its power, the government developed a system of *espionage* that penetrated every household.

es-pouse \is-'pau̇z\ (*v*) adopt; support. She was always ready to *espouse* a worthy cause.

es-prit de corps \is-ˌprēd-ə-'kō(ə)r\ (*n*) comradeship; spirit. West Point cadets are proud of their *esprit de corps.*

es-trange \is-'trānj\ (*v*) alienate. The wife was *estranged* from her husband and sought a divorce.

e-the-re-al \i-'thir-ē-əl\ (*adj*) light; heavenly; unusually refined. In Shakespeare's *The Tempest*, the spirit Ariel is an *ethereal* creature, too airy and unearthly for our mortal world.

eth-nic \'eth-nik\ (*adj*) relating to races. Intolerance between *ethnic* groups is deplorable; it usually is based on lack of information. also (*n*).

eth-nol-o-gy \eth-'näl-ə-jē\ (*n*) study of man. Sociology is one aspect of the science of *ethnology.*

et-y-mol-o-gy \ˌet-ə-'mäl-ə-jē\ (*n*) study of derivation, structure and development of words. A knowledge of *etymology* can help you on many English tests: if you know what the roots and prefixes mean, you can determine the meanings of unfamiliar words.

eu-gen-ic \yu̇-'jen-ik\ (*adj*) pertaining to the improvement of race. It is easier to apply *eugenic* principles to the raising of racehorses or prize cattle than to the development of human beings. **eu-gen-ics** \yu̇-'jen-iks\ (*n*)

\ŋ\ **sing** \ō\ **go** \ȯ\ **law** \ȯi\ **boy** \th\ **thin** \th̲\ **the** \ü\ **loot** \u̇\ **foot**
\y\ **yet** \zh\ **vision** \à, k̲, ⁿ, œ, œ̄, ue, ūe, ʸ\ *see* Pronunciation Symbols

eu·lo·gis·tic \ˌyü-lə-ˈjis-tik\ (*adj*) praising. To everyone's surprise, the speech was *eulogistic* rather than critical in tone.

eu·lo·gy \ˈyü-lə-jē\ (*n*) expression of praise, often on the occasion of someone's death. Instead of delivering a spoken *eulogy* at Genny's memorial service, Jeff sang a song he had written in her honor.

eu·phe·mism \ˈyü-fə-ˌmiz-əm\ (*n*) mild expression in place of an unpleasant one. The expression "He passed away" is a *euphemism* for "He died."

eu·pho·ni·ous \yu̇-ˈfō-nē-əs\ (*adj*) pleasing in sound. *Euphonious* even when spoken, Italian is particularly pleasing to the ear when sung.

eu·tha·na·sia \ˌyü-thə-ˈnā-zh(ē-)ə\ (*n*) mercy killing. Many people support *euthanasia* for terminally ill patients who wish to die.

ev·a·nes·cent \ˌev-ə-ˈnes-ᵊnt\ (*adj*) fleeting; vanishing. Brandon's satisfaction in his new job was *evanescent*, for he immediately began to notice its many drawbacks.

e·va·sive \i-ˈvā-siv\ (*adj*) not frank; eluding. Your *evasive* answers convinced the judge that you were withholding important evidence. e·vade \i-ˈvād\ (*v*)

e·vince \i-ˈvin(t)s\ (*v*) show clearly. When he tried to answer the questions, he *evinced* his ignorance of the subject matter.

e·vis·cer·ate \i-ˈvis-ə-ˌrāt\ (*v*) disembowel; remove entrails. The medicine man *eviscerated* the animal and offered the entrails to the angry gods.

e·voke \i-ˈvōk\ (*v*) call forth. Scent can be remarkably *evocative*: the aroma of pipe tobacco *evokes* the memory of my father; a whiff of talcum powder calls up images of my daughter as a child.

ex·ac·er·bate \ig-ˈzas-ər-ˌbāt\ (*v*) worsen; embitter. The latest bombing *exacerbated* England's already existing

---

\ə\ abut \ᵊ\ kitten, F table \ər\ further \a\ ash \ā\ ace \ä\ cot, cart
\au̇\ out \ch\ chin \e\ bet \ē\ easy \g\ go \i\ hit \ī\ ice \j\ job

bitterness against the IRA, causing the Prime Minister to break off the peace talks abruptly.

ex-alt \ig-'zólt\ (*v*) raise in rank or dignity; praise. The actor Alec Guinness was *exalted* to the rank of knighthood by the queen.

ex-as-per-ate \ig-'zas-pə-ˌrāt\ (*v*) vex. Johnny often *exasperates* his mother with his pranks.

ex-ci-sion \ik-'sizh-ən\ (*n*) act of cutting away. With the *excision* of the dead and dying limbs of this tree, you have not only improved its appearance but you have enhanced its chances of bearing fruit. ex-cise \ik-'sīz\ (*v*)

ex-co-ri-ate \ek-'skōr-ē-ˌāt\ (*v*) scold with biting harshness; strip the skin off. Seeing the rips in Bill's new pants, his mother furiously *excoriated* him for ruining his good clothes. The tight, starched collar chafed and *excoriated* his neck, rubbing it raw.

ex-cul-pate \'ek-(ˌ)skəl-ˌpāt\ (*v*) clear from blame. He was *exculpated* of the crime when the real criminal confessed.

ex-e-cra-ble \'ek-si-krə-bəl\ (*adj*) very bad. The anecdote was in such *execrable* taste that it disgusted the audience.

ex-e-crate \'ek-sə-ˌkrāt\ (*v*) curse; express abhorrence for. The world *execrates* the memory of Hitler and hopes that genocide will never again be the policy of any nation.

ex-e-cute \'ek-si-ˌkyüt\ (*v*) put into effect; carry out. The choreographer wanted to see how well she could *execute* a pirouette. (secondary meaning) ex-e-cu-tion \ˌek-si-'kyü-shən\ (*n*)

ex-e-ge-sis \ˌek-sə-'jē-səs\ (*n*) explanation, especially of Biblical passages. I can follow your *exegesis* of this passage to a limited degree; some of your reasoning eludes me.

ex-em-pla-ry \ig-'zem-plə-rē\ (*adj*) serving as a model; outstanding. Her *exemplary* behavior was praised at Commencement.

ex·haus·tive \ig-'zȯ-stiv\ (*adj*) thorough; comprehensive. We have made an *exhaustive* study of all published SAT tests and are happy to share our research with you.

ex·hort \ig-'zȯ(ə)rt\ (*v*) urge. The evangelist *exhorted* all the sinners in his audience to repent.

ex·hume \igz-'(y)üm\ (*v*) dig out of the ground; remove from a grave. Because of the rumor that he had been poisoned, his body was *exhumed* in order that an autopsy might be performed.

ex·i·gen·cy \'ek-sə-jən-sē\ (*n*) urgent situation. In this *exigency,* we must look for aid from our allies.

ex·ig·u·ous \ig-'zig-yə-wəs\ (*adj*) small; minute. Grass grew here and there, an *exiguous* outcropping among the rocks.

ex·o·dus \'ek-səd-əs\ (*n*) departure. The *exodus* from the hot and stuffy city was particularly noticeable on Friday evenings.

ex of·fi·ci·o \,ek-sə-'fish-ē-,ō\ (*adj*) by virtue of one's office. The mayor was *ex officio* chairman of the committee that decided the annual tax rate. also (*adv*).

ex·on·er·ate \ig-'zän-ə-,rāt\ (*v*) acquit; exculpate. The defense team feverishly sought fresh evidence that might *exonerate* their client.

ex·or·bi·tant \ig-'zȯr-bət-ənt\ (*adj*) excessive. The people grumbled at his *exorbitant* prices but paid them because he had a monopoly.

ex·or·cise \'ek-,sȯr-,sīz\ (*v*) drive out evil spirits. By incantation and prayer, the medicine man sought to *exorcise* the evil spirits that had taken possession of the young warrior.

ex·ot·ic \ig-'zät-ik\ (*adj*) not native; strange. Because of his *exotic* headdress, he was followed in the streets by small children who laughed at his strange appearance. also (*n*).

\ə\ **abut** \ᵊ\ **kitten, F table** \ər\ **further** \a\ **ash** \ā\ **ace** \ä\ **cot, cart**
\aů\ **out** \ch\ **chin** \e\ **bet** \ē\ **easy** \g\ **go** \i\ **hit** \ī\ **ice** \j\ **job**

ex-pa-ti-ate \ek-'spā-shē-ˌāt\ (*v*) talk at length. At this time, please give us a brief resumé of your work; we shall permit you to *expatiate* later.

ex-pa-tri-ate \ek-'spā-trē-ˌāt\ (*n*) exile; someone who has withdrawn from his native land. Henry James was an American *expatriate* who settled in England. also (*v, adj*).

ex-pe-di-en-cy \ik-'spēd-ē-ən-sē\ (*n*) that which is advisable or practical. He was guided by *expediency* rather than by ethical considerations.

ex-pe-di-tious-ly \ˌek-spə-'dish-əs-lē\ (*adv*) rapidly and efficiently. Please deliver our order as *expeditiously* as possible; we are working on a very tight schedule.

ex-per-tise \ˌek-₍₎spər-'tēz\ (*n*) specialized knowledge; expert skill. Although she was knowledgeable in a number of fields, she was hired for her particular *expertise* in computer programming.

ex-pi-ate \'ek-spē-ˌāt\ (*v*) make amends for (a sin). Jean Valjean tried to *expiate* his crimes by performing acts of charity.

ex-ple-tive \'ek-splət-iv\ (*n*) interjection; profane oath. The sergeant's remarks were filled with *expletives* that reflected on the intelligence and character of the new recruits. also (*adj*).

ex-plic-it \ik-'splis-ət\ (*adj*) totally clear; definite; outspoken. Don't just hint around that you're dissatisfied: be *explicit* about what's bugging you.

ex-ploit \'ek-ˌsplȯit\ (*n*) deed or action, particularly a brave deed. Raoul Wallenberg was noted for his *exploits* in rescuing Jews from Hitler's forces.

ex-ploit \ik-'splȯit\ (*v*) make use of, sometimes unjustly. Cesar Chavez fought attempts to *exploit* migrant farmworkers in California. ex-ploi-ta-tion \ˌek-ˌsplȯi-'tā-shən\ (*n*)

\ŋ\ si**ng**   \ō\ **go**   \ȯ\ **law**   \ȯi\ **boy**   \th\ **thin**   \t̲h̲\ **the**   \ü\ **loot**   \u̇\ **foot**
\y\ **yet**   \zh\ vi**sion**   \à, k̲, ⁿ, œ, œ̄, ue, ūe, ʸ\ *see* Pronunciation Symbols

ex-pos-tu-la-tion \ik-ˌspäs-chə-'lā-shən\ (*n*) remonstrance. Despite the teacher's scoldings and *expostulations,* the class remained unruly.

ex-punge \ik-'spənj\ (*v*) cancel; remove. If you behave, I will *expunge* this notation from your record.

ex-pur-gate \'ek-spər-ˌgāt\ (*v*) clean; remove offensive parts of a book. The editors felt that certain passages in the book had to be *expurgated* before it could be used in this classroom.

ex-tant \'ek-stənt\ (*adj*) still in existence. Although the book is out of print, some copies are *extant.* Unfortunately, all of them are in libraries or private collections; none are for sale.

ex-tem-po-ra-ne-ous \ˌ(ˌ)ek-ˌstem-pə-'rā-nē-əs\ (*adj*) not planned; impromptu. Because his *extemporaneous* remarks were misinterpreted, he decided to write all his speeches in advance.

ex-ten-sive \ik-'sten(t)-siv\ (*adj*) vast; comprehensive. The real estate magnate built up his *extensive* holdings over a number of years.

ex-ten-u-ate \ik-'sten-yə-ˌwāt\ (*v*) gloss over; whitewash; explain away; mitigate. It is easier for us to *extenuate* our own shortcomings than those of others.

ex-tir-pate \'ek-stər-ˌpāt\ (*v*) root up; blot out. We must *extirpate* and destroy this heretical philosophy.

ex-tol \ik-'stōl\ (*v*) praise; glorify. The president *extolled* the astronauts, calling them the pioneers of the Space Age.

ex-tort \ik-'stó(ə)rt\ (*v*) wring from; get money by threats, etc. The blackmailer *extorted* money from his victim.

ex-tra-di-tion \ˌek-strə-'dish-ən\ (*n*) surrender of prisoner by one state to another. The lawyers opposed the *extradition* of their client on the grounds that for more than five years he had been a model citizen.

---

ex-tra-ne-ous \ek-'strā-nē-əs\ (*adj*) not essential; external. His mind was so cluttered with *extraneous* details that he couldn't concentrate on the big picture.

ex-tra-vert \'ek-strə-ˌvərt\ (*n*) person interested mostly in external objects and actions. A good salesman is usually an *extravert,* who likes to mingle with people; also ex-tro-vert.

ex-tri-cate \'ek-strə-ˌkāt\ (*v*) free; disentangle. Icebreakers were needed to *extricate* the trapped whales from the icy floes that closed them in.

ex-trin-sic \ek-'strin-zik\ (*adj*) external; not essential; extraneous. A critically acclaimed *extrinsic* feature of the Chrysler Building is its ornate spire. The judge would not admit the testimony, ruling that it was *extrinsic* to the matter at hand.

ex-trude \ik-'strüd\ (*v*) force or push out. Much pressure is required to *extrude* these plastics.

ex-u-ber-ant \ig-'zü-b(ə-)rənt\ (*adj*) abundant; joyfully enthusiastic; flamboyant; lavish. I was bowled over by Amy's *exuberant* welcome. What an enthusiastic greeting!

ex-ude \ig-'züd\ (*v*) discharge; give forth. We obtain maple syrup from the sap that *exudes* from the trees in early spring. ex-u-da-tion \ˌek-s(y)ù-dā-shən\ (*n*)

ex-ult \ig-'zəlt\ (*v*) rejoice. We *exulted* when our team won the victory.

F

fab·ri·cate \\'fab-ri-ˌkāt\\ (*v*) build; lie. If we *fabricate* the buildings in this project out of standardized sections, we can reduce construction costs considerably. Because of Jack's tendency to *fabricate*, Jill had trouble believing a word he said.

fa·cade \\fə-'säd\\ (*n*) front (of building); superficial or false appearance. The ornate *facade* of the church was often photographed by tourists, who never bothered to walk around the building to view its other sides. Cher seemed superconfident, but that was just a *facade* she put on to hide her insecurity.

fac·et \\'fas-ət\\ (*n*) small plane surface (of a gem); a side. The stonecutter decided to improve the rough diamond by providing it with several *facets*.

fa·ce·tious \\fə-'sē-shəs\\ (*adj*) joking (often inappropriately); humorous. I'm serious about this project; I don't need any *facetious*, smart-alecky cracks about do-gooder little rich girls.

fac·ile \\'fas-əl\\ (*adj*) easily accomplished; ready or fluent; superficial. Words came easily to Jonathan: he was a *facile* speaker and prided himself on being ready to make a speech at a moment's notice.

fa·cil·i·tate \\fa-'sil-ə-ˌtāt\\ (*v*) help bring about; make less difficult. Rest and proper nourishment should *facilitate* the patient's recovery.

fac·tion \\'fak-shən\\ (*n*) party; clique; dissension. The quarrels and bickering of the two small *factions* within the club disturbed the majority of the members.

fac·tious \\'fak-shəs\\ (*adj*) inclined to form factions; causing dissension. Shaken by the extent of the disaster, lawmakers of both parties abandoned their *factious* quarrels and worked together to relieve the suffering of the victims.

\\ə\\ **abut** \\ᵊ\\ **kitten,** F **table** \\ər\\ **further** \\a\\ **ash** \\ā\\ **ace** \\ä\\ **cot, cart**
\\au̇\\ **out** \\ch\\ **chin** \\e\\ **bet** \\ē\\ **easy** \\g\\ **go** \\i\\ **hit** \\ī\\ **ice** \\j\\ **job**

fac·ti·tious \fak-'tish-əs\ (*adj*) artificial; sham. Hollywood actresses often create *factitious* tears by using glycerine.

fac·ul·ty \'fak-əl-tē\ (*n*) mental or bodily power; teaching staff. At seventy-five, Professor Twiggly was in full possession of his *faculties*; therefore, the school couldn't kick him off the *faculty*.

fal·la·cious \fə-'lā-shəs\ (*adj*) misleading. Paradoxically, *fallacious* reasoning does not always yield erroneous results: even though your logic may be faulty, the answer you get may nevertheless be correct.

fal·li·ble \'fal-ə-bəl\ (*adj*) liable to err. I know I am *fallible*, but I feel confident that I am right this time.

fal·low \'fal-(ˌ)ō\ (*adj*) plowed but not sowed; uncultivated. Farmers have learned that it is advisable to permit land to lie *fallow* every few years. also (*n, v*).

fal·ter \'fȯl-tər\ (*v*) hesitate. When told to dive off the high board, she did not *falter,* but proceeded at once.

fa·nat·i·cism \fə-'nat-ə-ˌsiz-əm\ (*n*) excessive zeal; extreme devotion to a belief or cause. When Islamic fundamentalists demanded the death of Salman Rushdie because his novel questioned their faith, world opinion condemned them for their *fanaticism*.

fan·cied \'fan(t)-sēd\ (*adj*) imagined; unreal. Don't upset yourself over *fancied* insults.

fan·ci·er \'fan(t)-sē-ər\ (*n*) breeder or dealer of animals. The dog *fancier* exhibited his prize collie at the annual Kennel Club show.

fan·ci·ful \'fan(t)-si-fəl\ (*adj*) whimsical; visionary. When Martin took a *fancy* to paint his toenails purple, his parents assumed he would outgrow such *fanciful* behavior.

fan·fare \'fan-ˌfa(ə)r\ (*n*) call by bugles or trumpets. The exposition was opened with a *fanfare* of trumpets and the firing of a cannon.

\ŋ\ sing \ō\ go \ȯ\ law \ȯi\ boy \th\ thin \th\ the \ü\ loot \u̇\ foot
\y\ yet \zh\ vision \à, k̲, ⁿ, œ, œ̅, ue, ūe, ʸ\ *see* Pronunciation Symbols

fan-tas-tic \fan-'tas-tik\ (*adj*) unreal; grotesque; whimsical. The painter Hieronymus Bosch depicted weird, *fantastic* creatures that could never have existed on earth.

farce \'färs\ (*n*) broad comedy; mockery. Nothing went right; the entire interview degenerated into a *farce*. far-ci-cal \'fär-si-kəl\ (*adj*)

fas-tid-i-ous \fa-'stid-ē-əs\ (*adj*) difficult to please; squeamish. Bobby was such a *fastidious* eater that he would eat a sandwich only if his mother first cut off every scrap of crust.

fa-tal-ism \'fāt-ᵊl-ˌiz-əm\ (*n*) belief that events are determined by forces beyond one's control. With *fatalism,* he accepted the hardships that beset him. fa-tal-is-tic \ˌfāt-ᵊl-'is-tik\ (*adj*)

fath-om \'fath-əm\ (*v*) comprehend; investigate. I find his motives impossible to *fathom.*

fat-u-ous \'fach-(ə-)wəs\ (*adj*) foolish; inane. He is far too intelligent to utter such *fatuous* remarks.

fau-na \'fȯn-ə\ (*n*) animals of a period or region. The scientist could visualize the *fauna* of the period by examining the skeletal remains and the fossils.

faux pas \'fō-ˌpä\ (*n*) an error or slip (in manners or behavior). Your tactless remarks during dinner were a *faux pas.*

fe-al-ty \'fē(-ə)l-tē\ (*n*) loyalty; faithfulness. The feudal lord demanded *fealty* of his vassals.

fea-si-ble \'fē-zə-bəl\ (*adj*) practical. Is it *feasible* to build a new stadium for the Yankees on New York's West Side? Without additional funding, the project is clearly unrealistic.

fe-cun-di-ty \fi-'kən-dət-ē\ (*n*) fertility; fruitfulness. The *fecundity* of his mind is manifested in the many vivid images in his poems.

---

feign \ˈfān\ (*v*) pretend. Bobby *feigned* illness, hoping that his mother would let him stay home from school.

feint \ˈfānt\ (*n*) trick; shift; sham blow. The boxer was fooled by his opponent's *feint* and dropped his guard. also (*v*).

fe·lic·i·tous \fi-ˈlis-ət-əs\ (*adj*) apt; suitably expressed, well chosen. Famous for his *felicitous* remarks, he was called on to serve as master of ceremonies at many a banquet.

fell \ˈfel\ (*adj*) cruel; deadly. Newspaper reports of SARS told of the tragic spread of the *fell* disease.

fell \ˈfel\ (*v*) cut or knock down; bring down (with a missile). Crying "Timber!" Paul Bunyan *felled* the mighty redwood tree. Robin Hood loosed his arrow and *felled* the king's deer.

fel·on \ˈfel-ən\ (*n*) person convicted of a grave crime. A convicted *felon* loses the right to vote.

fer·ment \ˈfər-ˌment\ (*n*) agitation; commotion. With the breakup of the Soviet Union, much of Eastern Europe was in a state of *ferment*. fer·ment \fər-ˈment\ (*v*)

fer·ret \ˈfer-ət\ (*v*) drive or hunt out of hiding. He *ferreted* out their secret. also (*n*).

fer·vent \ˈfər-vənt\ (*adj*) ardent; hot. She felt that their *fervent* praise was excessive and somewhat undeserved.

fer·vid \ˈfər-vəd\ (*adj*) ardent. His *fervid* enthusiasm inspired all of us to undertake the dangerous mission.

fer·vor \ˈfər-vər\ (*n*) glowing ardor; intensity of feeling. At the protest rally, the students cheered the strikers and booed the dean with equal *fervor*.

fes·ter \ˈfes-tər\ (*v*) rankle; produce irritation or resentment; generate pus. Joe's insult *festered* in Anne's mind for days, and made her too angry to speak to him.

fes·tive \ˈfes-tiv\ (*adj*) joyous; celebratory. Their wedding in the park was a *festive* occasion.

\ŋ\ sing \ō\ go \ȯ\ law \ȯi\ boy \th\ thin \th\ the \ü\ loot \u̇\ foot
\y\ yet \zh\ vision \à, k̲, ⁿ, œ, œ̄, ue, ūe, ʸ\ *see* Pronunciation Symbols

fete \\'fāt\ (*v*) honor at a festival. The returning hero was *feted* at a community supper and dance. also (*n*).

fet-id \\'fet-əd\ (*adj*) malodorous. The neglected wound became *fetid*.

fet-ter \\'fet-ər\ (*v*) shackle. The prisoner was *fettered* to the wall. also (*n*).

fi-as-co \fē-'äs-₍ᵢ₎kō\ (*n*) total failure. Tanya's attempt to look sophisticated by taking up smoking was a *fiasco*: she lit the filter, choked when she tried to inhale, and burned a hole in her boyfriend's couch.

fi-at \\'fē-ət\ (*n*) command. We cannot accept government by presidential *fiat;* Congress must be consulted.

fick-le \\'fik-əl\ (*adj*) changeable; faithless. As soon as Romeo saw Juliet, he forgot all about his old girlfriend Rosaline. Was Romeo *fickle*?

fic-ti-tious \fik-'tish-əs\ (*adj*) imaginary. Although this book purports to be a biography of George Washington, many of the incidents are *fictitious*.

fi-del-i-ty \fə-'del-ət-ē\ (*n*) loyalty. Iago wickedly manipulates Othello, arousing his jealousy and causing him to question his wife's *fidelity*.

fi-du-ci-ar-y \fe-'d(y)ü-shē-,er-ē\ (*adj*) pertaining to a position of trust. In his will, he stipulated that the bank act in a *fiduciary* capacity and manage his estate until his children became of age. also (*n*).

fig-ment \\'fig-mənt\ (*n*) invention; imaginary thing. Was he hearing real voices in the night, or were they just a *figment* of his imagination?

filch \\'filch\ (*v*) steal. The boys *filched* apples from the fruit stand.

fil-i-al \\'fil-ē-əl\ (*adj*) pertaining to a son or daughter. Many children forget their *filial* obligations and disregard the wishes of their parents.

fi-na-le \fə-'nal-ē\ (*n*) conclusion. It is not until we reach the *finale* of this play that we can understand the author's message.

\ə\ **abut** \ᵊ\ **kitten, F table** \ər\ **further** \a\ **ash** \ā\ **ace** \ä\ **cot, cart**
\aù\ **out** \ch\ **chin** \e\ **bet** \ē\ **easy** \g\ **go** \i\ **hit** \ī\ **ice** \j\ **job**

fi-nesse \fə-'nes\ (*n*) delicate skill. The *finesse* and adroitness with which the surgeon wielded her scalpel impressed all the observers in the operating room. also (*v*).

fin-ick-y \'fin-i-kē\ (*adj*) too particular; fussy. The little girl was *finicky* about her food, leaving over anything that wasn't to her taste.

fi-nite \'fī-ˌnīt\ (*adj*) having an end; limited. Though Bill wanted to win the pie-eating contest, the capacity of his stomach was *finite*: he had to call it quits after eating only seven pies.

fire-brand \'fī(ə)r-ˌbrand\ (*n*) hothead; troublemaker. The police tried to keep track of all the local *firebrands* when the president came to town.

fis-sure \'fish-ər\ (*n*) crevice. The mountain climbers secured footholds in tiny *fissures* in the rock. also (*v*).

fit-ful \'fit-fəl\ (*adj*) spasmodic; intermittent. After several *fitful* attempts, he decided to postpone the start of the project until he felt more energetic.

flac-cid \'flak-səd\ (*adj*) flabby. His sedentary life had left him with *flaccid* muscles.

fla-gel-late \'flaj-ə-ˌlāt\ (*v*) flog; whip. The Romans used to *flagellate* criminals with a whip that had three knotted strands. fla-gel-late \'flaj-ə-lət\ (*adj, n*)

flag-ging \'flag-iŋ\ (*adj*) weak; drooping. The encouraging cheers of the crowd lifted the team's *flagging* spirits.

fla-grant \'fla-grənt\ (*adj*) conspicuously wicked; blatant; outrageous. The governor's appointment of his brother-in-law to the State Supreme Court was a *flagrant* violation of the state laws against nepotism (favoritism based on kinship).

flail \'flā(ə)l\ (*v*) thresh grain by hand; strike or slap. In medieval times, warriors *flailed* their foe with a metal ball attached to a handle. also (*n*).

---

flair \ˈfla(ə)r\ (*n*) talent. He has an uncanny *flair* for discovering new artists before the public has become aware of their existence.

flam-boy-ant \flam-ˈbȯi-ənt\ (*adj*) ornate. Modern architecture has discarded the *flamboyant* trimming on buildings and emphasizes simplicity of line.

flaunt \ˈflȯnt\ (*v*) display ostentatiously. Mae West saw nothing wrong with showing off her considerable physical charms, saying, "Honey, if you've got it, *flaunt* it!"

flay \ˈflā\ (*v*) strip off skin; plunder. The criminal was condemned to be *flayed* alive.

fleck \ˈflek\ (*v*) spot. Her cheeks, *flecked* with tears, were testimony to the hours of weeping. also (*n*).

fledg-ling \ˈflej-liŋ\ (*adj*) inexperienced. The folk dance club set up an apprentice program to allow *fledgling* dance callers a chance to polish their skills. also (*n*).

fleece \ˈflēs\ (*n*) wool coat of a sheep. They shear sheep of their *fleece,* which they then comb into separate strands of wool.

fleece \ˈflēs\ (*v*) rob; plunder. The tricksters *fleeced* him of his inheritance.

flick \ˈflik\ (*n*) light stroke as with a whip. The horse needed no encouragement; only one *flick* of the whip was all the jockey had to apply to get the animal to run at top speed. also (*v*).

flinch \ˈflinch\ (*v*) hesitate; shrink. He did not *flinch* in the face of danger but fought back bravely.

flip-pan-cy \ˈflip-ən-sē\ (*n*) lack of proper seriousness. Mary refused to take Mark seriously, dismissing his earnest declaration of love with *flippancy*.

floe \ˈflō\ (*n*) mass of floating ice. The ship made slow progress as it battered its way through the ice *floes*.

flo-ra \ˈflōr-ə\ (*n*) plants of a region or era. Because she was a botanist, she spent most of her time studying the *flora* of the desert.

\ə\ **abut** \ᵊ\ **kitten, F table** \ər\ f**urther** \a\ **ash** \ā\ **ace** \ä\ **cot, cart** \aú\ **out** \ch\ **chin** \e\ **bet** \ē\ **easy** \g\ **go** \i\ **hit** \ī\ **ice** \j\ **job**

flor-id \'flȯr-əd\ (*adj*) flowery; ruddy. If you go to Florida and get a sunburn, your complexion looks *florid*. If your postcards about the trip praise Florida in flowery words, your prose sounds *florid*.

flo-til-la \flō-'til-ə\ (*n*) small fleet. It is always an exciting and interesting moment when the fishing *flotilla* returns to port.

flot-sam \'flät-səm\ (*n*) drifting wreckage. Beachcombers eke out a living by salvaging the *flotsam* and jetsam of the sea.

flout \'flaȯt\ (*v*) reject; mock. The headstrong youth *flouted* all authority; he refused to be curbed.

fluc-tu-a-tion \ˌflək-chə-'wā-shən\ (*n*) wavering. I'll never get used to the wild *fluctuations* of water pressure in our shower: one minute you're rinsing yourself off with a trickle, and two minutes later, a blast of water nearly knocks you down.

flu-en-cy \'flü-ən-sē\ (*n*) smoothness of speech. She spoke French with *fluency* and ease.

flus-ter \'fləs-tər\ (*v*) confuse. The teacher's sudden question *flustered* him and he stammered his reply. also (*n*).

flux \'fləks\ (*n*) flowing series of changes. While conditions are in such a state of *flux*, I do not wish to commit myself too deeply in this affair. also (*v*).

foi-ble \'fȯi-bəl\ (*n*) weakness; slight fault. We can overlook the *foibles* of our friends.

foil \'fȯi(ə)l\ (*n*) contrast. In *Star Wars,* dark, evil Darth Vader is a perfect *foil* for fair-haired, naive Luke Skywalker.

foil \'fȯi(ə)l\ (*v*) defeat; frustrate. In the end, Skywalker is able to *foil* Vader's diabolical schemes.

foist \'fȯist\ (*v*) force upon; insert improperly; palm off. When his dying brother begged Ralph Nickelby to care for his poor children, Nickelby harshly declared, "Those wretched brats shall never *foist* themselves upon me!"

\ŋ\ si**ng** \ō\ go \ȯ\ law \ȯi\ b**oy** \th\ **th**in \t̲h̲\ **the** \ü\ l**oo**t \u̇\ f**oo**t
\y\ **y**et \zh\ vi**s**ion \à, ḵ, ⁿ, œ, œ̄, ue, ūe, ʸ\ *see* Pronunciation Symbols

fo-ment \'fō-,ment\ (*v*) stir up; instigate. Cher's archene-my Heather spread some nasty rumors that *fomented* trouble in the club. Do you think Cher's foe meant to *foment* such discord?

fool-har-dy \'fül-,härd-ē\ (*adj*) rash. Don't be *foolhardy*. Get the advice of experienced people before undertak-ing this venture.

fop-pish \'fäp-ish\ (*adj*) vain about dress and appearance. He tried to imitate the *foppish* manner of the young men of the court.

for-ay \'for-,ā\ (*n*) raid. The company staged a midnight *foray* against the enemy outpost. also (*v*).

for-bear-ance \for-'bar-ən(t)s\ (*n*) patience. Be patient with John. Treat him with *forbearance*: he is still weak from his illness.

fore-bod-ing \for-'bōd-iŋ\ (*n*) premonition of evil. Suspecting no conspiracies against him, Caesar gently ridiculed his wife's *forebodings* about the Ides of March.

fo-ren-sic \fə-'ren(t)-sik\ (*adj*) suitable to debate or courts of law. In his best *forensic* manner, the lawyer addressed the jury. also (*n*).

fore-sight \'fō(ə)r-,sit\ (*n*) ability to foresee future happen-ings; prudence. A wise investor, she had the *foresight* to buy land just before the current real estate boom.

for-mal-i-ty \for-'mal-ət-ē\ (*n*) ceremonious quality; something done just for form's sake. The President received the visiting heads of state with due *formality*: flags waving, honor guards standing at attention, anthems sounding at full blast. Signing this petition is a mere *formality*; it does not obligate you in any way.

for-mi-da-ble \'for-məd-ə-bəl\ (*adj*) inspiring fear or apprehension; difficult; awe-inspiring. In the film *Meet the Parents*, the hero is understandably nervous about meeting his fiancee's father, a *formidable* CIA agent.

\ə\ **abut** \ə\ kitten, F table \ər\ **further** \a\ **ash** \ā\ **ace** \ä\ **cot, cart**
\au̇\ **out** \ch\ **chin** \e\ bet \ē\ **easy** \g\ **go** \i\ **hit** \ī\ **ice** \j\ **job**

forte \ˈfō(ə)rt\ (*n*)　strong point or special talent. I am not eager to play this rather serious role, for my *forte* is comedy.

for-ti-tude \ˈfȯrt-ə-ˌt(y)üd\ (*n*)　bravery; courage. He was awarded the medal for his *fortitude* in the battle.

for-tu-i-tous \fȯr-ˈt(y)ü-ət-əs\ (*adj*)　accidental; by chance. Though he pretended their encounter was *fortuitous*, he'd actually been hanging around her usual haunts for the past two weeks, hoping she'd turn up.

fos-ter \ˈfȯs-tər\ (*v*)　rear; encourage. According to the legend, Romulus and Remus were *fostered* by a she-wolf who raised the abandoned infants with her own cubs. also (*adj*).

fra-cas \ˈfrāk-əs\ (*n*)　brawl, melee. The military police stopped the *fracas* in the bar and arrested the belligerents.

frac-tious \ˈfrak-shəs\ (*adj*)　unruly. The *fractious* horse unseated its rider.

frail-ty \ˈfrā(-ə)l-tē\ (*n*)　weakness. The delicate child's *frailty* was evident as he struggled to lift the heavy carton.

fran-chise \ˈfran-ˌchīz\ (*n*)　right granted by authority; right to vote; business licensed to sell a product in a particular territory. The city issued a *franchise* to the company to operate surface transit lines on the streets for ninety-nine years. For most of American history women lacked the right to vote: not until the early twentieth century was the *franchise* granted to women. also (*v*).

fran-tic \ˈfrant-ik\ (*adj*)　wild. At the time of the collision, many people became *frantic* with fear.

fraud-u-lent \ˈfrȯ-jə-lənt\ (*adj*)　cheating; deceitful. The government seeks to prevent *fraudulent* and misleading advertising.

fraught \ˈfrȯt\ (*adj*)　filled. Since this enterprise is *fraught* with danger, I will ask for volunteers who are willing to assume the risks.

\ŋ\ si**ng**　\ō\ **go**　\ȯ\ **law**　\ȯi\ **boy**　\th\ **thin**　\t͟h\ **the**　\ü\ **loot**　\u̇\ **foot**
\y\ **yet**　\zh\ vi**sion**　\à, k̲, ⁿ, œ, œ̄, ue, ūe, ʸ\ *see* Pronunciation Symbols

fray \\'frā\ (*n*) brawl. The three musketeers were in the thick of the *fray*.

fre-net-ic \fri-'net-ik\ (*adj*) frenzied; frantic. His *frenetic* activities convinced us that he had no organized plan of operation.

fren-zied \\'fren-zēd\ (*adj*) madly excited. As soon as they smelled smoke, the *frenzied* animals milled about in their cages.

fres-co \\'fres-(ˌ)kō\ (*n*) painting on plaster (usually fresh). The cathedral is visited by many tourists who wish to admire the *frescoes* by Giotto.

fret \\'fret\ (*v*) to be annoyed or vexed. To *fret* over your poor grades is foolish; instead, decide to work harder in the future.

fric-tion \\'frik-shən\ (*n*) clash in opinion; rubbing against. At this time when harmony is essential, we cannot afford to have any *friction* in our group.

frieze \\'frēz\ (*n*) ornamental band on a wall. The *frieze* of the church was adorned with sculpture.

frig-id \\'frij-əd\ (*adj*) intensely cold. Alaska is in the *frigid* zone.

frit-ter \\'frit-ər\ (*v*) waste. He could not apply himself to any task and *frittered* away his time in idle conversation.

fri-vol-i-ty \friv-'äl-ət-ē\ (n) lack of seriousness. Though Nancy enjoyed Bill's *frivolity* and valued his lightheart-ed companionship, she sometimes wondered whether he could ever be serious. friv-o-lous \\'friv-(ə-)ləs\ (*adj*)

frol-ic-some \\'fräl-ik-səm\ (*adj*) prankish; gay. The *frolic-some* puppy tried to lick the face of its master.

fruc-ti-fy \\'frək-tə-ˌfī\ (*v*) bear fruit. This tree should *fruc-tify* in three years.

fru-gal-i-ty \frü-'gal-ət-ē\ (*n*) thrift; economy. In economi-cally hard times, anyone who doesn't learn to practice *frugality* risks bankruptcy.

fru-i-tion \frü-'ish-ən\ (*n*) bearing of fruit; fulfillment; re-alization. After years of saving and scrimping, her

---

\ə\ **abut** \ə\ **kitten,** F **table** \ər\ **further** \a\ **ash** \ā\ **ace** \ä\ **cot, cart**
\aů\ **out** \ch\ **chin** \e\ **bet** \ē\ **easy** \g\ **go** \i\ **hit** \ī\ **ice** \j\ **job**

dream of owning her own home finally came to *fruition*.

frus-trate \'frəs-ˌtrāt\ (*v*) thwart; defeat. Constant partisan bickering *frustrated* the governor's efforts to convince the legislature to approve his proposed budget.

ful-crum \'fu̇l-krəm\ (*n*) support on which a lever rests. If we use this stone as a *fulcrum* and the crowbar as a lever, we may be able to move this boulder.

ful-mi-nate \'fu̇l-mə-ˌnāt\ (*v*) thunder; explode. The Ayatollah *fulminated* against the wickedness of the United States, calling America the Great Satan.

ful-some \'fu̇l-səm\ (*adj*) disgustingly excessive. Disgusted by her fans' *fulsome* admiration, the movie star retreated from the public, crying, "I want to be alone!"

func-tion-ar-y \'fəŋ(k)-shə-ˌner-ē\ (*n*) official. As his case was transferred from one *functionary* to another, he began to despair of ever reaching a settlement.

fu-ne-re-al \fyu̇-'nir-ē-əl\ (*adj*) sad; solemn. On election night, the atmosphere at the Democratic candidate's headquarters was *funereal*: everyone present was sure the race was lost.

fu-ror \'fyu̇(ə)r-ˌȯ(ə)r\ (*n*) frenzy; great excitement. The story of his embezzlement of the funds created a *furor* on the Stock Exchange.

fur-tive \'fərt-iv\ (*adj*) stealthy; sneaky. Noticing the *furtive* glance the customer gave the diamond bracelet on the counter, the jeweler wondered whether he had a potential shoplifter on his hands.

fu-sion \'fyü-zhən\ (*n*) union; blending; synthesis. So-called rockabilly music represents a *fusion* of country western music with rock and roll.

fu-tile \'fyüt-ᵊl\ (*adj*) useless; hopeless; ineffectual. It is *futile* for me to try to get any work done around here while the telephone is ringing every thirty seconds.

\ŋ\ sing \ō\ go \ȯ\ law \ȯi\ boy \th\ thin \th\ the \ü\ loot \u̇\ foot
\y\ yet \zh\ vision \ä, ḵ, ⁿ, œ, œ̄, ue, ūe, ʸ\ *see* Pronunciation Symbols

G

gad-fly \'gad-ˌflī\ (*n*) animal-biting fly; an irritating person. Like a *gadfly*, he irritated all the guests at the hotel; within forty-eight hours, everyone regarded him as an annoying busybody.

gain-say \ gān-'sā\ (*v*) deny. Even though it reflected badly upon him, he was too honest to *gainsay* the truth of the report.

gait \'gāt\ (*n*) manner of walking or running; speed. The lame man walked with an uneven *gait*.

gal-a-xy \'gal-ək-sē\ (*n*) large, isolated system of stars, such as the Milky Way; any collection of brilliant personalities. Science fiction stories speculate about the possible existence of life in other *galaxies*. The deaths of such famous actors as John Candy and George Burns tell us that the *galaxy* of Hollywood superstars is rapidly disappearing.

gall \'gȯl\ (*n*) bitterness; nerve. The knowledge of his failure filled him with *gall*.

gall \'gȯl\ (*v*) annoy; chafe. Their taunts *galled* him.

gal-le-on \'gal-ē-ən\ (*n*) large sailing ship. The Spaniards pinned their hopes on the *galleon*, the large warship; the British, on the smaller and faster pinnace.

gal-va-nize \'gal-və-ˌnīz\ (*v*) stimulate by shock; stir up; revitalize. News that the prince was almost at their door *galvanized* Cinderella's ugly stepsisters into a frenzy of combing and primping.

gam-bit \'gam-bət\ (*n*) opening in chess in which a piece is sacrificed. The player was afraid to accept his opponent's *gambit* because he feared a trap that as yet he could not see.

gam-bol \'gam-bəl\ (*v*) skip; leap playfully. Watching the children *gambol* in the park, Betty marveled at their youthful energy and spirit. also (*n*).

\ə\ **abut** \ᵊ\ **kitten**, F **table** \ər\ **further** \a\ **ash** \ā\ **ace** \ä\ **cot, cart**
\au̇\ **out** \ch\ **chin** \e\ **bet** \ē\ **easy** \g\ **go** \i\ **hit** \ī\ **ice** \j\ **job**

game-ly \'gām-lē\ *(adv)* in a plucky manner. Because he had fought *gamely* against a much superior boxer, the crowd gave him a standing ovation when he left the arena.

gam-ut \'gam-ət\ *(n)* entire range. In a classic put-down of actress Katherine Hepburn, the critic Dorothy Parker wrote that the actress ran the *gamut* of emotion from A to B.

gape \'gāp\ *(v)* open widely. Slack-jawed in wonder, Huck *gaped* at the huge stalactites hanging down from the ceiling of the limestone cavern.

gar-ble \'gär-bəl\ *(v)* mix up; change meaning by distortion. A favorite party game involves passing a whispered message from one person to another, till, by the time it reaches the last player, the players have completely *garbled* the original wording.

gar-goyle \'gär-ˌgȯil\ *(n)* waterspout carved in grotesque figures on building. The *gargoyles* adorning the Cathedral of Notre Dame in Paris are amusing in their grotesqueness.

gar-ish \'ga(ə)r-ish\ *(adj)* overbright in color; gaudy. She wore a gaudy rhinestone necklace with an excessively *garish* gold lamé dress.

gar-ner \'gär-nər\ *(v)* gather; store up. In her long career as an actress, Hepburn *garnered* many awards, including the coveted Oscar.

gar-nish \'gär-nish\ *(v)* decorate. The chef *garnished* the boiled potatoes with a sprinkling of parsley.

gar-ru-li-ty \gə-'rü-lət-ē\ *(n)* talkativeness. The office manager fired her assistant because her *garrulity* distracted her coworkers.

gar-ru-lous \'gar-ə-ləs\ *(adj)* loquacious; wordy. My Uncle Henry is the most *garrulous* person in Cayuga County: he can outtalk any three people I know.

\ŋ\ sing \ō\ go \ȯ\ law \ȯi\ boy \th\ thin \t͟h\ the \ü\ loot \u̇\ foot
\y\ yet \zh\ vision \à, ḵ, ⁿ, œ, œ̄, ᵫ, ᵭ, ʸ\ *see* Pronunciation Symbols

o-my \ga-'strän-ə-mē\ (*n*) science of preparing rving good food. One of the by-products of his trip to ~~Eu~~rope was his interest in *gastronomy*; he enjoyed preparing and serving foreign dishes to his friends.

gauche \'gōsh\ (*adj*) clumsy; boorish. Compared to the sophisticated young ladies in their elegant gowns, tomboyish Jo felt *gauche* and out of place.

gaunt \'gȯnt\ (*adj*) lean and angular; barren. His once round face looked surprisingly *gaunt* after he had lost weight.

gaunt-let \'gȯnt-lət\ (*n*) leather glove. Now that we have been challenged, we must take up the *gauntlet* and meet our adversary fearlessly.

ge-ne-al-o-gy \jē-nē-äl-ə-jē\ (*n*) record of descent; lineage. He was proud of his *genealogy* and constantly referred to the achievements of his ancestors.

gen-er-al-i-ty \jen-ə-'ral-ət-ē\ (*n*) vague statement. This report is filled with *generalities*; you must be more specific in your statements.

ge-ner-ic \jə-'ner-ik\ (*adj*) characteristic of a class or species. Sue knew so many computer programmers who spent their spare time playing fantasy games that she began to think that playing Dungeons & Dragons was a *generic* trait.

ge-ni-al-i-ty \jē-nē-'al-ət-ē\ (*n*) cheerfulness; kindliness; sympathy. This restaurant is famous and popular because of the *geniality* of the proprietor who tries to make everyone happy.

gen-re \'zhän-rə\ (*n*) kind, sort; a category of artistic, musical, or literary composition characterized by a particular style, form, or content. Both a short story writer and a poet, Langston Hughes proved himself equally skilled in either *genre*.

gen-teel \jen-'tē(ə)l\ (*adj*) well-bred; elegant. We are looking for a man with a *genteel* appearance who can inspire confidence by his cultivated manner.

\ə\ **abut** \ᵊ\ **kitten, F table** \ər\ **further** \a\ **ash** \ā\ **ace** \ä\ **cot, cart**
\au̇\ **out** \ch\ **chin** \e\ **bet** \ē\ **easy** \g\ **go** \i\ **hit** \ī\ **ice** \j\ **job**

gen·til·i·ty \jen-'til-ət-ē\ (*n*) those of gentle birth; refinement. Her family was proud of its *gentility.*

gen·try \'jen-trē\ (*n*) people of standing; class of people just below nobility. The local *gentry* did not welcome the visits of the summer tourists and tried to ignore their presence in the community.

gen·u·flect \'jen-yə-ˌflekt\ (*v*) bend the knee as in worship. A proud democrat, he refused to *genuflect* to any man.

ger·mane \₍₎jər-'mān\ (*adj*) pertinent; bearing upon the case at hand. The judge refused to allow the testimony to be heard by the jury because it was not *germane* to the case.

ger·mi·nal \'jərm-nəl\ (*adj*) pertaining to a germ; creative. Such an idea is *germinal*; I am certain that it will influence thinkers and philosophers for many generations.

ger·mi·nate \'jər-mə-ˌnāt\ (*v*) cause to sprout; sprout. After the seeds *germinate* and develop their permanent leaves, the plants may be removed from the cold frames and transplanted to the garden.

ger·ry·man·der \ jer-ē-'man-dər\ (*v*) change voting district lines in order to favor a political party. The illogical pattern of the map of this congressional district is proof that the State Legislature *gerrymandered* this area in order to favor the majority party. also (*n*).

ges·tate \'jes-ˌtāt\ (*v*) evolve, as in prenatal growth. The author refused to discuss the book that he was currently working on, saying that the plot and characters were still *gestating.*

ges·tic·u·la·tion \je-ˌstik-yə-'lā-shən\ (*n*) motion; gesture. We were still too far off to make out what Mother was calling, but from her animated *gesticulations* we could tell she wanted us to hurry home instantly.

ghast·ly \'gast-lē\ (*adj*) horrible. The murdered man was a *ghastly* sight.

gib·ber \'jib-ər\ (*v*) babble; speak incoherently or foolishly. "Calm down and stop *gibbering* hysterically! No one can understand a word you say."

\ŋ\ si**ng**   \ō\ **go**   \ȯ\ **law**   \ȯi\ **boy**   \th\ **thin**   \t̲h̲\ **the**   \ü\ **loot**   \u̇\ **foot**
\y\ **yet**   \zh\ **vision**   \à, k̲, ⁿ, œ, œ̄, ᵫe, ᵫ̄e, ʸ\ *see* Pronunciation Symbols

gibe \\'jīb\\ (*v*) mock; taunt; scoff at. The ugly stepsisters constantly *gibed* at Cinderella, taunting her about her ragged clothes.

gig \\'gig\\ (*n*) two-wheeled carriage. As they drove down the street in their new *gig,* drawn by the dappled mare, they were cheered by the people who recognized them.

gin-ger-ly \\'jin-jər-lē\\ (*adv*) very carefully. To separate egg whites, first crack the egg *gingerly.* also (*adj*).

gist \\'jist\\ (*n*) essence. She was asked to give the *gist* of the essay in two sentences.

glaze \\'glāz\\ (*v*) cover with a thin and shiny surface. The freezing rain *glazed* the streets and made driving hazardous. also (*n*).

glean \\'glēn\\ (*v*) gather leavings. After the crops had been harvested by the machines, the peasants were permitted to *glean* the wheat left in the fields. glean-ings \\'gle-niŋz\\ (*n*)

glib \\'glib\\ (*adj*) fluent; facile; slick. Keeping up a steady patter to entertain his customers, the kitchen gadget salesman was a *glib* speaker, never at a loss for words.

gloat \\'glōt\\ (*v*) express evil satisfaction; view malevolently. As you *gloat* over your ill-gotten wealth, do you think of the many victims you have defrauded? also (*n*).

glos-sa-ry \\'gläs-(ə-)rē\\ (*n*) brief explanation of words used in the text. I have found the *glossary* in this book very useful; it has eliminated many trips to the dictionary.

glos-sy \\'gläs-ē\\ (*adj*) smooth and shining. I want this photograph printed on *glossy* paper. also (*n*).

glower \\'glau̇(-ə)r\\ (*v*) scowl. The angry boy *glowered* at his father.

glut \\'glət\\ (*v*) overstock; fill to excess. The manufacturers *glutted* the market and could not find purchasers for the many articles they had produced. also (*n*).

glu-ti-nous \\'glüt-nəs\\ (*adj*) sticky; viscous. Molasses is a *glutinous* substance.

glut-ton-ous \\'glət-nəs\\ (*adj*) greedy for food. The *gluttonous* boy ate all the cookies.

\\ə\\ **abut** \\ə\\ kitten, F table \\ər\\ **further** \\a\\ **ash** \\ā\\ **ace** \\ä\\ **cot, cart**
\\au̇\\ **out** \\ch\\ **chin** \\e\\ **bet** \\ē\\ **easy** \\g\\ **go** \\i\\ **hit** \\ī\\ **ice** \\j\\ **job**

gnarled \'när(-ə)ld\ (*adj*) twisted. The weatherbeaten old sailor was as *gnarled* and bent as an old oak tree.

gnome \'nōm\ (*n*) dwarf; underground spirit. In medieval mythology, *gnomes* were the special guardians and inhabitants of subterranean mines.

goad \'gōd\ (*v*) urge on; spur; incite. Mother was afraid that Ben's wild friends would *goad* him into doing something that would get him into trouble with the law. also (*n*).

gorge \'gȯ(ə)rj\ (*v*) stuff oneself. The gluttonous guest *gorged* himself, cramming food into his mouth with both hands.

gor-y \'gō(ə)r-ē\ (*adj*) bloody. The audience shuddered as they listened to the details of the *gory* massacre.

gos-sa-mer \'gäs-ə-mər\ (*adj*) sheer; like cobwebs. Nylon can be woven into *gossamer* or thick fabrics. also (*n*).

gouge \'gau̇j\ (*v*) tear out. In that fight, all the rules were forgotten; the adversaries bit, kicked, and tried to *gouge* each other's eyes out. also (*n*).

gour-mand \'gu̇(ə)r-ˌmänd\ (*n*) epicure; person who takes excessive pleasure in food and drink. *Gourmands* lack self-restraint; if they enjoy a particular cuisine, they eat far too much of it.

gour-met \'gu̇(ə)r-ˌmā\ (*n*) connoisseur of food and drink. The *gourmet* stated that this was the best onion soup he had ever tasted.

gra-na-ry \'grān-(ə-)rē\ (*n*) storehouse for grain. We have reason to be thankful, for our crops were good and our *granaries* are full.

gran-dil-o-quent \gran-'dil-ə-kwənt\ (*adj*) pompous; bombastic; using high-sounding language. The politician could never speak simply; he was always *grandiloquent*.

gran-di-ose \'gran-dē-ˌōs\ (*adj*) pretentious; high-flown; ridiculously exaggerated; impressive. The aged matinee idol still had *grandiose* notions of his supposed importance in the theatrical world.

\ŋ\ sing \ō\ go \ȯ\ law \ȯi\ boy \th\ thin \t͟h\ the \ü\ loot \u̇\ foot
\y\ yet \zh\ vision \à, k̲, ⁿ, œ, œ̄, ue, ūe, ʸ\ *see* Pronunciation Symbols

gran·u·late \\'gran-yə-ˌlāt\ (*v*) form into grains. Sugar that has been *granulated* dissolves more readily than lump sugar. **gran·ule** \\'gran-yü(ə)l⁽ʲ⁾\ (*n*).

graph·ic \\'graf-ik\ (*adj*) pertaining to the art of delineating; vividly described. I was particularly impressed by the *graphic* presentation of the winter storm; it was so vividly described that you could almost feel the hailstones. also (*n*).

gra·tis \\'grat-əs\ (*adv*) free. The company offered to give one package *gratis* to every purchaser of one of their products; also (*adj*).

gra·tu·i·tous \ grə-'t(y)ü-ət-əs\ (*adj*) given freely; unwarranted; uncalled for. Quit making *gratuitous* comments about my driving; no one asked you for your opinion.

gra·tu·i·ty \ grə-'t(y)ü-ət-ē\ (*n*) tip. Many service employees rely more on *gratuities* than on salaries for their livelihood.

gre·gar·i·ous \ gri-'gar-ē-əs\ (*adj*) sociable. Typically, partygoers are *gregarious*; hermits are not.

gri·mace \\'grim-əs\ (*n*) a facial distortion to show feeling such as pain, disgust, etc. Even though he remained silent, his *grimace* indicated his displeasure. also (*v*).

gris·ly \\'griz-lē\ (*adj*) ghastly. She shuddered at the *grisly* sight.

gro·tesque \ grō-'tesk\ (*adj*) fantastic; comically hideous. On Halloween people enjoy wearing *grotesque* costumes.

grot·to \\'grät-₍ᵢ₎ō\ (*n*) small cavern. The Blue *Grotto* in Capri can be entered only by small boats rowed by natives through a natural opening in the rocks.

grov·el \\'gräv-əl\ (*v*) crawl or creep on ground; remain prostrate. Mr. Wickfield was never harsh to his employees; he could not understand why Uriah would always cringe and *grovel* as if he expected a beating.

grudg·ing \\'grəj-iŋ\ (*adj*) unwilling; reluctant; stingy. We received only *grudging* support from the mayor despite his earlier promises of aid.

\ə\ **abut** \ᵊ\ **kitten**, F **table** \ər\ **further** \a\ **ash** \ā\ **ace** \ä\ **cot, cart**
\aú\ **out** \ch\ **chin** \e\ **bet** \ē\ **easy** \g\ **go** \i\ **hit** \ī\ **ice** \j\ **job**

gru-el-ing \'grü-ə-liŋ\ (*adj*) exhausting. The marathon is a *grueling* race.

grue-some \'grü-səm\ (*adj*) grisly. Freddy Kruger's face was the stuff of nightmares: all the children in the audience screamed when Kruger's *gruesome* countenance was flashed on the screen.

gruff \'grəf\ (*adj*) rough-mannered. Although he was blunt and *gruff* with most people, he was always gentle with children.

guf-faw \ (ı)gə-'fó\ (*n*) boisterous laughter. The loud *guffaws* that came from the closed room indicated that the members of the committee had not yet settled down to serious business. also (*v*).

guile \'gī(ə)l\ (*n*) deceit; duplicity; wiliness; cunning. Iago uses considerable *guile* to trick Othello into believing that Desdemona has been unfaithful.

guile-less \'gī(ə)l-ləs\ (*adj*) without deceit. He is naive, simple, and *guileless*; he cannot be guilty of fraud.

guise \'gīz\ (*n*) appearance; costume. In the *guise* of a plumber, the detective investigated the murder case.

gull-i-ble \'gəl-ə-bəl\ (*adj*) easily deceived. Overly *gullible* people have only themselves to blame if they fall for con artists repeatedly. As the saying goes, "Fool me once, shame on you. Fool me twice, shame on *me*."

gus-ta-to-ry \'gəs-tə-ˌtōr-ē\ (*adj*) affecting the sense of taste. This food has great *gustatory* appeal because of the spices it contains.

gus-to \'gəs-(ı)tō\ (*n*) enjoyment; enthusiasm. He accepted the assignment with such *gusto* that I feel he would have been satisfied with a smaller salary.

gus-ty \'gəs-tē\ (*adj*) windy. The *gusty* weather made sailing precarious.

gut-tur-al \'gət-ə-rəl\ (*adj*) pertaining to the throat. *Guttural* sounds are produced in the throat or in the back of the tongue and palate.

\ŋ\ si**ng** \ō\ g**o** \ò\ l**aw** \òi\ b**oy** \th\ **th**in \<u>th</u>\ **the** \ü\ l**oo**t \u̇\ f**oo**t
\y\ **y**et \zh\ vi**si**on \à, k̲, ⁿ, œ, œ̄, ue, ūe, ʸ\ *see* Pronunciation Symbols

H

hack-les \\'hak-əls\ (*n*) hairs on back and neck of a dog. The dog's *hackles* rose and he began to growl as the sound of footsteps grew louder. also (*v*).

hack-neyed \\'hak-nēd\ (*adj*) commonplace; trite. When the reviewer criticized the movie for its *hackneyed* plot, we agreed; we had seen similar stories hundreds of times before.

hag-gard \\'hag-ərd\ (*adj*) wasted away; gaunt. After his long illness, he was pale and *haggard*.

hag-gle \\'hag-əl\ (*v*) argue about prices. I prefer to shop in a store that has a one-price policy because whenever I *haggle* with a shopkeeper I am never certain that I paid a fair price for the articles I purchased. also (*n*).

hal-cy-on \\'hal-sē-ən\ (*adj*) calm; peaceful. In those *halcyon* days, people were not worried about sneak attacks and bombings.

hale \\'hā(ə)l\ (*adj*) healthy. After a brief illness, he was *hale* again.

hal-lowed \\'hal-ₒōd\ (*adj*) blessed; consecrated. Although the dead girl's parents had never been active churchgoers, they insisted that their daughter be buried in *hallowed* ground.

hal-lu-ci-na-tion \hə-ˌlüs-ᵊn-'ā-shən\ (*n*) delusion. I think you were frightened by an *hallucination* that you created in your own mind.

ham-per \\'ham-pər\ (*v*) obstruct. The new mother had not realized how much the effort of caring for an infant would *hamper* her ability to keep an immaculate house.

hap \\'hap\ (*n*) chance; luck. In his poem *Hap,* Thomas Hardy objects to the part chance plays in our lives.

hap-haz-ard \(ˈ)hap-'haz-ərd\ (*adj*) random; by chance. His *haphazard* style of reading left him unacquainted with many classic books.

---

hap·less \ˈhap-ləs\ (*adj*) unfortunate. This *hapless* creature had never known a moment's pleasure.

ha·rangue \hə-ˈraŋ\ (*n*) noisy speech. In a lengthy *harangue,* the principal berated the offenders. also (*v*).

ha·rass \hə-ˈras\ (*v*) to annoy by repeated attacks. When he could not pay his bills as quickly as he had promised, he was *harassed* by his creditors.

har·bin·ger \ˈhär-bən-jər\ (*n*) forerunner. The crocus is an early *harbinger* of spring. also (*v*).

har·bor \ˈhär-bər\ (*v*) provide a refuge for; hide. The church *harbored* illegal aliens who were political refugees.

harp·ing \ˈhärp-iŋ\ (*n*) tiresome dwelling on a subject. After he had reminded me several times about what he had done for me, I told him to stop *harping* on my indebtedness to him. harp \ˈhärp\ (*v*)

har·row·ing \ˈhar-ₒ̄ō-iŋ\ (*adj*) agonizing; distressing; traumatic. At first Jessica Lynch did not wish to discuss her *harrowing* days as a wounded American soldier captured by the Iraqi army.

har·ry \ˈhar-ē\ (*v*) raid; annoy. The guerrilla band *harried* the enemy nightly.

haugh·ti·ness \ˈhȯt-ē-nəs\ (*n*) pride; arrogance. When she realized that Darcy believed himself too good to dance with his inferiors, Elizabeth took great offense at his *haughtiness*.

haz·ard·ous \ˈhaz-ərd-əs\ (*adj*) dangerous. Your occupation is too *hazardous* for insurance companies to consider your application.

haz·y \ˈhā-zē\ (*adj*) slightly obscure. In *hazy* weather, you cannot see the top of this mountain.

heck·ler \ˈhek-(ə)lər\ (*n*) person who verbally harasses others. The *heckler* kept interrupting the speaker with rude remarks. heck·le \ˈhek-əl\ (*v*)

he·do·nism \ˈhēd-ᵊn-ˌiz-əm\ (*n*) belief that pleasure is the sole aim in life. Notorious for his *hedonism*, he consid-

---

...only his own pleasure and ignored any claims others had on his money or time.

heed·less \\'hēd-ləs\\ (*adj*) not noticing; disregarding. He drove on, *heedless* of the warnings placed at the side of the road that it was dangerous.

hei·nous \\'hā-nəs\\ (adj) atrocious; hatefully bad. Hitler's *heinous* crimes will never be forgotten.

her·biv·o·rous \\,(h)ər-'biv-ə-rəs\\ (*adj*) grain-eating. Some *herbivorous* animals have two stomachs for digesting their food. **her·bi·vore** \\'(h)ər-bə-,vō(ə)r\\ (*n*)

her·e·sy \\'her-ə-sē\\ (*n*) opinion contrary to popular belief; opinion contrary to accepted religion. Galileo's assertion that the earth moved around the sun directly contradicted the religious teachings of his day; as a result, he was tried for *heresy*.

her·e·tic \\'her-ə-,tik\\ (*n*) person who maintains opinions contrary to the doctrines of the church. She was tortured by the Spanish Inquisition because she was a *heretic*.

her·met·i·cal·ly \\,(,)hər-'met-i-k(ə-)lē\\ (*adv*) sealed by fusion so as to be airtight. After you sterilize the bandages, place them in a container and seal it *hermetically* to protect them from contamination by airborne bacteria.

her·mit·age \\'hər-mət-ij\\ (*n*) home of a hermit. Even in his remote *hermitage* he could not escape completely from the world.

het·er·o·ge·ne·ous \\,het-ə-rə-'jē-nē-əs\\ (*adj*) dissimilar; mixed. This year's entering class is remarkably *heterogeneous*: it includes students from 40 different states and 26 foreign countries, some the children of billionaires, others the offspring of welfare families.

hew \\'hyü\\ (*v*) cut to pieces with ax or sword. The cavalry rushed into the melee and *hewed* the enemy with their swords.

hi·a·tus \\hī-'āt-əs\\ (*n*) gap; interruption in duration or continuity; pause. Except for a brief two-year *hiatus*,

---

\\ə\\ **abut** \\ə\\ **kitten, F table** \\ər\\ **further** \\a\\ **ash** \\ā\\ **ace** \\ä\\ **cot, cart**
\\au̇\\ **out** \\ch\\ **chin** \\e\\ **bet** \\ē\\ **easy** \\g\\ **go** \\i\\ **hit** \\ī\\ **ice** \\j\\ **job**

during which she enrolled in the Peace Corps, Ms. Clements has devoted herself to her medical career.

hi-ber-nal \hī-'bərn-əl\ *(adj)* wintry. Bears prepare for their long *hibernal* sleep by overeating.

hi-ber-nate \'hī-bər-ˌnāt\ *(v)* sleep throughout the winter. Bears are one of the many species of animals that *hibernate*.

hi-er-ar-chy \'hī-(ə-)ˌrär-kē\ *(n)* body divided into ranks. To be low man on the totem pole is to have the most inferior place in the *hierarchy*.

hi-ero-glyph-ic \ˌhī-(ə-)rə-'glif-ik\ *(n)* picture writing. The discovery of the Rosetta Stone enabled scholars to read the ancient Egyptian *hieroglyphics*.

hi-lar-i-ty \hil-'ar-ət-ē\ *(n)* boisterous mirth. They could no longer contain their *hilarity*, but broke into great guffaws and whoops of laughter.

hind-most \'hīn(d)-ˌmōst\ *(adj)* furthest behind. The coward could always be found in the *hindmost* lines whenever a battle was being waged.

hire-ling \'hī(ə)r-liŋ\ *(n)* one who serves for hire [usually contemptuously]. In a matter of such importance, I do not wish to deal with *hirelings*; take me to your leader.

hir-sute \'hər-ˌsüt\ *(adj)* hairy. He was a *hirsute* individual with a heavy black beard.

his-tri-on-ic \ˌhis-trē-'än-ik\ *(adj)* theatrical. He was proud of his *histrionic* ability and dreamed of playing the role of Hamlet. **his-tri-on-ics** \ˌhis-tre-'än-iks\ *(n)*

hoar-y \'hō(ə)r-ē\ *(adj)* white with age. Old Father Time was *hoary* and wrinkled with age.

hoax \'hōks\ *(n)* trick; deception; fraud. In the case of Piltdown man, a scientific forgery managed to fool the experts for nearly half a century, when the *hoax* was finally unmasked. also *(v)*.

ho-lo-caust \'häl-ə-ˌkȯst\ *(n)* destruction by fire. Citizens of San Francisco remember that the destruction of the

\ŋ\ sing \ō\ go \ȯ\ law \ȯi\ boy \th\ thin \th\ the \ü\ loot \u̇\ foot
\y\ yet \zh\ vision \à, k̲, ⁿ, œ, œ̄, ue, ūe, ʸ\ *see* Pronunciation Symbols

city was caused not by the earthquake but by the *holocaust* that followed.

hom-age \\'(h)äm-ij\\ (*n*) honor; tribute. In her speech she tried to pay *homage* to a great man.

home-spun \\'hōm-,spən\\ (*adj*) domestic; made at home. *Homespun* wit like *homespun* cloth was often coarse and plain. also (*n*).

hom-i-ly \\'häm-ə-lē\\ (*n*) sermon; serious warning. His speeches were always *homilies,* warning his listeners to repent and reform.

ho-mo-ge-ne-ous \\,hō-mə-'jē-nē-əs\\ (*adj*) of the same kind. Because the student body at Elite Prep was so *homogeneous*, Sara and James decided to send their daughter to a school that offered greater cultural diversity. ho-mo-ge-ne-i-ty \\,hō-mə-jə-'nē-ət-ē\\ (*n*)

hone \\'hōn\\ (*v*) sharpen. To make shaving easier, he *honed* his razor with great care.

hood-wink \\'hùd-,wiŋk\\ (*v*) deceive; delude. Having been *hoodwinked* once by the fast-talking salesman, he was extremely cautious when he went to purchase a used car.

hor-ta-to-ry \\'hòrt-ə-,tōr-ē\\ (*adj*) encouraging; exhortive. *Hortatory* speeches exhort or urge, encouraging listeners to take action.

hor-ti-cul-tur-al \\,hòrt-ə-'kəlch(-ə)-rəl\\ (*adj*) pertaining to cultivation of gardens. When he bought his house, he began to look for flowers and decorative shrubs, and began to read books dealing with *horticultural* matters.

hov-el \\'həv-əl\\ (*n*) shack; small, wretched house. He wondered how poor people could stand living in such *hovels*.

hov-er \\'həv-ər\\ (*v*) hang about; wait nearby. The police helicopter *hovered* above the accident.

hub-bub \\'həb-,əb\\ (*n*) confused uproar. The marketplace was a scene of *hubbub* and excitement; in all the noise, we could not distinguish particular voices.

\\ə\\ abut \\ə\\ kitten, F table \\ər\\ further \\a\\ ash \\ā\\ ace \\ä\\ cot, cart
\\aù\\ out \\ch\\ chin \\e\\ bet \\ē\\ easy \\g\\ go \\i\\ hit \\ī\\ ice \\j\\ job

hu-bris \'hyü-brəs\ (*n*) arrogance; excessive self-conceit. Filled with *hubris,* Lear refused to heed his friends' warnings.

hue \'hyü\ (*n*) color; aspect. The aviary contained birds of every possible *hue.*

hu-mane \ hyü-'mān\ (*adj*) kind; marked by kindness or consideration. It is ironic that the *Humane* Society sometimes must show its compassion toward mistreated animals by killing them to put them out of their misery.

hum-drum \'həm-ˌdrəm\ (*adj*) dull; monotonous. After his years of adventure, he could not settle down to a *humdrum* existence.

hu-mid \'hyü-məd\ (*adj*) damp. Because Oakland's *humid* climate aggravated Richard's asthma, he decided to move to a drier area.

hu-mil-i-ty \ hyü-'mil-ət-ē\ (*n*) humbleness of spirit. Despite his fame as a Nobel Prize winner, Bishop Tutu spoke with a *humility* and lack of self-importance that immediately won over his listeners.

hur-tle \'hərt-ᵊl\ (*v*) rush headlong. The runaway train *hurtled* toward disaster.

hus-band-ry \'həz-bən-drē\ (*n*) frugality; thrift; agriculture. He accumulated his small fortune by diligence and *husbandry.*

hy-brid \'hī-brəd\ (*n*) mongrel; mixed breed. Mendel's formula explains the appearance of *hybrids* and pure species in breeding. also (*adj*).

hy-dro-pho-bi-a \ ˌhī-drə-'fō-bē-ə\ (*n*) rabies; fear of water. A dog that bites a human being must be observed for symptoms of *hydrophobia.*

hy-per-bo-le \ hī-'pər-bə-⁽ʲ⁾lē\ (*n*) exaggeration; overstatement. As far as I'm concerned, Apple's claims about the new computer are pure *hyperbole*: no machine is that good!

\ŋ\ sing \ō\ go \ò\ law \òi\ boy \th\ thin \t͟h\ the \ü\ loot \ u̇\ foot
\y\ yet \zh\ vision \à, ḵ, ⁿ, œ, œ̄, ue, ūe, ʸ\ *see* Pronunciation Symbols

hy-per-crit-i-cal \ˌhī-pər-'krit-i-kəl\ (*adj*) excessively exacting. You are *hypercritical* in your demands for perfection; we all make mistakes.

hy-po-chon-dri-ac \ˌhī-pə-'kän-drē-ˌak\ (*n*) person unduly worried about his or her health; worrier without cause about illness. The doctor prescribed chocolate pills for his patient who was a *hypochondriac*.

hyp-o-crit-i-cal \ˌhip-ə-'krit-i-kəl\ (*adj*) pretending to be virtuous; deceiving. It was *hypocritical* of Martha to say nice things about my poetry to me and then make fun of my verses behind my back.

hy-po-thet-i-cal \ˌhī-pə-'thet-i-kəl\ (*adj*) based on assumptions or hypotheses; supposed. Suppose you are accepted by Harvard, Stanford, and Brown. Which one would you choose to attend? Remember, this is only a *hypothetical* situation. hy-poth-e-sis \hī-'päth-ə-səs\ (*n*)

\ə\ **abut** \ᵊ\ **kitten**, F **table** \ər\ **further** \a\ **ash** \ā\ **ace** \ä\ **cot, cart**
\au̇\ **out** \ch\ **chin** \e\ **bet** \ē\ **easy** \g\ **go** \i\ **hit** \ī\ **ice** \j\ **job**

I

ich·thy·ol·o·gy \ˌik-thē-'äl-ə-jē\ (*n*) study of fish. Jacques Cousteau's programs about sea life have advanced the cause of *ichthyology.*

icon \'ī-ˌkän\ (*n*) religious image; idol. The *icons* on the walls of the church were painted in the thirteenth century.

i·con·o·clas·tic \ˌ(ˌ)ī-ˌkän-ə-'klas-tik\ (*adj*) attacking cherished traditions. Deeply *iconoclastic*, Jean Genet deliberately set out to shock conventional theatergoers with his radical plays.

i·de·ol·o·gy \ˌīd-ē-'äl-ə-jē\ (*n*) system of ideas of a group. For people who had grown up believing in the communist *ideology*, it was hard to adjust to capitalism.

id·i·om \'id-ē-əm\ (*n*) expression whose meaning as a whole differs from the meanings of its individual words; distinctive style. The phrase "to lose one's marbles" is an *idiom*: if I say that Joe's lost his marbles, I'm not asking you to find some for him. I'm telling you *idiomatically* that he's crazy.

id·i·o·syn·cra·sy \ˌid-ē-ə-'sin-krə-sē\ (*n*) individual trait, usually odd in nature; eccentricity. One of Richard Nixon's little *idiosyncracies* was his liking for ketchup on cottage cheese. One of Hannibal Lecter's little *idiosyncrasies* was his liking for human flesh.

id·i·o·syn·crat·ic \ˌid-ē-ō-ˌ(ˌ)sin-'krat-ik\ (*adj*) peculiar to an individual. Such behavior is *idiosyncratic;* it is as easily identifiable as a signature.

i·dol·a·try \ī-'däl-ə-trē\ (*n*) worship of idols; excessive admiration. Such *idolatry* of singers of popular ballads is typical of the excessive enthusiasm of youth.

i·dyl·lic \ī-'dil-ik\ (*adj*) charmingly carefree; simple. Far from the city, she led an *idyllic* existence in her rural retreat.

ig·ne·ous \'ig-nē-əs\ (*adj*) produced by fire; volcanic. Lava, pumice, and other *igneous* rocks are found in great abundance around Mount Vesuvius near Naples.

---

ig-no-ble \ig-'nō-bəl\ (*adj*) unworthy; base in nature; not noble. Sir Galahad was so pure in heart that he could never stoop to perform an *ignoble* deed.

ig-no-min-i-ous \ˌig-nə-'min-ē-əs\ (*adj*) deeply disgraceful; shameful. To lose the Ping-Pong match to a trained chimpanzee! How could Rollo stand such an *ignominious* defeat? ig-no-mi-ny \'ig-nə-ˌmin-ē\ (*n*)

il-lim-it-a-ble \⁽ⁱ⁾il-'⁽l⁾im-ət-ə-bəl\ (*adj*) infinite. Having explored the far corners of the earth, we are now reaching out into *illimitable* space.

il-lu-mi-nate \il-'ü-mə-ˌnāt\ (*v*) to light; make clear or understandable; enlighten. Just as a lamp can *illuminate* a dark room, a perceptive comment can *illuminate* a knotty problem.

il-lu-sion \il-'ü-zhən\ (*n*) misleading vision. It is easy to create an optical *illusion* in which lines of equal length appear different. il-lu-so-ry \il-'üs-(ə-)rē\ (*adj*)

il-lu-sive \il-'ü-siv\ (*adj*) deceiving. This mirage is an illusion; let us not be fooled by its *illusive* effect.

im-be-cil-i-ty \ˌim-bə-'sil-ət-ē\ (*n*) weakness of mind. I am amazed at the *imbecility* of the readers of these trashy magazines.

im-bibe \im-'bīb\ (*v*) drink in. The dry soil *imbibed* the rain quickly.

im-bro-glio \im-'brōl-⁽ⁱ⁾yō\ (*n*) complicated situation; painful or complex misunderstanding; entanglement; confused mass (as of papers). The humor of Shakespearean comedies often depends on cases of mistaken identity that involve the perplexed protagonists in one comic *imbroglio* after another.

im-bue \im-'byü\ (*v*) saturate, fill. His visits to the famous Gothic cathedrals *imbued* him with feelings of awe and reverence.

im-mac-u-late \im-'ak-yə-lət\ (*adj*) spotless; flawless; absolutely clean. Ken and Jessica were wonderful ten-

ants and left the apartment in *immaculate* condi
when they moved out.

im-mi-nent \ˈim-ə-nənt\ *(adj)* impending; near at hand.
Rosa was such a last-minute worker that she could never
start writing a paper until the deadline was *imminent*.

im-mo-bil-i-ty \ˌim-ₒō-ˈbil-ət-ē\ *(n)* state of being unable
to move. Peter's fear of snakes shocked him into *immobility*; then the use of his limbs returned to him and he
bolted from the room.

im-mo-late \ˈim-ə-ˌlāt\ *(v)* offer as a sacrifice. The tribal
king offered to *immolate* his daughter to quiet the angry
gods.

im-mune \im-ˈyün\ *(adj)* resistant to; free or exempt from.
Fortunately, Florence had contracted chicken pox as a
child and was *immune* to it when her baby came down
with spots.

im-mure \im-ˈyu̇(ə)r\ *(v)* imprison; shut up in confine-
ment. For the two weeks before the examination, the
student *immured* himself in his room and concentrated
upon his studies.

im-mu-ta-ble \⁽ˈ⁾im-ˈ(m)yüt-ə-bəl\ *(adj)* unchangeable. All
things change over time; nothing is *immutable*.

im-pair \im-ˈpa(ə)r\ *(v)* injure; hurt. Drinking alcohol can
impair your ability to drive safely; if you're going to
drink, don't drive.

im-pale \im-ˈpā(ə)l\ *(v)* pierce. He was *impaled* by the
spear hurled by his adversary.

im-pal-pa-ble \⁽ˈ⁾im-ˈpal-pə-bəl\ *(adj)* imperceptible;
intangible. The ash is so fine that it is *impalpable* to the
touch but it can be seen as a fine layer covering the
window ledge.

im-par-tial \⁽ˈ⁾im-ˈpär-shəl\ *(adj)* not biased; fair. Knowing
she could not be *impartial* about her own child,
Jo refused to judge any match in which Billy was
competing.

\ŋ\ **sing** \ō\ **go** \ȯ\ **law** \ȯi\ **boy** \th\ **thin** \t͟h\ **the** \ü\ **loot** \u̇\ **foot**
\y\ **yet** \zh\ **vision** \à, k̲, ⁿ, œ, œ̄, ᵫ, ᵫ̄, ʸ\ *see* Pronunciation Symbols

im-passe \ 'im-ˌpas\ (*n*) predicament offering no escape; deadlock; dead end. The negotiators reported they had reached an *impasse* in their talks and had little hope of resolving the deadlock swiftly.

im-pas-sive \ ⁽ᶦ⁾im-'pas-iv\ (*adj*) without feeling; imperturbable; stoical. Refusing to let the enemy see how deeply shaken he was by his capture, the prisoner kept his face *impassive*.

im-peach \ im-'pēch\ (*v*) charge with crime in office; indict. The angry congressman wanted to *impeach* the president.

im-pec-ca-ble \ ⁽ᶦ⁾im-'pek-ə-bəl\ (*adj*) faultless. The uncrowned queen of the fashion industry, Diana was acclaimed for her *impeccable* taste.

im-pe-cu-nious \ ˌim-pi-'kyü-nyəs\ (*adj*) without money. Though Scrooge claimed he was too *impecunious* to give alms, he easily could have afforded to be charitable.

im-pede \ im-'pēd\ (*v*) hinder; block; delay. A series of accidents *impeded* the launching of the space shuttle.

im-ped-i-ment \ im-'ped-ə-mənt\ (*n*) hindrance; stumbling-block. She had a speech *impediment* that prevented her speaking clearly.

im-pend-ing \ im-'pen-diŋ\ (*adj*) nearing; approaching. The entire country was saddened by the news of his *impending* death.

im-pen-i-tent \ ⁽ᶦ⁾im-'pen-ə-tənt\ (*adj*) not repentant. We could see from his tough guy attitude that he was *impenitent*.

im-pe-ri-ous \ im-'pir-ē-əs\ (*adj*) domineering; haughty. Jane rather liked a man to be masterful, but Mr. Rochester seemed so bent on getting his own way that he was actually *imperious*!

im-per-me-able \ ⁽ᶦ⁾im-'pər-mē-ə-bəl\ (*adj*) impervious; not permitting passage through its substance. Sue chose a raincoat made of Gore-Tex because the material was *impermeable* to liquids.

\ə\ **abut** \ᵊ\ **kitten, F table** \ər\ **further** \a\ **ash** \ā\ **ace** \ä\ **cot, cart**
\aů\ **out** \ch\ **chin** \e\ **bet** \ē\ **easy** \g\ **go** \i\ **hit** \ī\ **ice** \j\ **job**

im-per-ti-nent \\(ʰ)im-'pərt-ᵊn-ənt\ (*adj*) insolent. His neighbors' *impertinent* curiosity about his lack of dates angered Ted. He couldn't believe their rudeness, asking him such personal questions!

im-per-turb-a-ble \ˌim-pər-'tər-bə-bəl\ (*adj*) calm; placid. In the midst of the battle, the Duke of Wellington remained *imperturbable* and in full command of the situation despite the hysteria and panic all around him. im-per-turb-a-bil-i-ty \ˌim-pər-ˌtər-bə-'bil-ət-ē\ (*n*)

im-per-vi-ous \\(ʰ)im-'pər-vē-əs\ (*adj*) impenetrable; incapable of being damaged or distressed. The carpet salesman told Simone that his most expensive brand of floor covering was warranted to be *impervious* to ordinary wear and tear. Having read so many negative reviews of his acting, the movie star had learned to ignore them, and was now *impervious* to criticism.

im-pet-u-ous \im-'pech-(ə-)wəs\ (*adj*) violent; hasty; rash. "Leap before you look" was the motto suggested by one particularly *impetuous* young man.

im-pe-tus \'im-pət-əs\ (*n*) moving force; incentive; stimulus. A new federal highway program would create jobs and give added *impetus* to our economic recovery.

im-pi-e-ty \\(ʰ)im-'pī-ət-ē\ (*n*) irreverence; lack of respect for God. When members of the youth group draped the church in toilet paper one Halloween, the minister reprimanded them for their *impiety*.

im-pinge \im-'pinj\ (*v*) infringe; touch; collide with. How could they be married without *impinging* on one another's freedom?

im-pi-ous \'im-pē-əs\ (*adj*) irreverent. The congregation was offended by his *impious* remarks.

im-pla-ca-ble \\(ʰ)im-'plak-ə-bəl\ (*adj*) incapable of being pacified. Madame Defarge was the *implacable* enemy of the Evremonde family.

im-plau-si-ble \⁽ʰ⁾im-ˈplȯ-zə-bəl\ (*adj*) unlikely; unbelievable. Though her alibi seemed *implausible,* it in fact turned out to be true.

im-ple-ment \ˈim-plə-ˌmənt\ (*v*) supply what is needed; furnish with tools. I am unwilling to *implement* this plan until I have assurances that it has the full approval of your officials. **im-ple-ment** \ˈim-plə-mənt\ (*n*)

im-pli-ca-tion \ˌim-plə-ˈkā-shən\ (*n*) that which is hinted at or suggested. When Miss Watson said she hadn't seen her purse since the last time Jim was in the house, the *implication* was that she suspected Jim had taken it.

im-plic-it \im-ˈplis-ət\ (*adj*) understood but not stated. Jack never told Jill he adored her; he believed his love was *implicit* in his actions.

im-ply \im-ˈplī\ (*v*) suggest a meaning not expressed; signify. When Aunt Millie said, "My! That's a big piece of pie, young man!" was she *implying* that Bobby was being a glutton in helping himself to such a huge piece?

im-pol-i-tic \⁽ʰ⁾im-ˈpäl-ə-ˌtik\ (*adj*) not wise. I think it is *impolitic* to raise this issue at the present time because the public is too angry.

im-pon-der-a-ble \⁽ʰ⁾im-ˈpän-d(ə-)rə-bəl\ (*adj*) not able to be determined precisely. Psychology is not a precise science; far too many *imponderable* factors play a part in determining human behavior.

im-port \ˈim-ˌpō(ə)rt\ (*n*) importance; meaning. To Miss Manners, proper etiquette was a matter of great *import.* Because Tom knew so little about medical matters, it took a while before the full *import* of the doctor's words could sink in. **im-port** \im-ˈpō(ə)rt\ (*v*)

im-por-tu-nate \im-ˈpȯrch-(ə-)nət\ (*adj*) urging; demanding. He tried to hide from his *importunate* creditors until his allowance arrived.

im-por-tune \ˌim-pər-ˈt(y)ün\ (*v*) beg persistently. Democratic and Republican phone solicitors *impor-*

\ə\ **abut** \ᵊ\ **kitten, F table** \ər\ **further** \a\ **ash** \ā\ **ace** \ä\ **cot, cart**
\au̇\ **out** \ch\ **chin** \e\ **bet** \ē\ **easy** \g\ **go** \i\ **hit** \ī\ **ice** \j\ **job**

tuned her for contributions so frequently that she decided to give nothing to either party.

im-pos-ture \im-'päs-chər\ (*n*) assuming a false identity; masquerade. When the hospital staff discovered that Dr. Welby had no medical training and was passing himself off as a doctor, they were shocked by the *imposture*.

im-po-tent \'im-pət-ənt\ (*adj*) weak; ineffective. Although he wished to break the nicotine habit, he found himself *impotent* in resisting the craving for a cigarette.

im-pov-er-ished \im-'päv-(ə-)rishd\ (*adj*) poor. The loss of their farm left the family *impoverished* and hopeless.

im-pre-cate \'im-pri-ˌkāt\ (*v*) curse; pray that evil will befall. Shaking his fist at the stormy heavens, Macbeth *imprecated* the gods, cursing them for turning against him.

im-preg-na-ble \im-'preg-nə-bəl\ (*adj*) invulnerable. Until the development of the airplane as a military weapon, the fort was considered *impregnable*.

im-promp-tu \im-'präm(p)-ˌt(y)ü\ (*adj*) without previous preparation; off the cuff; on the spur of the moment. The judges were amazed that she could make such a thorough, well-supported presentation in an *impromptu* speech.

im-pro-pri-e-ty \ˌim-p(r)ə-'prī-ət-ē\ (*n*) improperness; unsuitableness. Because of the *impropriety* of the punk rocker's slashed T-shirt and jeans, the management refused to admit him to the hotel's very formal dining room.

im-prov-i-dent \⁽ᵒ⁾im-'präv-əd-ənt\ (*adj*) thriftless. He was constantly being warned to mend his *improvident* ways and begin to "save for a rainy day."

im-pro-vise \ˌim-prə-'vīz\ (*v*) compose on the spur of the moment. He would sit at the piano and *improvise* for hours on themes from Bach and Handel.

im-pru-dent \⁽ᵒ⁾im-'prüd-ᵊnt\ (*adj*) lacking caution; injudicious. It is *imprudent* to exercise vigorously and become overheated when you are unwell.

\ŋ\ sing \ō\ go \ȯ\ law \ȯi\ boy \th\ thin \th̲\ the \ü\ loot \u̇\ foot
\y\ yet \zh\ vision \à, k̲, ⁿ, œ, œ̄, ue, ūe, ʸ\ *see* Pronunciation Symbols

im-pugn \im-'pyün\ (*v*) dispute or contradict (often in an insulting way); challenge; gainsay. Our treasurer was furious when the finance committee's report *impugned* the accuracy of his financial records and recommended that he should take bonehead math.

im-pu-ni-ty \im-'pyü-nət-ē\ (*n*) freedom from punishment or harm. A 98-pound weakling can't attack a beachfront bully with *impunity*: the poor, puny guy is sure to get mashed.

im-pu-ta-tion \im-pyə-'tā-shən\ (*n*) accusation; charge; reproach. Paradoxically, the guiltier he was of the offense with which he was charged, the more he resented the *imputation*.

im-pute \im-'pyüt\ (*v*) attribute; ascribe. If I wished to *impute* blame to the officers in charge of this program, I would come out and state it definitely and without hesitation.

in-ad-ver-tence \in-əd-'vərt-ᵊn(t)s\ (*n*) oversight; carelessness. Judy's great fear was that by *inadvertence* she might fail to answer a question on the exam and mismark her whole answer sheet.

in-al-ien-a-ble \⁽ᵗ⁾in-'āl-yə-nə-bəl\ (*adj*) not to be taken away; nontransferable. The Declaration of Independence asserts that all people possess certain *inalienable* human rights that no powers on earth can take away.

in-ane \in-'ān\ (*adj*) silly; senseless. There's no point in what you're saying. Why are you bothering to make such *inane* remarks? in-an-i-ty \in-'an-ət-ē\ (*n*)

in-an-i-mate \⁽ᵗ⁾in-'an-ə-mət\ (adj) lifeless. She was asked to identify the still and *inanimate* body.

in-ar-tic-u-late \in-⁽ᵗ⁾är-'tik-yə-lət\ (*adj*) speechless; producing indistinct speech. He became *inarticulate* with rage and uttered sounds without meaning.

in-can-des-cent \in-kən-'des-ᵊnt\ (*adj*) strikingly bright; shining with intense heat. If you leave on an *incandescent* lightbulb, it quickly grows too hot to touch.

\ə\ abut \ᵊ\ kitten, F table \ər\ further \a\ ash \ā\ ace \ä\ cot, cart
\aú\ out \ch\ chin \e\ bet \ē\ easy \g\ go \i\ hit \ī\ ice \j\ job

in-can-ta-tion \ˌin-ˌkan-'tā-shən\ (*n*) singing or chanting of magic spells; magical formula. Uttering *incantations* to make the brew more potent, the witch doctor stirred the liquid in the caldron.

in-ca-pac-i-tate \ˌin-kə-'pas-ə-ˌtāt\ (*v*) disable. During the winter, many people were *incapacitated* by respiratory ailments.

in-car-cer-ate \in-'kär-sə-ˌrāt\ (*v*) imprison. The civil rights workers were willing to be arrested and even *incarcerated* if by their imprisonment they could serve the cause.

in-car-nate \in-'kär-nət\ (*adj*) endowed with flesh; personified. Your attitude is so fiendish that you must be a devil *incarnate*. also (*v*).

in-car-na-tion \ˌin-ˌkär-'nā-shən\ (*n*) act of assuming a human body and human nature. The *incarnation* of Jesus Christ is a basic tenet of Christian theology.

in-cen-di-ar-y \in-'sen-dē-ˌer-ē\ (*n*) arsonist. The fire spread in such an unusual manner that the fire department chiefs were certain that it had been set by an *incendiary*. also (*adj*).

in-cen-tive \in-'sent-iv\ (*n*) spur, motive. Mike's strong desire to outshine his big sister was all the *incentive* he needed to do well in school.

in-ces-sant \(ˌ)in-'ses-ᵊnt\ (*adj*) uninterrupted. The crickets kept up an *incessant* chirping that disturbed our attempts to fall asleep.

in-cho-ate \in-'kō-ət\ (*adj*) recently begun; rudimentary; elementary. Before the Creation, the world was an *inchoate* mass.

in-ci-dence \'in(t)-səd-ən(t)s\ (*n*) rate of occurrence; particular occurrence. Health workers expressed great concern over the high *incidence* of infant mortality in major urban areas.

\ŋ\ si**ng** \ō\ **go** \ȯ\ **law** \ȯi\ **boy** \th\ **thin** \th̲\ **the** \ü\ **loot** \u̇\ **foot**
\y\ **yet** \zh\ **vision** \à, k̲, ⁿ, œ, œ̄, ue, ue̅, ʸ\ *see* Pronunciation Symbols

in·ci·den·tal \ˌin(t)-sə-ˈdent-ᵊl\ *(adj)* not essential; minor. The scholarship covered his major expenses at college and some of his *incidental* expenses as well.

in·cip·i·ent \in-ˈsip-ē-ənt\ *(adj)* beginning; in an early stage. I will go to sleep early for I want to break an *incipient* cold.

in·ci·sive \in-ˈsī-siv\ *(adj)* cutting; sharp. His *incisive* remarks made us see the fallacy in our plans.

in·cite \in-ˈsīt\ *(v)* arouse to action; goad; motivate; induce to exist. In a fiery speech, Mario *incited* his fellow students to go out on strike to protest the university's anti-affirmative action stand.

in·clem·ent \⁽¹⁾in-ˈklem-ənt\ *(adj)* stormy; unkind. In *inclement* weather, I like to curl up on the sofa with a good book and listen to the storm blowing outside.

in·clu·sive \in-ˈklü-siv\ *(adj)* tending to include all. The comedian turned down the invitation to join the Players' Club, saying any club that would let him in was too *inclusive* for him.

in·cog·ni·to \ˌin-ˌkäg-ˈnēt-⁽¹⁾ō\ *(adv, adj)* with identity concealed; using an assumed name. The monarch enjoyed traveling through the town *incognito* and mingling with the populace. also *(n)*.

in·co·her·ence \ˌin-kō-ˈhir-ən(t)s\ *(n)* unintelligibility; lack of logic or relevance. "This essay makes no sense at all," commented the teacher, giving it an F because of its *incoherence*. in·co·her·ent \in-kō-ˈhir-ənt\ *(adj)*

in·com·mo·di·ous \ˌin-kə-ˈmōd-ē-əs\ *(adj)* not spacious. Couldn't you come up with better guest quarters than this *incommodious* attic, where I've barely enough room to stand?

in·com·pat·i·ble \ˌin-kəm-ˈpat-ə-bəl\ *(adj)* inharmonious. The married couple argued incessantly and finally decided to separate because they were *incompatible*.

\ə\ **abut** \ᵊ\ **kitten,** F **table** \ər\ **further** \a\ **ash** \ā\ **ace** \ä\ **cot, cart**
\au̇\ **out** \ch\ **chin** \e\ **bet** \ē\ **easy** \g\ **go** \i\ **hit** \ī\ **ice** \j\ **job**

in-con-gru-i-ty \ˌin-kən-ˈgrü-ət-ē\ (*n*) lack of harmony; absurdity. The ultramodern, glass-walled house was a complete *incongruity* in that neighborhood of Victorian painted mansions.

in-con-gru-ous \(ˈ)in-ˈkäŋ-grə-wəs\ (*adj*) not fitting; absurd. Dave saw nothing *incongruous* about wearing sneakers with a tuxedo; he couldn't understand why his date took one look at him and began to laugh.

in-con-se-quen-tial \ˌ(ˌ)in-ˌkän(t)-sə-kwən-chəl\ (*adj*) insignificant; unimportant. Brushing off Ali's apologies for having broken the wineglass, Tamara said, "Don't worry about it; it's *inconsequential*."

in-con-ti-nent \(ˈ)in-ˈkänt-ᵊn-ənt\ (*adj*) lacking self-restraint; licentious. His *incontinent* behavior off stage shocked many people so much that they refused to attend the plays and movies in which he appeared.

in-con-tro-vert-i-ble \ˌ(ˌ)in-ˌkän-trə-ˈvərt-ə-bəl\ (*adj*) indisputable; not open to question. Unless you find the evidence against my client absolutely *incontrovertible*, you must declare her not guilty of this charge.

in-cor-po-re-al \ˌin-(ˌ)kȯr-ˈpōr-ē-əl\ (*adj*) lacking a material body; insubstantial. While Casper the friendly ghost is an *incorporeal* being, nevertheless he and his fellow ghosts make quite an impact on the physical world.

in-cor-ri-gi-ble \(ˈ)in-ˈkȯr-ə-jə-bəl\ (*adj*) uncorrectable. Though Widow Douglass hoped to reform Huck, Miss Watson called him *incorrigible* and said he would come to no good end.

in-cre-du-li-ty \ˌin-kri-ˈd(y)ü-lət-ē\ (*n*) a tendency to disbelief. Your *incredulity* in the face of all the evidence is hard to understand.

in-cred-u-lous \(ˈ)in-ˈkrej-ə-ləs\ (*adj*) withholding belief; skeptical. When Jack claimed he hadn't eaten the jelly doughnut, Jill took an *incredulous* look at his red-smeared face and laughed.

\ŋ\ sing \ō\ go \ȯ\ law \ȯi\ boy \th\ thin \t̲h̲\ the \ü\ loot \u̇\ foot
\y\ yet \zh\ vision \à, k̲, ⁿ, œ, œ̄, ue, ūe, ʸ\ *see* Pronunciation Symbols

in-cre-ment \\'iŋ-krə-mənt\ (*n*) increase. The new contract calls for a 10 percent *increment* in salary for each employee for the next two years.

in-crim-i-nate \in-'krim-ə-ˌnāt\ (*v*) accuse. The evidence gathered against the racketeers *incriminates* some high public officials as well.

in-cu-bate \'iŋ-kyə-ˌbāt\ (*v*) hatch; scheme. Since our electricity is cut off, we shall have to rely on the hens to *incubate* these eggs.

in-cul-cate \in-'kəl-ˌkāt\ (*v*) teach. In an effort to *inculcate* religious devotion, the officials ordered that the school day begin with the singing of a hymn.

in-cum-bent \in-'kəm-bənt\ (*adj*) obligatory; currently holding an office. It is *incumbent* upon all *incumbent* elected officials to keep accurate records of expenses incurred in office. also (*n*).

in-cur \in-'kər\ (*v*) bring upon oneself. His parents refused to pay any future debt he might *incur.*

in-cur-sion \in-'kər-zhən\ (*n*) temporary invasion. The nightly *incursions* and hit-and-run raids of our neighbors across the border tried the patience of the country to the point where we decided to retaliate in force.

in-de-fat-i-ga-ble \ˌin-di-'fat-i-gə-bəl\ (*adj*) tireless. Although the effort of taking out the garbage tired Wayne out for the entire morning, when it came to partying, he was *indefatigable*.

in-dem-ni-fy \in-'dem-nə-ˌfī\ (*v*) make secure against loss; compensate for loss. The city will *indemnify* all home owners whose property is spoiled by this project.

in-den-ture \in-'den-chər\ (*v*) bind as servant or apprentice to master. Many immigrants could come to America only after they had *indentured* themselves for several years. also (*n*).

\ə\ **abut** \ᵊ\ kitten, F **table** \ər\ f**urther** \a\ **ash** \ā\ **ace** \ä\ **cot, cart**
\au̇\ **out** \ch\ **chin** \e\ **bet** \ē\ **easy** \g\ **go** \i\ **hit** \ī\ **ice** \j\ **job**

in-dict \in-'dīt\ (*v*) charge. The district attorney didn't want to *indict* the suspect until she was sure she had a strong enough case to convince a jury.

in-dig-e-nous \in-'dij-ə-nəs\ (*adj*) native. Cigarettes are made of tobacco, a plant *indigenous* to the New World.

in-di-gent \'in-di-jənt\ (*adj*) poor; destitute. Someone who is truly *indigent* can't even afford to buy a pack of cigarettes. [Don't mix up *indigent* and *indigenous*. See previous sentence.]

in-dig-ni-ty \in-'dig-nət-ē\ (*n*) offensive or insulting treatment. Although he seemed to accept cheerfully the *indignities* heaped upon him, he was inwardly very angry. in-dig-nant \in-'dig-nənt\ (*adj*)

in-dis-put-a-ble \,in-dis-'pyüt-ə-bəl\ (*adj*) too certain to be disputed. In the face of these *indisputable* statements, I withdraw my complaint.

in-dis-sol-u-ble \,in-dis-'äl-yə-bəl\ (*adj*) permanent. The *indissoluble* bonds of marriage are all too often being dissolved.

in-do-lence \'in-də-lən(t)s\ (*n*) laziness. Lying back on their Lazyboy recliners watching TV, couch potatoes lead a life of *indolence*.

in-dom-i-ta-ble \in-'däm-ət-ə-bəl\ (*adj*) unconquerable; unyielding. Focusing on her game despite all her personal problems, tennis champion Steffi Graf proved she had an *indomitable* will to win.

in-du-bi-ta-bly \(ˈ)in-'d(y)ü-bət-ə-blē\ (*adv*) beyond a doubt; unquestionably. Auditioning for the chorus line, Molly was *indubitably* a hit: the director fired the leading lady and hired Molly in her place!

in-duc-tive \in-'dək-tiv\ (*adj*) pertaining to induction or proceeding from the specific to the general. The discovery of the planet Pluto is an excellent example of the results that can be obtained from *inductive* reasoning.

\ŋ\ **sing**   \ō\ **go**   \ȯ\ **law**   \ȯi\ **boy**   \th\ **thin**   \th̲\ **the**   \ü\ **loot**   \u̇\ **foot**
\y\ **yet**   \zh\ **vision**   \à, k̲, ⁿ, œ, œ̄, ue, ūe, ʸ\ *see* Pronunciation Symbols

in·dul·gent \in-'dəl-jənt \ (*adj*) humoring; yielding; lenient. Jay's mom was excessively *indulgent*: she bought him every new toy on the market, and never scolded him, no matter what he did.

in·e·bri·et·y \ˌin-i-'brī-ət-ē\ (*n*) habitual intoxication. Drunk more often than sober, Abe was fired from his job as a bus driver because of his constant *inebriety*.

in·ef·fa·ble \⁽ⁱ⁾in-'ef-ə-bəl\ (*adj*) unutterable; unable to be expressed in speech. Looking down at her newborn daughter, Ruth felt such *ineffable* joy that, for the first time in her adult life, she had no words to convey what was in her heart

in·ef·fec·tu·al \ˌin-ə-'fek-chə(-wə)l\ (*adj*) not effective; weak. Because the candidate failed to get across his message to the public, his campaign was *ineffectual*.

in·e·luc·ta·ble \ˌin-i-'lək-tə-bəl\ (*adj*) irresistible; not to be escaped. Defeatists rage against the *ineluctable* nature of fate but are too disheartened to try to change their destiny.

in·ept \in-'ept\ (*adj*) lacking skill; unsuited; incompetent. The *inept* glovemaker was all thumbs.

in·eq·ui·ty \⁽ⁱ⁾in-'ek-wət-ē\ (*n*) unfairness. In demanding equal pay for equal work, women protest the basic *inequity* of a system that gives greater financial rewards to men.

in·er·tia \in-'ər-shə\ (*n*) state of being inert or indisposed to move. "Get up and get to work, you lazybones," Tina cried to Tony, protesting his *inertia*.

in·ex·o·ra·ble \⁽ⁱ⁾in-'eks-(ə-)rə-bəl\ (*adj*) relentless; unyielding; implacable. After listening to the pleas for clemency, the judge was *inexorable* and gave the convicted man the maximum punishment allowed by law.

in·fal·li·ble \⁽ⁱ⁾in-'fal-ə-bəl\ (*adj*) unerring. Jane refused to believe the pope was *infallible*, reasoning, "All human beings are capable of error. The pope is a human being. Therefore, the pope is capable of error."

\ə\ abut \ᵊ\ kitten, F table \ər\ **further** \a\ **ash** \ā\ **ace** \ä\ **cot, cart**
\au̇\ **out** \ch\ **chin** \e\ **bet** \ē\ **easy** \g\ **go** \i\ **hit** \ī\ **ice** \j\ **job**

in-fa-mous \ˈin-fə-məs\ (*adj*) notoriously bad. Charles Manson and Jeffrey Dahmer are both *infamous* killers.

in-fan-tile \ˈin-fən-ˌtīl\ (*adj*) childish; extremely immature. When will he outgrow such *infantile* behavior?

in-fer \in-ˈfər\ (*v*) deduce; conclude. From the glazed looks on the students' faces, I could easily *infer* that they were bored out of their minds.

in-fer-ence \ˌin-f(ə-)rən(t)s\ (*n*) conclusion drawn from data. I want you to check this *inference* because it may have been based on insufficient information.

in-fer-nal \in-ˈfərn-əl\ (*adj*) pertaining to hell; devilish. Batman was baffled: he could think of no way to hinder the Joker's *infernal* scheme to destroy the city.

in-fi-del \ˈin-fəd-əl\ (*n*) unbeliever. The Saracens made war against the *infidels*.

in-fin-i-tes-i-mal \ˌ(ˌ)in-ˌfin-ə-ˈtes-ə-məl\ (*adj*) exceedingly small; so small as to be almost nonexistent. Making sure everyone was aware she was on an extremely strict diet, Melanie said she would have only an *infinitesimal* sliver of pie.

in-fir-mi-ty \in-ˈfər-mət-ē\ (*n*) weakness. His greatest *infirmity* was lack of willpower.

in-flat-ed \in-ˈflāt-əd\ (*adj*) enlarged (with air or gas). After the balloons were *inflated*, they were distributed among the children.

in-flux \ˈin-ˌfləks\ (*n*) flowing into. The *influx* of refugees into the country has taxed the relief agencies severely.

in-frac-tion \in-ˈfrak-shən\ (*n*) violation (of a rule or regulation); breach. When basketball star Dennis Rodman butted heads with the referee, he committed a clear *infraction* of NBA rules.

in-fringe \in-ˈfrinj\ (*v*) violate; encroach. I think your machine *infringes* on my patent.

in-ge-nue \ˈan-jə-nü\ (*n*) an artless girl; an actress who plays such parts. Although she was forty, she still

---

insisted that she be cast as an *ingenue* and refused to play more mature roles.

in-gen-u-ous \in-'jen-yə-wəs\ (*adj*) naive; young; unsophisticated. The woodsman had not realized how *ingenuous* Little Red Riding Hood was until he heard that she had gone off for a walk in the woods with the Big Bad Wolf.

in-grate \'in-ˌgrāt\ (*n*) ungrateful person. That *ingrate* Bob sneered at the tie I gave him for his birthday.

in-gra-ti-ate \in-'grā-shē-ˌāt\ (*v*) make an effort to become popular with. In *All About Eve*, the heroine, an aspiring actress, wages a clever campaign to *ingratiate* herself with Margo Channing, an established star.

in-her-ent \in-'hir-ənt\ (*adj*) firmly established by nature or habit. Katya's *inherent* love of justice caused her to champion anyone she considered treated unfairly by society.

in-hib-it \in-'hib-ət\ (*v*) restrain; retard, or prevent. Only two things *inhibited* him from taking a punch at Mike Tyson: Tyson's left hook, and Tyson's right jab. The protective undercoating on my car *inhibits* the formation of rust. in-hi-bi-tion \ˌin-(h)ə-'bish-ən\ (*n*)

in-im-i-cal \in-'im-i-kəl\ (*adj*) unfriendly; hostile; harmful; detrimental. I've always been friendly to Martha. Why is she so *inimical* to me?

in-im-i-ta-ble \ (ⁱ)in-'im-ət-ə-bəl\ (*adj*) matchless; not able to be imitated. We admire Auden for his *inimitable* use of language; he is one of a kind.

in-iq-ui-tous \in-'ik-wət-əs\ (*adj*) wicked; immoral; unrighteous. Whether or not King Richard III was responsible for the murder of the two young princes in the Tower, it was an *iniquitous* deed. in-iq-ui-ty \in-'ik-wət-ē\ (*n*)

in-kling \'iŋ-kliŋ\ (*n*) hint. This came as a complete surprise to me as I did not have the slightest *inkling* of your plans.

---

in-nate \in-ˈāt\ *(adj)* inborn. Mozart's parents soon recognized young Wolfgang's *innate* talent for music.

in-noc-u-ous \in-ˈäk-yə-wəs\ *(adj)* harmless. An occasional glass of wine with dinner is relatively *innocuous* and should have no ill effect on you.

in-no-va-tion \ˌin-ə-ˈvā-shən\ *(n)* change; introduction of something new. Although Richard liked to keep up with all the latest technological *innovations*, he didn't always abandon tried-and-true techniques in favor of something new.

in-nu-en-do \ˌin-yə-ˈwen-₍ₐ₎dō\ *(n)* hint; insinuation. I can defend myself against direct accusations; *innuendos* and oblique attacks on my character are what trouble me.

in-op-por-tune \₍ₐ₎in-ˌäp-ər-ˈt(y)ün\ *(adj)* untimely; poorly chosen. A rock concert is an *inopportune* setting for a quiet conversation.

in-or-di-nate \in-ˈȯrd-ᵊn-ət\ *(adj)* unrestrained; excessive. She had an *inordinate* fondness for candy, eating two or three boxes in a single day.

in-sa-tia-ble \₍ᐟ₎in-ˈsā-shə-bəl\ *(adj)* not easily satisfied; unquenchable; greedy. The young writer's thirst for knowledge was *insatiable*; she was always in the library.

in-scru-ta-ble \in-ˈskrüt-ə-bəl\ *(adj)* incomprehensible; not to be discovered. I fail to understand the reasons for your outlandish behavior; your motives are *inscrutable*.

in-sen-sate \₍ᐟ₎in-ˈsen-ˌsāt\ *(adj)* without feeling. He lay there as *insensate* as a log.

in-sid-i-ous \in-ˈsid-ē-əs\ *(adj)* treacherous; stealthy; sly. The fifth column is *insidious* because it works secretly within our territory for our defeat.

in-sin-u-ate \in-ˈsin-yə-ˌwāt\ *(v)* hint; imply. When you said I was looking robust, did you mean to *insinuate* that I've gotten fat?

in-sip-id \in-ˈsip-əd\ *(adj)* lacking in flavor; dull. Flat prose and flat ginger are equally *insipid*: both lack sparkle.

\ŋ\ sing \ō\ go \ȯ\ law \ȯi\ boy \th\ thin \th̲\ the \ü\ loot \u̇\ foot
\y\ yet \zh\ vision \à, k̲, ⁿ, œ, œ̄, ue, ūe, ʸ\ *see* Pronunciation Symbols

in·so·lent \ˈin(t)-s(ə-)lənt\ (*adj*) haughty and contemptuous. How dare you treat me so rudely? I've never met such an *insolent* clerk.

in·sol·ven·cy \(ˈ)in-ˈsäl-vən-sē\ (*n*) bankruptcy; lack of ability to repay debts. When rumors of his *insolvency* reached his creditors, they began to press him for payment of the money due them.

in·som·ni·a \in-ˈsäm-nē-ə\ (*n*) wakefulness; inability to sleep. He refused to join us in a midnight cup of coffee because he claimed it gave him *insomnia.*

in·sou·ci·ant \in-ˈsü-sē-ənt\ (*adj*) indifferent; without concern or care. Nicole pretended to be *insouciant* and carefree, but in reality she was nowhere near as light-hearted as she seemed.

in·sti·gate \ˈin(t)-stə-ˌgāt\ (*v*) urge; start; provoke. Rumors of police corruption led the mayor to *instigate* an investigation into the department's activities.

in·su·lar \ˈin(t)s-(y)ə-lər\ (*adj*) like an island; narrow-minded. The widely traveled writer considered the islanders an *insular* group, suspicious of anything foreign.

in·su·per·a·ble \(ˈ)in-ˈsü-p(ə-)rə-bəl\ (*adj*) insurmountable; unbeatable. Though the odds against their survival seemed *insuperable*, the Apollo 13 astronauts reached earth safely.

in·sur·gent \in-ˈsər-jənt\ (*adj*) rebellious. Because the *insurgent* forces had occupied the capital and had gained control of the railway lines, several of the war correspondents covering the uprising predicted a rebel victory. also (*n*).

in·te·grate \ˈint-ə-ˌgrāt\ (*v*) make whole; combine; make into one unit. We hope to *integrate* the French, Spanish, and Italian programs into a combined Romance languages department.

in·teg·ri·ty \in-ˈteg-rət-ē\ (*n*) uprightness; wholeness. Lincoln, whose personal *integrity* has inspired millions,

---

\ə\ **abut** \ᵊ\ kitten, F table \ər\ **further** \a\ **ash** \ā\ **ace** \ä\ **cot, cart** \au̇\ **out** \ch\ **chin** \e\ bet \ē\ **easy** \g\ **go** \i\ hit \ī\ **ice** \j\ **job**

fought a civil war to maintain the *integrity* of the republic, that these United States might remain undivided for all time.

in-tel-lect \'int-ᵊl-ˌekt\ (*n*) higher mental powers. If you wish to develop your *intellect*, read the great books.

in-tel-li-gen-tsi-a \in-ˌtel-ə-'jen(t)-sē-ə\ (*n*) the intelligent and educated classes [often used derogatorily]. He preferred discussions about sports and politics to the literary conversations of the *intelligentsia*.

in-ter \in-'tər\ (*v*) bury. They are going to *inter* the body tomorrow.

in-ter-dict \ˌint-ər-'dikt\ (*v*) prohibit; forbid. Civilized nations must *interdict* the use of nuclear weapons if we expect our society to survive. in-ter-dict \'int-ər-ˌdikt\ (*n*)

in-ter-im \'int-ə-rəm\ (*n*) meantime. The company will not consider our proposal until next week; in the *interim*, let us proceed as we have in the past. also (*adj*).

in-ter-ment \in-'tər-mənt\ (*n*) burial. *Interment* will take place in the church cemetery at 2 P.M. Wednesday.

in-ter-mi-na-ble \⁽ⁱ⁾in-'tərm-(ə-)nə-bəl\ (*adj*) endless. Although his speech lasted for only twenty minutes, it seemed *interminable* to his bored audience.

in-ter-mit-tent \ˌint-ər-'mit-ᵊnt\ (*adj*) periodic; on and off. The outdoor wedding reception had to be moved indoors to avoid the *intermittent* showers that fell on and off all afternoon.

in-ter-ne-cine \ˌint-ər-'nes-ˌēn\ (*adj*) deadly; mutually destructive; relating to an internal conflict. The American Civil War was an *internecine* conflict in both senses of the word, for it was both an internal struggle and a war marked by great slaughter.

in-ter-stic-es \in-'tər-stə-ˌsēz\ (*n*) chinks; crevices. The mountain climber sought to obtain a foothold in the *interstices* of the cliff.

\ŋ\ sing \ō\ go \ȯ\ law \ȯi\ boy \th\ thin \t͟h\ the \ü\ loot \u̇\ foot
\y\ yet \zh\ vision \à, <u>k</u>, ⁿ, œ, œ̅, ue, ue̅, ʸ\ *see* Pronunciation Symbols

in-ti-mate \'int-ə-ˌmāt\ (*v*) hint. Did Jane mean to *intimate* that Tarzan had bad breath when she offered him a breath mint? in-ti-mate \'int-ə-mət\ (*adj, n*)

in-tim-i-da-tion \in-ˌtim-ə-'dā-shən\ (*n*) use of threats or violence to control someone's actions; state of being browbeaten. Before the civil rights movement, white Southerners often resorted to *intimidation* to keep blacks from the polls.

in-trac-ta-ble \⁽'⁾in-'trak-tə-bəl\ (*adj*) unruly; stubborn; unyielding. Charlie Brown's friend Pigpen was *intractable*: he absolutely refused to take a bath.

in-tran-si-gence \in-'tran(t)s-ə-jən(t)s\ (*n*) refusal of any compromise; stubbornness. The negotiating team had not expected such *intransigence* from the striking workers, who rejected any hint of a compromise.

in-tran-si-gent \in-'tran(t)s-ə-jənt\ (*adj*) refusing any compromise. The strike settlement has collapsed because both sides are *intransigent*.

in-trep-id \in-'trep-əd\ (*adj*) fearless. For her *intrepid* conduct nursing the wounded during the war, Florence Nightingale was honored by Queen Victoria.

in-tri-cate \'in-tri-kət\ (*adj*) complex; knotty; tangled. Philip spent many hours designing mazes so *intricate* that none of his classmates could solve them.

in-trin-sic \in-'trin-zik\ (*adj*) belonging to a thing in itself; inherent. Although my grandmother's china has little *intrinsic* value, I shall always cherish it for the memories it evokes.

in-tro-vert \'in-trə-ˌvərt\ (*n*) one who is introspective; inclined to think more about oneself. Uncommunicative by nature and disinclined to look outside himself, he was a classic *introvert*.

in-trude \in-'trüd\ (*v*) trespass; enter as an uninvited person. He hesitated to *intrude* on their conversation.

\ə\ **abut** \ᵊ\ **kitten,** F **table** \ər\ **further** \a\ **ash** \ā\ **ace** \ä\ **cot, cart**
\au̇\ **out** \ch\ **chin** \e\ **bet** \ē\ **easy** \g\ **go** \i\ **hit** \ī\ **ice** \j\ **job**

in-tu-i-tion \ˌin-t(y)ü-'ish-ən\ (*n*) immediate insight; power of knowing without reasoning. Even though Tony denied that anything was wrong, Tina trusted her *intuition* that something was bothering him. **in-tu-i-tive** \in-'t(y)ü-ət-iv\ (*adj*)

in-un-date \'in-(ˌ)ən-ˌdāt\ (*v*) overwhelm; flood; submerge. This semester I am *inundated* with work: piles of paperwork flood my desk. Until the great dam was built, the waters of the Nile used to *inundate* the river valley every year.

in-ure \in-'(y)ù(ə)r\ (*v*) accustom; harden. He was *inured* to the Alaskan cold.

in-val-i-date \(ˌ)in-'val-ə-ˌdāt\ (*v*) weaken; destroy. The relatives who received little or nothing sought to *invalidate* the will by claiming that the deceased had not been in his right mind when he had signed the document.

in-vec-tive \in-'vek-tiv\ (*n*) abuse. He had expected criticism but not the *invective* that greeted his proposal.

in-veigh \in-'vā\ (*v*) protest strongly; denounce; attack with words. The gubernatorial candidate *inveighed* against the smear tactics employed by his opponent's campaign staff.

in-vei-gle \in-'vā-gəl\ (*v*) entice; persuade; wheedle. Flattering Adam about his good taste in food, Eve *inveigled* him into taking a bite of her apple pie.

in-verse \(ˌ)in-'vərs\ (*adj*) opposite. There is an *inverse* ratio between the strength of light and its distance. **in-verse** \'in-ˌvərs\ (*n*)

in-vet-er-ate \in-'vet-ə-rət\ (*adj*) deep-rooted; habitual. An *inveterate* smoker, Bob cannot seem to break the habit, no matter how hard he tries

in-vid-i-ous \in-'vid-ē-əs\ (*adj*) designed to create ill will or envy. We disregarded her *invidious* remarks because we realized how jealous she was.

in-vin-ci-ble \⁽⁰⁾in-'vin(t)-sə-bəl\ (*adj*) unconquerable. Superman is *invincible*.

in-vi-o-la-bil-i-ty \⁽⁰⁾in-ˌvī-ə-lə-'bil-ət-ē\ (*n*) security from destruction or corruption; unassailability. Batman assured the people of Gotham City of the *inviolability* of his oath to keep them safe: nothing on earth could make him break this promise.

in-voke \in-'vōk\ (*v*) call upon; ask for. She *invoked* her advisor's aid in filling out her financial aid forms.

in-vul-ner-a-ble \⁽⁰⁾in-'vəln-(ə-)rə-bəl\ (*adj*) incapable of injury. Achilles was *invulnerable* except in his heel.

i-o-ta \ī-'ōt-ə\ (*n*) very small quantity. He hadn't an *iota* of common sense.

ir-as-ci-ble \ir-'as-ə-bəl\ (*adj*) irritable; easily angered. Miss Minchin's *irascible* temper intimidated the younger schoolgirls, who feared she'd burst into a rage at any moment.

i-rate \ī-'rāt\ (*adj*) angry. When John's mother found out he had overdrawn his checking account for the third month in a row, she was so *irate* she could scarcely speak to him.

ir-i-des-cent \ˌir-ə-'des-ᵊnt\ (*adj*) exhibiting rainbowlike colors. He admired the *iridescent* hues of the oil that floated on the surface of the water.

irk-some \'ərk-səm\ (*adj*) repetitious; tedious. He found working on the assembly line *irksome* because of the monotony of the operation he had to perform.

i-ron-i-cal \ī-'rän-i-kəl\ (*adj*) resulting in an unexpected and contrary manner. It is *ironical* that his success came when he least wanted it.

i-ro-ny \'ī-rə-nē\ (*n*) hidden sarcasm or satire; use of words that convey a meaning opposite to the literal meaning. Gradually his listeners began to realize that the excessive praise he was lavishing on his opponent was actually *irony*; he was in fact ridiculing the poor fool.

\ə\ abut \ᵊ\ kitten, F table \ər\ further \a\ ash \ā\ ace \ä\ cot, cart
\aù\ out \ch\ chin \e\ bet \ē\ easy \g\ go \i\ hit \ī\ ice \j\ job

ir-rec-on-ci-la-ble \ $_{(i)}$ir-,(r)ek-ən-'sī-lə-bəl\ (*adj*) incompatible; not able to be resolved. Because the separated couple were *irreconcilable,* the marriage counselor recommended a divorce.

ir-rel-e-vant \ $^{(i)}$ir-'(r)el-ə-vənt\ (*adj*) not applicable; unrelated. No matter how *irrelevant* the patient's mumblings may seem, they give us some indications of what he has on his mind.

ir-re-me-di-a-ble \,ir-i-'mēd-ē-ə-bəl\ (*adj*) incurable, uncorrectable. The error she made was *irremediable*; she could see no way to repair it.

ir-rep-a-ra-ble \ $^{(i)}$ir-'(r)ep-(ə-)rə-bəl\ (*adj*) not able to be corrected or repaired. Your apology cannot atone for the *irreparable* damage you have done to his reputation.

ir-rev-er-ent \ $^{(i)}$ir-'(r)ev-(ə-)rənt\ (*adj*) lacking proper respect. Some audience members were amused by the comedian's *irreverent* jokes about the pope; others felt offended by his lack of respect for the head of their church.

ir-rev-o-ca-ble \ $^{(i)}$ir-'(r)ev-ə-kə-bəl\ (*adj*) unalterable; irreversible. As Sue dropped the "Dear John" letter into the mailbox, she suddenly had second thoughts and wanted to take it back, but she could not: her action was *irrevocable*.

it-er-ate \'it-ə-,rāt\ (*v*) utter a second time; repeat. I will *iterate* the warning I have previously given to you.

i-tin-er-ant \ī-'tin-ə-rənt\ (*adj*) wandering; traveling. He was an *itinerant* peddler and traveled through Pennsylvania and Virginia selling his wares; also (*n*).

i-tin-er-ar-y \ī-'tin-ə-,rer-ē\ (n) plan of a trip. Disliking sudden changes in plans when she traveled abroad, Ethel refused to make any alterations to her *itinerary*.

\ŋ\ sing \ō\ go \ȯ\ law \ȯi\ boy \th\ thin \th\ the \ü\ loot \u̇\ foot
\y\ yet \zh\ vision \à, k̲, ⁿ, œ, œ̄, ue, ūe, ʸ\ *see* Pronunciation Symbols

J

jad-ed \'jād-əd\ (*adj*) fatigued; surfeited. He looked for exotic foods to stimulate his *jaded* appetite.

jar-gon \'jär-gən\ (*n*) language used by a special group; technical terminology; gibberish. The computer salesmen at the store used a *jargon* of their own that we simply couldn't follow; we had no idea what they were jabbering about.

jaun-diced \'jȯn-dəst\ (*adj*) prejudiced (envious, hostile, or resentful); yellowed. Because Sue disliked Carolyn, she looked at Carolyn's paintings with a *jaundiced* eye, calling them formless smears. Newborn infants afflicted with jaundice look slightly yellow: they have *jaundiced* skin.

jaunt \'jȯnt\ (*n*) trip; short journey. He took a quick *jaunt* to Atlantic City.

jaun-ty \'jȯnt-ē\ (*adj*) stylish; perky; carefree. She wore her beret at a *jaunty* angle.

jeop-ar-dy \'jep-ərd-ē\ (*n*) exposure to death or danger. We had supposedly won the war in Iraq, but our soldiers stationed there were still in *jeopardy*, exposed to terrorist bombs and sniper attacks.

jet-ti-son \'jet-ə-sən\ (*v*) throw overboard. In order to enable the ship to ride safely through the storm, the captain had to *jettison* much of his cargo; also (*n*).

jin-go-ism \'jiŋ-(ˌ)gō-ˌiz-əm\ (*n*) extremely aggressive and militant patriotism. Patriotism carried to extremes can turn into *jingoism*, with its warlike overtones and cries of "America first!"

jo-cose \jō-'kōs\ (*adj*) giving to joking. The salesman was so *jocose* that many of his customers suggested that he become a stand-up comic.

joc-u-lar \'jäk-yə-lər\ (*adj*) said or done in jest. Although Bill knew the boss hated jokes, he couldn't resist making one *jocular* remark.

jo·cund \'jäk-ənd\ (*adj*) merry; cheerful; blithe. Lighthearted as well as lightfooted, the folk dancers were a lively and *jocund* group.

ju·bi·la·tion \ jü-bə-'lā-shən\ (*n*) rejoicing. There was great *jubilation* when the armistice was announced.

ju·di·cious \ ju-'dish-əs\ (*adj*) wise; determined by sound judgment. At a key moment in her life, she made a *judicious* investment that was the foundation of her later wealth.

jug·ger·naut \'jəg-ər-ˌnȯt\ (*n*) irresistible crushing force. Nothing could survive in the path of the *juggernaut.*

junc·ture \'jəŋ(k)-chər\ (*n*) crisis; joining point. At this critical *juncture,* let us think carefully before determining the course we shall follow.

jun·ket \'jəŋ-kət\ (*n*) trip, especially one taken for pleasure by an official at public expense. Though she maintained she had gone abroad to collect firsthand data on the Common Market, the opposition claimed that her trip was merely a political *junket.* also (*v*).

jun·ta \'hȯn-tə\ (*n*) group of men joined in political intrigue; cabal. As soon as he learned of its existence, the dictator ordered the execution of all of the members of the *junta.*

ju·ris·pru·dence \ jur-ə-'sprüd-ᵊn(t)s\ (*n*) science of law. He was more a student of *jurisprudence* than a practitioner of the law.

jux·ta·pose \'jək-stə-ˌpōz\ (*v*) place side by side. You'll find it easier to compare the two paintings if you *juxtapose* them.

K

ka·lei·do·scope \kə-'lī-d-ə-ˌskōp\ (*n*) tube in which patterns made by the reflection in mirrors of colored pieces of glass, etc., produce interesting symmetrical effects. People found a new source of entertainment while peering through Sir David Brewster's invention, the *kaleidoscope*; they found the everchanging patterns fascinating.

ken \'ken\ (*n*) range of knowledge. I cannot answer your question since this matter is beyond my *ken*.

kin·dred \'kin-drəd\ (*adj*) related; similar in nature or character. Tom Sawyer and Huck Finn were two *kindred* spirits, born mischief makers who were always up to some new tomfoolery. also (*n*).

ki·net·ic \kə-'net-ik\ (*adj*) producing motion. Designers of the electric automobile find that their greatest obstacle lies in the development of light and efficient storage batteries, the source of the *kinetic* energy needed to propel the vehicle.

ki·osk \'kē-ˌäsk\ (*n*) booth; summerhouse; open pavilion. She waited at the subway *kiosk*.

kis·met \'kiz-ˌmet\ (*n*) fate. *Kismet* is the Arabic word for "fate."

klep·to·ma·ni·ac \ˌklep-tə-'mā-nē-ˌak\ (*n*) person who has a compulsive desire to steal. They discovered that the wealthy customer was a *kleptomaniac* when they caught her stealing some cheap trinkets.

knav·e·ry \'nāv-(ə-)rē\ (*n*) untrustworthiness; lack of principles; villainy. Any politician nicknamed Tricky Dick clearly has a reputation for *knavery*.

knead \'nēd\ (*v*) mix; work dough. Her hands grew strong from *kneading* bread.

knell \'nel\ (*n*) tolling of a bell at a funeral; sound of the funeral bell. "The curfew tolls the *knell* of parting day." also (*v*).

\ə\ **abut** \ᵊ\ **kitten, F table** \ər\ **further** \a\ **ash** \ā\ **ace** \ä\ **cot, cart**
\aù\ **out** \ch\ **chin** \e\ **bet** \ē\ **easy** \g\ **go** \i\ **hit** \ī\ **ice** \j\ **job**

knoll \'nōl\ (*n*) little round hill. Robert Louis Stevenson's grave is on a *knoll* in Samoa; to reach the grave site, you must climb uphill and walk a short distance along a marked path.

\ŋ\ **sing**   \ō\ **go**   \ò\ **law**   \òi\ **boy**   \th\ **thin**   \th̲\ **the**   \ü\ **loot**   \u̇\ **foot**
\y\ **yet**   \zh\ **vision**   \à, k̲, ⁿ, œ, œ̄, ue, ūe, ʸ\ *see* Pronunciation Symbols

L

lab-y-rinth \ˈlab-ə-ˌrin(t)th\ (*n*) maze. Hiding from Indian Joe, Tom and Becky soon lost themselves in the *labyrinth* of secret underground caves.

lac-er-ate \ˈlas-ə-ˌrāt\ (*v*) mangle; tear. The stock car driver needed stitches in his arm after it was *lacerated* in a car crash. lac-er-ate \ˈlas-ə-rət\ (*adj*)

lach-ry-mose \ˈlak-rə-ˌmōs\ (*adj*) producing tears. His voice has a *lachrymose* quality that is more appropriate at a funeral than a class reunion.

lack-a-dai-si-cal \ˌlak-ə-ˈdā-zi-kəl\ (*adj*) lacking purpose or zest; halfhearted; languid. Because Gatsby had his mind more on his love life than on his finances, he did a very *lackadaisical* job of managing his money.

lack-ey \ˈlak-ē\ (*n*) footman; toady. The duke was followed by his *lackeys*. also (*v*).

lack-lus-ter \ˈlak-ˌləs-tər\ (*adj*) dull. We were disappointed by the *lackluster* performance.

la-con-ic \lə-ˈkän-ik\ (*adj*) brief and to the point. Many of the characters portrayed by Clint Eastwood are *laconic* types: strong men of few words.

lag-gard \ˈlag-ərd\ (*adj*) slow; sluggish. The sailor had been taught not to be *laggard* in carrying out orders. also (*n*).

la-goon \lə-ˈgün\ (*n*) shallow body of water near a sea; lake. They enjoyed their swim in the calm *lagoon*.

la-i-ty \ˈlā-ət-ē\ (*n*) laymen; persons not connected with the clergy. The *laity* does not always understand the clergy's problems.

lam-i-nat-ed \ˈlam-ə-ˌnāt-əd\ (*adj*) made of thin plates or scales. Banded gneiss is a *laminated* rock, easily identified by its distinctive colored bands.

lam-poon \lam-ˈpün\ (*v*) ridicule. This hilarious article *lampoons* the pretensions of some pompous politicians. also (*n*).

\ə\ **abut** \ᵊ\ **kitten**, F **table** \ər\ **further** \a\ **ash** \ā\ **ace** \ä\ **cot, cart**
\aú\ **out** \ch\ **chin** \e\ **bet** \ē\ **easy** \g\ **go** \i\ **hit** \ī\ **ice** \j\ **job**

lan-guid \\'laŋ-gwəd\\ (*adj*) weary; sluggish; listless. Her siege of illness left her *languid* and pallid.

lan-guish \\'laŋ-gwish\\ (*v*) lose animation; lose strength. Left at Miss Minchin's school for girls while her father went off to war, Sarah Crewe refused to *languish*; instead, she hid her grief and actively befriended her less fortunate classmates.

lan-guor \\'laŋ-(g)ər\\ (*n*) lassitude; depression. His friends tried to overcome the *languor* into which he had fallen by taking him to parties and to the theater.

lank \\'laŋk\\ (*adj*) long and thin. *Lank,* gaunt, Abraham Lincoln was a striking figure.

lap-i-dar-y \\'lap-ə-ˌder-ē\\ (*n*) worker in precious stones. He employed a *lapidary* to cut the large diamond. also (*adj*).

lar-ce-ny \\'lärs-nē\\ (*n*) theft. Because of the prisoner's record, the district attorney refused to reduce the charge from grand *larceny* to petty *larceny*.

lar-gess \\lär-'zhes\\ (*n*) generous gift. Lady Bountiful distributed *largess* to the poor.

las-civ-i-ous \\lə-'siv-ē-əs\\ (*adj*) lustful. Because they might arouse *lascivious* impulses in students, the headmaster banned all lewd magazines and books from campus and threatened to destroy any that were found.

las-si-tude \\'las-ə-ˌt(y)üd\\ (*n*) languor; weariness. After a massage and a long soak in the hot tub, I gave in to my growing *lassitude* and lay down for a nap.

la-tent \\'lāt-ᵊnt\\ (*adj*) potential but undeveloped; dormant; hidden. Polaroid pictures were popular at parties, because you could see the *latent* photographic image gradually appear before your eyes.

lat-er-al \\'lat-ə-rəl\\ (*adj*) coming from the side. In order to get good plant growth, the gardener must pinch off all *lateral* shoots. also (*n, v*).

\\ŋ\\ si**ng**   \\ō\\ **go**   \\ȯ\\ **law**   \\ȯi\\ **boy**   \\th\\ **thin**   \\th\\ **the**   \\ü\\ **loot**   \\u̇\\ **foot**
\\y\\ **yet**   \\zh\\ **vision**   \\à, k̲, ⁿ, œ, œ̄, ᵫ, ᵫ̄, ʸ\\ *see* Pronunciation Symbols

\\'lat-ə-ˌt(y)üd\\ (*n*) freedom from narrow limita-
think you have permitted your son too much
latitude in his actions: keep him under better control.

laud-a-ble \\'lȯd-ə-bəl\\ (*adj*) praiseworthy; commendable.
Although her parents believed that Jill's ambition to
become a medical missionary was a *laudable* one, they
wished she could pursue her praiseworthy humanitarian
goals closer to home.

lau-da-to-ry \\'lȯ˙d-ə-ˌtōr-ē\\ (*adj*) expressing praise. The
critics' *laudatory* comments helped to make her a
star.

lav-ish \\'lav-ish\\ (*adj*) generous; openhanded; extravagant; wasteful. Her wealthy suitors wooed her with *lavish* gifts. also (*v*).

lech-er-ous \\'lech-(ə-)rəs\\ (*adj*) impure in thought and
act; lustful; unchaste. The villain of the play, a *lecher-
ous* old banker, lusted after the poor farmer's beautiful
daughter.

lech-er-y \\'lech-(ə-)rē\\ (*n*) gross lewdness; lustfulness. In
his youth he led a life of *lechery* and debauchery; he
did not mend his ways until middle age.

lec-tern \\'lek-tərn\\ (*n*) reading desk. The chaplain delivered his sermon from a hastily improvised *lectern*.

lee-way \\'lē-ˌwā\\ (*n*) room to move; margin. When you
set a deadline, allow a little *leeway*.

leg-a-cy \\'leg-ə-sē\\ (*n*) a gift made by a will; anything
handed down from the past. Part of my *legacy* from my
parents is an album of family photographs.

leg-end \\'lej-ənd\\ (*n*) explanatory list of symbols on a
map. The *legend* at the bottom of the map made it clear
which symbols stood for rest areas along the highway
and which stood for public campsites. (secondary
meaning)

leg-er-de-main \\ˌlej-ərd-ə-'mān\\ (*n*) sleight of hand. The
magician demonstrated his renowned *legerdemain*.

\\ə\\ **abut** \\ᵊ\\ **kitten**, F **table** \\ər\\ **further** \\a\\ **ash** \\ā\\ **ace** \\ä\\ **cot, cart**
\\au̇\\ **out** \\ch\\ **chin** \\e\\ **bet** \\ē\\ **easy** \\g\\ **go** \\i\\ **hit** \\ī\\ **ice** \\j\\ **job**

le-ni-en-cy \\'lē-nē-ən-sē\ (*n*) mildness; permissiveness. Considering the gravity of the offense, we were surprised by the *leniency* of the sentence.

le-o-nine \\'lē-ə-ˌnīn\ (*n*) like a lion. Paintings of Beethoven portray him with a *leonine* head and mane of hair.

le-sion \\'lē-zhən\ (*n*) unhealthy change in structure, injury. Many *lesions* are the result of disease.

le-thal \\'lē-thəl\ (*adj*) deadly. It is unwise to leave *lethal* weapons where children may find them.

le-thar-gic \lə-'thär-jik\ (*adj*) drowsy; dull. The stuffy room made her *lethargic*: she felt as if she was about to nod off.

lev-i-ty \\'lev-ət-ē\ (*n*) lack of seriousness; lightness. Stop giggling and wriggling around in the pew: such *levity* is improper in church.

lewd \\'lüd\ (*adj*) lustful. They found his *lewd* stories morally objectionable.

lex-i-cog-ra-pher \ˌlek-sə-'käg-rə-fər\ (*n*) compiler of a dictionary. The new dictionary is the work of many *lexicographers* who spent years compiling and editing the text.

lex-i-con \\'lek-sə-ˌkän\ (*n*) dictionary. I cannot find this word in any *lexicon* in the library.

li-ai-son \\'lē-ə-ˌzän\ (*n*) contact keeping parts of an organization in communication; go-between; secret love affair. As the *liaison* between the American and British forces during World War II, the colonel had to ease tensions between the leaders of the two armies. Romeo's romantic *liaison* with Juliet ended in tragedy.

li-ba-tion \lī-'bā-shən\ (*n*) drink. He offered a *libation* to the thirsty prisoner.

li-bel-ous \\'lī-b(ə-)ləs\ (*adj*) defamatory; injurious to the good name of a person. If Batman wrote that the Joker was a dirty, rotten, mass-murdering criminal, could Batman's statement be considered *libelous*?

\ŋ\ sing   \ō\ go   \ò\ law   \òi\ boy   \th\ thin   \<u>th</u>\ the   \ü\ loot   \u̇\ foot
\y\ yet   \zh\ vision   \à, <u>k</u>, ⁿ, œ, œ̄, ue, ūe, ʸ\ *see* Pronunciation Symbols

lib-er-tine \'lib-ər-₁tēn\ (*n*) debauched person, roué. Although she was aware of his reputation as a *libertine,* she felt she could reform him and help him break his dissolute way of life; also (*adj*).

li-bi-do \lə-'bēd-₍ᵢ₎ō\ (*n*) emotional urges behind human activity. The psychiatrist maintained that suppression of the *libido* often resulted in maladjustment and neuroses. li-bid-i-nous \lə-'bid-ᵊn əs\ (*adj*)

li-bret-to \lə-'bret-₍ᵢ₎ō\ (*n*) text of an opera. The composer of an opera's music is remembered more frequently than the author of its *libretto.*

li-cen-tious \lī-'sen-chəs\ (*adj*) amoral; lewd and lascivious; unrestrained. Unscrupulously seducing the daughter of his host, Don Juan felt no qualms about the immorality of his *licentious* behavior.

lieu \'lü\ (*n*) instead of. They accepted his check in *lieu* of cash.

lil-li-pu-tian \₁lil-ə-'pyü-shən\ (*adj*) extremely small. Tiny and delicate, the model was built on a *lilliputian* scale. also (*n*).

lim-ber \'lim-bər\ (*adj*) flexible. Hours of ballet classes kept him *limber.*

lim-bo \'lim-₍ᵢ₎bō\ (*n*) region near heaven or hell where certain souls are kept; a prison (slang). Among the divisions of Hell are Purgatory and *Limbo.*

lim-pid \'lim-pəd\ (*adj*) clear; transparent; lucid. We could see swarms of colorful tropical fish in the *limpid* waters of the peaceful cove.

lin-e-a-ments \'lin-ē-ə-mənts\ (*n*) features of the face. She quickly sketched the *lineaments* of his face.

lin-guis-tic \liŋ-'gwis-tik\ (*adj*) pertaining to language. Exposed to most modern European languages in childhood, she grew up to be a *linguistic* prodigy.

li-on-ize \'lī-ə-₁nīz\ (*v*) treat as a celebrity. She enjoyed being *lionized* and adored by the public.

\ə\ **abut** \ᵊ\ **kitten,** F **table** \ər\ **further** \a\ **ash** \ā\ **ace** \ä\ **cot, cart**
\aů\ **out** \ch\ **chin** \e\ **bet** \ē\ **easy** \g\ **go** \i\ **hit** \ī\ **ice** \j\ **job**

liq-ui-date \\'lik-wə-ˌdāt\\ (*v*) settle accounts; clear up. He was able to *liquidate* all his debts in a short period of time.

list-less \\'list-ləs\\ (*adj*) lacking in spirit or energy. We had expected him to be full of enthusiasm and were surprised by his *listless* attitude.

lit-a-ny \\'lit-ᵊn-ē\\ (*n*) supplicatory prayer. On this solemn day, the congregation responded to the prayers of the priest during the *litany* with fervor and intensity.

lithe \\'līth\\ (*adj*) flexible; supple. Her figure was *lithe* and willowy.

lit-i-ga-tion \\ˌlit-ə-'gā-shən\\ (*n*) lawsuit. Try to settle this without involving any lawyers; I do not want to become bogged down in *litigation*.

li-to-tes \\'līt-ə-ˌtēz\\ (*n*) understatement for emphasis. To say, "He little realizes," when we mean that he does not realize at all, is an example of the kind of understatement we call *litotes*.

liv-id \\'liv-əd\\ (*adj*) lead-colored; black and blue; enraged. His face was so *livid* with rage that we were afraid he might have an attack of apoplexy.

loath \\'lōth\\ (*adj*) reluctant; disinclined. Fearing for their son's safety, the overprotective parents were *loath* to let him go on the class trip.

loathe \\'lōth\\ (*v*) detest. Booing and hissing, the audience showed how much they *loathed* the wicked villain.

lode \\'lōd\\ (*n*) metal-bearing vein. If this *lode* that we have discovered extends for any distance, we have found a fortune.

lofty \\'lof-tē\\ (*adj*) very high. Though Barbara Jordan's fellow students used to tease her about her *lofty* ambitions, she rose to hold one of the highest positions in the land.

loi-ter \\'lȯit-ər\\ (*v*) hang around; linger. The policeman told him not to *loiter* in the alley.

\\ŋ\\ sing \\ō\\ go \\ȯ\\ law \\ȯi\\ boy \\th\\ thin \\th\\ the \\ü\\ loot \\u̇\\ foot
\\y\\ yet \\zh\\ vision \\à, ḵ, ⁿ, œ, œ̄, ue, ṻe, ʸ\\ *see* Pronunciation Symbols

loll \\'läl\\ (*v*) lounge about. They *lolled* around in their chairs watching television.

lon-gev-i-ty \\län-'jev-ət-ē\\ (*n*) long life. When she received congratulations from the White House on her hundredth birthday, she felt proud of her *longevity*.

lope \\'lōp\\ (*v*) gallop slowly. As the horses *loped* along, we had an opportunity to admire the ever-changing scenery. also (*n*).

lo-qua-cious \\lō-'kwā-shəs\\ (*adj*) talkative. Though our daughter barely says a word to us these days, put a phone in her hand and you'll see how *loquacious* she can be.

lout \\'laut\\ (*n*) clumsy person. That awkward *lout* dropped my priceless vase!

lu-cent \\'lüs-ᵊnt\\ (*adj*) shining. The moon's *lucent* rays silvered the river.

lu-cid \\'lü-səd\\ (*adj*) easily understood; clear; intelligible. She makes an excellent teacher: her explanations of technical points are *lucid* enough for a child to grasp.

lu-cra-tive \\'lü-krət-iv\\ (*adj*) profitable. He turned his hobby into a *lucrative* profession.

lu-cre \\'lü-kər\\ (*n*) money. Preferring *lucre* to fame, he wrote stories of popular appeal.

lu-di-crous \\'lüd-ə-krəs\\ (*adj*) ridiculous; laughable; absurd. Gwen tried to keep a straight face, but Bill's suggestion were so *ludicrous* that she finally had to laugh.

lu-gu-bri-ous \\lu-'gü-brē-əs\\ (*adj*) mournful. Gloomy Gus walked around town with a *lugubrious* expression on his face.

lu-mi-nous \\'lü-mə-nəs\\ (*adj*) shining; issuing light. The sun is a *luminous* body.

lu-nar \\'lü-nər\\ (*adj*) pertaining to the moon. *Lunar* craters can be plainly seen with the aid of a small telescope.

\\ə\\ **abut** \\ᵊ\\ **kitten**, F **table** \\ər\\ **further** \\a\\ **ash** \\ā\\ **ace** \\ä\\ **cot, cart**
\\au̇\\ **out** \\ch\\ **chin** \\e\\ **bet** \\ē\\ **easy** \\g\\ **go** \\i\\ **hit** \\ī\\ **ice** \\j\\ **job**

lu-rid \'lür-əd\ (*adj*) wild; sensational; graphic; gruesome. Do the *lurid* cover stories in the *Enquirer* actually attract people to buy that trashy tabloid?

lus-cious \'ləsh-əs\ (*adj*) pleasing to taste or smell. The ripe peach was *luscious.*

lus-ter \'ləs-tər\ (*n*) shine; gloss. The soft *luster* of the silk in the dim light was pleasing. also (*n*).

lus-trous \'ləs-trəs\ (*adj*) shining. Her large and *lustrous* eyes gave a touch of beauty to an otherwise drab face.

lux-u-ri-ant \ (ı)ləg-'zhur-ē-ənt\ (*adj*) abundant; rich and splendid; fertile. Lady Godiva was completely covered by her *luxuriant* hair.

M

ma·ca·bre \mə-'käb(-rə)\ *(adj)* gruesome; grisly. The city morgue is a *macabre* spot for the uninitiated.

mac·er·ate \'mas-ə-ˌrāt\ *(v)* to soften by soaking or steeping. The strawberries had been soaking in the champagne for so long that they had begun to *macerate*: they literally fell apart at the touch of a spoon.

Ma·chi·a·vel·li·an \ˌmak-ē-ə-'vel-ē-ən\ *(adj)* crafty; double-dealing. I do not think he will be a good ambassador because he is not accustomed to the *Machiavellian* maneuverings of foreign diplomats.

mach·i·na·tion \ˌmak-ə-'nā-shən\ *(n)* evil schemes or plots. Fortunately, Batman saw through the wily *machinations* of the Riddler and saved Gotham City from destruction by the forces of evil.

mad·ri·gal \'mad-ri-gəl\ *(n)* pastoral song. His program of folk songs included several *madrigals* that he sang to the accompaniment of a lute.

mael·strom \'mā(ə)l-strəm\ *(n)* whirlpool. The canoe was tossed about in the *maelstrom.*

mag·nan·i·mous \mag-'nan-ə-məs\ *(adj)* generous. In a *magnanimous* gesture, philanthropist Eugene Lang made a college education possible for a class of inner city youngsters.

mag·nate \'mag-ˌnāt\ *(n)* person of prominence or influence. Growing up in Pittsburgh, Annie Dillard was surrounded by the mansions of the great steel and coal *magnates* who set their mark on that city.

mag·nil·o·quent \mag-'nil-ə-kwənt\ *(adj)* boastful, pompous. In their stories of the trial, the reporters ridiculed the *magniloquent* speeches of the defense attorney.

mag·ni·tude \'mag-nə-ˌt(y)üd\ *(n)* greatness; extent. It is difficult to comprehend the *magnitude* of his crime.

maim \'mām\ *(v)* mutilate; injure. The hospital could not take care of all who had been wounded or *maimed* in the railroad accident.

---

mal-a-droit \ˌmal-ə-ˈdrȯit\ (*adj*) clumsy; bungling. "Oh! My stupid tongue!" exclaimed Jane, embarrassed at having said anything so *maladroit*.

mal-aise \mə-ˈlāz\ (*n*) uneasiness; vague feeling of ill health. Feeling slightly queasy before going onstage, Carol realized that this touch of *malaise* was merely stage fright.

mal-a-prop-ism \ˈmal-ə-ˌpräp-ˌiz-əm\ (*n*) comic misuse of a word. When Mrs. Malaprop criticizes Lydia for being "as headstrong as an allegory on the banks of the Nile," she confuses "allegory" and "alligator" in a typical *malapropism*.

mal-con-tent \ˌmal-kən-ˈtent\ (*n*) person dissatisfied with existing state of affairs. One of the few *malcontents* in Congress, he constantly voiced his objections to the President's programs. also (*adj*).

mal-e-dic-tion \ˌmal-ə-ˈdik-shən\ (*n*) curse. When the magic mirror revealed that Snow White was still alive, the wicked queen cried out in rage and uttered dreadful *maledictions*.

mal-e-fac-tor \ˈmal-ə-ˌfak-tər\ (*n*) evildoer; criminal. Mighty Mouse will save the day, hunting down *malefactors* and rescuing innocent mice from peril.

ma-lev-o-lent \mə-ˈlev-ə-lənt\ (*adj*) wishing evil. Iago is a *malevolent* villain who takes pleasure in ruining Othello.

ma-li-cious \mə-ˈlish-əs\ (*adj*) hateful; spiteful. Jealous of Cinderella's beauty, her *malicious* stepsisters expressed their spite by forcing her to do menial tasks.

ma-lign \mə-ˈlīn\ (*v*) speak evil of; bad-mouth; defame. Putting her hands over her ears, Rose refused to listen to Betty *malign* her friend Susan. also (*adj*).

ma-lig-nant \mə-ˈlig-nənt\ (*adj*) injurious; tending to cause death; aggressively malevolent. Though many tumors are benign, some are *malignant*, growing out of control and endangering the life of the patient.

\ŋ\ **sing** \ō\ **go** \ȯ\ **law** \ȯi\ **boy** \th\ **thin** \t͟h\ **the** \ü\ **loot** \u̇\ **foot**
\y\ **yet** \zh\ **vision** \ə, k̲, ⁿ, œ, œ̄, ᵫ, ᵫ̄, ʸ\ *see* Pronunciation Symbols

ma-lin-ger-er \mə-'liŋ-gər-ər\ (*n*) one who feigns illness to escape duty. The captain ordered the sergeant to punish all *malingerers* and force them to work.

mall \'mȯl\ (*n*) public walk. The *mall* in Central Park has always been a favorite spot for Sunday strollers.

mal-le-a-ble \'mal-ē-ə-bəl\ (*adj*) capable of being shaped by pounding; impressionable. Gold is a *malleable* metal, easily shaped into bracelets and rings. Fagin hoped Oliver was a *malleable* lad, easily shaped into a thief.

mam-mal \'mam-əl\ (*n*) a vertebrate animal whose female suckles its young. Many people regard the whale as a fish and do not realize that it is a *mammal.*

mam-moth \'mam-əth\ (*adj*) gigantic; enormous. To try to memorize every word on this vocabulary list would be a *mammoth* undertaking; take on projects that are more manageable in size. also (*n*).

man-date \'man-,dāt\ (*n*) order; charge. In his inaugural address, the president stated that he had a *mandate* from the people to seek an end to social evils such as poverty, poor housing, etc. also (*v*).

man-da-tor-y \'man-də-,tȯr-ē\ (*adj*) obligatory; compulsory. It is *mandatory* that, before graduation, all students must pass the swimming test.

man-gy \'mān-jē\ (*adj*) shabby; wretched. We finally threw out the *mangy* rug that the dog had destroyed.

ma-ni-a-cal \mə-'nī-ə-kəl\ (*adj*) raving mad; insane. Though Mr. Rochester had locked his mad wife in the attic, he could still hear her *maniacal* laughter echoing throughout the house.

man-i-fest \'man-ə-,fest\ (*adj*) understandable; clear. His evil intentions were *manifest* and yet we could not stop him. also (*v, n*).

man-i-fes-to \,man-ə-'fes-₍ₙ₎tō\ (*n*) declaration; statement of policy. This statement may be regarded as the *manifesto* of the party's policy.

\ə\ **abut** \ᵊ\ **kitten, F table** \ər\ **further** \a\ **ash** \ā\ **ace** \ä\ **cot, cart**
\au̇\ **out** \ch\ **chin** \e\ **bet** \ē\ **easy** \g\ **go** \i\ **hit** \ī\ **ice** \j\ **job**

man-i-fold \'man-ə-ˌfōld\ (*adj*) numerous; varied. I cannot begin to tell you how much I appreciate your *manifold* kindnesses. also (*adv, n*).

ma-nip-u-late \ mə-'nip-yə-ˌlāt\ (*v*) operate with one's hands; control or play upon (people, forces, etc.) artfully. Jim Henson understood how to *manipulate* the Muppets. Madonna understands how to *manipulate* publicity (and men).

ma-raud-er \mə-'rȯd-ər\ (*n*) raider; intruder. The sounding of the alarm frightened the *marauders*. ma-raud \mə-'rȯd\ (*v*)

mar-i-tal \'mar-ət-ᵊl\ (*adj*) pertaining to marriage. After the publication of her book of *marital* advice, she was often consulted by married couples on the verge of divorce.

mar-i-time \'mar-ə-ˌtīm\ (*adj*) bordering on the sea; nautical. The *Maritime* Provinces depend on the sea for their wealth.

marred \'märd\ (*adj*) damaged; disfigured. She had to refinish the *marred* surface of the table. mar \'mär\ (*v*)

mar-row \'mar-ₒō\ (*n*) soft tissue filling the bones. The frigid cold chilled the traveler to the *marrow*.

mar-su-pi-al \ mär-'sü-pē-əl\ (*n*) one of a family of mammals that nurse their offspring in a pouch. The most common *marsupial* in North America is the opossum. also (*adj*).

mar-tial \'mär-shəl\ (*adj*) warlike. The sound of *martial* music inspired the young cadet with dreams of military glory.

mar-ti-net \ˌmärt-ᵊn-'et\ (*n*) strict disciplinarian. No talking at meals! No mingling with the servants! Miss Minchin was a *martinet* who insisted that the schoolgirls in her charge observe each regulation to the letter.

mas-ti-cate \'mas-tə-ˌkāt\ (*v*) chew. We must *masticate* our food carefully and slowly in order to avoid stomach disorders.

---

ma-ter-nal \mə-'tərn-əl\ (*adj*) motherly. Many animals display *maternal* instincts only while their offspring are young and helpless.

ma-tri-arch \'mā-trē-ˌärk\ (*n*) woman who rules a family or larger social group. The *matriarch* ruled her gypsy tribe with a firm hand.

ma-trix \'mā-triks\ (*n*) point of origin; array of numbers or algebraic symbols; mold or die. Some historians claim the Nile Valley was the *matrix* of Western civilization.

maud-lin \'mȯd-lən\ (*adj*) effusively sentimental. Whenever a particularly *maudlin* tearjerker played at the movies, Marvin embarrassed himself by weeping copiously.

maul \'mȯl\ (*v*) handle roughly. The rock star was *mauled* by his overexcited fans.

mau-so-le-um \ˌmȯ-sə-'lē-əm\ (*n*) monumental tomb. His body was placed in the family *mausoleum*.

mav-er-ick \'mav-(ə-)rik\ (*n*) rebel; nonconformist. To the masculine literary establishment, George Sand with her insistence on wearing trousers and smoking cigars was clearly a *maverick* who fought her proper womanly role.

mawk-ish \'mȯ-kish\ (*adj*) mushy and gushy; icky-sticky sentimental; maudlin. Whenever Gigi and her boyfriend would sigh and get all lovey-dovey, her little brother would shout, "Yuck!," protesting their *mawkish* behavior.

max-im \'mak-səm\ (*n*) proverb; a truth pithily stated. Aesop's story of the hare and the tortoise illustrates the *maxim* "Slow and steady wins the race."

may-hem \'mā-ˌhem\ (*n*) injury to body. The riot was marked not only by *mayhem* with its attendant loss of life and limb but also by arson and pillage.

\ə\ abut \ᵊ\ kitten, F table \ər\ further \a\ ash \ā\ ace \ä\ cot, cart
\au̇\ out \ch\ chin \e\ bet \ē\ easy \g\ go \i\ hit \ī\ ice \j\ job

mea-ger \'mē-gər\ (*adj*) scanty; inadequate. Still hungry after his *meager* serving of porridge, Oliver Twist asked for a second helping.

me-an-der \mē-'an-dər\ (*v*) to wind or turn in its course. Needing to stay close to a source of water, he followed every twist and turn of the stream as it *meandered* through the countryside.

med-dle-some \'med-ᵊl-səm\ (*adj*) interfering. He felt his marriage was suffering because of his *meddlesome* mother-in-law.

me-di-ate \'mēd-ē-ˌāt\ (*v*) settle a dispute through the services of an outsider. King Solomon was asked to *mediate* a dispute between two women, each of whom claimed to be the mother of the same child. me-di-ate \'mēd-ē-ət\ (*adj*)

me-di-o-cre \ˌmēd-ē-'ō-kər\ (*adj*) ordinary; commonplace. We were disappointed because he gave a rather *mediocre* performance in this role.

med-i-ta-tion \ˌmed-ə-'tā-shən\ (*n*) reflection; thought. She reached her decision only after much *meditation*.

med-ley \'med-lē\ (*n*) mixture. To avoid boring dancers by playing any one tune for too long, bands may combine three or four tunes into a *medley*.

meg-a-lo-ma-ni-a \ˌmeg-ə-lō-'mā-nē-ə\ (*n*) mania for doing grandiose things. Developers who spend millions trying to build the world's tallest skyscraper suffer from *megalomania*.

mé-lange \mā-'läⁿzh\ (*n*) mixture of diverse, possibly incongruous items. The book was such a *mélange* of ill-assorted essays that, instead of plowing through it in a single sitting, I had to read it piecemeal.

me-lee \'mā-ˌlā\ (*n*) fight. The captain tried to ascertain the cause of the *melee* that had broken out among the crew members.

\ŋ\ sing   \ō\ go   \ȯ\ law   \ȯi\ boy   \th\ thin   \th̲\ the   \ü\ loot   \u̇\ foot
\y\ yet   \zh\ vision   \ə, k̲, ⁿ, œ, œ̄, ᵫ, ᵫ̄, ʸ\ *see* Pronunciation Symbols

mel·lif·lu·ous \me-'lif-lə-wəs\ (*adj*) sweetly or smoothly flowing; melodious. Italian is a *mellifluous* language, especially suited to being sung.

me·men·to \mi-'ment-ͺ(ͺ)ō\ (*n*) token; reminder. Take this book as a *memento* of your visit.

me·mo·ri·al·ize \mə-'mōr-ē-ə-ͺlīz\ (*v*) commemorate. Let us *memorialize* his great contribution by dedicating this library in his honor.

men·da·cious \men-'dā-shəs\ (*adj*) lying; habitually dishonest. Distrusting Huck from the start, Miss Watson assumed he was *mendacious* and refused to believe a word he said.

men·di·cant \'men-di-kənt\ (*n*) beggar. "O noble sir, give alms to the poor," cried Aladdin, playing the *mendicant*.

me·ni·al \'mē-nē-əl\ (*adj*) suitable for servants; lowly; mean. Her wicked stepmother forced Cinderella to do *menial* tasks around the house while her ugly stepsisters lolled around painting their toenails. also (*n*).

men·tor \'men-ͺtò(ə)r\ (*n*) teacher, guide. During this very trying period, he could not have had a better *mentor,* for the teacher was sympathetic and understanding.

mer·can·tile \'mər-kən-ͺtēl\ (*adj*) concerning trade. The East India Company sponsored *mercantile* ventures and established new trade routes to the East.

mer·ce·nar·y \'mərs-ᵊn-ͺer-ē\ (*adj*) motivated solely by money or gain. Andy's every act was prompted by *mercenary* motives: his first question was always "What's in it for me?" also (*n*).

mer·cu·ri·al \ͺ(ͺ)mər-'kyúr-ē-əl\ (*adj*) capricious; changing; fickle. Quick as quicksilver to change, he was *mercurial* in nature and therefore unreliable.

mer·e·tri·cious \ͺmer-ə-'trish-əs\ (*adj*) flashy; tawdry. Her jewels were inexpensive but not *meretricious*.

\ə\ **abut** \ᵊ\ **kitten, F table** \ər\ **further** \a\ **ash** \ā\ **ace** \ä\ **cot, cart**
\aú\ **out** \ch\ **chin** \e\ **bet** \ē\ **easy** \g\ **go** \i\ **hit** \ī\ **ice** \j\ **job**

me-sa \'mā-sə\ (*n*) high, flat-topped hill. The *mesa,* rising above the surrounding desert, was the most conspicuous feature of the area.

mes-mer-ize \'mez-mə-ˌrīz\ (*v*) hypnotize; fascinate. On a long stretch of road between Fresno and Los Angeles, the open highway began to *mesmerize* Richard; he pulled over to the side of the road and rested to free himself from highway hypnosis.

met-al-lur-gi-cal \ˌmet-əl-'ər-ji-kəl\ (*adj*) pertaining to the art of removing metals from ores. During the course of his *metallurgical* research, the scientist developed a steel alloy of tremendous strength.

met-a-mor-pho-sis \ˌmet-ə-'mȯr-fə-səs\ (*n*) change of form. The *metamorphosis* of caterpillar to butterfly is typical of many such changes in animal life.

met-a-phor \'met-ə-ˌfȯ(ə)r\ (*n*) implied comparison. "He soared like an eagle" is an example of a simile; "He is an eagle in flight," a *metaphor.*

met-a-phys-i-cal \ˌmet-ə-'fiz-i-kəl\ (*adj*) pertaining to speculative philosophy. The modern poets have gone back to the fanciful poems of the *metaphysical* poets of the seventeenth century for many of their images. met-a-phys-ics \ˌmet-ə-'fiz-iks\ (*n*)

mete \'mēt\ (*v*) measure; distribute. He tried to be impartial in his efforts to *mete* out justice.

me-thod-i-cal \mə-'thäd-i-kəl\ (*adj*) systematic. An accountant must be *methodical* and maintain order among his financial records.

me-tic-u-lous \mə-'tik-yə-ləs\ (*adj*) excessively careful; painstaking; scrupulous. Martha Stewart was a *meticulous* housekeeper, fussing about each and every detail that went into making up her perfect home.

me-trop-o-lis \mə-'träp-(ə-)ləs\ (*n*) large city. Every evening this terminal is filled with the thousands of commuters who are going from this *metropolis* to their homes in the suburbs.

\ŋ\ sing \ō\ go \ȯ\ law \ȯi\ boy \th\ thin \t̲h̲\ the \ü\ loot \ u̇\ foot
\y\ yet \zh\ vision \ȧ, k̲, ⁿ, œ, œ̄, ue, œ̄, ʸ\ *see* Pronunciation Symbols

met-tle \'met-ᵊl\ (*n*) courage; spirit. When challenged by the other horses in the race, the thoroughbred proved its *mettle* by its determination to hold the lead.

mi-as-ma \mī-'az-mə\ (*n*) swamp gas; heavy, vaporous atmosphere, often emanating from decaying matter; pervasive corrupting influence. The smog hung over Victorian London like a dark cloud; noisome, reeking of decay, it was a visible *miasma*.

mi-cro-cosm \'mī-krə-ˌkäz-əm\ (*n*) small world; the world in miniature. The small village community that Jane Austen depicts serves as a *microcosm* of English society in her time, for in this small world we see all the social classes meeting and mingling.

mien \'mēn\ (*n*) demeanor; bearing. She had the gracious *mien* of a queen.

mi-grant \'mī-grənt\ (*adj*) changing its habitat; wandering. *Migrant* workers return to the Central Valley each year at harvest time. also (*n*).

mi-gra-to-ry \'mī-grə-ˌtōr-ē\ (*adj*) wandering. The return of the *migratory* birds to the northern sections of this country is a harbinger of spring.

mi-lieu \mēl-'yə(r)\ (*n*) environment; means of expression. Surrounded by smooth preppies and arty bohemians, the country boy from Smalltown, USA, felt out of his *milieu*. Although he has produced excellent oil paintings and lithographs, his proper *milieu* is watercolor.

mil-i-tant \'mil-ə-tənt\ (*adj*) combative; bellicose. Although at this time he was advocating a policy of neutrality, one could usually find him adopting a more *militant* attitude. also (*n*).

mil-i-tate \'mil-ə-ˌtāt\ (*v*) work against. Your record of lateness and absence will *militate* against your chances of promotion.

mil-len-ni-um \mə-'len-ē-əm\ (*n*) thousand-year period; period of happiness and prosperity. At the end of the twentieth century, many people were uncertain whether the new *millennium* began in 2000 or in 2001.

mim·ic·ry \'mim-i-krē\ (*n*) imitation. Her gift for *mimicry* was so great that her friends said that she should be in the theater.

mi·na·to·ry \'min-ə-ˌtōr-ē\ (*adj*) menacing; threatening. Jabbing a *minatory* forefinger at Dorothy, the Wicked Witch cried, "I'll get you, and your little dog, too!"

minc·ing \'min(t)-siŋ\ (*adj*) affectedly dainty. Yum-Yum walked across the stage with *mincing* steps.

min·ion \'min-yən\ (*n*) servile dependent; subordinate. In "The Emperor's New Clothes," the emperor's *minions* fawn upon him, telling him how beautiful his new clothes are.

mi·nu·ti·ae \mə-'n(y)ü-shē-ˌē\ (*n*) petty details. She would have liked to ignore the *minutiae* of daily living.

mi·rage \mə-'räzh\ (*n*) unreal reflection; optical illusion. The lost prospector was fooled by a *mirage* in the desert.

mire \'mī(ə)r\ (*v*) entangle; stick in swampy ground. Their rear wheels became *mired* in mud. also (*n*).

mirth \'mərth\ (*n*) merriment; laughter. Sober Malvolio found Sir Toby's *mirth* improper.

mis·ad·ven·ture \ˌmis-əd-'ven-chər\ (*n*) mischance; ill luck. The young explorer met death by *misadventure*.

mis·an·thrope \'mis-ᵊn-ˌthrōp\ (*n*) one who hates mankind. In *Gulliver's Travels*, Swift portrays an image of humanity as vile, degraded beasts; for this reason, various critics consider him a *misanthrope*.

mis·ap·pre·hen·sion \ˌ(ˌ)mis-ˌap-ri-'hen-chən\ (*n*) error; misunderstanding. To avoid *misapprehension,* I am going to ask all of you to repeat the instructions I have given.

mis·cel·la·ny \'mis-ə-ˌlā-nē\ (*n*) mixture of writings on various subjects. This anthology is an interesting *miscellany* of nineteenth-century prose.

\ŋ\ **sing** \ō\ **go** \ȯ\ **law** \ȯi\ **boy** \th\ **thin** \t͟h\ **the** \ü\ **loot** \u̇\ **foot**
\y\ **yet** \zh\ **vision** \ə, k̲, ⁿ, œ, œ̄, ue, œ̄, ʸ\ *see* Pronunciation Symbols

mis-chance \⁽'⁾mis(h)-'chan(t)s\ (*n*) ill luck. By *mischance,* he lost his week's salary.

mis-con-cep-tion \ˌmis-kən-'sep-shən\ (*n*) misinterpretation; misunderstanding. I'm afraid you are suffering from a *misconception*, Mr. Collins: I do not want to marry you at all.

mis-con-strue \ˌmis-kən-'strü\ (*v*) interpret incorrectly; misjudge. She took the passage seriously rather than humorously because she *misconstrued* the author's ironic tone.

mis-cre-ant \'mis-krē-ənt\ (*n*) wretch; villain. What punishment does such a remorseless, uncaring *miscreant* deserve?

mis-de-mean-or \ˌmis-di-'mē-nər\ (*n*) minor crime. The culprit pleaded guilty to a *misdemeanor* rather than face trial for a felony.

mis-giv-ing \⁽'⁾mis-'giv-iŋ\ (*n*) doubt about a future event. Hamlet described his *misgivings* to Horatio but decided to fence with Laertes despite his foreboding of evil.

mis-hap \'mis-ˌhap\ (*n*) accident. With a little care you could have avoided this *mishap.*

mis-no-mer \⁽'⁾mis-'nō-mər\ (*n*) wrong name; incorrect designation. His tyrannical conduct proved to all that his nickname, King Eric the Just, was a *misnomer.*

mi-sog-a-my \'mə-'sä-ga-mē\ (*n*) hatred of marriage. He abhorred marriage as an outmoded, repressive institution, and even boasted of his *misogamy.*

mi-sog-y-nist \mə-'säj-ə-nəst\ (*n*) hater of women. Even though he belonged to several private clubs that barred women, Wallace claimed he was no *misogynist*, saying he liked women well enough in their proper place.

mis-sile \'mis-əl\ (*n*) object to be thrown or projected. After carefully folding his book report into a paper airplane, Beavis threw the *missile* across the classroom at

---

\ə\ **abut** \ᵊ\ **kitten,** F **table** \ər\ **further** \a\ **ash** \ā\ **ace** \ä\ **cot, cart**
\aù\ **out** \ch\ **chin** \e\ **bet** \ē\ **easy** \g\ **go** \i\ **hit** \ī\ **ice** \j\ **job**

Butthead. Rocket scientists build guided *missiles*; Beavis and Butthead can barely make unguided ones.

mis-sive \'mis-iv\ (*n*) letter. The ambassador received a *missive* from the secretary of state.

mite \'mīt\ (*n*) very small object or creature; small coin. Gnats are annoying *mites* that sting.

mit-i-gate \'mit-ə-ˌgāt\ (*v*) appease. Nothing Jason did could *mitigate* Medea's anger; she refused to forgive him for betraying her.

mne-mon-ic \ni-'män-ik\ (*adj*) pertaining to memory. He used *mnemonic* tricks to master new words. also (*n*).

mo-bile \'mō-bəl\ (*adj*) movable; not fixed. The *mobile* blood bank operated by the Red Cross visited our neighborhood today. mo-bil-i-ty \mō-'bil-ət-ē\ (*n*)

mode \'mōd\ (*n*) prevailing style; manner; way of doing something. The rock star had to have her hair done in the latest *mode*: frizzed, with occasional moussed spikes for variety. Henry plans to adopt a simpler *mode* of life: he is going to become a mushroom hunter and live off the land.

mod-i-cum \'mäd-i-kəm\ (*n*) limited quantity. Although his story is based on a *modicum* of truth, most of the events he describes are fictitious.

mod-ish \'mōd-ish\ (*adj*) fashionable. She always discarded all garments that were no longer *modish*.

mod-u-la-tion \ˌmäj-ə-'lā-shən\ (*n*) toning down; changing from one key to another. Always singing at the top of her lungs, the budding Brunhilde had no liking for restraint or *modulation*.

mo-gul \'mō-ˌ(ˌ)gəl\ (*n*) powerful person. The oil *moguls* made great profits when the price of gasoline rose.

moi-e-ty \'mȯi-ət-ē\ (*n*) half; part. On his death, his estate was divided into two equal *moieties*.

mol-e-cule \'mäl-i-ˌkyü(ə)l\ (*n*) the smallest part of a homogeneous substance. In chemistry, we study how atoms and *molecules* react to form new substances.

\ŋ\ si**ng** \ō\ go \ȯ\ law \ȯi\ boy \th\ thin \t͟h\ the \ü\ loot \u̇\ foot
\y\ yet \zh\ vision \ə, k̲, ⁿ, œ, œ̄, ᵫ, ᵫ̄, ʸ\ *see* Pronunciation Symbols

mol-li-fy \\'mäl-ə-ˌfī\\ (*v*) soothe. The airline customer service representative tried to *mollify* the angry passenger by offering her a seat in first class.

molt \\'mōlt\\ (*v*) shed or cast off hair or feathers. When Molly's canary *molted*, he shed feathers all over the house. also (*n*).

mol-ten \\'mōlt-ᵊn\\ (*adj*) melted. The city of Pompeii was destroyed by volcanic ash rather than by *molten* lava flowing from Mount Vesuvius.

mo-men-tous \\mō-'ment-əs\\ (*adj*) very important. When Marie and Pierre Curie discovered radium, they had no idea of the *momentous* impact their discovery would have upon society.

mo-men-tum \\mō-'ment-əm\\ (*n*) quantity of motion of a moving body; impetus. The car lost *momentum* as it tried to ascend the steep hill.

mon-ar-chy \\'män-ər-kē\\ (*n*) government under a single ruler. Though England today is a *monarchy*, there is some question whether it will be one in twenty years, given the present discontent at the prospect of Prince Charles as king.

mo-nas-tic \\mə-'nas-tik\\ (*adj*) related to monks or monasteries; removed from worldly concerns. Withdrawing from the world, Thomas Merton joined a contemplative religious order and adopted the *monastic* life.

mon-e-tar-y \\'män-ə-ˌter-ē\\ (*adj*) pertaining to money. Jane held the family purse strings: she made all *monetary* decisions affecting the household.

mon-o-lith-ic \\ˌmän-ᵊl-'ith-ik\\ (*adj*) solidly uniform; unyielding. Knowing the importance of appearing resolute, the patriots sought to present a *monolithic* front.

mon-o-the-ism \\'män-ə-ˌ₍ᵢ₎thē-ˌiz-əm\\ (*n*) belief in one God. Abraham was the first to proclaim his belief in *monotheism*.

\\ə\\ **abut** \\ᵊ\\ kitten, F table \\ər\\ **further** \\a\\ ash \\ā\\ **ace** \\ä\\ cot, cart
\\aú\\ **out** \\ch\\ **chin** \\e\\ bet \\ē\\ **easy** \\g\\ go \\i\\ **hit** \\ī\\ ice \\j\\ **job**

mo-not-o-ny \mə-'nät-ᵊn-ē\ (*n*) sameness leading to boredom. What could be more deadly dull than the *monotony* of punching numbers into a computer hour after hour?

mon-u-men-tal \ˌmän-yə-'ment-ᵊl\ (*adj*) massive. Writing a dictionary is a *monumental* task.

mood-i-ness \'müd-ē-nəs\ (*n*) fits of depression or gloom. Her recurrent fits of *moodiness* left her feeling as if she had fallen into a black hole.

moor \'mu̇(ə)r\ (*n*) marshy wasteland. These *moors* can only be used for hunting; they are too barren for agriculture. also (*v*).

moot \'müt\ (*adj*) debatable; controversial; hypothetical. In *moot* court, law students debate hypothetical cases; it is *moot* how much they learn from the process.

mor-a-to-ri-um \ˌmȯr-ə-'tōr-ē-əm\ (*n*) legal delay of payment. If we declare a *moratorium* and delay collection of debts for six months, I am sure the farmers will be able to meet their bills.

mor-bid \'mȯr-bəd\ (*adj*) given to unwholesome thought; moody; characteristic of disease. People who come to disaster sites just to peer at the grisly wreckage are indulging their *morbid* curiosity.

mor-dant \'mȯrd-ᵊnt\ (*adj*) biting; sarcastic; stinging. Actors feared the critic's *mordant* pen.

mo-res \'mȯ(ə)r-ˌāz\ (*n*) conventions; moral standards; customs. In America, Benazir Bhutto dressed as Western women did; in Pakistan, however, she followed the *mores* of her people, dressing in traditional veil and robes.

mor-i-bund \'mȯr-ə-₍ı₎bənd\ (*adj*) at the point of death. Hearst took a *moribund*, failing weekly newspaper and transformed it into one of the liveliest, most profitable daily papers around.

\ŋ\ **sing**   \ō\ **go**   \ȯ\ **law**   \ȯi\ **boy**   \th\ **thin**   \th̲\ **the**   \ü\ **loot**   \u̇\ **foot**
\y\ **yet**   \zh\ **vision**   \à, k̲, ⁿ, œ, œ̄, ue, ūe, ʸ\ *see* Pronunciation Symbols

mo·rose \mə-'rōs\ (*adj*) ill-humored; sullen; melancholy. Forced to take early retirement, Bill acted *morose* for months; then, all of a sudden, he shook off his gloom and was his usual cheerful self.

mor·ti·cian \mȯr-'tish-ən\ (*n*) undertaker. The *mortician* prepared the corpse for burial.

mor·ti·fy \'mȯrt-ə-ˌfī\ (*v*) humiliate; punish the flesh. She was so *mortified* by her blunder that she ran to her room in tears.

mote \'mōt\ (*n*) small speck. The tiniest *mote* in the eye is very painful.

mo·tif \mō-'tēf\ (*n*) theme. This simple *motif* runs throughout the entire score.

mot·ley \'mät-lē\ (*adj*) multicolored; mixed. The jester wore a *motley* tunic, red and green and blue and gold all patched together haphazardly. Captain Ahab had gathered a *motley* crew to sail the vessel: old sea dogs and runaway boys, pillars of the church and drunkards, even a tattooed islander who terrified the rest of the crew.

mot·tled \'mät-əld\ (*adj*) blotched in coloring; spotted. When old Falstaff blushed, his face was *mottled* with embarrassment, all pink and purple and red.

moun·te·bank \'maunt-i-ˌbaŋk\ (*n*) charlatan; boastful pretender. The patent medicine man was a *mountebank*.

mud·dle \'məd-əl\ (*v*) confuse; mix up. His thoughts were *muddled* and chaotic; also (*n*).

mug·gy \'məg-ē\ (*adj*) warm and damp. August in New York City is often *muggy*.

mulct \'məlkt\ (*v*) defraud a person of something. The lawyer was accused of trying to *mulct* the boy of his legacy. also (*n*).

mul·ti·far·i·ous \ˌməl-tə-'far-ē-əs\ (*adj*) varied; greatly diversified. A career woman and mother, she was constantly busy with the *multifarious* activities of her daily life.

\ə\ **abut** \ᵊ\ **kitten, F table** \ər\ **further** \a\ **ash** \ā\ **ace** \ä\ **cot, cart**
\au̇\ **out** \ch\ **chin** \e\ **bet** \ē\ **easy** \g\ **go** \i\ **hit** \ī\ **ice** \j\ **job**

mul-ti-form \'məl-ti-ˌförm\ (*adj*) having many forms. Snowflakes are *multiform* but always hexagonal.

mul-ti-lin-gual \ˌməl-ti-'liŋ-g(yə-)wəl\ (*adj*) having many languages. Because Switzerland is surrounded by France, Germany, Italy, and Austria, many Swiss people are *multilingual*.

mul-ti-plic-i-ty \ˌməl-tə-'plis-ət-ē\ (*n*) state of being numerous. He was appalled by the *multiplicity* of details he had to complete before setting out on his mission.

mun-dane \ˌmən-'dān\ (*adj*) worldly as opposed to spiritual; everyday. Uninterested in philosophical or spiritual discussions, Tom talked only of *mundane* matters such as the daily weather forecast or the latest basketball results.

mu-nif-i-cent \myu˙-'nif-ə-sənt\ (*adj*) very generous. The Annenberg Trust made a *munificent* gift to the city that generously supported art programs in the public schools.

murk-i-ness \'mər-kē-nəs\ (*n*) darkness; gloom. The *murkiness* of the swamp was so complete that in that gloom you couldn't tell the vines and branches from the snakes.

muse \'myüz\ (*v*) ponder. For a moment he *mused* about the beauty of the scene, but his thoughts soon changed as he recalled his own personal problems. also (*n*).

musk-y \'məs-kē\ (*adj*) having the odor of musk. She left a trace of *musky* perfume behind her.

must-y \'məs-tē\ (*adj*) stale; spoiled by age. The mildew-ridden attic was dank and *musty*.

mu-ta-ble \'myüt-ə-bəl\ (*adj*) changing in form; fickle. Going from rags to riches, and then back to rags again, the bankrupt financier was a victim of fortune's *mutable* ways.

mu-ti-late \'myüt-ᵊl-ˌāt\ (*v*) maim. The torturer threatened to *mutilate* his victim.

\ŋ\ sing \ō\ go \ö\ law \öi\ boy \th\ thin \t̲h̲\ the \ü\ loot \u̇\ foot
\y\ yet \zh\ vision \à, k̲, ⁿ, œ, œ̄, ue, ɶ, ʸ\ *see* Pronunciation Symbols

mu-ti-nous \\'myüt-ᵊn-əs\ (*adj*) unruly; rebellious. The captain had to use force to quiet his *mutinous* crew.

my-o-pic \mī-'ō-pik\ (*adj*) nearsighted; lacking foresight. Stumbling into doors despite the coke bottle lenses on his glasses, the nearsighted Mr. Magoo is markedly *myopic*. In playing all summer long and neglecting to store up food for winter, the grasshopper in Aesop's fable was *myopic* as well. my-o-pi-a \mī-'ō-pē-ə\ (*n*)

myr-i-ad \\'mir-ē-əd\ (*n*) very large number. *Myriads* of mosquitoes from the swamps invaded our village every twilight. also (*adj*).

\ə\ abut \ᵊ\ kitten, F table \ər\ **further** \a\ **ash** \ā\ **ace** \ä\ cot, cart
\aù\ **out** \ch\ **chin** \e\ bet \ē\ **easy** \g\ **go** \i\ hit \ī\ ice \j\ job

N

na-dir \\'nā-,di(ə)r\\ (*n*) lowest point. Although few people realized it, the Dow-Jones average had reached its *nadir* and would soon begin an upward surge.

na-iv-e-té \\(ₒ)nä-,ēv(-ə)-'tā\\ (*n*) quality of being unsophisticated; simplicity; artlessness; gullibility. Touched by the *naiveté* of sweet, convent-trained Cosette, Marius pledges himself to protect her innocence.

nar-cis-sist \\'när-sə-səst\\ (*n*) conceited, self-centered person. A *narcissist* is his own best friend. **nar-cis-sism** \\'när-sə-siz-əm\\ (*n*); **nar-cis-sis-tic** \\,när-sə-'sis-tik\\ (*adj*)

na-scent \\'nas-ᵊnt\\ (*adj*) incipient; coming into being. If we could identify these revolutionary movements in their *nascent* state, we would be able to eliminate serious trouble in later years.

na-tal \\'nāt-ᵊl\\ (*adj*) pertaining to birth. The Fourth of July is America's *natal* day, for on that date in 1776 the republic was born.

nau-se-ate \\'nȯ-z(h)ē-,āt\\ (*v*) cause to become sick; fill with disgust. The foul smells began to *nauseate* him.

nau-ti-cal \\'nȯt-i-kəl\\ (*adj*) pertaining to ships or navigation. The Maritime Museum contains many models of clipper ships, logbooks, anchors, and many other items of a *nautical* nature.

nave \\'nāv\\ (*n*) main body of a church. The *nave* of the cathedral was empty at this hour.

neb-u-lous \\'neb-yə-ləs\\ (*adj*) vague; hazy; cloudy. Phil and Dave tried to come up with a clear, intelligible business plan, not some hazy, *nebulous* proposal.

ne-crol-o-gy \\nə-'kräl-ə-jē\\ (*n*) obituary notice; list of the dead. The *necrology* of those buried in this cemetery is available in the office.

nec-ro-man-cy \\'nek-rə-,man(t)-sē\\ (*n*) black magic; dealings with the dead. The evil sorcerer performed feats of *necromancy*, calling on the spirits of the dead to tell the future.

---

ne-far-i-ous \ni-'far-ē-əs\ (*adj*) very wicked. The villain's crimes, though various, were one and all *nefarious*.

ne-ga-tion \ni-'gā-shən\ (*n*) denial; contradiction. At the age of two, Molly knew only one word: "No!" She wasn't merely negative, she was pure *negation*.

neg-li-gence \'neg-li-jən(t)s\ (*n*) neglect; failure to take reasonable care. Tommy failed to put back the cover on the well after he fetched his pail of water; because of his *negligence*, Kitty fell in.

nem-e-sis \'nem-ə-səs\ (*n*) revenging agent. Abandoned at sea in a small boat, the vengeful Captain Bligh vowed to be the *nemesis* of Fletcher Christian and his fellow mutineers.

ne-o-phyte \'nē-ə-ˌfīt\ (*n*) recent convert; beginner. This mountain slope contains slides that will challenge experts as well as *neophytes*.

nep-o-tism \'nep-ə-ˌtiz-əm\ (*n*) favoritism (to a relative). John left his position with the company because he felt that advancement was based on *nepotism* rather than ability.

net-tle \'net-ᵊl\ (*v*) annoy; vex. Do not let him *nettle* you with his sarcastic remarks.

nex-us \'nek-səs\ (*n*) connection. No one can study the legislative process without becoming aware of the *nexus* of Washington lobbyists and politicians.

nib \'nib\ (*n*) beak; pen point. The *nibs* of fountain pens often became clotted and corroded.

ni-ce-ty \'nī-sət-ē\ (*n*) subtlety; precision; minute distinction; fine point. This word list provides excellent illustrative sentences for each entry word; it cannot, however, explain all the *niceties* of current English usage.

nig-gard-ly \'nig-ərd-lē\ (*adj*) meanly stingy; parsimonious. The *niggardly* pittance the widow receives from the government cannot keep her from poverty.

\ə\ **abut** \ᵊ\ **kitten**, F **table** \ər\ **further** \a\ **ash** \ā\ **ace** \ä\ **cot, cart**
\au̇\ **out** \ch\ **chin** \e\ **bet** \ē\ **easy** \g\ **go** \i\ **hit** \ī\ **ice** \j\ **job**

nig-gle \'nig-əl\ (*v*) spend too much time on minor points; carp. Let's not *niggle* over details. nig-gling \'nig-(ə-)liŋ\ (*adj*)

ni-hil-ism \'nī-(h)ə-ˌliz-əm\ (*n*) philosophy that traditional beliefs are groundless and existence meaningless; absolute skepticism; terrorism. In his final days, Hitler abandoned himself to *nihilism*, showing himself prepared to annihilate all of Western Europe, even to destroy Germany itself, in order that his will might prevail. The root of the word *nihilism* is *nihil*, Latin for *nothing*.

nir-va-na \ni(ə)r-'vän-ə\ (*n*) in Buddhist teachings, the ideal state in which the individual becomes lost in the attainment of an impersonal beatitude. Despite his desire to achieve *nirvana*, the young Buddhist found that even the buzzing of a fly could distract him from his meditation.

noc-tur-nal \näk-'tərn-əl\ (*adj*) done at night. Mr. Jones obtained a watchdog to prevent the *nocturnal* raids on his chicken coops.

noi-some \'nȯi-səm\ (*adj*) foul smelling; unwholesome. The *noisome* atmosphere downwind of the oil refinery not only stank, it damaged the lungs of everyone living in the area.

no-mad-ic \nō-'mad-ik\ (*adj*) wandering. Several *nomadic* tribes of Indians would hunt in this area each year.

no-men-cla-ture \'nō-mən-ˌklā-chər\ (*n*) terminology; system of names. Sharon found her knowledge of Latin and Greek word parts useful in translating medical *nomenclature*: terms like bilateral myringotomy and splenectomy came easily to her.

non-age \'nän-ij\ (*n*) immaturity. She was embarrassed by the *nonage* of her contemporaries who never seemed to grow up.

non-cha-lance \ˌnän-shə-'län(t)s\ (*n*) indifference; lack of concern; composure. Cool, calm, and collected under

---

\ŋ\ **sing** \ō\ **go** \ȯ\ **law** \ȯi\ **boy** \th\ **thin** \t̲h̲\ **the** \ü\ **loot** \u̇\ **foot**
\y\ **yet** \zh\ **vision** \à, k̲, ⁿ, œ, œ̄, ue, ue̅, ʸ\ *see* Pronunciation Symbols

fire, James Bond shows remarkable *nonchalance* in the face of danger.

non-com-mit-tal \ˌnän-kə-ˈmit-ᵊl\ (*adj*) neutral; unpledged; undecided. We were annoyed by his *noncommittal* reply for we had been led to expect definite assurances of his approval.

non-en-ti-ty \nä-ˈnen(t)-ət-ē\ (*n*) nonexistence; person of no importance. Don't dismiss John as a *nonentity*; in his quiet, understated way, he's very important to the firm.

non-plus \ˈnän-ˈpləs\ (*v*) bring to a halt by confusion; perplex. Jack's uncharacteristic rudeness *nonplussed* Jill, leaving her uncertain how to react. also (*n*).

non se-qui-tur \⁽ˈ⁾nän-ˈsek-wət-ər\ (*n*) a conclusion that does not follow from the facts stated. Your term paper is full of *non sequiturs*; I cannot see how you reached the conclusions you state.

nose-gay \ˈnōz-ˌgā\ (*n*) fragrant bouquet. These spring flowers will make an attractive *nosegay.*

nos-tal-gia \nä-ˈstal-jə\ (*n*) homesickness; longing for the past. My grandfather seldom spoke of life in the old country, or of the good old days, when he first arrived in America; he had little patience with *nostalgia.*

no-to-ri-ous \nō-ˈtōr-ē-əs\ (*adj*) outstandingly bad; unfavorably known. To the starlet, any publicity was good publicity; if she couldn't have a good reputation, she'd settle for being *notorious.*

nov-el-ty \ˈnäv-əl-tē\ (*n*) something new; newness. The computer is no longer a *novelty* around the office. **nov-el** \ˈnäv-əl\ (*adj*)

nov-ice \ˈnäv-əs\ (*n*) beginner. Even a *novice* at working with computers can install *Barron's Computer Study Program for the SAT* by following the easy steps outlined in the user's manual.

nox-ious \ˈnäk-shəs\ (*adj*) harmful. We must trace the source of these *noxious* gases before they asphyxiate us.

\ə\ **abut** \ᵊ\ **kitten, F table** \ər\ **further** \a\ **ash** \ā\ **ace** \ä\ **cot, cart**
\aů\ **out** \ch\ **chin** \e\ **bet** \ē\ **easy** \g\ **go** \i\ **hit** \ī\ **ice** \j\ **job**

nu-ance \'n(y)ü-ˌän(t)s\ (*n*) shade of difference in meaning or color. Jody gazed at the Monet landscape for an hour, appreciating every subtle *nuance* of color in the painting.

nu-bile \'n(y)ü-bəl\ (*adj*) marriageable. Mrs. Bennet, in *Pride and Prejudice* by Jane Austen, was worried about finding suitable husbands for her five *nubile* daughters.

nu-ga-to-ry \'n(y)ü-gə-ˌtōr-ē\ (*adj*) futile; worthless. This agreement is *nugatory* for no court will enforce it.

nu-mis-ma-tist \n(y)ü-'miz-mət-əst\ (*n*) person who collects coins. The *numismatist* had a splendid collection of antique coins.

nup-tial \'nəp-shəl\ (*adj*) related to marriage. Reluctant to be married in a traditional setting, they chose to hold their *nuptial* ceremony at the carousel in Golden Gate Park.

nur-ture \'nər-chər\ (*v*) bring up; feed; educate. The Head Start program attempts to *nurture* prekindergarten children so that they will do well when they enter public school. also (*n*).

nu-tri-ent \'n(y)ü-trē-ənt\ (*n*) nourishing substance. As a budding nutritionist, Kim has learned to design diets that contain foods rich in important basic *nutrients*. also (*adj*).

O

oaf \\'ōf\\ (*n*) stupid, awkward person. "Watch what you're doing, you clumsy *oaf!*" Bill shouted at the waiter who had drenched him with iced coffee.

ob-du-rate \\'äb-d(y)ə-rət\\ (*adj*) stubborn. The manager was *obdurate* in refusing to discuss the workers' grievances.

o-bei-sance \\ō-'bās-ᵊn(t)s\\ (*n*) bow. She made an *obeisance* as the king and queen entered the room.

ob-e-lisk \\'äb-ə-ˌlisk\\ (*n*) tall column tapering and ending in a pyramid. Cleopatra's Needle is an *obelisk* in Central Park, New York City.

o-bese \\ō-'bēs\\ (*adj*) fat. It is advisable that *obese* people try to lose weight.

ob-fus-cate \\'äb-fə-ˌskāt\\ (*v*) confuse; muddle; cause confusion; make unnecessarily complex. Was the president's spokesman trying to clarify the hidden weapons mystery, or was he trying to *obfuscate* the issue so the voters would never figure out what had gone on?

o-bit-u-ar-y \\ə-'bich-ə-ˌwer-ē\\ (*n*) death notice. I first learned of his death when I read the *obituary* in the newspaper.

ob-jec-tive \\əb-'jek-tiv\\ (*adj*) not influenced by emotions; fair. Even though he was her son, she tried to be *objective* about his behavior.

ob-jec-tive \\əb-'jek-tiv\\ (*n*) goal; aim. A degree in medicine was her ultimate *objective*.

o-blig-a-to-ry \\ə-'blig-ə-ˌtōr-ē\\ (*adj*) binding; required. It is *obligatory* that books borrowed from the library be returned within two weeks.

o-blique \\ō-'blēk\\ (*adj*) slanting; deviating from the perpendicular or from a straight line. The sergeant ordered the men to march "*Oblique* Right"; also (*n*).

o-bliq-ui-ty \\ō-'blik-wət-ē\\ (*n*) indirectness; deviation from a vertical or horizontal position; obscurity of ver-

---

bal expression; perversity. Preferring indirection to straightforwardness, James was a master of *obliquity*.

o-blit-er-ate \ə-'blit-ə-ˌrāt\ (*v*) destroy completely. The tidal wave *obliterated* several island villages.

o-bliv-i-on \ə-'bliv-ē-ən\ (*n*) obscurity; forgetfulness. After a brief period of popularity, Hurston's works fell into *oblivion*; no one bothered to reprint them, or even to read them anymore.

ob-liv-i-ous \ə-'bliv-ē-əs\ (*adj*) inattentive or unmindful; wholly absorbed. Deep in her book, Nancy was *oblivious* of the noisy squabbles of her brother and his friends.

ob-lo-quy \'äb-lə-kwē\ (*n*) slander; disgrace; infamy. Condemned by the press, his political reputation in tatters, Eden declared, "I have had enough *obloquy* for one lifetime!"

ob-nox-ious \äb-'näk-shəs\ (*adj*) offensive; objectionable. A sneak and a tattletale, Sid was an *obnoxious* little brat.

ob-scure \äb-'skyu̇(ə)r, əb\ (*adj*) dark; vague; unclear. Even after I read the poem for the fourth time, its meaning was still *obscure*.

ob-scure \äb-'skyü(ə)r, əb\ (*v*) darken; make unclear. At times he seemed purposely to *obscure* his meaning, preferring mystery to clarity.

ob-se-qui-ous \əb-'sē-kwē-əs\ (*adj*) slavishly attentive; servile; sycophantic. Helen valued people who behaved as if they respected themselves; nothing irritated her more than an excessively *obsequious* waiter or a fawning salesclerk.

ob-ses-sion \äb-'sesh-ən\ (*n*) preoccupation; fixation. Ballet, which had been a pastime, began to dominate his life; his love of dancing became an *obsession*.

ob-so-lete \ˌäb-sə-'lēt\ (*adj*) outmoded. The invention of the pocket calculator made the slide rule used by generations of engineers *obsolete*.

\ŋ\ **sing** \ō\ **go** \ȯ\ **law** \ȯi\ **boy** \th\ **thin** \<u>th</u>\ **the** \ü\ **loot** \u̇\ **foot**
\y\ **yet** \zh\ **vision** \à, <u>k</u>, ⁿ, œ, œ̄, ue, ᵫ, ʸ\ *see* Pronunciation Symbols

ob-ste-tri-cian \ˌäb-stə-ˈtrish-ən\ (*n*) physician specializing in delivery of babies. Unlike midwives, who care for women giving birth at home, *obstetricians* generally work in a hospital setting.

ob-strep-er-ous \əb-ˈstrep-(ə-)rəs\ (*adj*) boisterous; noisy. The crowd became *obstreperous* and shouted their disapproval of the proposals made by the speaker.

ob-trude \əb-ˈtrüd\ (*v*) push (oneself or one's ideas) forward or intrude; butt in; stick out or extrude. Because Fanny was reluctant to *obtrude* her opinions about child-raising upon her daughter-in-law, she kept a close watch on her tongue.

ob-tru-sive \əb-ˈtrü-siv\ (*adj*) pushy and presumptuous; blatant; projecting. Mother's *obtrusive* helpfulness infuriated Jim, who insisted he could take care of himself. An *obtrusive* error definitely sticks out.

ob-tuse \äb-ˈt(y)üs\ (*adj*) blunt; stupid. Because Mr. Collins was too *obtuse* to take a hint, Elizabeth finally had to tell him she wouldn't marry him if he were the last man on earth.

ob-vi-ate \ˈäb-vē-ˌāt\ (*v*) prevent; make unnecessary. In the twentieth century people believed electronic communications would *obviate* the need for hard copy; they dreamed of a paperless society.

oc-cult \ə-ˈkəlt\ (*adj*) mysterious; secret; supernatural. Madame Blavatsky's claims to have *occult* knowledge impressed gullible souls who believed in supernatural powers. also (*n*).

oc-u-list \ˈäk-yə-ləst\ (*n*) physician who specializes in treatment of the eyes. In many states, an *oculist* is the only one who may apply medicinal drops to the eyes for the purpose of examining them.

o-di-ous \ˈōd-ē-əs\ (*adj*) hateful; vile. Cinderella's ugly stepsisters had the *odious* habit of popping their zits in public.

\ə\ **abut** \ᵊ\ **kitten**, F **table** \ər\ **further** \a\ **ash** \ā\ **ace** \ä\ **cot, cart**
\aù\ **out** \ch\ **chin** \e\ **bet** \ē\ **easy** \g\ **go** \i\ **hit** \ī\ **ice** \j\ **job**

o-di-um \ˈōd-ē-əm\ (*n*) strong dislike or contempt; hatefulness; disrepute. Unable to bear the *odium* attached to their family name, the killer's parents changed their name and moved away from their hometown.

o-dor-if-er-ous \ˌōd-ə-ˈrif-(ə-)rəs\ (*adj*) giving off an odor. The *odoriferous* spices stimulated his jaded appetite.

o-dor-ous \ˈōd-ə-rəs\ (*adj*) having an odor. This variety of hybrid tea rose is more *odorous* than the one you have in your garden.

of-fi-cious \ə-ˈfish-əs\ (*adj*) meddlesome; excessively pushy in offering one's services. After her long flight, Jill just wanted to nap, but the *officious* bellboy was intent on showing her all the special features of the deluxe suite.

o-gle \ˈōg-əl\ (*v*) look at amorously; make eyes at. At the coffee house, Walter was too shy to *ogle* the pretty girls openly; instead, he peeked out at them from behind his magazine.

ol-fac-to-ry \äl-ˈfak-t(ə-)rē\ (*adj*) concerning the sense of smell. A wine taster must have a discriminating palate and a keen *olfactory* sense, for a good wine appeals both to the taste buds and to the nose.

ol-i-gar-chy \ˈäl-ə-ˌgär-kē\ (*n*) government by a privileged few. One small clique ran the student council: what had been intended as a democratic governing body had become an *oligarchy*.

om-i-nous \ˈäm-ə-nəs\ (*adj*) threatening. Those clouds are *ominous*: they suggest a severe storm is on the way.

om-nip-o-tent \äm-ˈnip-ət-ənt\ (*adj*) all-powerful. Under Stalin, the Soviet government seemed *omnipotent*: no one dared defy the all-powerful State. also (*n*).

om-ni-pres-ent \ˌäm-ni-ˈprez-ᵊnt\ (*adj*) universally present; ubiquitous. The Beatles are a major musical force, whose influence is *omnipresent* in all contemporary popular music.

\ŋ\ sing   \ō\ go   \ȯ\ law   \ȯi\ boy   \th\ thin   \th̲\ the   \ü\ loot   \u̇\ foot
\y\ yet   \zh\ vision   \à, k̲, ⁿ, œ, œ̄, ue, ue̅, ʸ\ *see* Pronunciation Symbols

om·ni·scient \äm-'nish-ənt\ (*adj*) all-knowing. I may not be *omniscient*, but I know a bit more than you do, young man!

om·niv·o·rous \äm-'niv-(ə-)rəs\ (*adj*) eating both plant and animal food, devouring everything. Some animals, including man, are *omnivorous* and eat both meat and vegetables; others are either carnivorous or herbivorous.

on·er·ous \'än-ə-rəs\ (*adj*) burdensome. He asked for an assistant because his work load was too *onerous*. o-nus \'ō-nəs\ (*n*)

on·o·mat·o·poe·ia \,än-ə-,mat-ə-'pē-(y)ə\ (*n*) words formed in imitation of natural sounds. Words like "rustle" and "gargle" are illustrations of *onomatopoeia*.

on·slaught \'än-,slȯt\ (*n*) vicious assault. We suffered many casualties during the unexpected *onslaught* of the enemy troops.

o·nus \'ō-nəs\ (*n*) burden; responsibility. The emperor was spared the *onus* of signing the surrender papers; instead, he relegated the assignment to his generals.

o·pal·es·cent \,ō-pə-'les-ᵊnt\ (*adj*) iridescent; lustrous. The oil slick on the water had an *opalescent*, rainbowlike sheen.

o·paque \ō-'pāk\ (*adj*) dark; not transparent. The *opaque* window shade kept the sunlight out of the room.

o·pi·ate \'ō-pē-ət\ (*n*) sleep producer; deadener of pain. To say that religion is the *opiate* of the people is to condemn religion as a drug that keeps people quiet and submissive to those in power.

op·por·tune \,äp-ər-'t(y)ün\ (*adj*) timely; well chosen. You have come at an *opportune* moment for I need a new secretary.

op·por·tun·ist \,äp-ər-'t(y)ü-nəst\ (*n*) individual who sacrifices principles for expediency by taking advantage of circumstances. Joe is such an *opportunist* that he tripled the price of bottled water and bandages at his store right after the earthquake struck.

\ə\ **abut** \ᵊ\ **kitten, F table** \ər\ **further** \a\ **ash** \ā\ **ace** \ä\ **cot, cart**
\au̇\ **out** \ch\ **chin** \e\ **bet** \ē\ **easy** \g\ **go** \i\ **hit** \ī\ **ice** \j\ **job**

op-pro-bri-ous \ə-'prō-brē-əs\ (*adj*) despicable; disgraceful. Shocked by the students' *opprobrious* conduct, the headmaster had no recourse but to recommend they be expelled.

op-pro-bri-um \ə-'prō-brē-əm\ (*n*) public disgrace or reproach; vilification. How did the Republicans manage to turn the once-honored name of "liberal" into a term of *opprobrium*?

op-ti-cian \äp-'tish-ən\ (*n*) maker and seller of eyeglasses. The patient took the prescription given him by his oculist to the *optician*.

op-ti-mal \'äp-tə-məl\ (*adj*) most favorable. If you wait for the *optimal* moment to act, you may never begin your project. op-ti-mum \äp-tə-məm\ (*n*)

op-ti-mist \'äp-tə-məst\ (*n*) person who looks on the bright side. The pessimist says the glass is half-empty; the *optimist* says it is half-full.

op-tom-e-trist \äp-'täm-ə-trəst\ (*n*) one who fits glasses to remedy visual defects. Although an *optometrist* is qualified to treat many eye disorders, he may not use medicines or surgery in his examinations.

op-u-lence \'äp-yə-lən(t)s\ (*n*) extreme wealth; luxuriousness; abundance. The glitter and *opulence* of the ballroom took Cinderella's breath away.

o-pus \'ō-pəs\ (*n*) work. Although many critics hailed his Fifth Symphony as his greatest work, he did not regard it as his major *opus*.

or-a-to-ri-o \ˌȯr-ə-'tōr-ē-ˌō\ (*n*) dramatic poem set to music. The Glee Club decided to present an *oratorio* during their recital.

or-di-nance \'ȯrd-nən(t)s\ (*n*) decree. Running a red light is a violation of a city *ordinance*.

o-ri-en-ta-tion \ˌōr-ē-ən-'tā-shən\ (*n*) act of finding oneself in society. Freshman *orientation* provides incoming students with an opportunity to learn about their new environment and their place in it.

\ŋ\ sing \ō\ go \ȯ\ law \ȯi\ boy \th\ thin \th\ the \ü\ loot \u̇\ foot
\y\ yet \zh\ vision \ȧ, k̲, ⁿ, œ, œ̄, ue, ūe, y\ *see* Pronunciation Symbols

or-i-fice \\'òr-ə-fəs\ (*n*) mouthlike opening; small opening. The Howe Caverns were discovered when someone observed that a cold wind was issuing from an *orifice* in the hillside.

or-nate \ òr-'nāt\ (*adj*) excessively or elaborately decorated. With its elaborately carved, convoluted lines, furniture of the Baroque period was highly *ornate*.

or-ni-thol-o-gist \ ˌòr-nə-'thäl-ə-jəst\ (*n*) scientific student of birds. Audubon's drawings of American bird life have been of interest not only to the *ornithologists* but also to the general public.

or-ni-thol-o-gy \ ˌòr-nə-'thäl-ə-jē\ (*n*) study of birds. Audubon's studies of American birds greatly influenced the course of *ornithology* in this country.

or-o-tund \ 'òr-ə-ˌtənd\ (*adj*) having a round, resonant quality; inflated speech. The politician found his deep *orotund* voice an asset when he spoke to his constituents.

or-thog-ra-phy \ òr-'thäg-rə-fē\ (*n*) correct spelling. Many of us find English *orthography* difficult to master because so many of our words are not written phonetically.

os-cil-late \ 'äs-ə-ˌlāt\ (*v*) vibrate pendulumlike; waver. It is interesting to note how public opinion *oscillates* between the extremes of optimism and pessimism.

os-si-fy \ 'äs-ə-ˌfī\ (*v*) change or harden into bone. When he called his opponent a "bonehead," he implied that his adversary's brain had *ossified* and that he was not capable of clear thinking.

os-ten-si-ble \ ä-'sten(t)-sə-bəl\ (*adj*) apparent; professed; pretended. Although the *ostensible* purpose of this expedition is to discover new lands, we are really interested in finding new markets for our products.

os-ten-ta-tious \ ˌäs-tən-'tā-shəs\ (*adj*) showy; pretentious; trying to attract attention. Trump's latest casino in Atlantic City is the most *ostentatious* gambling palace in the East: it easily outglitters its competitors.

\ə\ **abut** \ᵊ\ **kitten**, F **table** \ər\ **further** \a\ **ash** \ā\ **ace** \ä\ **cot, cart** \aů\ **out** \ch\ **chin** \e\ **bet** \ē\ **easy** \g\ **go** \i\ **hit** \ī\ **ice** \j\ **job**

os-tra-cize \ˈäs-trə-ˌsīz\ (*v*) exclude from public favor; ban. As soon as the newspapers carried the story of his connection with the criminals, his friends began to *ostracize* him. **os-tra-cism** \ˈäs-trə-ˌsiz-əm\ (*n*)

oust \ˈaůst\ (*v*) expel; drive out. The world wondered if the United States could *oust* Saddam Hussein from power.

o-vert \ō-ˈvərt\ (*adj*) open to view. According to the United States Constitution, a person must commit an *overt* act before he may be tried for treason.

o-ver-ween-ing \ˌō-vər-ˈwē-niŋ\ (*adj*) presumptuous; arrogant. His *overweening* pride in his accomplishments was unjustified.

o-vine \ˈō-ˌvīn\ (*adj*) like a sheep. Cows are bovine, sheep are *ovine*: Little Bo Peep watched over an *ovine* flock, not a bovine herd.

o-void \ˈō-ˌvȯid\ (*adj*) egg-shaped. At Easter she had to cut out hundreds of brightly colored *ovoid* shapes.

P

pach-y-derm \'pak-i-,dərm\ (*n*) thick-skinned animal. The elephant is probably the best-known *pachyderm*.

pac-i-fist \'pas-ə-fəst\ (*n*) one opposed to force; anti-militarist. During the war, *pacifists*, though they refused to bear arms, nevertheless served in the front lines as ambulance drivers and medical corpsmen.

pad-dock \'pad-ək\ (*n*) saddling enclosure at race track; lot for exercising horses. The *paddock* is located directly in front of the grandstand so that all may see the horses being saddled and the jockeys mounted.

pae-an \'pē-ən\ (*n*) song of praise or joy. *Paeans* celebrating the great victory filled the air.

pains-tak-ing \'pān-,stā-kiŋ\ (*adj*) showing hard work; taking great care. The new high-frequency word list is the result of *painstaking* efforts on the part of our research staff.

pal-at-able \'pal-ət-ə-bəl\ (*adj*) agreeable; pleasing to the taste. Neither Jack's underbaked opinions nor his over-cooked casseroles were *palatable* to Jill.

pa-la-tial \pə-'lā-shəl\ (*adj*) magnificent. He proudly showed us through his *palatial* home.

pa-la-ver \pə-'lav-ər\ (*v*) chatter; talk idly; flatter. Don't you have anything better to do than stand on the street corner listening to idle fools *palaver*? also (*n*).

pal-ette \'pal-ət\ (*n*) flat surface on which a painter mixes pigments; range of colors commonly used by a particular artist. The artist's apprentices had the messy job of cleaning his brushes and *palette*. Through chromatic analysis, the forgers were able to match all the colors in Monet's *palette*.

pal-let \'pal-ət\ (*n*) small, poor bed. The weary traveler went to sleep on his straw *pallet*.

pal-li-ate \'pal-ē-,āt\ (*v*) lessen violence (of a disease); alleviate; moderate intensity; gloss over with excuses.

\ə\ abut \ᵊ\ kitten, F table \ər\ further \a\ ash \ā\ ace \ä\ cot, cart
\aú\ out \ch\ chin \e\ bet \ē\ easy \g\ go \i\ hit \ī\ ice \j\ job

Not content merely to *palliate* the patient's sores and cankers, the researcher sought a means of wiping out the disease. pal-li-a-tion \ˌpal-ē-ˈā-shən\ (*n*)

pal-lid \ˈpal-əd\ (*adj*) pale; wan. Because his occupation required that he work at night and sleep during the day, he had an exceptionally *pallid* complexion.

pal-pa-ble \ˈpal-pə-bəl\ (*adj*) tangible; easily perceptible; unmistakable. The patient's enlarged spleen was *palpable*: even the first year medical student could feel it. pal-pa-bly \ˈpal-pə-blē\ (*adv*)

pal-pi-tate \ˈpal-pə-ˌtāt\ (*v*) throb; flutter. As he became excited, his heart began to *palpitate* more and more erratically.

pal-try \ˈpȯl-trē\ (*adj*) insignificant; petty; trifling. One hundred dollars for a genuine imitation Rolex watch! Lady, this is a *paltry* sum to pay for such a high-class piece of jewelry.

pan-a-ce-a \ˌpan-ə-ˈsē-ə\ (*n*) cure-all; remedy for all diseases. The rich youth cynically declared that the *panacea* for all speeding tickets was a big enough bribe.

pan-de-mo-ni-um \ˌpan-də-ˈmō-nē-əm\ (*n*) wild tumult. When the ships collided in the harbor, *pandemonium* broke out among the passengers.

pan-der \ˈpan-dər\ (*v*) cater to the low desires of others. The reviewer accused the makers of *Lethal Weapon* of *pandering* to the masses' taste for violence.

pan-e-gy-ric \ˌpan-ə-ˈjir-ik\ (*n*) formal praise. Blushing at all the praise heaped upon him by the speakers, the modest hero said, "I don't deserve such *panegyrics*."

pan-o-ply \ˈpan-ə-plē\ (*n*) full set of armor. The medieval knight in full *panoply* found his movements limited by the weight of his armor.

pan-o-ra-ma \ˌpan-ə-ˈram-ə\ (*n*) unobstructed view; comprehensive survey; range. From Inspiration Point we

---

\ŋ\ **sing** \ō\ **go** \ȯ\ **law** \ȯi\ **boy** \th\ **thin** \th̲\ **the** \ü\ **loot** \u̇\ **foot** \y\ **yet** \zh\ **vision** \à, k̲, ⁿ, œ, œ̄, ue, ūe, ʸ\ *see* Pronunciation Symbols

viewed the magnificent *panorama* of the Marin headlands and San Francisco Bay.

pan-to-mime \pant-ə-ˌmīm\ (*n*) acting without dialogue. Artists in *pantomime* need no words to communicate with their audience; their only language is gesture. also (*v*).

pa-py-rus \pə-ˈpī-rəs\ (*n*) ancient paper made from stem of papyrus plant. The ancient Egyptians were among the first to write on *papyrus*.

par-a-ble \ˈpar-ə-bəl\ (*n*) short, simple story teaching a moral. Let us apply to our own conduct the lesson that this *parable* teaches.

par-a-digm \ˈpar-ə-ˌdīm\ (*n*) model; example; pattern. Pavlov's experiment in which he trains a dog to salivate on hearing a bell is a *paradigm* of the conditioned-response experiment in behavioral psychology.

par-a-dox \ˈpar-ə-ˌdäks\ (*n*) something apparently contradictory in nature; statement that looks false but is actually correct. Richard presents a bit of a *paradox*, for he is a card-carrying member of both the National Rifle Association and the relatively pacifist American Civil Liberties Union. par-a-dox-i-cal \ par-ə-ˈdäk-si-kəl\ (*adj*); par-a-dox-i-cal-ly \ˌpar-ə-ˈdäk-si-k(ə-)lē\ (*adv*)

par-a-gon \ˈpar-ə-ˌgän\ (*n*) model of perfection. The class disliked her because the teacher was always pointing her out as a *paragon* of virtue.

par-al-lel-ism \ˈpar-ə-ˌlel-ˌiz-əm\ (*n*) state of being parallel; similarity. Although the twins were separated at birth and grew up in different adoptive families, a striking *parallelism* exists between their lives.

pa-ram-et-er \pə-ˈram-ət-ər\ (*n*) boundary; limiting factor; distinguishing characteristic. According to feminist Andrea Dworkin, men have defined the *parameters* of every subject; now women must redefine the limits of each field.

\ə\ **abut** \ᵊ\ **kitten**, F **table** \ər\ **further** \a\ **ash** \ā\ **ace** \ä\ **cot, cart**
\aů\ **out** \ch\ **chin** \e\ **bet** \ē\ **easy** \g\ **go** \i\ **hit** \ī\ **ice** \j\ **job**

par-a-mour \'par-ə-ˌmu̇(ə)r\ (*n*) illicit lover. In Bellini's opera *Norma*, the seduced heroine learns that her faithless *paramour* is seeking to lead astray her friend and fellow priestess.

par-a-noi-a \ˌpar-ə-'noi-ə\ (*n*) psychosis marked by delusions of grandeur or persecution. Suffering from *paranoia*, the patient claimed everyone was out to get him; ironically, his claim was accurate: even *paranoids* have enemies.

par-a-pet \'par-ə-pət\ (*n*) low wall at edge of roof or balcony. The best way to attack the soldiers fighting behind the *parapets* on the roof is by bombardment from the air.

par-a-pher-na-lia \ˌpar-ə-fə(r)-'nāl-yə\ (*n*) equipment; odds and ends. His desk was cluttered with paper, pen, ink, a dictionary, and other *paraphernalia* of the writing craft.

par-a-phrase \'par-ə-ˌfrāz\ (*v*) restate a passage in one's own words while retaining thought of author. In 250 words or less, *paraphrase* this article; also (*n*).

par-a-site \'par-ə-ˌsīt\ (*n*) animal or plant living on another; toady; sycophant. The tapeworm is an example of the kind of *parasite* that may infest the human body. par-a-sit-ic \ˌpar-ə-'sit-ik\ (*adj*); par-a-sit-ism \ par-ə-sə-ˌtiz-əm\ (*n*); par-a-sit-ize \'par-ə-sə-ˌtīz\ (*v*)

pa-ri-ah \pə-'rī-ə\ (*n*) social outcast. If everyone ostracized singer Mariah Carey, would she then be Mariah the *pariah*?

par-i-ty \'par-ət-ē\ (*n*) equality in status or amount; close resemblance. Unfortunately, some doubt exists whether women's salaries will ever achieve *parity* with men's.

par-lance \'pär-lən(t)s\ (*n*) language; idiom. All this legal *parlance* confuses me; I need an interpreter.

par-ley \'pär-lē\ (*n*) conference. The peace *parley* has not produced the anticipated truce. also (*v*).

par-o-dy \'par-əd-ē\ (*n*) humorous imitation; spoof; take-off; travesty. The show *Forbidden Broadway* presents *parodies* spoofing the year's new productions playing on Broadway. also (*v*).

par-ox-ysm \'par-ək-ˌsiz-əm\ (*n*) fit or attack of pain, laughter, rage. When he heard of his sons' misdeeds, he was seized by a *paroxysm* of rage. **par-ox-ys-mal** \ˌpar-ək-'siz-məl\ (*adj*)

par-ry \'par-ē\ (*v*) ward off a blow; deflect. Unwilling to injure his opponent in such a pointless clash, Dartagnan simply tried to *parry* his rival's thrusts. What fun it was to watch Katharine Hepburn and Spencer Tracy *parry* each other's verbal thrusts in their classic screwball comedies!

par-si-mo-ni-ous \ˌpär-sə-'mō-nē-əs\ (*adj*) stingy; excessively frugal. Silas Marner's *parsimonious* nature did not allow him to indulge himself in any luxuries. **par-si-mo-ny** \'pär-sə-ˌmō-nē\ (*n*); **par-si-mo-ni-ous-ly** \ˌpar-sə-'mō-nē-əs-lē\ (*adv*)

par-ti-al-i-ty \ˌpär-shē-'al-ət-ē\ (*n*) inclination; bias. As a judge, not only must I be unbiased, but I must also avoid any evidence of *partiality* when I award the prize. **par-tial** \'pär-shəl\ (*adj*); **par-tial-ly** \'pärsh-(ə-)lē\ (*adv*)

par-ti-san \'pärt-ə-zən\ (*adj*) one-sided; prejudiced; committed to a party. Rather than joining forces to solve our nation's problems, the Democrats and Republicans spend their time on *partisan* struggles. also (*n*).

par-tu-ri-tion \ˌpärt-ə-'rish-ən\ (*n*) delivery; childbirth. The difficulties anticipated by the obstetricians at *parturition* did not materialize; it was a normal delivery.

par-ve-nu \'pär-və-ˌn(y)ü\ (*n*) upstart; newly rich person. Although extremely wealthy, he was regarded as a *parvenu* by the aristocratic members of society.

pas-sé \pa-'sā\ (*adj*) outmoded; old-fashioned. Later choreographers, finding Busby Berkeley's musical

---

\ə\ abut \ᵊ\ kitten, F table \ər\ further \a\ ash \ā\ ace \ä\ cot, cart
\aù\ out \ch\ chin \e\ bet \ē\ easy \g\ go \i\ hit \ī\ ice \j\ job

spectacles *passé*, sought fresh ways to bring music and dance to film.

pas-sive \\'pas-iv\\ (*adj*) not active; acted upon. Mahatma Gandhi urged his followers to pursue a program of *passive* resistance rather than resorting to violence and acts of terrorism. pas-sive-ly \\'pas-iv-lē\\ (*adv*); pas-siv-i-ty \\pa-'siv-ət-ē\\ (*n*)

pas-tiche \\pas-'tēsh\\ (*n*) piece of writing or music made up of borrowed bits and pieces; hodgepodge. Her essay was a *pastiche* of fragments of articles she had found on the Internet.

pas-to-ral \\'pas-t(ə-)rəl\\ (*adj*) rural; simple and peaceful; idyllic; related to shepherds. Tired of city living, Dana dreamed of moving to the country and enjoying a simple *pastoral* life.

pa-tent \\'pat-ᵊnt\\ (*adj*) open for the public to read; obvious. It was *patent* to everyone that the witness spoke the truth. also (*n*).

pa-thet-ic \\pa-'thet-ik\\ (*adj*) causing sadness, compassion, pity; touching. Everyone in the auditorium was weeping by the time he finished his *pathetic* tale about the orphaned boy. pa-thet-i-cal-ly \\pə-'thet-i-k(ə-)lē\\ (*adv*)

path-o-log-i-cal \\,path-ə-'läj-i-kəl\\ (*adj*) related to the study of disease; diseased or markedly abnormal. Jerome's *pathological* fear of germs led him to wash his hands a hundred times a day. pa-thol-o-gy \\pə-'thäl-ə-jē\\ (*n*); pa-thol-o-gist \\pə-'thäl-ə-jəst\\ (*n*)

pa-thos \\'pā-,thäs\\ (*n*) tender sorrow; pity; quality in art or literature that produces these feelings. The quiet tone of *pathos* that ran through the novel never degenerated into the maudlin or the overly sentimental.

pa-ti-na \\pə-'tē-nə\\ (*n*) green crust on old bronze works; tone slowly taken by varnished painting. Judging by the *patina* on this bronze statue, we can conclude that this is the work of a medieval artist.

---

pa-tois \'pa-ˌtwä\ (*n*) local or provincial dialect. His years of study of the language at the university did not enable him to understand the *patois* of the natives.

pa-tri-arch \'pā-trē-ˌärk\ (*n*) father and ruler of a family or tribe. In many primitive tribes, the leader and lawmaker was the *patriarch*. pa-tri-ar-chal \ˌpā-trē-'är-kəl\ (*adj*); pa-tri-arch-ate \'pā-trē-ˌär-kət\ (*n*); pa-tri-ar-chy \'pā-trē-ˌär-kē\ (*n*)

pa-tri-mo-ny \'pa-trə-ˌmō-nē\ (*n*) inheritance from father. As predicted by his critics, he spent his *patrimony* within two years of his father's death. pat-ri-mo-ni-al \ˌpa-trə-'mo-nē-əl\ (*adj*)

pa-tron-ize \'pā-trə-ˌnīz\ (*v*) support; act superior toward; be a customer of. Penniless artists hope to find some wealthy art lover who will *patronize* them. If some condescending wine steward *patronized* me because he saw I knew nothing about fine wine, I'd refuse to *patronize* his restaurant.

pau-ci-ty \'pȯ-sət-ē\ (*n*) scarcity; lack. They closed the restaurant because the *paucity* of customers meant that it was a losing proposition to operate.

pec-ca-dil-lo \ˌpek-ə-'dil-ˌ(ˌ)ō\ (*n*) slight offense. When Peter Piper picked a peck of Polly Potter's pickles, did Pete commit a major crime or just a *peccadillo*?

pe-cu-ni-ar-y \pi-'kyü-nē-ˌer-ē\ (*adj*) pertaining to money. Seldom earning enough to cover their expenses, folk dance teachers work because they love dancing, not because they expect any *pecuniary* reward.

ped-a-gogue \'ped-ə-ˌgäg\ (*n*) teacher; dull and formal teacher. He could never be a stuffy *pedagogue;* his classes were always lively and filled with humor.

ped-ant \'ped-ᵊnt\ (*n*) scholar who overemphasizes book learning or technicalities. His insistence that the book be memorized marked the teacher as a *pedant* rather than a scholar. ped-ant-ry \'ped-ᵊn-trē\ (*n*)

\ə\ **abut** \ᵊ\ **kitten**, F **table** \ər\ **further** \a\ **ash** \ā\ **ace** \ä\ **cot, cart**
\au̇\ **out** \ch\ **chin** \e\ **bet** \ē\ **easy** \g\ **go** \i\ **hit** \ī\ **ice** \j\ **job**

pe-dan-tic \pi-'dant-ik\ (*adj*) showing off learning; bookish. Leavening her decisions with humorous, down-to-earth anecdotes, Judge Judy was not at all the *pedantic* legal scholar. ped-ant \'ped-ᵊnt\ (*n*)

pe-des-tri-an \pə-'des-trē-ən\ (*adj*) ordinary; unimaginative. Unintentionally boring, he wrote page after page of *pedestrian* prose.

pe-di-a-tri-cian \ˌpēd-ē-ə-'trish-ən\ (*n*) expert in children's diseases. The family doctor advised the parents to consult a *pediatrician* about their child's ailment. pe-di-at-rics \ˌpēd-ē-'a-triks\ (*n*); pe-di-at-ric \ˌpēd-ē-'a-trik\ (*n*)

pe-jo-ra-tive \pi-'jȯr-ət-iv\ (*adj*) negative in connotation; having a belittling effect. Instead of criticizing Schwarzenegger's policies, the Democrats made *pejorative* comments about his character.

pell-mell \'pel-'mel\ (*adv*) in confusion; disorderly. The excited students dashed *pell-mell* into the stadium to celebrate the victory.

pel-lu-cid \pe-'lü-səd\ (*adj*) transparent; limpid; easy to understand. After reading these stodgy philosophers, I find Bertrand Russell's witty and *pellucid* prose both entertaining and clear.

pen-ance \'pen-ən(t)s\ (*n*) self-imposed punishment for sin. The Ancient Mariner said, "I have *penance* done and *penance* more will do," to atone for the sin of killing the albatross.

pen-chant \'pen-chənt\ (*n*) strong inclination; liking. Dave has a *penchant* for taking risks: one semester he went steady with three girls, two of whom were stars on the school karate team.

pen-dant \'pen-dənt\ (*adj*) hanging down from something. Her *pendant* earrings glistened in the light.

pen-dent \'pen-dənt\ (*adj*) suspended; jutting; pending. The *pendent* rock hid the entrance to the cave.

---

pen·du·lous \\'pen-jə-ləs\\ *(adj)* hanging; suspended. The *pendulous* chandeliers swayed in the breeze and gave the impression that they were about to fall from the ceiling.

pen·i·tent \\'pen-ə-tənt\\ *(adj)* repentant. When he realized the enormity of his crime, he became remorseful and *penitent;* also *(n).* **pen·i·tence** \\'pen-ə-ten(t)s\\ *(n);* **pen·i·ten·tial** \\ˌpen-ə-'ten-chəl\\ *(adj)*

pen·sive \\'pen(t)-siv\\ *(adj)* dreamily thoughtful; thoughtful with a hint of sadness. The *pensive* lover gazed at the portrait of his beloved and deeply sighed. **pen·sive·ly** \\'pen(t)-siv-lē\\ *(adv)*

pen·um·bra \\pə-'nəm-brə\\ *(n)* partial shadow (in an eclipse). During an eclipse, we can see an area of total darkness and a lighter area that is the *penumbra.*

pe·nu·ri·ous \\pə-'n(y)ur-ē-əs\\ *(adj)* stingy; parsimonious. Constantly worrying about the economy, he became such a penny-pincher that he turned into a close-fisted, *penurious* miser.

pen·u·ry \\'pen-yə-rē\\ *(n)* severe poverty; stinginess. When his pension fund failed, George feared he would end his days in *penury.*

pe·on \\'pē-ˌän\\ *(n)* landless agricultural laborer; bond servant. The land reformers sought to liberate the *peons* and establish them as independent farmers.

per·cus·sion \\pər-'kəsh-ən\\ *(adj)* striking one object against another sharply. The drum is a *percussion* instrument.

per·di·tion \\pər-'dish-ən\\ *(n)* damnation; complete ruin. Praying for salvation, young Daedalus feared he was damned to eternal *perdition.*

per·e·gri·na·tion \\ˌper-ə-grə-'nā-shən\\ *(n)* journey. Auntie Mame was a world traveler whose *peregrinations* took her from Tijuana to Timbuktu.

pe·remp·to·ry \\pə-'rem(p)-t(ə-)rē\\ *(adj)* demanding and leaving no choice. From Jack's *peremptory* knock on

---

\\ə\\ **abut** \\ᵊ\\ **kitten, F table** \\ər\\ **further** \\a\\ **ash** \\ā\\ **ace** \\ä\\ **cot, cart** \\au̇\\ **out** \\ch\\ **chin** \\e\\ **bet** \\ē\\ **easy** \\g\\ **go** \\i\\ **hit** \\ī\\ **ice** \\j\\ **job**

the door, Jill could tell he would not give up until she let him in. pe-remp-to-ri-ly \pə-'rem(p)-t(ə-)rə-ly\ (*adv*)

pe-ren-ni-al \pə-'ren-ē-əl\ (*n*) something long-lasting. These plants are hardy *perennials* and will bloom for many years. also (*adj*). pe-ren-ni-al-ly \pə-'ren-ē-ə-lē\ (*adv*)

per-fid-i-ous \₍ᵢ₎pər-'fid-ē-əs\ (*adj*) treacherous; disloyal. When Caesar realized that Brutus had betrayed him, he reproached his *perfidious* friend. per-fid-i-ous-ly \pər-'fid-ē-əs-lē\ (*adv*)

per-fi-dy \'pər-fəd-ē\ (*n*) violation of a trust. When we learned of his *perfidy,* we were shocked and dismayed.

per-force \pər-'fō(ə)rs\ (*adv*) of necessity. I must *perforce* leave, as my train is about to start.

per-func-to-ry \pər-'fəŋ(k)-t(ə-)rē\ (*adj*) superficial; not thorough; lacking interest, care, or enthusiasm. The auditor's *perfunctory* inspection of the books over-looked many errors. Giving the tabletop only a *perfunctory* swipe with her dust cloth, Betty promised herself she'd clean it more thoroughly tomorrow. per-func-to-ri-ly \pər-'fəŋ(k)-t(ə-)rə-lē\ (*adv*)

pe-rim-e-ter \pə-'rim-ət-ər\ (*n*) outer boundary. To find the *perimeter* of any quadrilateral, we add the four sides.

per-i-pa-tet-ic \ˌper-ə-pə-'tet-ik\ (*adj*) walking about; moving. The *peripatetic* school of philosophy derives its name from the fact that Aristotle walked with his pupils while discussing philosophy with them.

pe-riph-e-ry \pə-'rif-(ə-)rē\ (*n*) edge, especially of a round surface. He sensed that there was something just beyond the *periphery* of his vision. pe-riph-er-al \pə-'rif-(ə-)rəl\ (*adj*)

per-ju-ry \pərj-(ə-)rē\ (*n*) false testimony while under oath. Rather than lie under oath and perhaps be indicted for *perjury*, the witness chose to take the Fifth

---

\ŋ\ **sing**   \ō\ **go**   \ȯ\ **law**   \ȯi\ **boy**   \th\ **thin**   \t͟h\ **the**   \ü\ **loot**   \u̇\ **foot**
\y\ **yet**   \zh\ **vision**   \à, k̲, ⁿ, œ, œ̄, ue, ūe, ʸ\ *see* Pronunciation Symbols

Amendment, refusing to answer any questions on the grounds that he might incriminate himself. per-jure \pər-jər\ (*v*); per-jur-er \'pər-jər-ər\ (*n*)

per-me-a-ble \'pər-mē-ə-bəl\ (*adj*) penetrable; porous; allowing liquids or gas to pass through. If your jogging clothes weren't made out of *permeable* fabric, you'd drown in your own sweat (figuratively speaking). per-me- a-bil-i-ty \,pər-mē-ə-'bil-ət-ē\ (*n*)

per-me-ate \'pər-mē-,āt\ (*v*) pass through, spread. The odor of frying onions *permeated* the air. per-me-a-tion \,pər-mē-'ā-shən\ (*n*)

per-ni-cious \pər-'nish-əs\ (*adj*) very destructive. Crack cocaine has had a *pernicious* effect on urban society: it has destroyed families, turned children into drug dealers, and increased the spread of violent crimes. per-ni-cious-ly \pər-'nish-əs-lē\ (*adv*)

per-or-a-tion \'per-ər-,ā-shən\ (*n*) conclusion of an oration. The largely hortatory *peroration* brought the audience to its feet clamoring for action at its close.

per-pe-trate \'pər-pə-,trāt\ (*v*) commit an offense. Only an insane person could *perpetrate* such a horrible crime. per-pe-tra-tion \,pər-pə-'trā-shən\ (*n*); per-pe-tra-tor \'pər-pə-,trāt-ər\ (*n*)

per-pet-u-al \pər-'pech-(ə-)wəl\ (*adj*) everlasting. Ponce de Leon hoped to find the legendary fountain of *perpetual* youth. per-pet-u-al-ly \pər-'pech-(ə-)wəl-lē\ (*adv*)

per-qui-site \'pər-kwə-zət\ (*n*) any gain above stipulated salary. The *perquisites* attached to this job make it even more attractive than the salary indicates.

per-se-vere \,pər-sə-'vi(ə)r\ (*v*) to persist in an attempt to accomplish a goal, despite difficulty. Despite the church's threats to excommunicate him for heresy, Galileo *persevered* in his belief that the earth moved around the sun.

\ə\ **abut** \ᵊ\ kitten, F table \ər\ **further** \a\ **ash** \ā\ **ace** \ä\ **cot, cart**
\aú\ **out** \ch\ **chin** \e\ bet \ē\ **easy** \g\ **go** \i\ hit \ī\ ice \j\ **job**

per-si-flage \\'pər-si-ˌfläzh\\ (*n*) flippant conversation; banter. Peter Wimsey's constant stream of light *persiflage* and banter disguised his underlying seriousness of mind.

per-sist \\ pər-'sist\\ (*v*) to continue; endure. You will receive poor grades if you *persist* in your poor study habits.

per-son-a-ble \\'pərs-nə-bəl\\ (*adj*) attractive. Though not as strikingly handsome as a movie star, James was nonetheless a *personable* young man.

per-spi-ca-cious \\ˌpər-spə-'kā-shəs\\ (*adj*) having insight; penetrating; astute. "Absolutely brilliant, Holmes!" cried Watson, as Holmes made yet another *perspicacious* deduction. per-spi-cac-i-ty \\ˌpər-spə-'kas-ət-ē\\ (*n*)

per-spi-cu-i-ty \\ˌpər-spə-'kyü-ət-ē\\ (*n*) clearness of expression; freedom from ambiguity. One outstanding feature of this book is its author's *perspicuity*: her meaning is always clear.

per-spic-u-ous \\ pər-'spik-yə-wəs\\ (*adj*) plainly expressed. His *perspicuous* comments eliminated all possibility of misinterpretation.

pert \\'pərt\\ (*adj*) impertinent; forward. The matron in charge of the orphanage thought Annie was *pert* and disrespectful.

per-ti-na-cious \\ˌpərt-ᵊn-'ā-shəs\\ (*adj*) stubborn; persistent. He is bound to succeed because his *pertinacious* nature will not permit him to quit. per-ti-nac-i-ty \\ˌpərt-ᵊn-'as-ət-ē\\ (*n*)

per-ti-nent \\'pərt-ᵊn-ənt\\ (*adj*) to the point; relevant. Virginia Woolf's words on women's rights are as *pertinent* today as they were when she wrote them nearly a century ago. per-ti-nence \\'pərt-ᵊn-ən(t)s\\ (*n*)

per-turb \\ pər-'tərb\\ (*v*) disturb greatly. The thought that electricity might be leaking out of the empty lightbulb sockets *perturbed* Thurber's aunt so much that every night she crept about the house screwing fresh bulbs in the vacant sockets. per-tur-ba-tion \ˌpərt-ər-'bā-shən\ (*n*)

pe-rus-al \pə-'rü-zəl\ (*n*) close reading. Concerned about the possibility of forest fires in her area, Joan decided she needed a careful *perusal* of her home insurance policy to discover exactly what benefits her coverage might provide her. pe-ruse \pə-'rüz\ (*v*)

per-va-sive \pər-'vā-siv\ (*adj*) spread throughout; permeating. The *pervasive* odor of mothballs clung to the clothes and did not fade away until they had been thoroughly aired. per-vade \pər-'vād\ (*adj*)

per-verse \ˌ(ˌ)pər-'vərs\ (*adj*) stubbornly wrongheaded; wicked and perverted. When Jack was in a *perverse* mood, he would do the opposite of whatever Jill asked him. When Hannibal Lecter was in a *perverse* mood, he ate the flesh of his victims. per-verse-ly \pər-'vərs-lē\ (*adv*); per-verse-ness \pər-'vərs-nəs\ (*n*)

per-ver-sion \pər-'vər-zhən\ (*n*) corruption; turning from right to wrong. Hannibal Lecter's cannibalism was an act of *perversion*.

per-ver-si-ty \pər-'vər-sət-ē\ (*n*) stubborn maintenance of a wrong cause. In stubbornly refusing to accede to Jill's reasonable request, Jack acted out of *perversity*.

pes-si-mism \'pəs-ə-ˌmiz-əm\ (*n*) belief that life is basically bad or evil; gloominess. Considering how well you have done in the course so far, you have no real reason for such *pessimism* about your final grade. pes-si-mist \'pəs-ə-məst\ (*n*); pes-si-mis-tic \ˌpes-ə-'mis-tik\ (*adj*)

pes-ti-len-tial \ˌpes-tə-'len-chəl\ (*adj*) causing plague; baneful. People were afraid to explore the *pestilential* swamp. pes-ti-lence \'pes-tə-lən(t)s\ (*n*); pes-ti-len-tial-ly \ˌpes-tə-'lench-(ə-)lē\ (*adv*)

pet-ri-fy \'pe-trə-ˌfī\ (*v*) turn to stone. His sudden, unexpected appearance shocked her into immobility: she was *petrified*. pet-ri-fac-tion \ˌpe-trə-'fak-shən\ (*n*)

\ə\ **abut** \ᵊ\ kitten, F table \ər\ **further** \a\ ash \ā\ **ace** \ä\ cot, cart
\au̇\ **out** \ch\ **chin** \e\ bet \ē\ **easy** \g\ **go** \i\ **hit** \ī\ ice \j\ **job**

pet-u-lant \ 'pech-ə-lənt\ (*adj*) touchy; peevish. If you'd had hardly any sleep for three nights and people kept on phoning and waking you up, you'd sound pretty *petulant*, too. pet-u-lance \ 'pech-ə-lən(t)s\ (*n*); pet-u-lant-ly \ 'pech-ə-lənt-lē\ (*adv*)

phi-al \ 'fī(-ə)l\ (*n*) small bottle. Even though it is small, this *phial* of perfume is expensive.

phi-lan-der \ fə-'lan-dər\ (*v*) make love lightly, flirt. Swearing he had never so much as looked at another woman, Jack assured Jill he was not one to *philander*. phi-lan-der-er \ fə-'lan-dər-ər\ (*n*)

phi-lan-thro-pist \ fə-'lan(t)-thrə-pəst\ (*n*) lover of mankind; doer of good. In his role as *philanthropist* and public benefactor, John D. Rockefeller, Sr., donated millions to charity; as an individual, however, he was a tight-fisted old man. phi-lan-thro-py \ fə-'lan(t)-thrə-pē\ (*n*); phil-an-throp-ic \ ˌfil-ən-'thräp-ik\ (*adj*)

phi-lis-tine \ 'fil-ə-ˌstēn\ (*n*) narrow-minded person, uncultured and exclusively interested in material gain. A *philistine* knows the price of everything, but the value of nothing. also (*adj*).

phi-lol-o-gy \ fə-'läl-ə-jē\ (*n*) study of language. The professor of *philology* advocated the use of Esperanto as an international language. phil-o-log-i-cal \ ˌfil-ə-'läj-i-kəl\ (*adj*); phi-lol-o-gist \ fə-'läl-ə-jəst\ (*n*)

phleg-mat-ic \ fleg-'mat-ik\ (*adj*) calm; not easily disturbed. The nurse was a cheerful but *phlegmatic* person, unexcited in the face of sudden emergencies.

pho-bi-a \ 'fō-bē-ə\ (*n*) morbid fear. His fear of flying was more than mere nervousness; it was a real *phobia.*

phys-i-og-no-my \ ˌfiz-ē-'ä(g)-nə-mē\ (*n*) face. He prided himself on his ability to analyze a person's character by studying his *physiognomy.*

phys-i-o-log-i-cal \ ˌfiz-ē-ə-'läj-i-kəl\ (*adj*) pertaining to the science of the function of living organisms. To

---

\ŋ\ si**ng** \ō\ **go** \o\ **law** \oi\ **boy** \th\ **thin** \<u>th</u>\ **the** \ü\ **loot** \u\ **foot**
\y\ **yet** \zh\ vi**sion** \à, <u>k</u>, ⁿ, œ, œ̄, ue, ū̄e, ʸ\ *see* Pronunciation Symbols

understand this disease fully, we must examine not only its *physiological* aspects but also its psychological elements. phys-i-ol-o-gist \\,fiz-ē-'äl-ə-jəst\ (*n*); phys-i-ol-o-gy \\,fiz-ē-'äl-ə-jē\ (*n*)

pi-ca-resque \\,pik-ə-'resk\ (*adj*) pertaining to rogues in literature. *Tom Jones* has been hailed as one of the best *picaresque* novels in the English language.

pie-bald \'pī-,bȯld\ (*adj*) mottled; spotted. You should be able to identify Polka Dot in this race; it is the only *piebald* horse running. also (*n*).

pied \'pīd\ (*adj*) variegated; multicolored. The *Pied* Piper of Hamelin got his name from the multicolored clothing he wore.

pil-lage \'pil-ij\ (*v*) plunder. The enemy *pillaged* the quiet village and left it in ruins; also (*n*).

pil-lo-ry \'pil-(ə-)rē\ (*v*) punish by placing in a wooden frame and subjecting to ridicule. Even though he was mocked and *pilloried,* he maintained that he was correct in his beliefs. also (*n*).

pin-ion \'pin-yən\ (*v*) restrain. They *pinioned* his arms against his body but left his legs free so that he could move about; also (*n*).

pin-na-cle \'pin-i-kəl\ (*n*) peak. We could see the morning sunlight illuminate the *pinnacle* while the rest of the mountain lay in shadow.

pi-ous \'pī-əs\ (*adj*) devout; religious. The challenge for church people today is how to be *pious* in the best sense, that is, to be devout without becoming hypocritical or sanctimonious. pi-ous-ly \'pī-əs-lē\ (*adv*)

pi-quant \'pē-kənt\ (*adj*) pleasantly tart-tasting; stimulating. The *piquant* sauce added to our enjoyment of the meal. pi-quan-cy \'pē-kən-sē\ (*n*)

pique \'pēk\ (*n*) irritation; resentment. She showed her *pique* by her refusal to appear with the other contestants at the end of the contest. also (*v*).

\ə\ **abut** \ə\ **kitten**, F **table** \ər\ **further** \a\ **ash** \ā\ **ace** \ä\ **cot, cart**
\au̇\ **out** \ch\ **chin** \e\ **bet** \ē\ **easy** \g\ **go** \i\ **hit** \ī\ **ice** \j\ **job**

pith-y \\'pith-ē\ (*adj*) concise; meaningful; substantial; meaty. While other girls might have gone on and on about how uncool Elton was, Cher summed it up in one *pithy* remark: "He's bogus!"

pit-tance \\'pit-ᵊn(t)s\ (*n*) a small allowance or wage. He could not live on the *pittance* he received as a pension and had to look for an additional source of revenue.

pla-cate \\'plāk-ˌāt\ (*v*) pacify; conciliate. The store manager tried to *placate* the angry customer, offering to replace the damaged merchandise or to give back her money right away. pla-ca-ble \\'plak-ə-bəl\ (*adj*)

plac-id \\'plas-əd\ (*adj*) peaceful; calm. Looking at the storm-tossed waters of the lake, Bob wondered how people had ever come to call it Lake *Placid*. pla-cid-i-ty \\pla-'sid-ət-ē\ (*n*); plac-id-ly \\'plas-əd-lē\ (*adv*)

pla-gia-rism \\'plā-jə-ˌriz-əm\ (*n*) theft of another's ideas or writings passed on as original. The teacher could tell that the student had committed *plagiarism* in writing his book report; she could recognize whole paragraphs straight from *Barron's Book Notes*. pla-gia-rize \\'plā-jə-ˌrīz\ (*v*); pla-gia-rist \\'plā-jə-ˌrəst\ (*n*)

plain-tive \\'plānt-iv\ (*adj*) mournful. The dove has a *plaintive* and melancholy call. plain-tive-ly \\'plānt-iv-lē\ (*adv*)

plat-i-tude \\'plat-ə-ˌt(y)üd\ (*n*) trite remark; commonplace statement. In giving advice to his son, old Polonius expressed himself only in *platitudes*; every word out of his mouth was commonplace. plat-i-tu-di-nous \\ˌplat-ə-'t(y)üd-nəs\ (*adj*)

pla-ton-ic \\plə-'tän-ik\ (*adj*) purely spiritual; theoretical; without sensual desire. Accused of impropriety in his dealings with female students, the professor maintained he had only a *platonic* interest in the women involved.

plau-di-to-ry \\'plȯ-də-ˌtȯr-ē\ (*adj*) approving; applauding. The theatrical company reprinted the *plauditory* comments of the critics in its advertisement.

---

plau-si-ble \'plȯ-zə-bəl\ (*adj*) having a show of truth but open to doubt; specious. Your mother made you stay home from school because she needed you to program the VCR? I'm sorry, you'll have to come up with a more *plausible* excuse than that. plau-sibil-i-ty \,plȯ-zə-'bil-ət-ē\ (*n*); plau-si-bly \'plȯ-zə-blē\ (*adv*)

ple-be-ian \pli-'bē-(y)ən\ (*adj*) common; pertaining to the common people. Aristocratic Lady Bracknell scorned the *plebeian* background of her daughter Gwendolyn's suitor: no mere commoner could dare to aspire to the hand of her only child!

pleb-i-scite \'pleb-ə-,sīt\ (*n*) expression of the will of a people by direct election. A matter so important should be decided not by a handful of legislators but by a *plebiscite* of the entire nation.

ple-na-ry \'plē-nə-rē\ (*adj*) complete; full. The union leader was given *plenary* power to negotiate a new contract with the employers.

plen-i-po-ten-tia-ry \,plen-ə-pə-'tench-(ə-)rē\ (*adj*) fully empowered. Since he was not given *plenipotentiary* powers by his government, he could not commit his country without consulting his superiors. also (*n*).

plen-i-tude \'plen-ə-,t(y)üd\ (*n*) abundance; completeness. Looking in the pantry, we admired the *plenitude* of fruits and pickles we had preserved during the summer.

pleth-o-ra \'pleth-ə-rə\ (*n*) excess; overabundance. She offered a *plethora* of reasons for her shortcomings.

plumb \'pləm\ (*v*) examine critically in order to understand; measure depth (by sounding). Try as he would, Watson could never fully *plumb* the depths of Holmes's thought processes.

po-di-a-trist \pə-'dī-ə-trəst\ (*n*) doctor who treats ailments of the feet. He consulted a *podiatrist* about his fallen arches. po-di-a-try \pə-'dī-ə-trē\ (*n*)

\ə\ **abut** \ᵊ\ **kitten,** F **table** \ər\ **further** \a\ **ash** \ā\ **ace** \ä\ **cot, cart**
\au̇\ **out** \ch\ **chin** \e\ **bet** \ē\ **easy** \g\ **go** \i\ **hit** \ī\ **ice** \j\ **job**

po·di·um \\'pōd-ē-əm\\ (*n*) pedestal; raised platform. The audience applauded as the conductor made his way to the *podium.*

poi·gnant \\'poi-nyənt\\ (*adj*) deeply moving; keenly affecting. Watching the tearful reunion of the long-separated mother and child, the social worker was touched by the *poignant* scene. poi·gnan·cy \\'poi-nyən-sē\\ (*n*)

po·lem·ic \\pə-'lem-ik\\ (*n*) controversy; argument in support of a point of view. Lexy was a master of *polemics*; she should have worn a T-shirt with the slogan "Born to Debate." also (*adj*). po·lem·i·cist \\pə-'lem-ə-səst\\ (*n*)

pol·i·tic \\'päl-ə-ˌtik\\ (*adj*) expedient; prudent; well devised. Even though he was disappointed by the size of the bonus he was offered, he did not think it *politic* to refuse it.

pol·i·ty \\'päl-ət-ē\\ (*n*) form of government of a state, nation, church, etc.; body politic. Since each Presbyterian congregation selects its own minister and ruling elders, it is clear the Presbyterian *polity* is fundamentally democratic.

po·lyg·a·mist \\pə-'lig-ə-məst\\ (*n*) one who has more than one spouse at a time. He was arrested as a *polygamist* when his two wives filed complaints about him. po·lyg·a·my \\pə-'lig-ə-mē\\ (*n*); po·lyg·a·mous \\pə-'lig-ə-məs\\ (*adj*)

pol·y·glot \\'päl-i-ˌglät\\ (*adj*) speaking several languages. New York City is a *polyglot* community because of the thousands of immigrants who settle there. also (*n*).

pon·der·ous \\'pän-d(ə-)rəs\\ (*adj*) weighty; unwieldy. His humor lacked the light touch; his jokes were always *ponderous.*

por·tend \\pȯr-'tend\\ (*v*) foretell; presage. The king did not know what these omens might *portend* and asked his soothsayers to interpret them.

\\ŋ\\ **sing** \\ō\\ **go** \\ȯ\\ **law** \\ȯi\\ **boy** \\th\\ **thin** \\<u>th</u>\\ **the** \\ü\\ **loot** \\u̇\\ **foot**
\\y\\ **yet** \\zh\\ **vision** \\à, <u>k</u>, ⁿ, œ, œ̄, ue, ūe, ʸ\\ *see* Pronunciation Symbols

por-tent \'pȯ(ə)r-ˌtent\ (*n*) sign; omen; forewarning. He regarded the black cloud as a *portent* of evil. por-ten-tous \pȯr-'tent-əs\ (*adj*)

port-ly \'pōrt-lē\ (*adj*) stately; stout. The overweight gentleman was shown a size 44 *portly* suit.

pos-ter-i-ty \pä-'ster-ət-ē\ (*n*) descendants; future generations. We hope to leave a better world to *posterity*.

post-hu-mous \'päs-chə-məs\ (*adj*) after death (as of child born after father's death or book published after author's death). The critics ignored his works during his lifetime; it was only after the *posthumous* publication of his last novel that they recognized his great talent.

pos-tu-late \'päs-chə-lət\ (*n*) essential premise; underlying assumption. The basic *postulate* of democracy, set forth in the Declaration of Independence, is that all men are created equal. also (*v*).

po-ta-ble \'pȯt-ə-bəl\ (*adj*) suitable for drinking. The recent drought in the Middle Atlantic states has emphasized the need for extensive research in ways of making seawater *potable*. also (*n*).

po-tent \'pōt-ᵊnt\ (adj) powerful; persuasive; greatly influential. Looking at the expiration date on the cough syrup bottle, we wondered whether the medication would still be *potent*. po-ten-cy \'pōt-ᵊn-sē\ (*n*)

po-ten-tate \'pōt-ᵊn-ˌtāt\ (*n*) monarch; sovereign. The *potentate* spent more time at Monte Carlo than he did at home with his people.

po-ten-tial \pə-'ten-chəl\ (*adj*) expressing possibility; latent.The cello teacher looked on every new pupil as a *potential* Yo-Yo Ma. po-ten-ti-al-i-ty \pə-ˌten-chē-'al-ət-ē\ (*n*); po-ten-tial-ly \pə-'tench-(ə-)lē\ (*adv*)

po-tion \'pō-shən\ (*n*) dose (of liquid). Tristan and Isolde drink a love *potion* in the first act of the opera.

pot-pour-ri \ˌpō-pu̇-'rē\ (*n*) heterogeneous mixture; medley. He offered a *potpourri* of folk songs from many lands.

\ə\ **abut** \ᵊ\ **kitten**, F **table** \ər\ **further** \a\ **ash** \ā\ **ace** \ä\ **cot, cart**
\au̇\ **out** \ch\ **chin** \e\ **bet** \ē\ **easy** \g\ **go** \i\ **hit** \ī\ **ice** \j\ **job**

poul-tice \'pōl-təs\ (*n*) soothing application applied to sore and inflamed portions of the body. The wise woman advised him to apply a flaxseed *poultice* to the inflammation. also (*v*).

prac-ti-ca-ble \'prak-ti-kə-bəl\ (*adj*) feasible. The board of directors decided that the plan was *practicable* and agreed to undertake the project. prac-ti-ca-bil-i-ty \,prak-ti-kə-'bil-ət-ē\ (*n*)

prac-ti-cal \'prak-ti-kəl\ (*adj*) based on experience; useful. He was a *practical* man, opposed to theory. prac-ti-cal-i-ty \,prak-ti-'kal-ət-ē\ (*n*); prac-ti-cal-ly \'prak-ti-k(ə-)lē\ (*adv*)

prag-mat-ic \prag-'mat-ik\ (*adj*) practical (as opposed to idealistic); concerned with the practical worth or impact of something. This coming trip to France should provide me with a *pragmatic* test of the value of my conversational French class.

prag-ma-tist \'prag-mət-əst\ (*n*) practical person. No *pragmatist* enjoys becoming involved in a game he can never win.

prate \'prāt\ (*v*) speak foolishly; boast idly. Despite Elizabeth's obvious disinclination for the topic, Mr. Collins *prated* on and on about his wonderful prospects as a husband, thanks to his noble patron, Lady Catherine de Burgh.

prat-tle \'prat-ᵊl\ (*v*) babble. The little girl *prattled* endlessly about her dolls. also (*n*).

pre-am-ble \'prē-,am-bəl\ (*n*) introductory statement. In the *Preamble* to the Constitution, the purpose of the document is set forth.

pre-car-i-ous \pri-'kar-ē-əs\ (*adj*) uncertain; risky. Saying the stock would be a *precarious* investment, the broker advised her client against purchasing it. pre-car-i-ous-ly \pri-'kar-ē-əs-lē\ (*adv*); pre-car-i-ous-ness \pri-'kar-ē-əs-nəs\ (*n*)

\ŋ\ si**ng**   \ō\ **go**   \ȯ\ **law**   \ȯi\ **boy**   \th\ **thin**   \t̲h̲\ **the**   \ü\ **loot**   \u̇\ **foot**
\y\ **yet**   \zh\ **vision**   \à, ḵ, ⁿ, œ, œ̄, ue, ūe, ʸ\ *see* Pronunciation Symbols

prec-e-dent \'pres-əd-ənt\ (*n*) something preceding in time that may be used as an authority or guide for future action. If I buy you a car for your sixteenth birthday, your brothers will want me to buy them cars when they turn sixteen, too; I can't afford to set such an expensive *precedent*.

pre-cept \'prē-ˌsept\ (*n*) practical rule guiding conduct. "Love thy neighbor as thyself" is a worthwhile *precept*.

prec-i-pice \'pres-(ə-)pəs\ (*n*) cliff; dangerous position. Suddenly Indiana Jones found himself dangling from the edge of a *precipice*.

pre-cip-i-tate \pri-'sip-ət-ət\ (*adj*) rash; premature; hasty; sudden. Though I was angry enough to resign on the spot, I had enough sense to keep myself from quitting a job in such a *precipitate* fashion. pre-cip-i-tate-ly \pri-'sip-ət-ət-lē\ (*adv*); pre-cip-i-tate-ness \pri-'sip-ət-ət-nəss\ (*n*)

pre-cip-i-tate \pri-'sip-ə-ˌtāt\ (*v*) cause to happen; throw headlong; hasten. The removal of American political support *precipitated* the downfall of the Marcos regime.

pre-cip-i-tous \pri-'sip-ət-əs\ (*adj*) steep; overhasty. This hill is difficult to climb because it is so *precipitous*; one slip, and our descent will be *precipitous* as well. pre-cip-i-tous-ly \pri-'sip-ət-əs-lē\ (*adv*)

pre-clude \pri-'klüd\ (*v*) make impossible; eliminate. Because the band was already booked to play in Hollywood on New Year's Eve, that *precluded* their accepting the New Year's Eve gig in London they were offered.

pre-co-cious \pri-'kō-shəs\ (*adj*) advanced in development. Listening to the grown-up way the child discussed serious topics, we couldn't help remarking how *precocious* she was. pre-co-cious-ly \pri-'kō-shəs-lē\ (*adv*); pre-coc-i-ty \pri-'käs-ət-ē\ (*n*)

\ə\ abut \ʼə\ kitten, F table \ər\ further \a\ ash \ā\ ace \ä\ cot, cart
\au̇\ out \ch\ chin \e\ bet \ē\ easy \g\ go \i\ hit \ī\ ice \j\ job

pre-cur-sor \pri-'kər-sər\ (*n*) forerunner. Though Gray and Burns share many traits with the Romantic poets who followed them, most critics consider them *precursors* of the Romantic Movement, not true Romantics.

pred-a-to-ry \'pred-ə-ˌtōr-ē\ (*adj*) devouring; preying upon others; plundering. Not just cats, but a wide variety of *predatory* creatures—owls, hawks, weasels, foxes—catch mice for dinner. A carnivore is by definition *predatory*, for it *preys* on weaker creatures. pred-a-tor \'pred-ət-ər\ (*n*)

pre-di-lec-tion \ˌpred-əl-'ek-shən\ (*n*) partiality; preference. Although Nash wrote all sorts of poetry over the years, he had a definite *predilection* for limericks.

pre-em-i-nent \prē-'em-ə-nənt\ (*adj*) outstanding; superior. The king traveled to Boston because he wanted the *preeminent* surgeon in the field to perform the operation. pre-em-i-nence \prē-'em-ə-nən(t)s\ (*n*); pre-em-i-nent-ly \prē-'em-ə-nənt-lē\ (*adv*)

pre-empt \prē-'em(p)t\ (*v*) head off; forestall by acting first; appropriate for oneself; supplant. Hoping to *preempt* any attempts by the opposition to make educational reform a hot political issue, the candidate set out her own plan to revitalize the public schools. pre-emp-tion \prē-'em(p)-shən\ (*n*)

pref-a-to-ry \'pref-e-ˌtōr-ē\ (*adj*) introductory. The chairman made a few *prefatory* remarks before he called on the first speaker.

pre-hen-sile \prē-'hen(t)-səl\ (*adj*) capable of grasping or holding. Monkeys use not only their arms and legs but also their *prehensile* tails in traveling through the trees.

pre-lude \'prel-ˌ(y)üd\ (*n*) introduction; forerunner. I am afraid that this border raid is the *prelude* to more serious attacks.

pre-med-i-tate \pri-'med-ə-tāt\ (*v*) plan in advance. She had *premeditated* the murder for months, reading about common poisons and buying weed killer that contained arsenic.

pre·mo·ni·tion \ˌprē-mə-ˈnish-ən\ (*n*) forewarning. In horror movies, the hero often has a *premonition* of danger, which he foolishly ignores.

pre·mon·i·to·ry \pri-ˈmän-ə-ˌtor-ē\ (*adj*) serving to warn. You should have visited a doctor as soon as you felt these *premonitory* chest pains.

pre·pon·der·ance \pri-ˈpän-d(ə-)rən(t)s\ (*n*) superiority of power, quantity, etc. The rebels sought to overcome the *preponderance* of strength of the government forces by engaging in guerrilla tactics. pre·pon·der·ant \pri-ˈpänd(ə-)rənt\ (*adj*); pre·pon·der·ant·ly \pri-ˈpän-d(ə-)rənt-lē\ (*adv*); pre·pon·der·ate \pri-ˈpän-də-ˌrāt\ (*v*)

pre·pos·ter·ous \pri-ˈpäs-t(ə-)rəs\ (*adj*) absurd; ridiculous. When he tried to downplay his youthful experiments with marijuana by saying he hadn't inhaled, we all thought, "What a *preposterous* excuse!"

pre·rog·a·tive \pri-ˈräg-ət-iv\ (*n*) privilege; unquestionable right. The president cannot levy taxes; that is the *prerogative* of the legislative branch of government.

pres·age \ˈpres-ij\ (*v*) foretell. The vultures flying overhead *presaged* the discovery of the corpse in the desert.

pre·sen·ti·ment \pri-ˈzent-ə-mənt\ (*n*) feeling something will happen; anticipatory fear; premonition. Saying goodbye at the airport, Jack had a sudden *presentiment* that this was the last time he would see Jill.

pres·tige \pre-ˈstēzh\ (*n*) impression produced by achievements or reputation. Many students want to go to Harvard College not for the education offered but for the *prestige* of Harvard's name. pres·ti·gious \pre-ˈstij-əs\ (*adj*)

pre·sump·tion \pri-ˈzəm(p)-shən\ (*n*) arrogance; effrontery. impertinent boldness; assumption that something is true. You mean you interrupted Bishop Tutu's talk

---

\ə\ **abut** \ᵊ\ **kitten,** F **table** \ər\ **further** \a\ **ash** \ā\ **ace** \ä\ **cot, cart**
\aů\ **out** \ch\ **chin** \e\ **bet** \ē\ **easy** \g\ **go** \i\ **hit** \ī\ **ice** \j\ **job**

with Senator Clinton just to ask for their autographs?
What *presumption*! pre-sump-tive \pri-'zəm(p)-tiv\ (*adj*)

pre-ten-tious \pri-'ten-chəs\ (*adj*) ostentatious; pompous;
making unjustified claims; overly ambitious. None of the
other prize winners are wearing their medals; isn't it a
bit *pretentious* of you to wear yours? pre-ten-tious-ly \
pri-'ten-chəs-lē\ (*adv*); pre-ten-tious-ness \pri-'ten-chəs-
nəs\ (*n*)

pre-ter-nat-u-ral \ˌprēt-ər-'nach(-ə)-rəl\ (*adj*) beyond that
which is normal in nature. John's mother's ability to tell
when he was lying struck him as almost *preternatural.*

pre-text \'prē-ˌtekst\ (*n*) excuse. He looked for a good *pre-
text* to get out of paying a visit to his aunt.

pre-vail \pri-'vā(e)l\ (*v*) induce; triumph over. He tried to
prevail on her to type his essay for him.

prev-a-lent \'prev(-ə)-lənt\ (*adj*) widespread; generally
accepted. A radical committed to social change, Reed
had no patience with the conservative views *prevalent*
in the America of his day.

pre-var-i-cate \pri-'var-ə-ˌkāt\ (*v*) lie. Some people believe
that to *prevaricate* in a good cause is justifiable and
regard the statement as a "white lie." pre-var-i-ca-tion
\pri-ˌvar-ə-'kā-shən\ (*n*); pre-var-i-ca-tor \pri-'var-ə-ˌkāt-
ər\ (*n*)

prim \'prim\ (*adj*) very precise and formal; exceedingly
proper. Never having worked as a governess before,
Jane thought it best to assume a very *prim* and proper
manner, so that her charges would not take liberties with
her. prim-ly \'prim-lē\ (*adv*); prim-ness \'prim-nəs\ (*n*)

pri-mo-gen-i-ture \ˌprī-mō-'jen-ə-ˌchu̇(ə)r\ (*n*) seniority by
birth. By virtue of *primogeniture,* the first-born child
has many privileges denied his brothers and sisters.

pri-mor-di-al \prī-'mȯrd-ē-əl\ (*adj*) existing at the beginning (of time); rudimentary. The Neanderthal Man is
one of our *primordial* ancestors.

\ŋ\ **sing**　\ō\ **go**　\ȯ\ **law**　\ȯi\ **boy**　\th\ **thin**　\t̲h̲\ **the**　\ü\ **loot**　\u̇\ **foot**
\y\ **yet**　\zh\ **vision**　\à, k̲, ⁿ, œ, œ̄, ue, ūe, ʸ\ *see* Pronunciation Symbols

primp \\'primp\\ (*v*) dress or groom oneself with care. She *primps* for hours before a dance.

pris-tine \\'pris-ˌtēn\\ (*adj*) characteristic of earlier times; primitive; unspoiled. This area has been preserved in all its *pristine* wildness.

pri-va-tion \\prī-'vā-shən\\ (*n*) hardship; want. In his youth, he knew hunger and *privation.*

privy \\'priv-ē\\ (*adj*) knowing about something secret; ꞏsecret or hidden; not public. People read fan magazines because they enjoy the feeling of being *privy* to the secrets of the stars. priv-i-ly \\'priv-ə-lē\\ (*adv*)

probe \\'prōb\\ (*v*) explore with tools. The surgeon *probed* the wound for foreign matter before suturing it. also (*n*).

pro-bi-ty \\'prō-bət-ē\\ (*n*) uprightness; incorruptibility. Everyone took his *probity* for granted; his misuse of funds, therefore, shocked us all.

prob-lem-at-ic \\ˌpräb-lə-'mat-ik\\ (*adj*) doubtful; unsettled; questionable; perplexing. Given the way building costs have exceeded estimates for the job, whether the arena will ever be completed is *problematic.*

pro-bos-cis \\prə-'bäs-əs\\ (*n*) long snout; nose. The elephant uses its *proboscis* to handle things and carry them from place to place.

pro-cliv-i-ty \\prō-'kliv-ət-ē\\ (*n*) inclination; natural tendency. Watching the two-year-old voluntarily put away his toys, I was amazed by his *proclivity* for neatness.

pro-cras-ti-nate \\p(r)ə-'kras-tə-ˌnāt\\ (*v*) postpone; delay or put off. Looking at four years of receipts and checks he still had to sort through, Bob was truly sorry he had *procrastinated* for so long and not finished filing his taxes ages ago. pro-cras-ti-na-tion \\p(r)ə-ˌkras-tə-'nā-shən\\ (*n*); pro-cras-ti-na-tor \\p(r)ə-'kras-tə-ˌnāt-ər\\ (*n*)

prod \\'präd\\ (*v*) poke; stir up; urge. If you *prod* him hard enough, he'll eventually clean his room.

\\ə\\ **abut** \\ᵊ\\ **kitten,** F **table** \\ər\\ **further** \\a\\ **ash** \\ā\\ **ace** \\ä\\ **cot, cart**
\\aú\\ **out** \\ch\\ **chin** \\e\\ **bet** \\ē\\ **easy** \\g\\ **go** \\i\\ **hit** \\ī\\ **ice** \\j\\ **job**

prod-i-gal \'präd-i-gəl\ (*adj*) wasteful; reckless with money. Don't be so *prodigal* spending my money; when you've earned some money, you can waste it as much as you want! also (*n*). prod-i-gal-i-ty \,präd-ə-'gal-ət-ē\ (*n*)

pro-di-gious \prə-'dij-əs\ (*adj*) marvelous; enormous. Watching the champion weight lifter heave the weighty barbell to shoulder height and then boost it overhead, we marveled at his *prodigious* strength. pro-di-gious-ly \prə-'dij-əs-lē\ (*adv*)

prod-i-gy \'präd-ə-jē\ (*n*) marvel; highly gifted child. Menuhin was a *prodigy,* performing wonders on his violin when he was barely eight years old.

pro-fane \prō-'fān\ (*v*) violate; desecrate; treat unworthily. The members of the mysterious Far Eastern cult sought to kill the British explorer because he had *profaned* the sanctity of their holy goblet by using it as an ashtray. also (*adj*). prof-a-na-tion \,präf-ə-'nā-shən\ (*n*)

prof-li-gate \'präf-li-gət\ (*adj*) dissipated; wasteful; wildly immoral. Although surrounded by wild and *profligate* companions, she nevertheless managed to retain some sense of decency. also (*n*). prof-li-ga-cy \'präf-li-gə-sē\ (*n*); prof-li-gate-ly \'präf-li-gət-lē\ (*adv*)

pro-fu-sion \prə-'fyü-zhən\ (*n*) overabundance; lavish expenditure; excess. Freddy was so overwhelmed by the *profusion* of choices on the menu that he knocked over his wineglass and soaked his host. Flustered, he made *profuse* apologies to everyone in sight. pro-fuse \prə-'fyüs\ (*adj*); pro-fuse-ly \prə-'fyüs-lē\ (*adv*)

pro-gen-i-tor \prō-'jen-ət-ər\ (*n*) ancestor. The Roth family, whose *progenitors* emigrated from Germany early in the nineteenth century, settled in Peru, Illinois.

prog-e-ny \'präj-(ə-)nē\ (*n*) children; offspring. He was proud of his *progeny* but regarded George as the most promising of all his children.

\ŋ\ sing   \ō\ go   \ȯ\ law   \ȯi\ boy   \th\ thin   \t͟h\ the   \ü\ loot   \u̇\ foot
\y\ yet   \zh\ vision   \à, k̲, ⁿ, œ, œ̄, ue, ūe, ʸ\ *see* Pronunciation Symbols

prog-no-sis \präg-'nō-səs\ (*n*) forecasted course of a disease; prediction. If the doctor's *prognosis* is correct, the patient will be in a coma for at least twenty-four hours.

prog-nos-ti-cate \präg-'näs-tə-ˌkāt\ (*v*) predict. Practitioners of phrenology claimed to be able to *prognosticate* people's moral nature by examining the bumps on their skulls. prog-nos-ti-ca-tion \ₒₗpräg-ˌnäs-tə-'kā-shən\ (*n*); prog-nos-ti-ca-tor \präg-'näs-tə-ˌkāt-ər\ (*n*)

pro-jec-tile \prə-'jek-tᵊl\ (*n*) missile. Man has always hurled *projectiles* at his enemy, whether in the form of stones or of highly explosive shells.

pro-le-tar-i-an \ˌprō-lə-'ter-ē-ən\ (*n*) member of the working class. The aristocrats feared mob rule and gave the right to vote only to the wealthy, thus depriving the *proletarians* of a voice in government; also (*adj*).

pro-lif-ic \prə-'lif-ik\ (*adj*) abundantly fruitful. My editors must assume I'm a *prolific* writer: they expect me to revise six books this year! pro-lif-i-cal-ly \prə-'lif-i-k(ə-)lē\ (*adv*)

pro-lix \prō-'liks\ (*adj*) wordy, to the point of tediousness; verbose. A *prolix* writer, he inevitably tells his readers far more than they ever wanted to know about his subject. pro-lix-i-ty \prō-'lik-sət-ē\ (*n*)

pro-mis-cu-ous \prə-'mis-kyə-wəs\ (*adj*) indiscriminate (often sexually); haphazard; irregular. In the opera *La Bohème,* we get a picture of the *promiscuous* life led by the young artists of Paris. pro-mis-cu-it-y \ˌpräm-əs-'kyü-ət-ē\ (*n*); pro-mis-cu-ous-ly \prə-'mis-kyə-wəs-lē\ (*adv*); pro-mis-cu-ous-ness \pra-'mis-kyə-wəs-nəs\ (*n*)

prom-on-to-ry \'präm-ən-ˌtōr-ē\ (*n*) headland. They erected a lighthouse on the *promontory* to warn approaching ships of their nearness to the shore.

pro-mote \prə-'mōt\ (*v*) help to flourish; advance in rank; publicize. Founder of the Children's Defense Fund,

---

\ə\ **abut** \ᵊ\ **kitten,** F **table** \ər\ **further** \a\ **ash** \ā\ **ace** \ä\ **cot, cart**
\aú\ **out** \ch\ **chin** \e\ **bet** \ē\ **easy** \g\ **go** \i\ **hit** \ī\ **ice** \j\ **job**

Marian Wright Edelman ceaselessly *promotes* the welfare of young people everywhere.

pro·mul·gate \ˈpräm-əl-ˌgāt\ (*v*) proclaim a doctrine or law; make known by official publication. When Moses came down from the mountaintop all set to *promulgate* God's commandments, he was appalled to discover his followers worshipping a golden calf. pro·mul·ga·tion \ˌpräm-əl-ˈgā-shən\ (*n*)

prone \ˈprōn\ (*adj*) inclined to; prostrate. She was *prone* to sudden fits of anger during which she would lie *prone* on the floor, screaming and kicking her heels.

prop·a·gate \ˈpräp-ə-ˌgāt\ (*v*) multiply; spread. Since bacteria *propagate* more quickly in unsanitary environments, it is important to keep hospital rooms clean. prop·a·ga·tion \ˌpräp-ə-ˈgā-shən\ (*n*)

pro·pel·lants \prə-ˈpel-ənts\ (*n*) substances that propel or drive forward. The development of our missile program has forced our scientists to seek more powerful *propellants*.

pro·pen·si·ty \prə-ˈpen(t)-sət-ē\ (*n*) natural inclination. Convinced of his own talent, Sol has an unfortunate *propensity* to belittle the talents of others.

pro·phy·lac·tic \ˌprō-fə-ˈlak-tik\ (*adj*) used to prevent disease. Despite all *prophylactic* measures introduced by the authorities, the epidemic raged until cool weather set in. also (*n*).

pro·pin·qui·ty \pra-ˈpiŋ-kwət-ē\ (*n*) nearness; kinship. Their relationship could not be explained as being based on mere *propinquity*: they were more than relatives; they were true friends.

pro·pi·ti·ate \prō-ˈpish-ē-ˌāt\ (*v*) appease. The natives offered sacrifices to *propitiate* the angry gods. pro·pi·ti·a·tion \prō-ˌpis(h)-ē-ˈā-shən\ (*n*); pro·pi·ti·a·to·ry \prō-ˈpish-(ē-)ə-ˌtōr-ē\ (*adj*)

\ŋ\ **sing** \ō\ **go** \ȯ\ **law** \ȯi\ **boy** \th\ **thin** \t͟h\ **the** \ü\ **loot** \u̇\ **foot**
\y\ **yet** \zh\ **vision** \à, k̲, ⁿ, œ, œ̄, ue, ūe, ʸ\ *see* Pronunciation Symbols

pro-pi-tious \prə-'pish-əs\ (*adj*) favorable; fortunate; advantageous. Chloe consulted her horoscope to see whether Tuesday would be a *propitious* day to dump her boyfriend.

pro-pound \prə-'paúnd\ (*v*) put forth for analysis. In your discussion, you have *propounded* several questions; let us consider each one separately.

pro-pri-ety \p(r)ə-'pri-ət-ē\ (*n*) fitness; correct conduct. Miss Manners counsels her readers so that they may behave with due *propriety* in any social situation and not embarrass themselves.

pro-pul-sive \prə-'pel-siv\ (*adj*) driving forward. The jet plane has a greater *propulsive* power than the engine-driven plane. pro-pul-sion \prə-'pel-shən\ (*n*)

pro-sa-ic \prō-'zā-ik\ (*adj*) dull and unimaginative; matter-of-fact; factual. Though the ad writers came up with a highly creative campaign to publicize the product, the head office rejected it for a more *prosaic*, ordinary approach.

pro-scribe \prō-'skrīb\ (*v*) ostracize; banish; outlaw. Antony, Octavius, and Lepidus *proscribed* all those who had conspired against Julius Caesar. pro-scrip-tion \prō-'skrip-shən\ (*n*)

pros-e-ly-tize \'präs-(ə-)lə-ˌtīz\ (*v*) convert to a religion or belief. In these interfaith meetings, there must be no attempt to *proselytize;* we must respect all points of view.

pros-o-dy \'präs-əd-ē\ (*n*) the art of versification. This book on *prosody* contains a rhyming dictionary as well as samples of the various verse forms.

pros-trate \'präs-ˌtrāt\ (*v*) stretch out full on ground. He *prostrated* himself before the idol. also (*adj*). pros-tra-tion \prä-'strā-shən\ (*n*)

pro-té-gé \'prōt-ə-ˌzhā\ (*n*) person receiving protection and support from a patron. Born with an independent spirit, Cyrano de Bergerac refused to be a *protégé* of Cardinal Richelieu. pro-té-gée \'prōt-ə-ˌzhā\ (*n*)

\ə\ **abut** \ᵊ\ **kitten,** F **table** \ər\ **further** \a\ **ash** \ā\ **ace** \ä\ **cot, cart**
\aú\ **out** \ch\ **chin** \e\ **bet** \ē\ **easy** \g\ **go** \i\ **hit** \ī\ **ice** \j\ **job**

pro-to-col \\'prōt-ə-ˌkol\\ (*n*) diplomatic etiquette. We must run this state dinner according to *protocol* if we are to avoid offending any of our guests.

pro-to-type \\'prōt-ə-ˌtīp\\ (*n*) original work used as a model by others. The National Air and Space Museum displays the Wright brothers' first plane, the *prototype* of all the American aircraft that came after.

pro-tract \\ prō-'trakt\\ (*v*) prolong. Seeking to delay the union members' vote, the management team tried to *protract* the negotiations endlessly.

pro-trude \\ prō-'trüd\\ (*v*) stick out. His fingers *protruded* from the holes in his gloves. pro-tru-sion \\ prō-'trü-zhən\\ (*n*); pro-tru-sive \\ prō-'trü-siv\\ (*adj*)

prov-e-nance \\'präv(-ə)-nən(t)s\\ (*n*) origin or source of something. Scholars argue about the *provenance* of the Bayeux tapestry, with some attributing the embroidery to Queen Matilda and her handmaidens, and others to an unknown group of English embroiderers.

prov-en-der \\'präv-ən-dər\\ (*n*) dry food; fodder. I am not afraid of a severe winter because I have stored a large quantity of *provender* for the cattle.

prov-i-dent \\'präv-əd-ənt\\ (*adj*) displaying foresight; thrifty; preparing for emergencies. In his usual *provident* manner, he had insured himself against this type of loss. prov-i-dent-ly \\'präv-əd-ənt-lē\\ (*adv*)

pro-vin-cial \\ pra-'vin-chəl\\ (*adj*) pertaining to a province; limited in outlook; unsophisticated. As *provincial* governor, Sir Henry administered the Queen's law in his remote corner of Canada. Caught up in local problems, out of touch with London news, he became sadly *provincial*. pro-vin-cial-ism \\ prə-'vin-chəl-ˌiz-əm\\ (*n*)

pro-vi-so \\ prə-'vī-ˌ(ˌ)zo\\ (*n*) stipulation. I am ready to accept your proposal with the *proviso* that you meet your obligations within the next two weeks.

prov-o-ca-tion \\ˌpräv-ə-'kā-shən\\ (*n*) cause for anger or retaliation. In a typical act of *provocation*, the bully kicked sand into the weaker man's face. pro-voc-a-tive \prə-'väk-ət-iv\ (*n*)

prox-im-i-ty \präk-'sim-ət-ē\ (*n*) nearness. Blind people sometimes develop a compensatory ability to sense the *proximity* of objects around them.

prox-y \'präk-sē\ (*n*) authorized agent. Please act as my *proxy* and vote for this slate of candidates. also (*adj*).

pru-dent \'prüd-ᵊnt\ (*adj*) cautious; careful. A miser hoards money not because he is *prudent* but because he is greedy. pru-dence \'prüd-ᵊn(t)s\ (*n*)

prune \'prün\ (*v*) cut away; trim. With the help of her editor, she was able to *prune* her manuscript into publishable form.

pru-ri-ent \'prur-ē-ənt\ (*adj*) having or causing lustful thoughts and desires. Aroused by his *prurient* impulses, the dirty old man leered at the sweet young thing and offered to give her a sample of his "prowess." pru-ri-ence \'prur-ē-ən(t)s\ (*n*)

pseud-o-nym \'süd-ᵊn-ˌim\ (*n*) pen name. Samuel Clemens's *pseudonym* was Mark Twain. pseud-on-y-mous \sü-'dän-ə-məs\ (*adj*)

psy-che \'sī-kē\ (*n*) soul; mind. It is difficult to delve into the *psyche* of a human being.

psy-chi-a-trist \sə-'kī-ə-trəst\ (*n*) a doctor who treats mental diseases. *Psychiatrists* often need long conferences with their patients before they can diagnose their patients' mental twists. psy-chi-a-try \sə-'kī-ə-trē\ (*n*); psy-chi-at-ric \ˌsī-kē-'a-trik\ (*adj*)

psy-cho-path-ic \ˌsī-kə-'path-ik\ (*adj*) pertaining to mental derangement. The *psychopathic* patient suffers more frequently from a disorder of the nervous system than from a diseased brain. psy-cho-path \'sī-kə-ˌpath\ (*n*)

psy-cho-sis \sī-'kō-səs\ (*n*) mental disorder. Szasz brilliantly sums up the difference between neurosis and *psychosis* by asserting that, while the neurotic has problems, the *psychotic* has solutions.

\ə\ **abut** \ᵊ\ **kitten,** F **table** \ər\ **further** \a\ **ash** \ā\ **ace** \ä\ **cot, cart**
\aů\ **out** \ch\ **chin** \e\ **bet** \ē\ **easy** \g\ **go** \i\ **hit** \ī\ **ice** \j\ **job**

pu·er·ile \\'pyu̇(-ə)r-al\\ (*adj*) childish; immature. Throwing tantrums! You should have outgrown such *puerile* behavior years ago. pu-eril-i-ty \\,pyu̇(-ə)r-'il-ət-ē\\ (*n*)

pu·gi·list \\'pyü-jə-ləst\\ (*n*) boxer. The famous *pugilist* Cassius Clay changed his name to Muhammad Ali.

pug·na·cious \\,pəg-'nā-shəs\\ (*adj*) combative; disposed to fight. "Put up your dukes!" he cried, doubling up his fists to show how *pugnacious* he was. pug-nac-i-ty \\,pəg-'nas-ət-ē\\ (*n*)

puis·sant \\'pwis-ᵊnt\\ (*adj*) powerful; strong; potent. "All bow," cried the herald, "to the most mighty and *puissant* Emperor of Japan!" puis-sance \\'pwis-ᵊn(t)s\\ (*n*)

pul·chri·tude \\'pəl-krə-,t(y)üd\\ (*n*) beauty; comeliness. I do not envy the judges who have to select this year's Miss America from this collection of female *pulchritude.* pul-chri-tu-di-nous \\,pəl-krə-'t(y)üd-nəs\\ (*adj*)

pul·mo·nar·y \\'pu̇l-mə-,ner-ē\\ (*adj*) pertaining to the lungs. Smoking tobacco can exacerbate many chronic *pulmonary* conditions, such as asthma and emphysema.

pul·sate \\'pəl-,sāt\\ (*v*) throb. We could see the blood vessels in his temple *pulsate* as he became more angry. pul-sa-tion \\,pəl-'sā-shən\\ (*n*)

pum·mel \\'pəm-əl\\ (*v*) beat or pound with fists. Swinging wildly, Pammy *pummeled* her brother around the head and shoulders.

punc·til·i·ous \\,pəŋ(k)-'til-ē-əs\\ (*adj*) laying stress on niceties of conduct or form; minutely attentive to fine points (perhaps too much so). Percy is *punctilious* about observing the rules of etiquette whenever Miss Manners invites him to stay.

pun·dit \\'pən-dət\\ (*n*) authority on a subject; learned person; expert. Some authors who write about the SAT and GRE as if they are *pundits* actually know very little about the tests.

pun·gent \\'pən-jənt\\ (*adj*) stinging; caustic. The *pungent* odor of ripe Gorgonzola cheese appealed to Simone but

\\ŋ\\ sing \\ō\\ go \\ȯ\\ law \\ȯi\\ boy \\th\\ thin \\<u>th</u>\\ the \\ü\\ loot \\u̇\\ foot
\\y\\ yet \\zh\\ vision \\à, <u>k</u>, ⁿ, œ, œ̄, ue, ūe, ʸ\\ *see* Pronunciation Symbols

made Stanley gag. **pun·gen·cy** \\'pən-jən-sē\ (*n*); **pun·gent·ly** \pən-jənt-lē\ (*adv*)

pu·ni·tive \\'pyü-nət-iv\ (*adj*) punishing. He asked for *punitive* measures against the offender.

pu·ny \\'pyü-nē\ (*adj*) insignificant; tiny; weak. Our *puny* efforts to stop the flood were futile.

pur·ga·to·ry \\'pər-gə-ˌtōr-ē\ (*n*) place of spiritual expiation. Do modern celebrities agree with Bulwer-Lytton's comment that to have fame is *purgatory*, but to lose it is hell? **pur·ga·tor·i·al** \ˌpər-gə-'tōr-ē-əl\ (*adj*)

purge \\'pərj\ (*v*) remove or get rid of something unwanted; free from blame or guilt; cleanse or purify. When the Communist government *purged* the party to get rid of members suspected of capitalist sympathies, they sent the disloyal members to labor camps in Siberia. also (*n*).

pur·loin \ˌ(ˌ)pər-'lȯin\ (*v*) steal. In the story, "The *Purloined* Letter," Poe points out that the best hiding place is often the most obvious place.

pur·port \\'pər-ˌpō(ə)rt \ (*n*) intention; meaning. If the *purport* of your speech was to arouse the rabble, you succeeded admirably. also (*v*).

pur·vey·or \ ˌ(ˌ)pər-'vā-ər\ (*n*) furnisher of foodstuffs; caterer. As a *purveyor* of rare wines and viands, he traveled through France and Italy every year in search of new products to sell. **pur·vey** \ ˌ(ˌ)pər-'vā\ (*v*); **pur·vey·ance** \ˌ(ˌ)pər-'vā-ən(t)s\ (*n*)

pur·view \\'pər-ˌvyü\ (*n*) scope. The sociological implications of these inventions are beyond the *purview* of this book.

pu·sil·lan·i·mous \ˌpyü-sə-'lan-ə-məs\ (*adj*) cowardly; fainthearted. In *The Wizard of Oz*, Dorothy's friend the Cowardly Lion wishes he were brave and not *pusillanimous*. **pu·sil·la·nim·i·ty** \ˌpyü-sə-lə-'nim-ət-ē\ (*n*)

\ə\ **abut** \ᵊ\ **kitten**, F **table** \ər\ **further** \a\ **ash** \ā\ **ace** \ä\ **cot, cart**
\au̇\ **out** \ch\ **chin** \e\ **bet** \ē\ **easy** \g\ **go** \i\ **hit** \ī\ **ice** \j\ **job**

pu-ta-tive \'pyüt-ət-iv\ (*adj*) supposed; reputed. Although scholars have their doubts, the *putative* author of this work is Massinger.

pu-trid \'pyü-trəd\ (*adj*) foul; rotten; decayed. From the *putrid* smell when we removed the bandage, we could tell the wound had turned gangrenous. pu-trid-i-ty \pyü-'trid-ət-ē\ (*n*)

py-ro-ma-ni-ac \ˌpī-rō-'mā-nē-ˌak\ (*n*) person with an irresistible desire to set things on fire. The detectives searched the area for the *pyromaniac* who had set these costly fires. py-ro-ma-ni-a \ˌpī-rō-'mā-nē-ə\ (*n*)

Q

quack \'kwak\ (*n*) charlatan; imposter. Don't let this *quack* fool you with his extravagant claims: he can't cure you. also (*adj*).

quad-ru-ped \'kwäd-,rə-ped\ (*n*) four-footed animal. Most mammals are *quadrupeds*.

quaff \'kwäf\ (*v*) drink with relish. As we *quaffed* our ale, we listened to the gay songs of the students in the tavern. also (*n*).

quag-mire \'kwag-,mī(ə)r\ (*n*) soft wet boggy land; complex or dangerous situation from which it is difficult to free oneself. Up to her knees in mud, Myra wondered how on earth she was going to extricate herself from this *quagmire*.

quail \'kwā(ə)l\ (*v*) cower; lose heart. He was afraid that he would *quail* in the face of danger.

qual-i-fied \'kwäl-ə-,fīd\ (*adj*) limited; restricted. Unable to give the candidate full support, the mayor gave him only a *qualified* endorsement. (secondary meaning) qual-i-fy \'kwäl-ə-,fī\ (*v*)

qualm \'kwäm\ (*n*) misgiving; uneasy fear, especially about matters of conscience. I have no *qualms* about giving this assignment to Helen; I know she will handle it admirably.

quan-da-ry \'kwän-d(ə-)rē\ (*n*) dilemma. When the two colleges to which he had applied accepted him, he was in a *quandary* as to which one he should attend.

quar-an-tine \'kwȯr-ən-,tēn\ (*n*) isolation of person or ship to prevent spread of infection. We will have to place this house under *quarantine* until we determine the exact nature of the disease. also (*v*).

quar-ry \'kwȯr-ē\ (*n*) victim; object of a hunt. The police closed in on their *quarry*.

quar-ry \'kwȯr-ē\ (*v*) dig into. They *quarried* blocks of marble out of the hillside. also (*n*).

\ə\ **abut** \ʾ\ **kitten, F table** \ər\ **further** \a\ **ash** \ā\ **ace** \ä\ **cot, cart**
\au̇\ **out** \ch\ **chin** \e\ **bet** \ē\ **easy** \g\ **go** \i\ **hit** \ī\ **ice** \j\ **job**

quay \kē\ (*n*) dock; landing place. Because of the captain's carelessness, the ship crashed into the *quay*.

quea-sy \'kwē-zē\ (*adj*) easily nauseated; squeamish. As the ship left the harbor, he became *queasy* and thought that he was going to suffer from seasickness.

quell \'kwel\ (*v*) extinguish; put down; quiet. Miss Minchin's demeanor was so stern and forbidding that she could *quell* any unrest among her students with one intimidating glance.

quer-u-lous \'kwer-(y)ə-ləs\ (*adj*) fretful; whining. Even the most cheerful and agreeable toddlers can begin to act *querulous* if they miss their nap.

queue \'kyü\ (*n*) line. They stood patiently in the *queue* outside the movie theater.

quib-ble \'kwib-əl\ (*n*) minor objection or complaint. Aside from a few hundred teensy-weensy *quibbles* about the set, the script, the actors, the director, the costumes, the lighting, and the props, the hypercritical critic loved the play. also (*v*).

qui-es-cent \kwī-'es-ᵊnt\ (*adj*) at rest; dormant; temporarily inactive. After the great eruption, fear of Mount Etna was great; people did not return to cultivate its rich hillside lands until the volcano had been *quiescent* for a full two years.

qui-e-tude \'kwī-ə-ˌt(y)üd\ (*n*) tranquillity. He was impressed by the air of *quietude* and peace that pervaded the valley.

quin-tes-sence \kwin-'tes-ᵊn(t)s\ (*n*) purest and highest embodiment. Gandhi maintains that to befriend someone who regards himself as your enemy is the *quintessence* of true religion.

quip \'kwip\ (*n*) taunting remark. She was a bit too free with her *quips* and sarcastic comments. also (*v*).

quirk \'kwərk\ (*n*) startling twist; caprice. By a *quirk* of fate, he found himself working for the man whom he had discharged years before.

\ŋ\ si**ng** \ō\ g**o** \ȯ\ l**aw** \ȯi\ b**oy** \th\ **th**in \t͟h\ **th**e \ü\ l**oo**t \u̇\ f**oo**t
\y\ **y**et \zh\ vi**s**ion \à, k̲, ⁿ, œ, ō͞e, ue, ū͞e, ʸ\ *see* Pronunciation Symbols

quix·ot·ic \kwik-'sät-ik\ *(adj)* idealistic but impractical. Constantly coming up with *quixotic*, unworkable schemes to save the world, Simon has his heart in the right place, but his head somewhere off in the clouds.

quiz·zi·cal \'kwiz-i-kəl\ *(adj)* teasing; bantering; mocking; curious. When the skinny teenager tripped over his own feet stepping into the bullpen, Coach raised one *quizzical* eyebrow, shook his head, and said, "Okay, kid. You're here, let's see what you've got."

quo·rum \'kwōr-əm\ *(n)* number of members necessary to conduct a meeting. The senator asked for a roll call to determine whether a *quorum* was present.

R

ra-bid \rab-əd\ (*adj*) like a fanatic; furious. He was a *rabid* follower of the Dodgers and watched them play whenever he could go to the ball park.

ra-con-teur \rak-ˌän-'tər\ (*n*) storyteller. My father was a gifted *raconteur* with an unlimited supply of anecdotes.

rail \rā(ə)l\ (*v*) scold; rant. You may *rail* at him all you want; you will never change him.

rai-ment \rā-mənt\ (*n*) clothing. "How can I go to the ball?" asked Cinderella. "I have no *raiment* fit to wear."

rak-ish \rā-kish\ (*adj*) stylish; sporty. He wore his hat at a *rakish* and jaunty angle.

ram-i-fi-ca-tion \ˌram-ə-fə-'kā-shən\ (*n*) branching out; subdivision. We must examine all the *ramifications* of this problem.

ram-i-fy \ram-ə-ˌfī\ (*v*) divide into branches or subdivisions. When the plant begins to *ramify,* it is advisable to nip off most of the new branches.

ramp \ramp\ (*n*) slope; inclined plane. The nursing home was built with *ramps* instead of stairs in order to enable people in wheelchairs to move easily from room to room and floor to floor.

ram-pant \ram-pənt\ (*adj*) rearing up on hind legs; unrestrained. The *rampant* weeds in the garden killed all the flowers that had been planted in the spring.

ram-part \ram-ˌpärt\ (*n*) defensive mound of earth. From the *ramparts* we watched the fighting continue.

ran-cid \ran(t)-səd\ (*adj*) having the odor of stale fat. The *rancid* odor filling the ship's galley nauseated the crew.

ran-cor \raŋ-kər\ (*n*) bitterness; hatred. Thirty years after the war, she could not let go of the past but was still consumed with *rancor* against the foe.

ran-kle \raŋ-kəl\ (*v*) irritate; fester. The memory of having been jilted *rankled* him for years.

rant \rant\ (*v*) rave; talk excitedly; scold; make a grandiloquent speech. When he heard that I'd totaled the family car, Dad began to *rant* at me like a complete madman. also (*n*).

ra-pa-cious \rə-'pā-shəs\ (*adj*) predatory; greedy; plundering. Hawks and other *rapacious* birds play an important role in the "balance of nature"; therefore, they are protected throughout North America.

rap-proche-ment \rap-ˌrōsh-'mäⁿ\ (*n*) reconciliation. Both sides were eager to effect a *rapprochement* but did not know how to bring about harmony.

rar-e-fied \rar-ə-ˌfīd\ (*adj*) made less dense [of a gas]. The mountain climbers had difficulty breathing in the *rarefied* atmosphere.

raspy \ras-pē\ (*adj*) grating; harsh. The sergeant's *raspy* voice grated on the recruits' ears.

ra-ti-o-ci-na-tion \ˌrat-ē-ˌōs-ᵊn-'ā-shən\ (*n*) reasoning; act of drawing conclusions from premises. While Watson was a man of average intelligence, Holmes was a genius, whose gift for *ratiocination* made him a superb detective.

ra-tio-na-lize \rash-nə-ˌlīz\ (*v*) give a plausible reason for an action in place of a true, less admirable one; offer an excuse. When David told gabby Gabrielle he couldn't give her a ride to the dance because he had no room in the car, he was *rationalizing*; actually, he couldn't stand being cooped up in a car with anyone who talked as much as she did.

rau-cous \rȯ-kəs\ (*adj*) harsh and shrill; disorderly and boisterous. The *raucous* crowd of New Year's Eve revelers got progressively noisier as midnight drew near.

rav-age \rav-ij\ (*v*) plunder; despoil. The marauding army *ravaged* the countryside. also (*n*).

rav-en-ous \rav-(ə-)nəs\ (*adj*) extremely hungry. The *ravenous* dog upset several garbage pails in its search for food.

\ə\ **abut** \ᵊ\ kitten, F table \ər\ f**urther** \a\ ash \ā\ ace \ä\ cot, cart
\au̇\ **out** \ch\ chin \e\ bet \ē\ easy \g\ go \i\ hit \ī\ ice \j\ job

raze \'rāz \ (*v*) destroy completely. The owners intend to *raze* the hotel and erect an office building on the site.

re·ac·tion·ar·y \rē-'ak-shə-ˌner-ē\ (*adj*) recoiling from progress; politically ultraconservative. Opposing the use of English in worship services, *reactionary* forces in the church fought to reinstate the mass in Latin. also (*n*).

realm \'relm\ (*n*) kingdom; field or sphere. In the animal *realm*, the lion is the king of beasts.

re·bate \'re-ˌbāt\ (*n*) discount. We offer a *rebate* of ten percent to those who pay cash. also (*v*).

re·buff \ri-'bəf\ (*v*) reject sharply; snub. She *rebuffed* his invitation so smoothly that he did not realize he had been snubbed.

re·cal·ci·trant \ri-'kal-sə-trənt\ (*adj*) obstinately stubborn; determined to resist authority; unruly. Which animal do you think is more *recalcitrant*, a pig or a mule?

re·cant \ri-'kant\ (*v*) disclaim or disavow; retract a previous statement; openly confess error. Hoping to make Joan of Arc *recant* her sworn testimony, her English captors tried to convince her that her visions had been sent to her by the Devil.

re·ca·pit·u·late \ˌrē-kə-'pich-ə-ˌlāt\ (*v*) summarize. Let us *recapitulate* what has been said thus far before going ahead.

re·ces·sion \ri-'sesh-ən\ (*n*) withdrawal; retreat; time of low economic activity. The slow *recession* of the flood waters created problems for the crews working to restore power to the area.

re·cid·i·vism \ri-'sid-ə-ˌviz-əm\ (*n*) habitual return to crime. Prison reformers in the United States are disturbed by the high rate of *recidivism;* the number of men serving second and third terms in prison indicates the failure of the prisons to rehabilitate the inmates.

re·cip·i·ent \ri-'sip-ē-ənt\ (*n*) receiver. Although he had been the *recipient* of many favors, he was not grateful to his benefactor.

\ŋ\ sing \ō\ go \ò\ law \òi\ boy \th\ thin \th\ the \ü\ loot \u̇\ foot
\y\ yet \zh\ vision \à, k̲, ⁿ, œ, œ̄, ue, ue̅, ʸ\ *see* Pronunciation Symbols

re-cip-ro-cal \ri-'sip-rə-kəl\ *(adj)* mutual; exchangeable; interacting. The two nations signed a *reciprocal* trade agreement. also *(n)*.

re-cip-ro-cate \ri-'sip-rə-ˌkāt\ *(v)* repay in kind. If they invite us to dinner, we shall have to *reciprocate* and invite them here.

re-cluse \rek-ˌlüs\ *(n)* hermit; loner. Disappointed in love, Miss Emily became a *recluse*; she shut herself away in her empty mansion and refused to see another living soul.

rec-on-cile \rek-ən-ˌsīl\ *(v)* correct inconsistencies; become friendly after a quarrel. Each month when we try to *reconcile* our checkbook with the bank statement, we quarrel. However, despite these monthly lovers' quarrels, we always manage to *reconcile*.

re-con-dite \rek-ən-ˌdīt\ *(adj)* abstruse; profound; hidden from view. He read many obscure and *recondite* books in order to obtain the material for his scholarly thesis.

re-con-nais-sance \ri-'kän-ə-zən(t)s\ *(n)* survey of enemy by soldiers; reconnoitering. If you encounter any enemy soldiers during your *reconnaissance,* capture them for questioning.

re-count \(ˈ)re-'kaủnt\ *(v)* tell; narrate. We always looked forward to our visits to my grandfather's home because he would *recount* fascinating stories from his youth. also *(n)*.

re-course \ˈrē-ˌkō(ə)rs\ *(n)* resorting to help when in trouble. The boy's only *recourse* was to appeal to his father for aid.

rec-re-ant \ˈrek-rē-ənt\ *(n)* coward; betrayer of faith. The disciples shunned him as a *recreant* who had abandoned their faith. also *(adj)*.

re-crim-i-na-tion \ri-ˌkrim-ə-'nā-shən\ *(n)* countercharges. Loud and angry *recriminations* were her answer to his accusations.

---

rec-ti-fy \'rek-tə-ˌfī\ (*v*) set right; correct. You had better send a check to *rectify* your account before American Express cancels your credit card.

rec-ti-tude \'rek-tə-ˌt(y)üd\ (*n*) uprightness; moral virtue; correctness of judgment. The Eagle Scout was a model of *rectitude*.

re-cum-bent \ri-'kəm-bənt\ (*adj*) reclining; lying down completely or in part. The command "AT EASE" does not permit you to take a *recumbent* position.

re-cu-per-ate \ri-'k(y)ü-pə-ˌrāt\ (*v*) recover. The doctors were worried because the patient did not *recuperate* as rapidly as they had expected.

re-cur-rent \ri-'kər-ənt\ (*adj*) occurring again and again. A motif is a *recurrent* theme or melodic passage that crops up again and again in an artist's or composer's work.

re-cu-sant \'rek-yə-zənt\ (*adj*) refusing to comply (applied specifically to those who refused to conform to Church of England practices). In the sixteenth century, *recusant* Roman Catholics who refused to attend Church of England services faced heavy fines and possible confiscation of their property. also (*n*). re-cu-san-cy \'rek-yə-zən-sē\ (*n*)

red-o-lent \'red-əl-ənt\ (*adj*) fragrant; odorous; suggestive of an odor. Even though it is February, the air is *redolent* of spring.

re-doubt-a-ble \ri-'daut-ə-bəl\ (*adj*) formidable; causing fear. During the Cold War period, neighboring countries tried not to offend the Russians because they could be *redoubtable* foes.

re-dress \ri-'dres\ (*n*) remedy; compensation. Do you mean to tell me that I can get no *redress* for my injuries? also (*v*).

re-dun-dant \ri-'dən-dənt\ (*adj*) superfluous; repetitious; excessively wordy. The bottle of wine I brought to

---

\ŋ\ sing \ō\ go \ò\ law \òi\ boy \th\ thin \t͟h\ the \ü\ loot \u̇\ foot
\y\ yet \zh\ vision \à, ǩ, ⁿ, œ, œ̄, ue, ūe, ʸ\ *see* Pronunciation Symbols

Bob's was certainly *redundant*: how was I to know Bob owned a winery? In your essay, you repeat several points unnecessarily; try to be less *redundant* in the future.

reek \rēk\ (*v*) emit (odor). The room *reeked* with stale tobacco smoke. also (*n*).

re-fec-to-ry \ri-'fek-t(ə-)rē\ (*n*) dining hall. In this huge *refectory,* we can feed the entire monastic order at one sitting.

re-frac-tion \ri-'frak-shən\ (*n*) bending of a ray of light. When you look at a stick inserted in water, it looks bent because of the *refraction* of the light by the water.

re-frac-to-ry \ri-'frak-t(ə-)rē\ (*adj*) stubborn; unmanageable. Though his jockey whipped him, the *refractory* horse stubbornly refused to enter the starting gate.

re-fur-bish \ri-'fər-bish\ (*v*) renovate; make bright by polishing. The furniture in the lobby was worn, the paint faded; clearly, it was time to *refurbish* the lobby.

ref-u-ta-tion \ˌref-yủ-'tā-shən\ (*n*) disproof of opponents' arguments. Cooley's aphorism, "Sleaze is a point-by-point *refutation* of elegance," sums up the inherent conflict between vulgarity and refinement.

re-fute \ri-'fyüt\ (*v*) disprove. The defense called several respectable witnesses who were able to *refute* the false testimony of the prosecution's only witness.

re-gal \'rē-gəl\ (*adj*) royal. The young prince has a *regal* manner.

re-gale \ri-'gā(ə)l\ (*v*) entertain. John *regaled* us with tales of his adventures in Africa.

re-gat-ta \ri-'gät-ə\ (*n*) boat or yacht race. Many boating enthusiasts followed the *regatta* in their own yachts.

re-gen-er-a-tion \ri-jen-ə-'rā-shən\ (*n*) renewal or restoration (of a bodily part); spiritual rebirth. Hoping for insights into healing human injuries, biologists study the process of *regeneration* in lizards that regrow lost tails.

\ə\ **abut** \ᵊ\ **kitten,** F **table** \ər\ **further** \a\ **ash** \ā\ **ace** \ä\ **cot, cart**
\aů\ **out** \ch\ **chin** \e\ **bet** \ē\ **easy** \g\ **go** \i\ **hit** \ī\ **ice** \j\ **job**

reg·i·cide \'rej-ə-ˌsīd\ (*n*) murder of a king or queen. The death of Mary Queen of Scots was an act of *regicide.*

re·gime \rā-'zhēm\ (*n*) method or system of government. When a Frenchman mentions the Old *Regime,* he refers to the government existing before the revolution.

reg·i·men \'rej-ə-mən\ (*n*) systematic plan, especially for improving health. I hope the results warrant our living under this strict and inflexible *regimen* of exercise.

re·ha·bil·i·tate \ˌrē-(h)ə-'bil-ə-ˌtāt\ (*v*) restore to proper condition. We must *rehabilitate* those whom we send to prison.

re·im·burse \ˌrē-əm-'bərs\ (*v*) repay. Let me know what you have spent and I will *reimburse* you.

re·it·er·ate \rē-'it-ˌə-rāt\ (*v*) repeat. She *reiterated* her instructions to make sure everyone understood them.

re·ju·ve·nate \ri-'jü-və-ˌnāt\ (*v*) make young again. The charlatan claimed that his elixir would *rejuvenate* the aged and weary.

rel·e·gate \'rel-ə-ˌgāt\ (*v*) banish to an inferior position; delegate; assign. After Ralph dropped his second tray of drinks that week, the manager swiftly *relegated* him to a minor post cleaning up behind the bar.

rel·e·van·cy \'rel-ə-vən-sē\ (*n*) pertinence; reference to the case in hand. Consider the *relevancy* of Virginia Woolf's essays to women today; it's as if Woolf in the 1930s foresaw our current struggles. rel·e·vant \'rel-ə-vənt\ (*adj*)

re·lin·quish \ri-'liŋ-kwish\ (*v*) give up something with reluctance; yield. Once you become accustomed to fringe benefits like expense account meals and a company car, it's very hard to *relinquish* them.

rel·ish \'rel-ish\ (*v*) savor; enjoy. Watching Peter enthusiastically chow down, I thought, "Now there's a man who *relishes* a good dinner!" also (*n*).

re·luc·tant \ri-'lək-tənt\ (*adj*) unwilling; hesitant. I was *reluctant* to run for office a second time after my first unsuccessful attempt.

\ŋ\ si**ng** \ō\ **go** \ȯ\ **law** \ȯi\ **boy** \th\ **thin** \<u>th</u>\ **the** \ü\ **loot** \u̇\ **foot**
\y\ **yet** \zh\ **vision** \à, <u>k</u>, ⁿ, œ, œ̄, ue, ūe, ʸ\ *see* Pronunciation Symbols

re-me-di-a-ble \ri-'mēd-ē-ə-bəl\ (*adj*) reparable. Let us be grateful that the damage is *remediable*.

re-me-di-al \ri-'mēd-ē-əl\ (*adj*) curative; corrective. Because he was a slow reader, he decided to take a course in *remedial* reading.

rem-i-nis-cence \,rem-ə-'nis-ᵊn(t)s\ (*n*) recollection. Her *reminiscences* of her experiences are so fascinating that she ought to write a book.

re-miss \ri-'mis\ (*adj*) negligent. When the prisoner escaped, the guard was charged with having been *remiss* in his duty.

rem-nant \'rem-nənt\ (*n*) remainder. I suggest that you wait until the store places the *remnants* of these goods on sale.

re-mon-strate \ri-'män-,strāt \ (*v*) protest. Although the pastor tried to *remonstrate* about the lack of police protection in the area, the authorities were deaf to his *remonstrances*.

re-morse \ri-'mȯ(ə)rs\ (*n*) guilt; self-reproach. The murderer felt no *remorse* for his crime.

re-mu-ner-a-tive \ri-'myü-nə-rət-iv\ (*adj*) compensating; rewarding. I find my new work so *remunerative* that I may not return to my previous employment. re-mu-ner-a-tion \ri-,myü-nə-rā-shən\ (*n*)

rend \'rend\ (*v*) split; tear apart. In his grief, he tried to *rend* his garments.

ren-der \'ren-dər\ (*v*) deliver; provide; represent. He *rendered* aid to the needy and indigent.

ren-dez-vous \'rän-di-,vü\ (*n*) meeting place. The two fleets met at the *rendezvous* at the appointed time. also (*v*).

ren-di-tion \ren-'dish-ən\ (*n*) artistic interpretation of a song, etc.; translation. The audience enthusiastically cheered her *rendition* of the aria.

ren-e-gade \'ren-i-,gād\ (*n*) deserter; traitor. Because he had abandoned his post and joined forces with the

---

\ə\ **abut** \ᵊ\ **kitten, F table** \ər\ **further** \a\ **ash** \ā\ **ace** \ä\ **cot, cart**
\aú\ **out** \ch\ **chin** \e\ **bet** \ē\ **easy** \g\ **go** \i\ **hit** \ī\ **ice** \j\ **job**

Indians, his fellow officers considered the hero of *Dances with Wolves* a *renegade*. also (*adj*).

re-nounce \ri-'naùn(t)s\ (*v*) abandon; disown; repudiate. Even though she knew she would be burned at the stake as a witch, Joan of Arc refused to *renounce* her belief that her voices came from God.

ren-o-vate \'ren-ə-ˌvāt\ (*v*) restore to good condition; renew. We *renovated* our kitchen, replacing the old cabinets and countertop and installing new appliances.

re-nun-ci-a-tion \ri-ˌnən(t)-sē-ˌā-shən\ (*n*) giving up; renouncing. Do not sign this *renunciation* of your right to sue until you have consulted a lawyer.

rep-a-ra-ble \'rep-(ə-)rə-bəl\ (*adj*) capable of being repaired. Fortunately, the damage to our car was *reparable*, and after two weeks in the shop it looks brand new.

rep-a-ra-tion \ˌrep-ə-'rā-shən\ (*n*) amends; compensation. At the peace conference, the defeated country promised to pay *reparations* to the victors.

rep-ar-tee \ˌrep-ər-'tē\ (*n*) clever reply. Always quick with a clever comeback, Dorothy Parker had the gift of *repartee*.

re-pel-lent \ri-'pel-ənt\ (*adj*) driving away; unattractive. Mosquitoes find the odor so *repellent* that they leave any spot where this liquid has been sprayed. also (*n*).

re-per-cus-sion \ˌrē-pər-'kəsh-ən\ (*n*) result or impact (of an event, etc.); rebound; reverberation. The brothers' quarrel had serious *repercussions*, for it led to their estrangement.

rep-er-toire \'rep-ə(r)-ˌtwär\ (*n*) list of works of music, drama, etc., a performer is prepared to present. The opera company decided to include *Madame Butterfly* in its *repertoire* for the following season.

re-plen-ish \ri-'plen-ish\ (*v*) fill up again. Before she could take another backpacking trip, Carla had to *replenish* her stock of freeze-dried foods.

\ŋ\ sing   \ō\ go   \ò\ law   \òi\ boy   \th\ thin   \ŧħ\ the   \ü\ loot   \ù\ foot
\y\ yet   \zh\ vision   \à, ḵ, ⁿ, œ, œ̄, ue, ūe, ʸ\ *see* Pronunciation Symbols

re-plete \ri-'plēt\ (*adj*) filled to the brim or to the point of being stuffed; abundantly supplied. The movie star's memoir was *replete* with juicy details about the love life of half of Hollywood.

rep-li-ca \'rep-li-kə\ (*n*) copy. Are you going to hang this *replica* of the Declaration of Independence in the classroom or in the auditorium?

re-pos-i-to-ry \ri-'päz-ə-ˌtōr-ē\ (*n*) storehouse. Libraries are *repositories* of the world's best thoughts.

rep-re-hen-si-ble \ˌrep-ri-'hen(t)-sə-bəl\ (*adj*) deserving blame. Shocked by the viciousness of the bombing, politicians of every party uniformly condemned the terrorists' *reprehensible* act.

re-prieve \ri-'prēv\ (*n*) temporary stay. During the twenty-four-hour *reprieve,* the lawyers sought to make the stay of execution permanent. also (*v*).

rep-ri-mand \'rep-rə-ˌmand\ (*v*) reprove severely. She was afraid that her parents would *reprimand* her when they saw her report card. also (*n*).

re-pri-sal \ri-'prī-zəl\ (*n*) retaliation. I am confident that we are ready for any *reprisals* the enemy may undertake.

rep-ro-bate \'rep-rə-ˌbāt\ (*n*) person hardened in sin, devoid of a sense of decency. I cannot understand why he has so many admirers if he is the *reprobate* you say he is.

rep-ro-ba-tion \ˌrep-rə-'bā-shən\ (*n*) severe disapproval. The students showed their *reprobation* of his act by refusing to talk with him.

re-prove \ri-'prüv\ (*v*) censure; rebuke. Though Aunt Bea at times had to *reprove* Opie for inattention in church, she believed he was at heart a God-fearing lad.

re-pu-di-ate \ri-'pyüd-ē-ˌāt\ (*v*) disown; disavow. On separating from Tony, Tina announced that she would *repudiate* all debts incurred by her soon-to-be ex-husband.

re-pug-nance \ri-'pəg-nən(t)s\ (*n*) loathing. While some people like earthworms, others find them disgusting and view them with *repugnance*.

\ə\ abut \ᵊ\ kitten, F table \ər\ **further** \a\ **ash** \ā\ **ace** \ä\ cot, **cart**
\aů\ **out** \ch\ **chin** \e\ bet \ē\ **easy** \g\ go \i\ hit \ī\ ice \j\ job

re-qui-em \'rek-wē-əm\ (*n*) mass for the dead; dirge. They played Mozart's *Requiem* at the funeral.

req-ui-site \'rek-wə-zət\ (*n*) necessary requirement. Many colleges state that a student must offer three years of a language as a *requisite* for admission; also (*adj*).

re-quite \ri-'kwīt\ (*v*) repay; revenge. The wretch *requited* his benefactors by betraying them.

re-scind \ri-'sind \ (*v*) cancel. Because of the public outcry against the new taxes, the senator proposed a bill to *rescind* the unpopular financial measure. re-scis-sion \ri-'sizh-ən\ (*n*)

re-serve \ri-'zərv\ (*n*) self-control; care in expressing oneself. She was outspoken and uninhibited; he was cautious and inclined to *reserve*. (secondary meaning) re-served \ri-'zərvd\ (*adj*)

res-i-due \'rez-ə-ˌd(y)ü\ (*n*) remainder; balance. In his will, he requested that after payment of debts, taxes, and funeral expenses, the *residue* be given to his wife.

re-signed \ri-'zīnd\ (*adj*) unresisting; patiently submissive. Bob Cratchit was too *resigned* to his downtrodden existence to protest Scrooge's bullying. res-ig-na-tion \rez-ig-'nā-shən\ (*n*)

re-sil-ient \ri-'zil-yənt\ (*adj*) elastic; having the power of springing back. Highly *resilient*, steel makes excellent bedsprings.

re-solve \ri-'zälv\ (*v*) decide; settle; solve. Holmes *resolved* to travel to Bohemia to *resolve* the dispute between Irene Adler and the King.

re-solve \ri-'zälv\ (*n*) determination. Nothing could shake his *resolve* that his children would get the best education that money could buy; also (*v*).

res-o-nant \'rez-ᵊn-ənt\ (*adj*) echoing; resounding; deep and full in sound. The deep, *resonant* voice of actor James Earl Jones makes him particularly effective on stage.

---

re-spite \'res-pət\ (*n*) interval of relief; time for rest; delay in punishment. For David, the two weeks vacationing in New Zealand were a delightful *respite* from the pressures of his job.

re-splen-dent \ri-'splen-dənt\ (*adj*) dazzling; glorious; brilliant. While all the adults were commenting how glorious the emperor looked in his *resplendent* new clothes, one little boy was heard to say, "But he's naked!"

re-spon-sive-ness \ri-'spän(t)-siv-nəs\ (*n*) state of reacting readily to appeals, orders, etc. The audience cheered and applauded, delighting the performers by its *responsiveness.*

res-ti-tu-tion \res-tə-'t(y)ü-shən\ (*n*) reparation; indemnification. He offered to make *restitution* for the window broken by his son.

res-tive \'res-tiv\ (*adj*) restlessly impatient; obstinately resisting control. Waiting impatiently in line to see Santa Claus, even the best-behaved children grow *restive* and start to fidget.

re-strained \ri-'strānd\ (*adj*) held in check; under control; limited. The artist's *restrained* use of color was considered subtle by some, and dull by others.

re-sur-gent \ri-'sər-jənt\ (*adj*) experiencing renewal; rising again. Tourists who had shunned Times Square for its seediness are once again flocking to the *resurgent* midtown area.

re-sus-ci-tate \ri-'səs-ə-ˌtāt\ (*v*) revive. The lifeguard managed to *resuscitate* the drowning victim by applying artificial respiration.

re-tal-i-ate \ri-'tal-ē-ˌāt\ (*v*) repay in kind (usually for bad treatment). Because everyone knew the Princeton Band had stolen Brown's mascot, the entire Princeton student body expected Brown to *retaliate*.

re-ten-tive \ri-'tent-iv\ (*adj*) able to retain or keep; able to remember. Priding herself on her *retentive* memory, she claimed she never forgot a face.

\ə\ **abut** \ᵊ\ **kitten,** F **table** \ər\ **further** \a\ **ash** \ā\ **ace** \ä\ **cot, cart**
\au̇\ **out** \ch\ **chin** \e\ **bet** \ē\ **easy** \g\ **go** \i\ **hit** \ī\ **ice** \j\ **job**

ret·i·cence \'ret-ə-sən(t)s\ (*n*) reserve; uncommunicativeness; inclination to be silent. The other students' attempts to get Silent Sam to speak only increased Sam's *reticence.*

ret·i·nue \'ret-ᵊn-,(y)ü\ (*n*) following; attendants. The queen's *retinue* followed her down the aisle.

re·tir·ing \ri-'tī(ə)r-iŋ\ (*adj*) modest; shy. Given Susan's *retiring* personality, no one expected her to take up public speaking.

re·tort \ri-'tó(ə)rt\ (*n*) quick, sharp reply. Even when it was advisable for her to keep her mouth shut, she was always ready with a quick *retort.* also (*v*).

re·trac·tion \ri-'trak-shən\ (*n*) withdrawal. He dropped his libel suit after the newspaper published a *retraction* of its statement.

re·trench \ri-'trench\ (*v*) cut down; economize. If they were to be able to afford to send their children to college, they would have to *retrench.*

ret·ri·bu·tion \re-trə-'byü-shən\ (*n*) vengeance; compensation; punishment for offenses. The evangelist maintained that an angry deity would exact *retribution* from the sinners.

re·trieve \ri-'trēv\ (*v*) recover; find and bring in. The intelligent dog quickly learned to *retrieve* the game killed by the hunter. also (*n*).

ret·ro·ac·tive \re-trō-'ak-tiv\ (*adj*) taking effect prior to its enactment (as a law) or imposition (as a tax). Because the new pension law was *retroactive* to the first of the year, even though Martha had retired in February she was eligible for the pension.

ret·ro·grade \'re-trə-,grād\ (*v*) go backwards; degenerate. Instead of advancing, academic standards today have *retrograded.* also (*adv, adj*).

ret·ro·spec·tive \re-trə-'spek-tiv\ (*adj*) looking back on the past. The Museum of Graphic Arts is holding a *ret-*

---

rospective showing of the paintings of Michael Whelan over the past two decades. also (*n*).

rev-el-ry \'rev-əl-rē\ (*n*) boisterous merrymaking. New Year's Eve is a night of *revelry.*

re-ver-ber-ate \ri-'vər-bə-ˌrāt\ (*v*) echo; resound. The entire valley *reverberated* with the sound of the church bells.

re-vere \ri-'vi(ə)r\ (*v*) respect; honor. In Asian societies, people *revere* their elders.

rev-er-ie \'rev-(ə-)rē\ (*n*) daydream; musing. He was awakened from his *reverie* by the teacher's question.

re-vile \ri-'vī(ə)l\ (*v*) attack with abusive language; vilify. Though most of his contemporaries *reviled* Captain Kidd as a notorious, bloody-handed pirate, some of his fellow merchant-captains believed him innocent of his alleged crimes.

re-vul-sion \ri-'vəl-shən\ (*n*) sudden violent change of feeling; reaction. Many people in this country who admired dictatorships underwent a *revulsion* when they realized what Hitler and Mussolini were trying to do.

rhap-so-dize \'rap-sə-ˌdīz\ (*v*) to speak or write in an exaggeratedly enthusiastic manner. She greatly enjoyed her Hawaiian vacation and *rhapsodized* about it for weeks.

rhet-o-ric \'ret-ə-rik\ (*n*) art of effective communication; insincere language. All writers, by necessity, must be skilled in *rhetoric*. rhe-tor-i-cal \ri-'tòr-i-kəl\ (*adj*)

rheum-y \'rü-mē\ (*adj*) pertaining to a discharge from nose and eyes. His *rheumy* eyes warned us that he was coming down with a cold.

rib-ald \'rib-əld\ (*adj*) wanton; profane. He sang a *ribald* song that offended many of us.

rife \'rīf \ (*adj*) abundant; current. Discontent was *rife* among the early settlers, who had not foreseen the harshness of life in the New World.

\ə\ abut \ᵊ\ kitten, F table \ər\ **further** \a\ **ash** \ā\ **ace** \ä\ **cot, cart**
\aù\ **out** \ch\ **chin** \e\ **bet** \ē\ **easy** \g\ **go** \i\ **hit** \ī\ **ice** \j\ **job**

rift \rift\ (*n*) opening; break. The plane was lost in the stormy sky until the pilot saw the city through a *rift* in the clouds.

rig-or \rig-ər\ (*n*) severity. Many settlers could not stand the *rigors* of the New England winters.

ris-i-ble \riz-ə-bəl\ (*adj*) inclined to laugh; ludicrous. His remarks were so *risible* that the audience howled with laughter. ris-i-bil-i-ty \riz-ə-'bil-ət-ē\ (*n*)

ris-qué \ri-'skā\ (*adj*) verging upon the improper; off-color. Please do not tell your *risqué* anecdotes at this party.

roan \rōn\ (*adj*) brown mixed with gray or white. She was given her choice of three horses: a dark-tailed bay, a glossy brown chestnut, a *roan* with its coat flecked with white. also (*n*).

ro-bust \rō-'bəst\ (*adj*) vigorous; strong. The candidate for the football team had a *robust* physique.

ro-co-co \rə-'kō-(ˌ)kō\ (*adj*) ornate; highly decorated. The *rococo* style in furniture and architecture, marked by scrollwork and excessive decoration, flourished during the middle of the eighteenth century. also (*n*).

ro-se-ate \'rō-zē-ət\ (*adj*) rose-colored; overly optimistic. Seeing the *roseate* sunset, she made a *roseate* prediction of fine weather the next day; unfortunately, it poured.

ros-ter \räs-tər\ (*n*) list. They print the *roster* of players in the season's program.

ros-trum \räs-trəm\ (*n*) platform for speech-making; pulpit. The crowd murmured angrily and indicated that they did not care to listen to the speaker who was approaching the *rostrum.*

rote \rōt\ (*n*) repetition. He recited the passage by *rote,* giving no indication he understood what he was saying.

ro-tun-da \rō-'tən-də\ (*n*) circular building or hall covered with a dome. His body lay in state in the *rotunda* of the Capitol.

\ŋ\ sing   \ō\ go   \ȯ\ law   \ȯi\ boy   \th\ thin   \t͟h\ the   \ü\ loot   \u̇\ foot
\y\ yet   \zh\ vision   \à, ḵ, ⁿ, œ, œ̄, ue, ūe, ʸ\ *see* Pronunciation Symbols

ro-tun-di-ty \rō-'tən-dət-ē\ (*n*) roundness; sonorousness of speech. Short, squat, round as a bowling ball, he was the very model of *rotundity*. ro-tund \rō-'tənd\ (*adj*)

rout \raüt\ (*v*) stampede; drive out; defeat decisively. The reinforcements were able to *rout* the enemy. also (*n*).

rub-ble \rəb-əl\ (*n*) fragments. Ten years after World War II, some of the *rubble* left by enemy bombings could still be seen.

ru-bi-cund \rü-bi-ₚkənd\ (*adj*) having a healthy reddish color; ruddy; florid. Flushed from his labors, the farmer owed his *rubicund* complexion to his active outdoor life.

rud-dy \rəd-ē\ (*adj*) reddish; healthy-looking. His *ruddy* features indicated that he had spent much time in the open.

ru-di-men-ta-ry \ˌrüd-ə-'ment ə-rē\ (*adj*) not developed; elementary. His dancing was limited to a few *rudimentary* steps.

rue-ful \rü-fəl\ (*adj*) regretful (often quizzically); sorrowful; pitiable. Looking at the stack of dirty dishes awaiting her, she gave a *rueful* grin, shrugged, and set to work.

ruf-fi-an \rəf-ē-ən\ (*n*) bully; scoundrel. The *ruffians* threw stones at the police.

ru-mi-nate \rü-mə-ˌnāt\ (*v*) chew over and over (mentally, or, like cows, physically); mull over; ponder. Unable to assimilate the baffling events of the day, Reuben *ruminated* about them till four in the morning.

rum-mage \rəm-ij\ (*v*) ransack; thoroughly search. When we *rummaged* through the trunks in the attic, we found many souvenirs of our childhood days. also (*n*).

ruse \rüs\ (*n*) trick; stratagem. You will not be able to fool your friends with such an obvious *ruse*.

rus-tic \rəs-tik\ (*adj*) pertaining to country people; uncouth. The backwoodsman looked out of place in his *rustic* attire. also (*n*).

\ə\ abut \ˀ\ kitten, F table \ər\ **further** \a\ ash \ā\ **ace** \ä\ cot, cart
\aù\ **out** \ch\ **chin** \e\ bet \ē\ **easy** \g\ **go** \i\ hit \ī\ ice \j\ **job**

rus-ti-cate \'rəs-ti-ˌkāt\ (*v*) banish to the country, dwell in the country. I like city life so much that I can never understand how people can *rusticate* in the suburbs.

ruth-less \'rüth-ləs\ (*adj*) pitiless; cruel. Captain Hook was a dangerous, *ruthless* villain who would stop at nothing to destroy Peter Pan.

S

sac-cha-rine \\'sak-(ə-)rən\\ *(adj)* cloyingly sweet. She tried to ingratiate herself, speaking sweetly and smiling a *saccharine* smile.

sac-er-do-tal \\sas-ər-'dōt-ᵊl\\ *(adj)* priestly. The priest decided to abandon his *sacerdotal* duties and enter the field of politics.

sac-ri-le-gious \\sak-rə-'lij-əs\\ *(adj)* desecrating; profane. To steal an altar cloth is a *sacrilegious* act.

sac-ro-sanct \\'sak-rō-,saŋ(k)t\\ *(adj)* most sacred; inviolable. The brash insurance salesman invaded the *sacrosanct* privacy of the office of the president of the company.

sa-dis-tic \\sə-'dis-tik\\ *(adj)* inclined to cruelty. If we are to improve conditions in this prison, we must first get rid of the *sadistic* warden. **sa-dism** \\'sa-,diz-əm\\ *(n)*

saf-fron \\'saf-rən\\ *(adj)* orange-colored; colored like the autumn crocus. The Halloween cake was decorated with *saffron*-colored icing.

sa-ga \\'säg-ə\\ *(n)* Scandinavian myth; any legend. This is a *saga* of the sea and the men who risk their lives on it.

sa-ga-cious \\sə-'gā-shəs\\ *(adj)* perceptive; shrewd; having insight. My father was a *sagacious* judge of character: he could spot a phony a mile away.

sa-lient \\'sā-lyənt\\ *(adj)* protruding; strikingly conspicuous; jumping. Good readers quickly grasp the *salient* and significant points of a passage; indeed, the ideas almost leap out at them, demanding their attention. also *(n)*.

sa-line \\'sā-,lēn\\ *(adj)* salty. For a viral sore throat, gargle with a warm *saline* solution; the salt reduces swelling and discomfort.

sal-low \\'sal-(,)ō\\ *(adj)* yellowish; sickly in color. Never dress someone with *sallow* skin in pale blue or apple green: they'll look as if they have jaundice.

---

sa·lu·bri·ous \sə-'lü-brē-əs\ (*adj*) promoting good health; healthful. The health resort advertised the *salubrious* properties of the waters of its famous hot springs.

sal·u·ta·ry \'sal-yə-ˌter-ē\ (*adj*) tending to improve; beneficial; wholesome. The punishment had a *salutary* effect on the boy, who became a model student. also (*n*).

sal·vage \'sal-vij\ (*v*) rescue from loss. All attempts to *salvage* the wrecked ship failed; also (*n*).

sanc·ti·mo·ni·ous \ ˌsaŋ(k)-tə-'mō-nē-əs\ (*adj*) falsely holy; feigning piety. Mark Twain mocked pious hypocrites, calling one a *sanctimonious* old iceberg that looked like he was waiting for a vacancy in the Trinity.

sanc·tion \'saŋ(k)-shən\ (*v*) approve; ratify. Nothing will convince me to *sanction* the engagement of my daughter to such a worthless young man.

san·gui·nar·y \'saŋ-gwə-ˌner-ē\ (*adj*) bloody. In pre–Civil War days, Kansas was the scene of so many *sanguinary* clashes between proslavery and antislavery factions that it was called "Bleeding Kansas."

san·guine \'saŋ-gwən\ (*adj*) cheerful; hopeful. Let's not be too *sanguine* about the outcome of the election; we may still lose.

sa·pi·ent \'sā-pē-ənt\ (*adj*) wise; shrewd. The students learned more from the professor's *sapient* digressions than from the textbook.

sar·casm \'sär-ˌkaz-əm\ (*n*) scornful remarks; stinging rebuke. Though Ralph pretended to ignore the mocking comments of his supposed friends, their *sarcasm* wounded him deeply. **sar·cas·tic** \ sär-'kas-tik\ (*adj*)

sar·coph·a·gus \sär-'käf-ə-gəs\ (*n*) stone coffin, often highly decorated. When the archaeologists opened the *sarcophagus*, they discovered the tomb raiders had been there before them: the coffin was empty, the mummy gone.

sar·don·ic \sär-'dän-ik\ (*adj*) cynically mocking; sarcastic. Dorothy Parker's wry couplet, "Men seldom make passes at girls who wear glasses," epitomizes her *sardonic* wit.

sar-to-ri-al \sär-'tōr-ē-əl\ (*adj*) pertaining to tailors or tailored clothes. *GQ Magazine* provides *sartorial* advice for the not-so-well-dressed man.

sate \'sāt\ (*v*) satisfy to the full; cloy. Its hunger *sated,* the lion dozed.

sat-el-lite \'sat-ᵊl-ˌīt\ (*n*) small body revolving around a larger one. During the first few years of the Space Age, hundreds of *satellites* were launched by Russia and the United States.

sa-ti-ate \'sā-shē-ˌāt\ (*v*) satisfy fully. Having stuffed themselves until they were *satiated*, the guests were so full they were ready for a nap. **sa-ti-ate** \'sā-sh(ē-)ət\ (*adj*) **sa-ti-e-ty** \sə-'tī-ət-ē\ (*n*)

sat-ire \'sa-ˌtī(ə)r\ (*n*) form of literature in which irony, sarcasm, and ridicule are employed to attack vice and folly. *Gulliver's Travels,* which is regarded by many as a tale for children, is actually a bitter *satire* attacking man's folly.

sat-u-rate \'sach-ə-ˌrāt\ (*v*) soak. Thorough watering is the key to lawn care: you must *saturate* your new lawn well to encourage its growth. **sat-u-rate** \'sach-(ə-)rət\ (*adj*)

sat-ur-nine \'sat-ər-ˌnīn\ (*adj*) gloomy. Do not be misled by his *saturnine* countenance; he is not as gloomy as he looks.

sa-tyr \'sāt-ər\ (*n*) half-human, half-bestial being in the court of Dionysos, portrayed as wanton and cunning. He was like a *satyr* in his lustful conduct.

saun-ter \'sȯnt-ər\ (*v*) stroll slowly. As we *sauntered* through the park, we stopped frequently to admire the spring flowers.

sa-vant \sa-'vänt\ (*n*) learned scholar. Despite all her academic honors, Dr. Diamond disliked being classed as a *savant*: considering herself a simple researcher, she refused to describe herself in such grandiose terms.

sa·voir faire \\sav-ˌwär-'fa(ə)r\ (*n*) tact; poise; sophistication. I envy his *savoir faire*; he always knows exactly what to do and say.

sa·vor \\'sā-vər\ (*v*) enjoy; have a distinctive flavor, smell, or quality. Relishing his triumph, Costner especially *savored* the chagrin of the critics who had predicted his failure. also (*n*).

scant·y \\'skant-ē\ (*adj*) meager; insufficient. Thinking his helping of food was *scanty*, Oliver Twist asked for more.

scape·goat \\'skāp-ˌgōt\ (*n*) someone who bears the blame for others. After the *Challenger* disaster, NASA searched for *scapegoats* on whom it could cast the blame.

scav·en·ger \\'skav-ən-jər\ (*n*) collector and disposer of refuse; animal that devours refuse and carrion. The Oakland *Scavenger* Company is responsible for the collection and disposal of the community's garbage.

schism \\'siz-əm\ (*n*) division; split. His reforms led to a *schism* in the church and the establishment of a new sect opposing the old order.

scin·til·la \\sin-'til-ə\ (*n*) shred; least bit. You have not produced a *scintilla* of evidence to support your argument.

scin·til·late \\'sint-ᵊl-ˌāt\ (*v*) sparkle; flash. I enjoy her dinner parties because the food is excellent and the conversation *scintillates*.

sci·on \\'sī-ən\ (*n*) offspring. The farm boy felt out of place in the school attended by the *scions* of wealthy and prominent families.

scourge \\'skərj\ (*n*) cause of widespread devastation; severe punishment; whip. Abraham Lincoln wrote "Fondly do we hope, fervently do we pray, that this mighty *scourge* of war speedily may pass away." also (*v*).

---

scru-pu-lous \\'skrü-pyə-ləs\\ (*adj*) conscientious; extremely thorough. Though Alfred is *scrupulous* in fulfilling his duties at work, he is less conscientious about his obligations to his family and friends.

scru-ti-nize \\'skrüt-ᵊn-ˌīz\\ (*v*) examine closely and critically. Searching for flaws, the sergeant *scrutinized* every detail of the private's uniform.

scur-ri-lous \\'skər-ə-ləs\\ (*adj*) vulgar; coarse; foul-mouthed; obscene. Politicians often face *scurrilous* attacks from foul-mouthed, angry constituents.

scut-tle \\'skət-ᵊl\\ (*v*) sink by cutting holes in. The sailors decided to *scuttle* their vessel rather than surrender it to the enemy. also (*n*).

se-ba-ceous \\si-'bā-shəs\\ (*adj*) oily; fatty. The *sebaceous* glands secrete oil to the hair follicles.

se-ces-sion \\si-'sesh-ən\\ (*n*) withdrawal. The *secession* of the Southern states provided Lincoln with his first major problem after his inauguration.

sec-u-lar \\'sek-yə-lər\\ (*adj*) worldly; not pertaining to church matters; temporal. The church leaders decided not to interfere in *secular* matters. also (*n*).

se-date \\si-'dāt\\ (*adj*) calm and composed; dignified. To calm the agitated pony, we teamed him with a *sedate* mare that easily accepted the harness. also (*v*).

sed-en-tar-y \\'sed-ᵊn-ˌter-ē\\ (*adj*) requiring sitting. Sitting all day at the computer, Sharon grew to resent the *sedentary* nature of her job.

se-di-tion \\si-'dish-ən\\ (*n*) resistance to authority; insubordination. His words, though not treasonous in themselves, were calculated to arouse thoughts of *sedition*.

sed-u-lous \\'sej-ə-ləs\\ (*adj*) diligent; hard-working. After weeks of *sedulous* labor, we completed our detailed analysis of every published SAT examination.

seethe \\'sē_th_\\ (*v*) be disturbed; boil. France *seethed* with discontent as the noblemen continued their arrogant ways.

\\ə\\ **abut** \\ᵊ\\ **kitten, F table** \\ər\\ **further** \\a\\ **ash** \\ā\\ **ace** \\ä\\ **cot, cart**
\\aů\\ **out** \\ch\\ **chin** \\e\\ **bet** \\ē\\ **easy** \\g\\ **go** \\i\\ **hit** \\ī\\ **ice** \\j\\ **job**

sem-blance \'sem-blən(t)s\ (*n*) outward appearance; trace; copy. The new owners hope to restore the mansion to some *semblance* of its original magnificence.

se-nil-i-ty \si-'nil-ət-ē\ (*n*) old age; feeblemindedness of old age. Keeping mentally and physically active may help delay the onset of *senility*.

sen-su-al \'sench-(ə-)wəl\ (*adj*) devoted to the pleasures of the senses; carnal; voluptuous. Giving in to his *sensual* appetites, he sampled the carnal delights of the fleshpots.

sen-su-ous \'sench-(ə-)wəs\ (*adj*) pertaining to the physical senses; operating through the senses. Yeats's early verse abounds with *sensuous* images: the sound of water lapping, or of a bee-loud glade; the scent of rose-breath, or of odorous twilight.

sen-ten-tious \sen-'ten-chəs\ (*adj*) terse; concise; aphoristic. After reading so many redundant speeches, I find his *sententious* style particularly pleasing.

sep-tic \'sep-tik\ (*adj*) putrid; producing putrefaction. The hospital was in such a filthy state that we were afraid that many of the patients would suffer from *septic* poisoning.

sep-ul-cher \'sep-əl-kər\ (*n*) tomb. Suryavarman II planned the great temple at Angkor Wat as a *sepulcher* in which he would someday be buried.

se-ques-ter \si-'kwes-tər\ (*v*) isolate; retire from public life; segregate; seclude. Banished from his kingdom, the wizard Prospero *sequestered* himself on a desert island.

ser-en-dip-i-ty \ser-ən-'dip-ət-ē\ (*n*) gift for finding valuable or desirable things by accident; accidental good fortune or luck. Many scientific discoveries are a matter of *serendipity*: Newton was not sitting there thinking about gravity when the apple dropped on his head.

se-ren-i-ty \sə-'ren-ət-ē\ (*n*) calmness; placidity. The *serenity* of the sleepy town was shattered by a tremendous explosion.

\ŋ\ sing \ō\ go \ò\ law \òi\ boy \th\ thin \th\ the \ü\ loot \ù\ foot
\y\ yet \zh\ vision \à, k, ⁿ, œ, œ̄, ue, ūe, ʸ\ *see* Pronunciation Symbols

ser-pen-tine \'sər-pən-ˌtēn\ (*adj*) winding; twisting. The car swerved at every curve in the *serpentine* road.

ser-rat-ed \'se(ə)r-ˌāt-əd\ (*adj*) having a sawtoothed edge. I cut my finger on the *serrated* edge of the bread knife. ser-rate \se-'rāt\ (*v*)

ser-vile \'sər-vəl\ (*adj*) slavish; cringing. Constantly fawning on his employer, humble Uriah Heep was unvaryingly *servile*.

sev-er-ance \'sev-(ə-)rən(t)s\ (*n*) the act of dividing or separating. A factory accident resulted in the *severance* of two of the worker's fingers. sev-er \'sev-ər\ (*v*)

se-ver-i-ty \sə-'ver-ət-ē\ (*n*) harshness; intensity; austerity; rigidity. The *severity* of Jane's migraine attack was so great that she took to her bed for a week.

shack-le \'shak-əl\ (*v*) chain; fetter. In a chain gang, convicts are *shackled* together to prevent their escape. also (*n*).

sham \'sham\ (*v*) pretend. He *shammed* sickness to get out of going to school. also (*n*).

sham-bles \'sham-bəlz\ (*n*) wreck; mess. After the hurricane, the Carolina coast was a *shambles*. After the New Year's Eve party, the apartment was a *shambles*.

sheaf \'shēf\ (*n*) bundle of stalks of grain; any bundle of things tied together. The lawyer picked up a *sheaf* of papers as he rose to question the witness.

sheathe \'shēth\ (*v*) place into a case. As soon as he recognized the approaching men, he *sheathed* his dagger and hailed them as friends.

sher-bet \'shər-bət\ (*n*) flavored dessert ice. I prefer raspberry *sherbet* to ice cream since it is less fattening.

shib-bo-leth \'shib-ə-ləth\ (*n*) word or pronunciation used by one group but not by another; catchword. To many Standard English users, the pronunciation "noo-kyuh-luhr" instead of "noo-klee-uhr" is a *shibboleth*: if you inadvertently use the minority pronunciation, you lay yourself open to sneers and mockery.

\ə\ **abut** \ᵊ\ **kitten, F table** \ər\ **further** \a\ **ash** \ā\ **ace** \ä\ **cot, cart**
\au̇\ **out** \ch\ **chin** \e\ **bet** \ē\ **easy** \g\ **go** \i\ **hit** \ī\ **ice** \j\ **job**

shim-mer \\'shim-ər\\ (*v*) glimmer intermittently. The moonlight *shimmered* on the water as the moon broke through the clouds for a moment. also (*n*).

shoal \\'shōl\\ (*n*) shallow place. Stranded on a *shoal*, the ship had to be pulled off by tugs. also (*v*).

shod-dy \\'shäd-ē\\ (*adj*) inferior; trashy; cheap. Grumbling, "They don't make things the way they used to," Grandpa complained about the *shoddy* workmanship nowadays.

shrew \\'shrü\\ (*n*) scolding woman. No one wanted to marry Shakespeare's Kate because she was a *shrew*.

sib-ling \\'sib-ling\\ (*adj*) related to brothers and/or sisters. Brotherly love is a complex emotion, with *sibling* rivalry its natural corollary. also (*n*).

sib-yl-line \\'sib-ə-ˌlīn\\ (*adj*) prophetic; oracular. Until their destruction by fire in 83 B.C., the *sibylline* books were often consulted by Romans seeking supernatural guidance.

si-de-re-al \\sī-'dir-ē-əl\\ (*adj*) relating to the stars. Although hampered by optical and mechanical flaws, the orbiting Hubble space telescope has relayed extraordinary images of distant *sidereal* bodies.

silt \\'silt\\ (*n*) sediment deposited by running water. The harbor channel must be dredged annually to remove the *silt*. also (*v*).

sim-i-an \\'sim-ē-ən\\ (*adj*) monkeylike. Lemurs are nocturnal mammals that have many *simian* characteristics, although they are less intelligent than monkeys. also (*n*).

sim-i-le \\'sim-ə-ˌlē\\ (*n*) comparison of one thing with another, using the word *like* or *as*. "My love is like a red, red rose" is a *simile*.

si-mil-i-tude \\sə-'mil-ə-ˌt(y)üd\\ (*n*) similarity; using comparisons such as similes, etc. Although the critics deplored his use of mixed metaphors, he continued to write in *similitudes*.

---

sim-per \\sim-pər\ (*v*) smirk; smile affected. Compliment-ed on her appearance, Stella self-consciously *simpered*.

sim-u-late \\sim-yə-,lāt\ (*v*) feign. He *simulated* insanity in order to avoid punishment for his crime.

si-ne-cure \\sī-ni-,kyu̇(ə)r\ (*n*) well-paid position with lit-tle responsibility. My job is no *sinecure*; I work long hours and have much responsibility.

sin-ew-y \\sin-yə-wē\ (*adj*) tough; strong and firm. The steak was too *sinewy* to chew.

sin-is-ter \\sin-əs-tər\ (*adj*) evil; conveying a sense of ill omen. Aware of the Penguin's *sinister* purpose, Batman wondered how he could save Gotham City from the ravages of his evil enemy.

sin-u-ous \\sin-yə-wəs\ (*adj*) winding; bending in and out; not morally honest. The snake moved in a *sinuous* manner.

skep-tic \\skep-tik\ (*n*) doubter; person who suspends judgment until having examined the evidence support-ing a point of view. I am a *skeptic* about the new health plan; I want some proof that it can work.

skimp \\skimp\ (*v*) provide scantily; live very economical-ly. They were forced to *skimp* on necessities in order to make their limited supplies last the winter.

skit-tish \\skit-ish\ (*adj*) lively; frisky. He is as *skittish* as a kitten playing with a piece of string.

skul-dug-ge-ry \\skəl-'dəg-(ə-)rē\ (*n*) dishonest behavior. The investigation into municipal corruption turned up new instances of *skulduggery* daily.

skulk \\skəlk\ (*v*) move furtively and secretly. He *skulked* through the less fashionable sections of the city in order to avoid meeting any of his former friends. also (*n*).

slack-en \\slak-ən\ (*v*) slow up; loosen. As they passed the finish line, the runners *slackened* their pace.

slake \\slāk\ (*v*) quench; sate. When we reached the oasis, we were able to *slake* our thirst.

\ə\ **abut** \ᵊ\ **kitten, F table** \ər\ **further** \a\ **ash** \ā\ **ace** \ä\ **cot, cart**
\au̇\ **out** \ch\ **chin** \e\ **bet** \ē\ **easy** \g\ **go** \i\ **hit** \ī\ **ice** \j\ **job**

slan-der \\slan-dər\ (*n*) defamation; utterance of false and malicious statements. Considering the negative comments politicians make about each other, it's a wonder that more of them aren't sued for *slander*. also (*v*).

slea-zy \\slē-zē\ (*adj*) flimsy; unsubstantial. This is a *sleazy* fabric; it will not wear well.

sleep-er \\slē-pər\ (*n*) something originally of little value or importance that in time becomes very valuable. Unnoticed by the critics at its publication, the eventual Pulitzer Prize winner was a classic *sleeper.*

sleight \\slīt\ (*n*) dexterity. The magician amazed the audience with his *sleight* of hand.

slith-er \\slith-ər\ (*v*) slip or slide. During the recent ice storm, many people *slithered* down the hill as they walked to the station.

sloth \\slȯth\ (*n*) laziness. Lying idly on the sofa while others worked, Reggie defended his *sloth*: "I just supervise better lying down."

slough \\sləf\ (*v*) cast off. Each spring, the snake *sloughs* off its skin. also (*n*).

slov-en-ly \\sləv-ən-lē\ (*adj*) untidy; careless in work habits. Unshaven, sitting around in his bathrobe all afternoon, Gus didn't seem to care about the *slovenly* appearance he presented.

slug-gard \\sləg-ərd\ (*n*) lazy person. Someone who leaps happily out of bed first thing in the morning and cheerfully sets off to work is no *sluggard*.

slug-gish \\sləg-ish\ (*adj*) slow; lazy; lethargic. After two nights without sleep, she felt *sluggish* and incapable of exertion.

sluice \\slüs\ (*n*) artificial channel for directing or controlling the flow of water. This *sluice* gate is opened only in times of drought to provide water for irrigation. also (*v*).

---

smat-ter-ing \\'smat-ə-riŋ\\ (*v*) slight knowledge. I don't know whether it is better to be ignorant of a subject or to have a mere *smattering* of information about it.

smirk \\'smərk\\ (*n*) conceited smile. Wipe that *smirk* off your face! also (*v*).

smol-der \\'smōl-dər\\ (*v*) burn without flame; be liable to break out at any moment. The rags *smoldered* for hours before they burst into flame.

snick-er \\'snik-ər\\ (*n*) half-stifled laugh. The boy could not suppress a *snicker* when the teacher sat on the tack. also (*v*).

sniv-el \\'sniv-əl\\ (*v*) run at the nose; snuffle; whine. Don't you come *sniveling* to me complaining about your big brother.

so-bri-e-ty \\sə-'brī-ət-ē\\ (*n*) moderation (especially regarding indulgence in alcohol); seriousness. Neither falling-down drunks nor stand-up comics are noted for *sobriety*.

so-bri-quet \\'sō-bri-ˌkā\\ (*n*) nickname. Despite all his protests, his classmates continued to call him by that unflattering *sobriquet*.

sod-den \\'säd-ᵊn\\ (*adj*) soaked; dull, as if from drink. He set his *sodden* overcoat near the radiator to dry.

so-journ \\'sō-jərn\\ (*n*) temporary stay. After his *sojourn* in Florida, he began to long for the colder climate of his native New England home. also (*v*).

so-lace \\'säl-əs\\ (*n*) comfort in trouble. I hope you will find *solace* in the thought that all of us share your loss.

so-le-cism \\'säl-ə-ˌsiz-əm\\ (*n*) construction that is flagrantly incorrect grammatically. I must give this paper a failing mark because it contains many *solecisms*.

so-lem-ni-ty \\sə-'lem-nət-ē\\ (*n*) seriousness; gravity. The minister was concerned that nothing should disturb the *solemnity* of the marriage service. sol-emn \\'säl-əm\\ (*adj*)

---

so·lic·i·tous \sə-'lis-ət-əs\ (*adj*) worried; concerned. Dora was delicate, David knew, and he was very *solicitous* about her health during her pregnancy.

so·lil·o·quy \sə-'lil-ə-kwē\ (*n*) the act of talking to oneself. Dramatists use the *soliloquy* as a device to reveal a character's innermost thoughts and emotions.

sol·stice \'säl-stəs\ (*n*) point at which the sun is farthest from the equator. The winter *solstice* usually occurs on December 21.

sol·vent \'säl-vənt\ (*adj*) able to pay all debts. By dint of very frugal living, he was finally able to become *solvent* and avoid bankruptcy proceedings.

sol·vent \'säl-vənt\ (*n*) substance that dissolves another. Dip a cube of sugar into a cup of water; note how the water acts as a *solvent*, causing the cube to break down.

so·mat·ic \sō-'mat-ik\ (*adj*) pertaining to the body; physical. Your mental state can influence your physical health, affecting *somatic* disorders such as cancer and heart disease.

som·nam·bu·list \säm-'nam-byə-ləst\ (*n*) sleepwalker. The most famous *somnambulist* in literature is Lady Macbeth, whose monologue in the sleepwalking scene is a highlight of Shakespeare's play.

som·no·lent \'säm-nə-lənt\ (*adj*) half asleep. The heavy meal and the overheated room made us all *somnolent* and indifferent to the speaker.

so·no·rous \sə-'nōr-əs\ (*adj*) resonant. His *sonorous* voice resounded through the hall.

soph·ist \'säf-əst\ (*n*) quibbler; employer of fallacious reasoning. You argue like a *sophist*: speciously, not soundly.

so·phis·ti·ca·tion \sə-ˌfis-tə-'kā-shən\ (*n*) complexity; refinement. Last year's new IBM laptop with the butterfly keyboard and the built-in quadspeed FAX modem seemed the height of computer *sophistication*.

soph·ist·ry \'säf-ə-strē\ (*n*) seemingly plausible but fallacious reasoning. Instead of advancing valid argu-

---

\ŋ\ **sing** \ō\ **go** \ȯ\ **law** \ȯi\ **boy** \th\ **thin** \th\ **the** \ü\ **loot** \u̇\ **foot**
\y\ **yet** \zh\ **vision** \à, ḵ, ⁿ, œ, œ̄, ue, ūe, ʸ\ *see* Pronunciation Symbols

ments, he tried to overwhelm his audience with a flood of *sophistries*. soph-ist \\'säf-əst\ (*n*)

soph-o-mor-ic \\,säf-ə-'mȯr-ik\ (*adj*) immature; half-baked, like a sophomore. When Sophy makes wisecracks, she thinks she sounds sophisticated, but instead she sounds *sophomoric*.

so-po-rif-ic \\säp-ə-'rif-ik\ (*adj*) sleep-causing; marked by sleepiness. Professor Pringle's lectures were so *soporific* that even he fell asleep in class. also *(n)*.

sor-did \\'sȯrd-əd\ (*adj*) vile; filthy; wretched; mean. Talk show hosts seem willing to discuss any topic, no matter how *sordid* and disgusting it may be.

soup-çon \\süp-'sōⁿ\ (*n*) suggestion; hint; taste. A *soupçon* of garlic will improve this dish.

span-gle \\'spaŋ-gəl\ (*n*) small metallic piece sewn to clothing for ornamentation. The thousands of *spangles* on her dress sparkled in the glare of the stage lights. also *(v)*.

sparse \\'spärs\ (*adj*) not thick; thinly scattered; scanty. No matter how carefully Albert combed his hair to make it look as full as possible, it still looked *sparse*.

spas-mod-ic \\spaz-'mäd-ik\ (*adj*) fitful; periodic. The *spasmodic* coughing in the auditorium annoyed the performers.

spate \\'spāt\ (*n*) sudden flood or strong outburst; a large number or amount. After the *spate* of angry words that came pouring out of him, Mary was sure they would never be reconciled.

spa-tial \\'spā-shəl\ (*adj*) relating to space. NASA is engaged in an ongoing program of *spatial* exploration. Certain exercises test your sense of *spatial* relations by asking you to identify two views of an object seen from different points in space.

spat-u-la \\'spach-(ə-)lə\ (*n*) broad-bladed instrument used for spreading or mixing. The manufacturers of this fry-

---

\ə\ **abut** \ᵊ\ **kitten, F table** \ər\ **further** \a\ **ash** \ā\ **ace** \ä\ **cot, cart**
\au̇\ **out** \ch\ **chin** \e\ **bet** \ē\ **easy** \g\ **go** \i\ **hit** \ī\ **ice** \j\ **job**

ing pan recommend the use of a rubber *spatula* to avoid scratching the specially treated surface.

spawn \'spȯn\ (*v*) lay eggs. Fish ladders had to be built in the dams to assist the salmon returning to *spawn* in their native streams. also (*n*).

spe-cious \'spē-shəs\ (*adj*) seemingly reasonable but incorrect; misleading (often intentionally). To claim that, because houses and birds both have wings, both can fly, is extremely *specious* reasoning.

spec-tral \'spek-trəl\ (*adj*) ghostly. In stormy weather the Flying Dutchman sails his *spectral* ship of the doomed off the Cape of Good Hope.

spec-trum \'spek-trəm\ (*n*) colored band produced when beam of light passes through a prism. The visible portion of the *spectrum* includes red at one end and violet at the other.

spec-u-la-tion \spek-yə-'lā-shən\ (*n*) conjecture; contemplation. The discovery of Hester's pregnancy caused much *speculation* as to the identity of the father of her child.

sple-net-ic \spli-'net-ik\ (*adj*) spiteful; irritable; peevish. Ill and *splenetic*, the irritable patient viewed his surroundings with an increasingly jaundiced eye. **spleen** \'splēn\ (*n*)

spo-rad-ic \spə-'rad-ik\ (*adj*) occurring irregularly. Although you can still hear *sporadic* outbursts of laughter and singing outside, the big Halloween parade has passed; the party's over till next year.

sport-ive \'spȯrt-iv\ (*adj*) playful. Half man, half goat, the mischievous, *sportive* fauns gamboled on the green.

spume \'spyüm\ (*n*) froth; foam. The *spume* at the base of the waterfall extended for a quarter of a mile downriver. also (*v*).

spu-ri-ous \'spyur-ē-əs\ (*adj*) false; counterfeit; forged; illogical. Natasha's claim to be the lost heir of the Romanoffs was *spurious*: the only thing Russian about her was the vodka she drank. The hero of Jonathan Gash's mystery novels is an antiques dealer who gives the reader advice on how to tell *spurious* antiques from the real thing.

spurn \\'spərn\ (*v*) reject; scorn. The heroine *spurned* the villain's advances.

squal-id \\'skwäl-əd\ (*adj*) dirty; neglected; poor. Tar paper peeling from the roof, trash piled up on the porch, the *squalid* shack was a depressing sight.

squan-der \\'skwän-dər\ (*v*) waste. If you *squander* your allowance on candy, you won't have any money left to buy the new comic book you want.

stac-ca-to \sta-'kät-ₐ)ō\ (*adj*) played in an abrupt manner; marked by abrupt sharp sound. His *staccato* speech reminded one of the sound of a machine gun.

stag-nant \\'stag-nənt\ (*adj*) motionless; stale; dull. Mosquitoes commonly breed in ponds of *stagnant* water. Mike's career was *stagnant*; it wasn't going anywhere, and neither was he! stag-nate \\'stag-ˌnāt\ (*v*)

staid \\'stād \ (*adj*) sober; sedate. My Harry may be *staid* and sober, but at least he's not stodgy and dull like your Tom!

stale-mate \\'stā(ə)l-ˌmāt\ (*n*) deadlock. Negotiations between the union and the employers have reached a *stalemate;* neither side is willing to budge from previously stated positions. also (*v*).

stal-wart \\'stȯl-wərt\ (*adj*) strong and vigorous; unwaveringly dependable. We thought the congressman was a *stalwart* Republican until he voted against President Bush's Medicare reform bill. also (*n*).

stam-i-na \\'stam-ə-nə\ (*n*) strength; staying power. I doubt that he has the *stamina* to run the full distance of the marathon race.

stanch \\'stȯnch\ (*v*) check flow of. It is imperative that we *stanch* the gushing wound before we attend to the other injuries.

\ə\ **abut** \ᵊ\ **kitten,** F **table** \ər\ **further** \a\ **ash** \ā\ **ace** \ä\ **cot, cart**
\au̇\ **out** \ch\ **chin** \e\ **bet** \ē\ **easy** \g\ **go** \i\ **hit** \ī\ **ice** \j\ **job**

stat-ic \\'stat-ik\\ (*adj*) unchanging; lacking development. Why watch chess on TV? I like watching a game with action, not something *static* where nothing seems to be going on. **sta-sis** \\'stā-səs\\ (*n*)

stat-ute \\'stach-ˌüt\\ (*n*) law enacted by the legislature. The *statute* of limitations sets the limits on how long you have to take legal action in specific cases. **stat-u-to-ry** \\'stach-ə-ˌtōr-ē\\ (*adj*)

stead-fast \\'sted-ˌfast\\ (*adj*) loyal; unswerving. Penelope was *steadfast* in her affections, faithfully waiting for Ulysses to return from his wanderings.

stein \\'stīn\\ (*n*) beer mug. At Munich's Hofbrau House, David bought a beer *stein* as a souvenir of his trip to Germany.

stel-lar \\'stel-ər\\ (*adj*) pertaining to the stars; outstanding. He was the *stellar* attraction of the entire performance.

sten-to-ri-an \\sten-'tōr-ē-ən\\ (*adj*) extremely loud. The town crier had a *stentorian* voice.

ste-re-o-type \\'ster-ē-ə-ˌtīp\\ (*n*) fixed and unvarying representation; standardized mental picture, often reflecting prejudice. Critics object to the character of Jim in *The Adventures of Huckleberry Finn* because he seems to reflect the *stereotype* of the happy, ignorant slave.

stig-ma \\'stig-mə\\ (*n*) token of disgrace; brand. I do not attach any *stigma* to the fact that you were accused of this crime; the fact that you were acquitted clears you completely.

stig-ma-tize \\'stig-mə-ˌtīz\\ (*v*) brand; mark as wicked. I do not want to *stigmatize* this young offender for life by sending him to prison.

stilt-ed \\'stil-təd\\ (*adj*) bombastic; inflated. His *stilted* rhetoric did not impress the college audience; they were immune to bombastic utterances.

stint \'stint\ (*n*) supply; allotted amount; assigned portion of work. After his *stint* in the Army he will join his father's company. (*v*) be thrifty; set limits. "Spare no expense," the bride's father said, refusing to *stint* on the wedding arrangements.

sti-pend \'stī-,pend\ (*n*) pay for services. There is a nominal *stipend* attached to this position.

sto-ic \'stō-ik\ (*adj*) impassive; unmoved by joy or grief. I wasn't particularly *stoic* when I had my flu shot; I squealed like a stuck pig. also (*n*).

stoke \'stōk\ (*v*) provide with fuel; feed abundantly. They swiftly *stoked* themselves, knowing they would not have another meal until they reached camp.

stol-id \'stäl-əd\ (*adj*) unruffled; impassive; dull. Marianne wanted a romantic, passionate suitor like Willoughby, not a *stolid*, unimaginative one like Colonel Brandon.

strat-a-gem \'strat-ə-jəm\ (*n*) deceptive scheme. Though Wellington's forces seemed in full retreat, in reality their withdrawal was a *stratagem* intended to lure the enemy away from its sheltered position.

stra-tum \'strāt-əm\ (*n*) layer of earth's surface; layer of society. Neither an elitist nor a reverse snob, Mitch had friends from every social *stratum*.

stri-at-ed \'strī-,āt-əd\ (*adj*) marked with parallel bands. The glacier left many *striated* rocks.

stric-ture \'strik-chər\ (*n*) critical comments; severe and adverse criticism. His *strictures* on the author's style are prejudiced and unwarranted.

stri-dent \'strīd-ᵊnt\ (*adj*) loud and harsh; insistent. Whenever Sue became angry, she tried not to raise her voice; she disliked appearing *strident*.

strin-gent \'strin-jənt\ (*adj*) severe; rigid; constricted. Fearing the rapid spread of the SARS virus, the Canadian government imposed *stringent* quarantine measures.

\ə\ **abut** \ᵊ\ **kitten**, F **table** \ər\ **further** \a\ **ash** \ā\ **ace** \ä\ **cot, cart**
\aú\ **out** \ch\ **chin** \e\ **bet** \ē\ **easy** \g\ **go** \i\ **hit** \ī\ **ice** \j\ **job**

strut \'strət\ (*n*) pompous walk. His *strut* as he marched about the parade ground revealed him for what he was: a pompous buffoon. also (*v*).

strut \'strət\ (*n*) supporting bar. The engineer calculated that the *strut* supporting the rafter needed to be reinforced. (secondary meaning)

stul-ti-fy \'stəl-tə-ˌfī\ (*v*) cause to appear or become stupid or inconsistent; frustrate or hinder. His long hours in the blacking factory left young Dickens numb and incurious, as if the menial labor had *stultified* his mind.

stu-por \'st(y)ü-pər\ (*n*) state of apathy; daze; lack of awareness. The paramedics shook the unconscious man but could not rouse him from his *stupor*.

sty-gi-an \'stij-(ē-)ən\ (*adj*) gloomy; hellish; deathly. Shielding the flickering candle from any threatening draft, Tom and Becky descended into the *stygian* darkness of the underground cavern. *Stygian* derives from *Styx*, the chief river in the subterranean land of the dead.

sty-mie \'stī-mē\ (*v*) present an obstacle; stump. The detective was *stymied* by the contradictory evidence in the robbery investigation. also (*n*).

suave \'swäv\ (*adj*) smooth; bland. He is the kind of individual who is more easily impressed by a *suave* approach than by threats or bluster.

sua-vi-ty \'swäv-ət-ē\ (*n*) urbanity; polish. He is particularly good in roles that require *suavity* and sophistication.

sub-al-tern \sə-'ból-tərn\ (*n*) subordinate. The captain treated his *subalterns* as though they were children rather than commissioned officers. also (*adj*).

sub-jec-tive \ˌ(ˌ)səb-'jek-tiv\ (*adj*) occurring or taking place within the subject; unreal. Your analysis is highly *subjective*; you have permitted your emotions and your opinions to color your thinking.

---

sub·ju·gate \'səb ji-ˌgāt\ (*v*) conquer; bring under control. Alexander the Great conquered most of the known world of his time, first *subjugating* the Persians under Darius, then defeating the armies of India's King Porus.

sub·li·mate \'səb-lə-ˌmāt\ (*v*) refine; purify. Is it truly possible to *sublimate* one's sexual drives, diverting the energy into artistic creation?

sub·lime \sə-'blīm\ (*adj*) exalted or noble and uplifting; utter. Lucy was in awe of Desi's *sublime* musicianship, while he was in awe of her *sublime* naiveté.

sub·lim·i·nal \ₐsəb-'lim-ən-ᵊl\ (*adj*) below conscious awareness. The pulse of the music began to work in the crowd in a *subliminal* way: they rocked to the rhythm unconsciously.

sub·se·quent \'səb-si-kwənt\ (*adj*) following; later. In *subsequent* lessons, we shall take up more difficult problems.

sub·ser·vi·ent \səb-'sər-vē-ənt\ (*adj*) behaving like a slave; servile; obsequious. He was proud and dignified; he refused to be *subservient to* anyone.

sub·sid·i·ar·y \səb-'sid-ē-ˌer-ē\ (*n*) something secondary in importance or subordinate; auxiliary. The Turner Broadcasting System is a wholly owned *subsidiary* of AOL Time Warner. First deal with the critical issues, then with the *subsidiary* ones. also (*adj*).

sub·si·dy \'səb-səd-ē\ (*n*) direct financial aid by government, etc. Without this *subsidy,* American ship operators would not be able to compete in world markets.

sub·sis·tence \səb-'sis-tən(t)s\ (*n*) means needed to support life; existence. Farming those barren, depleted fields, he raised barely enough food for his family's *subsistence.*

sub·stan·ti·ate \səb-'stan-chē-ˌāt\ (*v*) establish by evidence; verify; support. These endorsements from satisfied customers *substantiate* our claim that Barron's

---

\ə\ **abut** \ᵊ\ **kitten,** F **table** \ər\ **further** \a\ **ash** \ā\ **ace** \ä\ **cot, cart**
\aú\ **out** \ch\ **chin** \e\ **bet** \ē\ **easy** \g\ **go** \i\ **hit** \ī\ **ice** \j\ **job**

Pocket Guide to Vocabulary is the best vocabulary text on the market.

sub-stan-tive \\'səb-stən-tiv\\ *(adj)* real, as opposed to imaginary; essential; solidly based; substantial. Bishop Tutu received the Nobel Peace Prize in recognition of his *substantive* contributions to the peace movement in South Africa.

sub-ter-fuge \\'səb-tər-ˌfyüj\\ *(n)* deceitful stratagem; trick; pretense. Hiding from his pursuers, the fugitive used every *subterfuge* he could think of to get them off his track.

sub-tle-ty \\'sət-ᵊl-tē\\ *(n)* perceptiveness; ingenuity; delicacy. Never obvious, she expressed herself with such *subtlety* that her remarks went right over the heads of most of her audience.

sub-ver-sive \\səb-'vər-siv\\ *(adj)* tending to overthrow; destructive. At first hearing, the notion that Styrofoam cups may actually be more ecologically sound than paper cups strikes most environmentalists as *subversive*. also *(n)*.

suc-cinct \\₍ₗ₎sək-'siŋ(k)t\\ *(adj)* brief; terse; compact. Don't bore your audience with excess verbiage: be *succinct*.

suc-cor \\'sək-ər\\ *(v)* aid; assist; comfort. If you believe that con man has come here to *succor* you in your hour of need, you're an even bigger sucker than I thought. also *(n)*.

suc-cu-lent \\'sək-yə-lənt\\ *(adj)* juicy; full of richness. To some people, Florida citrus fruits are more *succulent* than those from California. also *(n)*.

suc-cumb \\sə-'kəm\\ *(v)* yield; give in; die. I *succumb* to temptation whenever it comes my way.

suf-fuse \\sə-'fyüz\\ *(v)* spread over. A blush *suffused* her cheeks when we teased her about her love affair.

sul-ly \\'səl-ē\\ *(v)* tarnish; soil. He felt that it was beneath his dignity to *sully* his hands in such menial labor.

\\ŋ\\ sing \\ō\\ go \\ȯ\\ law \\ȯi\\ boy \\th\\ thin \\t͟h\\ the \\ü\\ loot \\u̇\\ foot
\\y\\ yet \\zh\\ vision \\à, k̲, ⁿ, œ, œ̄, ue, ūe, ʸ\\ *see* Pronunciation Symbols

sul-try \\'səl-trē\ (*adj*) sweltering. He could not adjust himself to the *sultry* climate of the tropics.

sum-ma-tion _(ₒ)sə-'mā-shən\ (*n*) act of finding the total; summary. In her *summation,* the lawyer emphasized the testimony given by the two witnesses.

sump-tu-ous \\'səm(p)-ch(ə-w)əs\ (*adj*) lavish; rich. I cannot recall when I have had such a *sumptuous* Thanksgiving feast.

sun-der \\'sən-dər\ (*v*) separate; part. Northern and southern Ireland are politically and religiously *sundered.*

sun-dry \\'sən-drē\ (*adj*) various; several. Her briefcase bulged with her cell phone, Palm pilot, journal, and *sundry* other items.

su-per-an-nu-at-ed \\sü-pə-'ran-yə-ˌwāt-əd\ (*adj*) retired on pension because of age. Don't call me *superannuated*! I can still put in a good day's work.

su-per-cil-i-ous \\ˌsü-pər-'sil-ē-əs\ (*adj*) arrogant; condescending; patronizing. The *supercilious* headwaiter sneered at customers whom he thought did not fit in at his ultrafashionable restaurant.

su-per-fi-cial \\ˌsü-pər-'fish-əl\ (*adj*) trivial; shallow. Since your report gave only a *superficial* analysis of the problem, I cannot give you more than a passing grade.

su-per-flu-it-y \\ˌsü-per-'flü-ət-ē\ (*n*) excess; overabundance. Please try not to include such a *superfluity* of details in your report; just give me the bare facts.

su-per-im-pose \\ˌsü-pə-rim-'pōz\ (*v*) place over something else. The filmmakers *superimposed* the credits over the movie's opening scene.

su-per-nal \\sù-'pərn-ᵊl\ (*adj*) heavenly; celestial. Angels, archangels, and all the *supernal* powers were ranged in battle against Lucifer's infernal hosts.

su-per-nu-mer-ar-y \\sü-pər-'n(y)ü-mə-ˌrer-ē\ (*n*) person or thing in excess of what is necessary; extra. His first appearance on the stage was as a *supernumerary* in a Shakespearean tragedy.

\\ə\ **abut** \\ᵊ\ **kitten,** F **table** \\ər\ **further** \\a\ **ash** \\ā\ **ace** \\ä\ **cot, cart**
\\aú\ **out** \\ch\ **chin** \\e\ **bet** \\ē\ **easy** \\g\ **go** \\i\ **hit** \\ī\ **ice** \\j\ **job**

su-per-sede \ˌsü-pər-'sēd\ (*v*) cause to be set aside; replace; make obsolete. Bulk mailing postal regulation 326D *supersedes* bulk mailing postal regulation 326C. If, in bundling your bulk mailing, you follow regulation 326C and not regulation 326D, your bulk mailing will be returned.

su-pine \sü-'pīn\ (*adj*) lying on back. The defeated pugilist lay *supine* on the canvas.

sup-plant \sə-'plant\ (*v*) replace; usurp. Did Camilla actually *supplant* Princess Diana in Prince Charles's affections, or did Charles never love Diana at all?

sup-ple \'səp-əl\ (*adj*) flexible; pliant. Years of yoga exercises made Grace's body *supple*.

sup-pli-ant \'səp-lē-ənt\ (*n*) petitioner; one who entreats. O king, I come before you as a *suppliant*, begging for the life of my misguided son. also (*adj*).

sup-pli-cate \'səp-lə-ˌkāt\ (*v*) petition humbly; pray to grant a favor. We *supplicate* your majesty to grant him amnesty.

sup-pos-i-ti-tious \sə-ˌpäz ə-'tish-əs\ (*adj*) fraudulent; counterfeit; hypothetical. Refusing to recognize Caesarion as the rightful son of Julius Caesar, Caesar's nephew Octavian persisted in treating him as *supposititious*.

sup-press \sə-'pres\ (*v*) crush; subdue; inhibit. Too polite to laugh in anyone's face, Roy did his best to *suppress* his amusement at Ed's inane remark.

sur-cease \'sər-ˌsēs\ (*n*) end; cessation. Sir! Cease pestering me: grant me *surcease* from your unwanted attentions. sur-cease \ˌ(ˌ)sər-'sēs\ (*v*)

sur-feit \'sər-fət\ (*v*) satiate; stuff; indulge to excess in anything. Every Thanksgiving we are *surfeited* with an overabundance of holiday treats. also (*n*).

sur-ly \'sər-lē\ (*adj*) rude; cross. Because of his *surly* attitude, many people avoided his company.

\ŋ\ sing \ō\ go \ȯ\ law \ȯi\ boy \th\ thin \t̲h̲\ the \ü\ loot \u̇\ foot
\y\ yet \zh\ vision \à, k̲, ⁿ, œ, œ̄, ue, ūe, ʸ\ *see* Pronunciation Symbols

sur-mise \sər-'mīz \ (*v*) suspect; guess; imagine. I *surmise* that Suzanne will be late for this meeting; I've never known her to be on time. also (*n*).

sur-mount \sər-'maunt\ (*v*) overcome. Could Helen Keller, blind and deaf since childhood, *surmount* her physical disabilities and lead a productive life?

sur-rep-ti-tious \sər-əp-'tish-əs\ (*adj*) secret; furtive; sneaky; hidden. Hoping to discover where his mom had hidden the Christmas presents, Timmy took a *surreptitious* peek into the master bedroom closet.

sur-ro-gate \'sər-ə-ˌgät\ (*n*) substitute. For a fatherless child, a male teacher may become a father *surrogate.*

sur-veil-lance \sər-'vā-lən(t)s\ (*n*) watching; guarding. The FBI kept the house under constant *surveillance* in the hope of capturing all the criminals at one time.

sus-te-nance \'səs-tə-nən(t)s\ (*n*) means of support, food, nourishment. In the tropics, the natives find *sustenance* easy to obtain.

su-ture \'sü-chər\ (*n*) stitches sewn to hold the cut edges of a wound or incision; material used in sewing. We will remove the *sutures* as soon as the wound heals. also (*v*).

swar-thy \'swȯr-thē\ (*adj*) dark; dusky. Despite the stereotypes, not all Italians are *swarthy;* many are fair-skinned and blond-haired.

swathe \'swäth\ (*v*) wrap around; bandage. When I visited him in the hospital, I found him *swathed* in bandages.

swel-ter \'swel-tər\ (*v*) be oppressed by heat. I am going to buy an air conditioning unit for my apartment as I do not intend to *swelter* through another hot and humid summer. also (*n*).

swin-dler \'swin-(d)lər\ (*n*) cheat. She was gullible and trusting, an easy victim for the first *swindler* who came along.

syb-a-rite \'sib-ə-ˌrīt\ (*n*) lover of luxury. Rich people are not always *sybarites*; some of them have little taste for a life of luxury.

\ə\ **abut** \ᵊ\ **kitten**, F **table** \ər\ **further** \a\ **ash** \ā\ **ace** \ä\ **cot, cart**
\au̇\ **out** \ch\ **chin** \e\ **bet** \ē\ **easy** \g\ **go** \i\ **hit** \ī\ **ice** \j\ **job**

sy·co·phant \ˌsik-ə-ˈfant\ (*n*) servile flatterer; bootlicker; yes man. Fed up with the toadies and flatterers who made up his entourage, the star cried, "Get out, all of you! I'm sick of *sycophants!*"

syl·lo·gism \ˈsil-ə-jiz-əm\ (*n*) logical formula utilizing a major premise, a minor premise, and a conclusion. "All humans are fallible. The pope is a human. Therefore, the pope is fallible." This is an example of a *syllogism.*

syl·van \ˈsil-vən\ (*adj*) pertaining to the woods; rustic. He painted wood nymphs in their *sylvan* setting, shyly peeping between the leaves of the trees.

sym·me·try \ˈsim-ə-trē\ (*n*) arrangement of parts so that balance is obtained; congruity. Something lopsided by definition lacks *symmetry.*

syn·chro·nous \ˈsiŋ-krə-nəs\ (*adj*) similarly timed; simultaneous with. The swimmers executed a series of *synchronous* movements, lifting their arms out of the water in unison.

syn·the·sis \ˈsin(t)-thə-səs\ (*n*) combining parts into a whole. Now that we have succeeded in isolating this drug, our next challenge is to plan its *synthesis* in the laboratory.

syn·thet·ic \sin-ˈthet-ik\ (*adj*) artificial; resulting from synthesis. During the late twentieth century, many *synthetic* products replaced their natural counterparts.

T

tac-it \'tas-ət\ (*adj*) understood; not put into words. We have a *tacit* agreement based on only a handshake.

tac-i-turn \'tas-ə-ˌtərn\ (*adj*) habitually silent; talking little. The stereotypical cowboy is a *taciturn* soul, answering lengthy questions with a "Yep" or "Nope."

tact \'takt\ (*n*) diplomacy; good taste. One must use *tact* when providing criticism in order to avoid hurting the feelings of the person one is trying to help.

tac-tile \'tak-tᵊl\ (*adj*) pertaining to the organs or sense of touch. His calloused hands had lost their *tactile* sensitivity.

taint \'tānt\ (*v*) contaminate; cause to lose purity; modify with a trace of something bad. One speck of dirt on your utensils may contain enough germs to *taint* an entire batch of preserves.

tal-is-man \'tal-ə-smən\ (*n*) charm to bring good luck and avert misfortune. Joe believed that the carved pendant he found in Vietnam served him as a *talisman* and brought him safely through the war.

tal-on \'tal-ən\ (*n*) claw of a bird. The falconer wore a leather gauntlet to avoid being clawed by the hawk's *talons*.

tan-ta-lize \'tant-ᵊl-ˌīz\ (*v*) tease; torture with disappointment. Tom *tantalized* his younger brother, holding the ball just too high for Jimmy to reach.

tan-ta-mount \'tant-ə-ˌmaủnt\ (*adj*) equivalent in effect or value. Because so few Southern blacks could afford to pay the poll tax, the imposition of this tax on prospective voters was *tantamount* to disenfranchisement for black voters.

tan-trum \'tan-trəm\ (*n*) fit of petulance; caprice. The child learned that he could have almost anything if he went into a *tantrum*.

---

ta-ran-tu-la \tə-'ranch-(ə-)lə\ (*n*) venomous spider. We need an antitoxin to counteract the bite of the *tarantula.*

taut \'tòt\ (*adj*) tight; ready. The captain maintained that he ran a *taut* ship.

tau-to-log-i-cal \,tòt-ᵊl-'äj-i-kəl\ (*adj*) needlessly repetitious. In the sentence "It was visible to the eye," the phrase "to the eye" is *tautological.*

taw-dry \'tòd-rē\ (*adj*) cheap and gaudy. He won a few *tawdry* trinkets at the amusement park in Coney Island. also (*n*).

te-di-um \'tēd-ē-ə-əm\ (*n*) boredom; weariness. The repetitious nature of work on the assembly line added to the *tedium* of Martin's job.

te-mer-i-ty \tə-'mer-ət-ē\ (*n*) boldness; rashness. Do you have the *temerity* to argue with me?

tem-per \'tem-pər\ (*v*) moderate; tone down or restrain; toughen (steel). Not even her supervisor's grumpiness could *temper* Nancy's enthusiasm for her new job.

tem-po \'tem-₍ᵢ₎pō\ (*n*) speed of music. I found the band's *tempo* too slow for such a lively, energetic dance.

tem-po-ral \'tem-p(ə-)rəl\ (*adj*) not lasting forever; limited by time; secular. At one time in our history, *temporal* rulers assumed that they had been given their thrones by divine right.

tem-po-rize \'tem-pə-,rīz\ (*v*) act evasively to gain time; avoid committing oneself. Ordered by King John to drive Robin Hood out of Sherwood Forest, the sheriff *temporized*, hoping to put off any confrontation with the outlaw band.

te-na-cious \tə-'nā-shəs\ (*adj*) holding fast. I had to struggle to break his *tenacious* hold on my arm.

te-nac-i-ty \tə-'nas-ət-ē\ (*n*) firmness; persistency; adhesiveness. Jean Valjean could not believe the *tenacity* of Inspector Javert. Here all Valjean had done was to steal a loaf of bread, and the inspector had pursued him doggedly for twenty years!

\ŋ\ sing \ō\ go \ò\ law \òi\ boy \th\ thin \th\ the \ü\ loot \u̇\ foot
\y\ yet \zh\ vision \à, k̲, ⁿ, œ, œ̄, ue, ūe, ʸ\ *see* Pronunciation Symbols

te-net \'ten-ət\ (*n*) doctrine; dogma. The agnostic did not accept the *tenets* of their faith.

ten-sile \'ten(t)-səl\ (*adj*) capable of being stretched. Mountain climbers must know the *tensile* strength of their ropes.

ten-ta-tive \'tent-ət-iv\ (*adj*) hesitant; not fully worked out or developed; experimental; not definite or positive. Unsure of his welcome at the Christmas party, Scrooge took a *tentative* step into his nephew's drawing room.

ten-u-ous \'ten-yə-wəs\ (*adj*) thin; rare; slim. The allegiance of our allies is based on rather *tenuous* ties; let us hope they remain loyal.

ten-ure \'ten-yər\ (*n*) holding of an office; time during which such an office is held. A special recall election put a sudden end to Gray Davis's *tenure* in office as governor of California.

tep-id \'tep-əd\ (*adj*) lukewarm. To avoid scalding the baby at bath time, make sure the bathwater is *tepid*, not hot.

ter-mi-nol-o-gy \ ˌtər-mə-'näl-ə-jē\ (*n*) terms used in a science or art. In talking to patients, doctors should either avoid medical *terminology* altogether or take time to explain the technical terms they use.

ter-mi-nus \'tər-mə-nəs\ (*n*) last stop of railroad. After we reached the railroad *terminus,* we continued our journey into the wilderness on saddle horses.

ter-res-tri-al \tə-'res-t(r)ē-əl\ (*adj*) earthly (as opposed to celestial); pertaining to the land. In many science fiction movies, alien invaders from outer space plan to destroy all *terrestrial* life.

terse \'tərs\ (*adj*) concise; abrupt; pithy. There is a fine line between speech that is *terse* and to the point and speech that is too abrupt.

ter-ti-ar-y \'tər-shē-ˌer-ē\ (*adj*) third in rank or order. There are four levels of stress in spoken English: primary, secondary, *tertiary*, and unstressed.

\ə\ abut \ᵊ\ kitten, F table \ər\ **further** \a\ ash \ā\ **ace** \ä\ **cot, cart**
\au̇\ **out** \ch\ **chin** \e\ bet \ē\ **easy** \g\ go \i\ hit \ī\ **ice** \j\ **job**

tes·sel·lat·ed \'tes-ə-ˌlāt-əd\ (*adj*) inlaid; mosaic. The tour guide pointed out the intricate geometric pattern of colored stones seen in the chapel's *tesselated* floor.

tes·ta·tor \'tes-ˌtāt-ər\ (*n*) maker of a will. The attorney called in his secretary and his partner to witness the signature of the *testator*.

tes·ty \'tes-tē\ (*adj*) irritable; short-tempered. My advice is to avoid discussing this problem with him today as he is rather *testy*.

teth·er \'teth-ər\ (*v*) tie with a rope. Before we went to sleep, we *tethered* the horses to prevent their wandering off during the night. also (*v*).

thau·ma·tur·gist \'thȯ-mə-ˌtər-jəst\ (*n*) miracle worker; magician. I would have to be a *thaumaturgist* and not a mere doctor to find a remedy for this disease.

the·oc·ra·cy \thē-'äk-rə-sē\ (*n*) government run by religious leaders. Though some Pilgrims aboard the *Mayflower* favored the establishment of a *theocracy* in New England, many of their fellow voyagers preferred a nonreligious form of government.

ther·a·peu·tic \ther-ə-'pyüt-ik\ (*adj*) curative. Now better known for its racetrack, Saratoga Springs first gained attention for the *therapeutic* qualities of its famous "healing waters."

ther·mal \'thər-məl\ (*adj*) pertaining to heat. On cold wintry days, Jack dresses for warmth, putting on his *thermal* underwear.

thrall \'thrȯl\ (*n*) slave; bondage. The nymph Nimue captivates Merlin, holding him in *thrall* to her beauty. The *thrall*, or bondsman, was bound in servitude to his master, the thane.

thren·o·dy \'thren-əd-ē\ (*n*) poem or song of lamentation; dirge. One of Emerson's most famous works is *Threnody*, his lament on the death of his son.

\ŋ\ **sing** \ō\ **go** \ȯ\ **law** \ȯi\ **boy** \th\ **thin** \t̲h̲\ **the** \ü\ **loot** \u̇\ **foot**
\y\ **yet** \zh\ **vision** \à, ḵ, ⁿ, œ, œ̄, ᵫ, ᵫ̄, ʸ\ *see* Pronunciation Symbols

thrifty \'thrif-tē\ (*adj*) careful about money; economical. A *thrifty* shopper compares prices before making major purchases.

throe \'thrō\ (*n*) violent anguish. The *throes* of despair can be as devastating as the spasms accompanying physical pain.

throng \'thrȯŋ\ (*n*) crowd. *Throngs* of shoppers jammed the aisles. also (*v*).

throt-tle \'thrät-ᵊl\ (*v*) strangle. The strangler tried to *throttle* his victim with his bare hands.

thwart \'thwȯ(ə)rt\ (*v*) prevent; frustrate; oppose and defeat. Batman searched for a way to *thwart* the Joker's evil plan to destroy Gotham City.

tim-bre \'tam-bər\ (*n*) quality of a musical tone produced by a musical instrument. The sousaphone has a deep, bass *timbre* that makes it ideally suited for performances outdoors.

ti-mid-i-ty \tə-'mid-ət-ē\ (*n*) lack of self-confidence or courage. If you are to succeed as a salesman, you must first lose your *timidity.*

tim-o-rous \'tim-(ə-)rəs\ (*adj*) fearful; demonstrating fear. His *timorous* manner betrayed the fear he felt at the moment.

ti-rade \tī-'rād\ (*n*) extended scolding; denunciation. The cigar smoker went into a bitter *tirade* denouncing the antismoking forces that had succeeded in banning smoking from most planes and restaurants.

ti-tan-ic \tī-'tan-ik\ (*adj*) gigantic. *Titanic* waves beat against the shore during the hurricane.

tithe \'tīth\ (*n*) tax of one-tenth. Because he was an agnostic, he refused to pay his *tithe* to the clergy. also (*v*).

tit-il-late \'tit-ᵊl-ˌāt\ (*v*) excite superficially; tickle. Talk show hosts *titillate* their audiences, amusing them without enlightening them.

tit-u-lar \'tich-(ə-)lər\ (*adj*) nominal holding of title without obligations. Although he was the *titular* head of the

---

\ə\ **abut** \ᵊ\ kitten, F table \ər\ **further** \a\ ash \ā\ **ace** \ä\ **cot, cart**
\au̇\ **out** \ch\ **chin** \e\ bet \ē\ **easy** \g\ go \i\ hit \ī\ ice \j\ job

company, the real decisions were made by his general manager.

toad-y \\'tōd-ē\ (*n*) servile flatterer; yes man. Never tell the boss anything he doesn't wish to hear: he doesn't want an independent adviser; he just wants a *toady*. also (*v*).

to-ga \\'tō-gə\ (*n*) Roman outer robe. Marc Antony pointed to the slashes in Caesar's *toga*.

tol-er-ant \\'täl(-ə)-rənt\ (*adj*) immune; forbearing. Because of restrictions on water use, we purchased drought-*tolerant* plants for our yard.

tome \\'tōm\ (*n*) large volume. He spent much time in the libraries poring over ancient *tomes*.

to-pog-ra-phy \\tə-'päg-rə-fē\ (*n*) physical features of a region. Before the generals gave the order to attack, they ordered a complete study of the *topography* of the region.

tor-por \\'tòr-pər\ (*n*) lethargy; sluggishness; dormancy. Throughout the winter, nothing aroused the bear from his *torpor*: he would not emerge from hibernation until spring. **tor-pid** \\'tòr-pəd\ (*adj*)

tor-so \\'tòr-ˌsō\ (*n*) trunk of statue with head and limbs missing; human trunk. This torso, found in the ruins of Pompeii, is now on exhibition in the museum in Naples.

tor-tu-ous \\'torch-(ə-)wəs\ (*adj*) winding; full of curves. Because this road is so *tortuous,* it is unwise to go faster than twenty miles an hour on it.

touch-stone \\'təch-ˌstōn\ (*n*) stone used to test the fineness of gold alloys; criterion. What *touchstone* can be used to measure the character of a person?

touchy \\'təch-ē\ (*adj*) sensitive; irascible. Do not discuss his acne with Archy; he is very *touchy* about it.

tox-ic \\'täk-sik\ (*adj*) poisonous. We must seek an antidote for whatever *toxic* substance he has eaten.

tract \\'trakt\ (*n*) pamphlet; a region of indefinite size. The king granted William Penn a *tract* of land in the New World.

\ŋ\ sing \ō\ go \ò\ law \òi\ boy \th\ thin \th̲\ the \ü\ loot \u̇\ foot
\y\ yet \zh\ vision \à, k̲, ⁿ, œ, œ̄, ue, ūe, ʸ\ *see* Pronunciation Symbols

trac-ta-ble \'trak-tə-bəl\ (*adj*) docile; easily managed. Although Susan seemed a *tractable* young woman, she had a stubborn streak of independence that occasionally led her to defy the powers-that-be when she felt they were in the wrong.

tra-duce \trə-'d(y)üs\ (*v*) expose to slander. His opponents tried to *traduce* the candidate's reputation by spreading rumors about his past.

tra-jec-to-ry \tra-'jek-t(ə-)rē\ (*n*) path taken by a projectile. The police tried to locate the spot from which the assassin had fired the fatal shot by tracing the *trajectory* of the bullet.

tran-quil-li-ty \tran-'kwil-ət-ē\ (*n*) calmness; peace. After the commotion and excitement of the city, I appreciate the *tranquillity* of these fields and forests.

tran-scend \tran(t)s-'end\ (*v*) exceed; surpass. This accomplishment *transcends* all our previous efforts. tran-scen-den-tal \tran(t)s-,en-'dent-ᵊl\ (*adj*)

tran-scribe \tran(t)s-'krīb\ (*v*) make a copy of. It took hours for the secretary to *transcribe* his shorthand notes of the conference into a form others could read. tran-scrip-tion \tran(t)s-'krip-shən\ (*n*)

trans-gres-sion \tran(t)s-'gresh-ən\ (*n*) violation of a law; sin. Although Widow Douglass was willing to forgive Huck's *transgressions*, Miss Watson refused to forgive and forget.

tran-sient \'tranch-ənt\ (*adj*) momentary; temporary; staying for a short time. Lexy's joy at finding the perfect Christmas gift for Phil was *transient*; she still had to find presents for the cousins and Uncle Bob. Located near the airport, this hotel caters to a largely *transient* trade. also (*n*).

tran-si-tion \tran(t)s-'ish-ən\ (*n*) going from one state of action to another. During the period of *transition* from oil heat to gas heat, the furnace will have to be shut off.

\ə\ **abut** \ᵊ\ **kitten, F table** \ər\ **further** \a\ **ash** \ā\ **ace** \ä\ **cot, cart**
\aú\ **out** \ch\ **chin** \e\ **bet** \ē\ **easy** \g\ **go** \i\ **hit** \ī\ **ice** \j\ **job**

trans·lu·cent \tran(t)s-'lüs-ᵊnt\ (*adj*) partly transparent. We could not recognize the people in the next room because of the *translucent* curtains that separated us.

trans·mute \tran(t)s-'myüt\ (*v*) change; convert to something different. He was unable to *transmute* his dreams into actualities.

trans·par·ent \tran(t)s-'par-ənt\ (*adj*) easily detected; permitting light to pass through freely. John's pride in his son is *transparent*; no one who sees the two of them together can miss it.

tran·spire \tran(t)s-'pī(ə)r\ (*v*) be revealed; happen. When Austen writes the sentence "It had just *transpired* that he had left gaming debts behind him," her meaning is not that the incident had just occurred, but that the shocking news had just leaked out.

trau·mat·ic \trə-'mat-ik\ (*adj*) pertaining to an injury caused by violence. In his nightmares, he kept recalling the *traumatic* experience of being wounded in battle.

tra·vail \trə-'vā(ə)l\ (*n*) painful physical or mental labor; drudgery; torment. Like every other high school she knew, Sherry hated the yearlong *travail* of cramming for the SAT. also (*v*).

tra·verse \trə-'vərs\ (*v*) go through or across. When you *traverse* this field, be careful of the bull. tra·verse \'tra-vərs\ (*n*)

trav·es·ty \'trav-ə-stē\ (*n*) harshly distorted imitation; parody; debased likeness. Phillips's translation of *Don Quixote* is so inadequate and clumsy that it seems a *travesty* of the original. also (*v*).

trea·tise \'trēt-əs\ (*n*) article treating a subject systematically and thoroughly. He is preparing a *treatise* on the Elizabethan playwrights for his graduate degree.

trek \'trek\ (*v*) travel with difficulty. The tribe *trekked* further north that summer in search of available game. also (*n*).

\ŋ\ **sing**   \ō\ **go**   \ô\ **law**   \ȯi\ **boy**   \th\ **thin**   \t͟h\ **the**   \ü\ **loot**   \u̇\ **foot**
\y\ **yet**   \zh\ **vision**   \à, k̲, ⁿ, œ, œ̄, ue, ūe, ʸ\ *see* Pronunciation Symbols

trem-or \'trem-ər\ (*n*) trembling; slight quiver. She had a nervous *tremor* in her right hand.

trem-u-lous \'trem-yə-ləs\ (*adj*) trembling; wavering. She was *tremulous* more from excitement than from fear.

tren-chant \'tren-chənt\ (*adj*) forceful and vigorous; cutting. With his *trenchant* wit, Rich cuts straight to the heart of the matter, panning a truly dreadful play.

tren-cher-man \'tren-chər-mən\ (*n*) good eater. He is not finicky about his food; he is a *trencherman.*

trep-i-da-tion \,trep-ə-'dā-shən\ (*n*) fear; trembling agitation. As she entered the office of the dean of admissions, Sharon felt some *trepidation* about how she would do in her interview.

trib-u-la-tion \,trib-yə-'lā-shən\ (*n*) distress; suffering. After all the trials and *tribulations* we have gone through, we need this rest.

tri-bu-nal \trī-,byün-ᵊl\ (*n*) court of justice. The decision of the *tribunal* was final.

trib-ute \'trib-₍ᵢ₎yüt\ (*n*) tax levied by a ruler; mark of respect. The colonists refused to pay *tribute* to a foreign despot.

tri-dent \'trīd-ᵊnt\ (*n*) three-pronged spear. Neptune is usually depicted as rising from the sea, carrying his *trident* on his shoulder. also (*adj*).

tril-o-gy \'tril-ə-jē\ (*n*) group of three works. Tolkien's novel *The Lord of the Rings* was published as a *trilogy.*

trite \'trīt\ (*adj*) hackneyed; commonplace. The *trite* and predictable situations in many television programs turn off many viewers, who, in turn, turn off their sets.

tri-vi-a \'triv-ē-ə\ (*n*) trifles; unimportant matters. Too many magazines ignore newsworthy subjects and feature *trivia.*

troth \'träth\ (*n*) pledge of good faith especially in betrothal. He gave her his *troth* and vowed he would cherish her always.

\ə\ **abut** \ᵊ\ **kitten**, F **table** \ər\ **further** \a\ **ash** \ā\ **ace** \ä\ **cot**, **cart**
\au̇\ **out** \ch\ **chin** \e\ **bet** \ē\ **easy** \g\ **go** \i\ **hit** \ī\ **ice** \j\ **job**

tru-cu-lent \'trək-yə-lənt\ (*adj*) aggressive; savage. Tynan's reviews were noted for their caustic attacks on performers and their generally *truculent* tone.

tru-ism \'trü-ˌiz-əm\ (*n*) self-evident truth. Many a *truism* is summed up in a proverb; for example, "Marry in haste, repent at leisure."

trum-pe-ry \'trəm-p(ə-)rē\ (*n*) objects that are showy, valueless, deceptive. All this finery is mere *trumpery*.

trun-cate \'trəŋ-ˌkāt\ (*v*) cut the top off. The top of a cone that has been *truncated* in a plane parallel to its base is a circle.

tryst \'trist\ (*n*) appointed meeting. The lovers kept their *tryst* even though they realized their danger.

tu-mult \'t(y)ü-ˌməlt\ (*n*) commotion; riot; noise. She could not make herself heard over the *tumult* of the mob.

tun-dra \'tən-drə\ (*n*) rolling, treeless plain in Siberia and arctic North America. Despite the cold, many geologists are trying to discover valuable mineral deposits in the *tundra*.

tur-bid \'tər-bəd\ (*adj*) muddy; having the sediment disturbed. The water was *turbid* after the children had waded through it.

tur-bu-lence \'tər-byə-lən(t)s\ (*n*) state of violent agitation. Warned of approaching *turbulence* in the atmosphere, the pilot told the passengers to fasten their seat belts.

tu-reen \tə-'rēn\ (*n*) deep table dish for holding soup. The waiters brought the soup to the tables in silver *tureens*.

tur-gid \'tər-jəd\ (*adj*) swollen; distended. The *turgid* river threatened to overflow the levees and flood the countryside.

turn-key \'tərn-ˌkē\ (*n*) jailer. By bribing the *turnkey*, the prisoner arranged to have better food brought to him in his cell.

\ŋ\ **sing** \ō\ **go** \ȯ\ **law** \ȯi\ **boy** \th\ **thin** \t͟h\ **the** \ü\ **loot** \u̇\ **foot** \y\ **yet** \zh\ **vision** \à, k̲, ⁿ, œ, œ̄, ᴜe, ᴜ̄e, ʸ\ *see* Pronunciation Symbols

tur-pi-tude \'tər-pə-ˌt(y)üd\ (*n*) depravity. A visitor may be denied admittance to this country if he has been guilty of moral *turpitude*.

tu-te-lage \'t(y)üt-ᵊl-ij\ (*n*) guardianship; training. Under the *tutelage* of such masters of the instrument, she made rapid progress as a virtuoso.

tu-te-lar-y \'t(y)üt-ᵊl-ˌer-ē\ (*adj*) protective; pertaining to a guardianship. I was acting in my *tutelary* capacity when I refused to grant you permission to leave the campus. also (*n*).

ty-ro \'tī-ₒrō\ (*n*) beginner; novice. For a mere *tyro*, you have achieved some wonderfully expert results.

U

u·biq·ui·tous \yü-'bik-wət-əs\ (*adj*) being everywhere; omnipresent. That Christmas "The Little Drummer Boy" seemed *ubiquitous*: David heard the tune everywhere.

ul·te·ri·or \ˌəl-'tir-ē-ər\ (*adj*) unstated; hidden; more remote. Suspicious of altruistic gestures, he looked for an *ulterior* motive behind every charitable deed.

ul·ti·mate \'əl-tə-mət\ (*adj*) final; not susceptible to further analysis. Scientists are searching for the *ultimate* truths. also (*n*).

ul·ti·ma·tum \ˌəl-tə-'māt-əm\ (*n*) last demand; warning. Since they have ignored our *ultimatum,* our only recourse is to declare war.

um·brage \'əm-brij\ (*n*) resentment; anger; sense of injury or insult. She took *umbrage* at his remarks and stormed away in a huff.

u·na·nim·i·ty \ˌyü-nə-'nim-ət-ē\ (*n*) complete agreement. We were surprised by the *unanimity* with which members of both parties accepted our proposals. u·nan·i·mous \yu̇-nan-ə-məs\ (*adj*)

un·as·suag·able \ˌən-ə-'swā-jə-bəl\ (*adj*) unable to be soothed. He was *unassuagable;* the apology did no good.

un·as·sum·ing \ˌən-ə-'sü-miŋ\ (*adj*) modest. He is so *unassuming* that some people fail to realize how great a man he really is.

un·bri·dled \ˌən-'brīd-ᵊld\ (*adj*) unrestrained. He had a sudden fit of *unbridled* rage.

un·can·ny \ən-'kan-ē\ (*adj*) strange; mysterious. You have the *uncanny* knack of reading my innermost thoughts.

un·con·scio·na·ble \ən-'känch-(ə-)nə-bəl\ (*adj*) unscrupulous; excessive. He found the loan shark's demands *unconscionable* and impossible to meet.

---

un·couth \ən-'küth\ (*adj*) outlandish; clumsy; boorish. Most biographers portray Lincoln as an *uncouth* and ungainly young man.

unc·tion \'əŋ(k)-shən\ (*n*) the act of anointing with oil. The anointing with oil of a person near death is called extreme *unction.*

unc·tu·ous \'əŋ(k)-chə(-wə)s\ (*adj*) oily; bland; insincerely suave. Uriah Heep disguised his nefarious actions by *unctuous* protestations of his "'umility."

un·du·late \'ən jə-‚lāt\ (*v*) move with a wavelike motion. The hula dancers *undulated* enticingly, moving their hips and arms sinuously. un·du·late \'ən-jə-lət\ (*adj*)

un·earth \‚ən-'ərth\ (*v*) dig up. When they *unearthed* the city, the archaeologists found many relics of an ancient civilization.

un·earth·ly \‚ən-'ərth-lē\ (*adj*) supernatural; weird; not earthly. The trick-or-treaters heard *unearthly* moans coming from the old haunted house.

un·e·quiv·o·cal \ ‚ən-i-'kwiv-ə-kəl\ (*adj*) plain; obvious. My answer to your proposal is an *unequivocal* and absolute "No."

un·err·ing·ly \‚ən-'e(ə)r-iŋ-lē\ (*adv*) infallibly. My teacher *unerringly* pounced on the one typographical error in my essay.

un·fal·ter·ing \‚ən-'föl-t(ə-)riŋ\ (*adj*) steadfast. She approached the guillotine with *unfaltering* steps.

un·feigned \ən-'fānd\ (*adj*) genuine; real. My grandmother genuinely loved company: her obvious delight at guests was *unfeigned.*

un·fledged \‚ən-'flejd\ (*adj*) immature. It is hard for an *unfledged* writer to find a sympathetic publisher.

un·gain·ly \ən 'gān-lē\ (*adj*) awkward; clumsy; unwieldy. "If you want proof that Nick's an *ungainly* dancer, check out my bruised feet," said Nora. Anyone who has ever tried to carry a bass fiddle knows it's an *ungainly* instrument.

un-guent \'ən-gwənt\ (*n*) ointment. Apply this *unguent* to the sore muscles before retiring.

u-ni-for-mi-ty \yü-nə-'fòr-mət-ē\ (*n*) sameness; consistency; monotony. After a while, the *uniformity* of TV situation comedies becomes boring. u-ni-form \'yü-nə-ˌfòrm\ (*adj*)

u-ni-lat-er-al \yü-ni-'lat-ə-rəl\ (*adj*) undertaken by only one side; involving one side; obligating only one side. Pacifists advocate *unilateral* disarmament, trusting that if one side discards its weapons, others will follow.

un-im-peach-a-ble \ˌən-im-'pē-chə-bəl\ (*adj*) blameless and exemplary. Her conduct in office was *unimpeachable*; her record, spotless.

un-in-hib-it-ed \ˌən-in-'hib-ət-əd\ (*adj*) unrepressed. The congregation was shocked by her *uninhibited* laughter during the sermon.

u-nique \yü-'nēk\ (*adj*) without an equal; single in kind. You have the *unique* distinction of being the first student whom I have had to fail in this course.

u-ni-son \'yü-nə-sən\ (*n*) unity of pitch; complete accord. The choir sang in *unison,* forty voices sounding as one.

un-kempt \ən-'kem(p)t\ (*adj*) disheveled; uncared for in appearance. Jeremy hated his neighbor's *unkempt* lawn: he thought its neglected appearance had a detrimental effect on neighborhood property values.

un-mit-i-gat-ed \ˌən-'mit-ə-ˌgāt-əd\ (*adj*) unrelieved or immoderate; absolute. After four days of *unmitigated* heat, I was ready to collapse from heat prostration. The congresswoman's husband was an *unmitigated* jerk: not only did he abandon her, he took her campaign funds, too!

un-ob-tru-sive \ˌən-əb-'trü-siv\ (*adj*) inconspicuous; not blatant. Reluctant to attract notice, the governess took a chair in a far corner of the room and tried to be as *unobtrusive* as possible.

\ŋ\ si**ng** \ō\ g**o** \ò\ l**aw** \òi\ b**oy** \th\ **th**in \th̲\ **th**e \ü\ l**oo**t \ù\ f**oo**t
\y\ **y**et \zh\ vi**s**ion \à, k̲, ⁿ, œ, œ̄, ue, ūe, ʸ\ *see* Pronunciation Symbols

un-prec-e-dent-ed \ˌən-'pres-ə-ˌdent-əd\ (*adj*) novel; unparalleled. Margaret Mitchell's novel *Gone with the Wind* was an *unprecedented* success that made publishing history.

un-ru-ly \ən-'rü-lē\ (*adj*) disobedient; lawless. The only way to curb this *unruly* mob is to use tear gas.

un-sa-vo-ry \ˌən-'sāv-(ə-)rē\ (*adj*) distasteful; morally offensive. People with *unsavory* reputations should not be allowed to work with young children.

un-seem-ly \ən-'sēm-lē\ (*adj*) unbecoming; indecent; in poor taste. When he put whoopie cushions on all the seats in the funeral parlor, Seymour's conduct was most *unseemly*.

un-sul-lied \ən-'səl-ēd\ (*adj*) spotlessly clean; unstained. The reputation of our school is *unsullied*, young ladies: conduct yourself modestly and discreetly, so that you never disgrace our good name.

un-ten-a-ble \ən-'ten-ə-bəl\ (*adj*) indefensible; not able to be maintained. Wayne is so contrary that, the more *untenable* a position is, the harder he'll try to defend it.

un-to-ward \ˌən-'tō(-ə)rd\ (*adj*) unfortunate or unlucky; adverse; unexpected. Trying to sneak out of the house, Huck had a most *untoward* encounter with Miss Watson, who thwarted his escape.

un-wit-ting \ən-'wit-iŋ\ (*adj*) unintentional; not knowing. Honest by nature, he was the *unwitting* tool of the swindlers.

un-wont-ed \ən-'wȯnt-əd\ (*adj*) unaccustomed by experience. He hesitated to assume the *unwonted* role of master of ceremonies at the dinner.

up-braid \ˌəp-'brād\ (*v*) severely scold; reprimand. Not only did Miss Minchin *upbraid* Ermengarde for her disobedience, but she hung her up by her braids from a coat rack in the classroom.

\ə\ **abut** \ᵊ\ **kitten,** F table \ər\ **further** \a\ **ash** \ā\ **ace** \ä\ **cot, cart**
\au̇\ **out** \ch\ **chin** \e\ **bet** \ē\ **easy** \g\ **go** \i\ **hit** \ī\ **ice** \j\ **job**

up-shot \'əp-ˌshät\ (*n*) outcome. The *upshot* of the rematch was that the former champion proved that he still possessed all the skills of his youth.

ur-bane \ˌər-'bān\ (*adj*) suave; refined; elegant. The courtier was *urbane* and sophisticated. ur-ban-i-ty \ˌər-'ban-ət-ē\ (*n*)

ur-chin \'ər-chən\ (*n*) mischievous child (usually a boy). Get out! This store is no place for grubby *urchins!*

ur-sine \'ər-ˌsīn\ (*adj*) bearlike; pertaining to a bear. Because of its *ursine* appearance, the great panda has been identified with the bears; actually, it is closely related to the raccoon.

u-sur-pa-tion \ˌyü-sər-'pā-shən\ (*n*) act of seizing power and rank of another. The revolution ended when the victorious rebel general succeeded in his *usurpation* of the throne.

u-su-ry \'yüzh-(ə-)rē\ (*n*) lending money at illegal rates of interest. The loan shark was found guilty of *usury.*

u-to-pi-a \yu-'tō-pē-ə\ (*n*) ideal place, state, or society. Fed up with this imperfect universe, Don would have liked to run off to Shangri-la or some other imaginary *utopia.*

V

vac·il·la·tion \\'vas-ə-'lā-shən\ (*n*) wavering; indecisiveness; fluctuation. Her parents grew impatient with Allison's *vacillation* between Harvard and Yale; they just wanted her to make up her mind which school she would attend.

vac·u·ous \\'vak-yə-wəs\ (*adj*) empty; inane. The *vacuous* remarks of the politician annoyed the audience, who had hoped to hear more than empty platitudes.

vag·a·bond \\'vag-ə-ˌbänd\ (*n*) wanderer; tramp. In summer, college students wander the roads of Europe like carefree *vagabonds*. also (*adj*).

va·ga·ry \\'vā-gə-rē\ (*n*) caprice; whim. She followed every *vagary* of fashion.

va·grant \\'vā-grənt\ (*adj*) stray; random. He tried to study, but could not collect his *vagrant* thoughts. va·gran·cy \\'vā-grən(t)-sē\ (*n*)

va·grant \\'vā-grənt\ (*n*) homeless wanderer. Because he was a stranger in town and had no visible means of support, Martin feared he would be jailed as a *vagrant*. va·gran·cy \\'va-grən(t)-sē\ (*n*)

vague \\'vāg\ (*adj*) unclear. The politician gave *vague* answers to the reporters' questions in order to avoid offending any voters.

vain·glo·ri·ous \⁽ⁱ⁾vān-'glōr-ē-əs\ (*adj*) boastful; excessively conceited. Puffed up with empty pride, someone *vainglorious* is vain enough to consider himself simply glorious.

val·e·dic·to·ry \\'val-ə-'dik-t(ə-)rē\ (*adj*) pertaining to farewell. I found the *valedictory* address too long; leave-taking should be brief. also (*n*).

val·i·date \\'val-ə-ˌdāt\ (*v*) confirm; ratify. I will not publish my findings until I *validate* my results.

val·or \\'val-ər\ (*n*) bravery. He received the Medal of Honor for his *valor* in battle. val·iant \\'val-yənt\ (*adj*)

\ə\ **abut** \ᵊ\ **kitten**, F **table** \ər\ **further** \a\ **ash** \ā\ **ace** \ä\ **cot, cart**
\aú\ **out** \ch\ **chin** \e\ **bet** \ē\ **easy** \g\ **go** \i\ **hit** \ī\ **ice** \j\ **job**

vam-pire \'vam-ˌpī(ə)r\ (*n*) ghostly being that sucks the blood of the living. Children were afraid to go to sleep at night because of the many legends of *vampires.*

van-guard \'van-ˌgärd\ (*n*) advance guard of a military force; forefront of a movement. When no enemy was in sight, the Duke of Plaza Toro marched in the *vanguard* of his troops, but once the bullets flew above, he headed for the rear.

van-tage \'vant-ij\ (*n*) position giving an advantage. They fired upon the enemy from behind trees, walls, and any other point of *vantage* they could find.

va-pid \'vap-əd\ (*adj*) dull and unimaginative; insipid and flavorless. "*Bor*-ing!" said Cher, as she suffered through yet another *vapid* lecture about Dead White Male Poets.

var-i-e-gat-ed \'ver-ē-ə-ˌgāt-əd\ (*adj*) many-colored. Without her glasses, Gretchen saw the fields of red and yellow and purple tulips as a *variegated* blur.

vas-sal \'vas-əl\ (*n*) in feudalism, one who held land of a superior lord. The lord demanded that his *vassals* contribute more to his military campaign.

vaunt-ed \'vȯnt-əd\ (*adj*) boasted; highly publicized. Our much-*vaunted* educational system fails as often as it succeeds; too many children are left behind.

veer \'vi(ə)r\ (*v*) change in direction. After what seemed an eternity, the wind *veered* to the east and the storm abated. also (*n*).

veg-e-tate \'vej-ə-ˌtāt\ (*v*) live in a monotonous way. I do not understand how you can *vegetate* in this quiet village after the adventurous life you have led.

ve-he-ment \'vē-ə-mənt\ (*adj*) forceful; intensely emotional; with marked vigor. Alfred became so *vehement* in describing what was wrong with the Internal Revenue Service that he began to froth at the mouth.

\ŋ\ **sing** \ō\ **go** \ȯ\ **law** \ȯi\ **boy** \th\ **thin** \th\ **the** \ü\ **loot** \u̇\ **foot**
\y\ **yet** \zh\ **vision** \à, k̲, ⁿ, œ, œ̄, ue, ūe, ʸ\ *see* Pronunciation Symbols

vel·lum \\'vel-əm\ (*n*) parchment. Bound in *vellum* and embossed in gold, this book is a beautiful example of the binder's craft. also (*adj*).

ve·loc·i·ty \və-'läs-ət-ē\ (*n*) speed. The train went by at a considerable *velocity*.

ve·nal \\'vēn-ᵊl\ (*adj*) capable of being bribed. The *venal* policeman accepted the bribe offered him by the speeding motorist whom he had stopped.

ven·det·ta \ven-'det-ə\ (*n*) feud; private warfare. Hoping to stop the street warfare disrupting his city, the Duke ordered the Capulet and Montague families to end their bitter *vendetta*.

ven·dor \\'ven-dər\ (*n*) seller. The fruit *vendor* sold her wares from a stall on the sidewalk.

ve·neer \və-'ni(ə)r\ (*n*) thin layer; cover. Casual acquaintances were deceived by his *veneer* of sophistication and failed to recognize his fundamental shallowness. also (*v*).

ven·er·a·ble \\'ven-ər(-ə)-bəl\ (*adj*) deserving high respect. We mean no disrespect when we refuse to follow the advice of our *venerable* leader.

ven·er·ate \\'ven-ə-ˌrāt\ (*v*) revere. In Tibet today, the common people still *venerate* their traditional spiritual leader, the Dalai Lama.

ve·ni·al \\'vē-nē-əl\ (*adj*) forgivable; trivial. From a modern viewpoint, when Jean Valjean stole a loaf of bread to feed his starving sister, he committed a *venial*, forgivable offense.

vent \\'vent\ (*n*) a small opening outlet. The wine did not flow because the air *vent* in the barrel was clogged. also (*v*).

ven·tril·o·quist \ven-'tril-ə-kwəst\ (*n*) someone who can make his or her voice seem to come from another person or thing. In the classic movie *Dead of Night*, the *ventriloquist* is possessed by his wooden dummy, which torments its master, driving him to madness and murder.

\ə\ **abut** \ᵊ\ **kitten**, F **table** \ər\ **further** \a\ **ash** \ā\ **ace** \ä\ **cot, cart**
\aú\ **out** \ch\ **chin** \e\ **bet** \ē\ **easy** \g\ **go** \i\ **hit** \ī\ **ice** \j\ **job**

ven·ture·some \'ven-chər-səm\ *(adj)* involving risks; audacious. Prudence preferred the small but steady interest she earned on her certificates of deposit to potentially greater but less certain profits from more *venturesome* investments.

ven·tur·ous \'vench-(ə-)rəs\ *(adj)* daring. Three *venturous* vessels—the *Nina*, the *Pinta*, and the *Santa Maria*—boldly set out to discover a new route to the fabled Indies.

ven·ue \'ven-ˌyü\ *(n)* location. The attorney asked for a change of *venue;* he thought his client would do better if the trial were held in a less conservative county.

ve·ra·cious \və-'rā-shəs\ *(adj)* truthful; accurate. Originally accepted as *veracious*, Mandeville's account of his travels has proven to be at best fanciful, at worst a pack of lies. **ve·rac·i·ty** \və-'ras-ət-ē\ *(n)*

ver·bal·ize \'vər-bə-ˌlīz\ *(v)* to put into words. I know you don't like to talk about these things, but please try to *verbalize* your feelings.

ver·ba·tim \ˌ(ˌ)vər-'bāt-əm\ *(adv)* word for word. Blessed with a retentive memory, he could repeat lengthy messages *verbatim*. also *(adj)*.

ver·bi·age \'vər-bē-ij\ *(n)* pompous array of words. After we had waded through all the *verbiage,* we discovered that the writer had said very little.

ver·bose \ˌ(ˌ)vər-'bōs\ *(adj)* wordy. Someone mute cannot talk; someone *verbose* can hardly stop talking.

ver·dant \'vərd-ᵊnt\ *(adj)* green; lush in vegetation. Monet's paintings of the *verdant* meadows were symphonies in green.

verge \'vərj\ *(n)* border; edge. Madame Curie knew she was on the *verge* of discovering the secrets of radioactive elements. also *(v)*.

ver·i·si·mil·i·tude \ver-ə-sə-'mil-ə-ˌt(y)üd\ *(n)* appearance of truth; likelihood. Critics praised her for the *verisimil-*

\ŋ\ **sing** \ō\ **go** \ȯ\ **law** \ȯi\ **boy** \th\ **thin** \t͟h\ **the** \ü\ **loot** \u̇\ **foot**
\y\ **yet** \zh\ **vision** \à, k̲, ⁿ, œ, œ̄, ɷe, œ̄e, ʸ\ *see* Pronunciation Symbols

itude of her performance as Lady Macbeth. She was completely believable.

ver-i-ty \'ver-ət-ē\ (*n*) quality of being true; lasting truth or principle. Do you question the *verity* of the witness's testimony about what he heard on the night of the murder? To the skeptic, everything was relative: there were no eternal *verities* in which one could believe.

ver-nac-u-lar \və(r)-'nak-yə-lər\ (*n*) living language; natural style. Cut out those old-fashioned thee's and thou's and write in the *vernacular;* also (*adj*).

ver-nal \'vərn-ᵊl\ (*adj*) pertaining to spring. We may expect *vernal* showers all during the month of April.

ver-sa-tile \'vər-sət-ᵊl\ (*adj*) having many talents; capable of working in many fields. She was a *versatile* athlete, earning varsity letters in basketball, hockey, and track.

ver-tex \'vər-ˌteks\ (*n*) summit. Let us drop a perpendicular line from the *vertex* of the triangle to the base.

ver-tig-i-nous \₍ᵤ₎vər-'tij-ə-nəs\ (*adj*) giddy; causing dizziness. Sufferers from Meniere's Syndrome, an inner ear disorder causing loss of balance, complain of its *vertiginous* effects.

ver-ti-go \'vərt-i-gō\ (*n*) dizziness. When you test potential plane pilots for susceptibility to spells of *vertigo*, be sure to hand out airsick bags.

verve \'vərv\ (*n*) energy in expressing ideas, especially artistically; liveliness. In his rhymes, Seuss writes with such *verve* and good humor that adults as well as children delight in the adventures of the Cat in the Hat.

ves-tige \'ves-tij\ (*n*) trace; remains. We discovered *vestiges* of early Indian life in the cave.

vex \'veks\ (*v*) annoy; distress. Please try not to *vex* your mother; she is doing the best she can.

vi-a-ble \'vī-ə-bəl\ (*adj*) practical or workable; capable of maintaining life. That idea won't work. Let me see whether I can come up with a *viable* alternative.

\ə\ **abut** \ᵊ\ **kitten**, F **table** \ər\ **further** \a\ **ash** \ā\ **ace** \ä\ **cot, cart**
\au̇\ **out** \ch\ **chin** \e\ **bet** \ē\ **easy** \g\ **go** \i\ **hit** \ī\ **ice** \j\ **job**

vi-ands \'vī-əndz\ (*n*) items of food; choice dishes; provisions. The elegant restaurant served only the most exquisite *viands* and the finest wines.

vi-car-i-ous \vī-'ker-ē-əs\ (*adj*) acting as a substitute; done by a deputy. Though Maud was too meek to talk back to anybody, she got a *vicarious* kick out of Rita's sharp retorts.

vi-cis-si-tude \və-'sis-ə-ˌt(y)üd\ (*n*) change of fortune. Humbled by life's *vicissitudes*, the last emperor of China worked as a lowly gardener in the palace over which he had once ruled.

vict-uals \'vit-ᵊlz\ (*n*) food supplies; provisions. We loaded the camper with enough *victuals* to last us the entire two weeks we'd be on the road.

vie \'vī\ (*v*) contend; compete. Politicians *vie* with one another, competing for donations and votes.

vig-i-lance \'vij-ə-lən(t)s\ (*n*) watchfulness. Eternal *vigilance* is the price of liberty.

vi-gnette \vin-'yet\ (*n*) picture; short literary sketch. *The New Yorker* published her latest *vignette*.

vig-or \'vig-ər\ (*n*) active strength. Although he was over seventy years old, Jack had the *vigor* of a man in his prime. **vig-or-ous** \'vig-(ə-)rəs\ (*adj*)

vil-i-fy \'vil-ə-ˌfī\ (*v*) slander. Waging a highly negative campaign, the candidate attempted to *vilify* his opponent's reputation.

vin-di-cate \'vin-də-ˌkāt\ (*v*) clear from blame; exonerate; justify or support. The lawyer's goal was to *vindicate* her client and prove him innocent on all charges. The critics' extremely favorable reviews *vindicate* my opinion that *The Madness of King George* is a brilliant movie.

vin-dic-tive \vin-'dik-tiv\ (*adj*) out for revenge; malicious. Divorce sometimes brings out a *vindictive* streak in people; when Tony told Tina he wanted a divorce, she poured green Jello into the aquarium and turned his tropical fish into dessert.

vi-per \'vī-pər\ (*n*) poisonous snake. The habitat of the horned *viper,* a particularly venomous snake, is in sandy regions like the Sahara or the Sinai peninsula.

vir-ile \'vir-əl\ (*adj*) manly. I do not accept the premise that a man is *virile* only when he is belligerent.

vir-tu-o-so \vər-chə-'wō-ₜ)sō\ (*n*) highly skilled artist. The promising young cellist Yo-Yo Ma grew into a *virtuoso* whose performances thrilled audiences throughout the world.

vir-u-lent \'vir-(y)ə-lənt\ (*adj*) extremely poisonous; hostile; bitter. Laid up with a *virulent* case of measles, Vera blamed her doctors because her recovery took so long. In fact, she became quite *virulent* on the subject of the quality of modern medical care.

vi-rus \'vī-rəs\ (*n*) disease communicator. The doctors are looking for a specific medicine to control this *virus.*

vis-age \'viz-ij\ (*n*) face; appearance. The stern *visage* of the judge indicated that he had decided to impose a severe penalty.

vis-cer-al \'vis-ə-rəl\ (*adj*) felt in one's inner organs. She disliked the *visceral* sensations she had whenever she rode the roller coaster.

vis-cous \'vis-kəs\ (*adj*) sticky; gluey. Melted tar is a *viscous* substance. **vis-cos-i-ty** \vis-'käs-ət-ē\ (*n*)

vi-sion-ar-y \'vizh-ə-ner-ē\ (*adj*) produced by imagination; fanciful; mystical. He was given to *visionary* schemes that never materialized. also (*n*).

vi-ti-ate \'vish-ē-ₐāt\ (*v*) spoil the effect of; make inoperative. Fraud will *vitiate* the contract.

vit-re-ous \'vi-trē-əs\ (*adj*) pertaining to or resembling glass. Although this plastic has many *vitreous* qualities such as transparency, it is unbreakable.

\ə\ **abut** \ᵊ\ **kitten, F table** \ər\ **further** \a\ **ash** \ā\ **ace** \ä\ **cot, cart**
\aů\ **out** \ch\ **chin** \e\ **bet** \ē\ **easy** \g\ **go** \i\ **hit** \ī\ **ice** \j\ **job**

vit-ri-ol-ic \vi-trē-'äl-ik\ (*adj*) corrosive; sarcastic. Oil of *vitriol*, or sulfuric acid, leaves scars on the flesh; *vitriolic* criticism leaves scars on the soul.

vi-tu-per-a-tive \vī-'t(y)ü-p(ə-)rət-iv\ (*adj*) abusive; scolding. He became more *vituperative* as he realized that we were not going to grant him his wish.

vi-va-cious \və-'vā-shəs\ (*adj*) animated; gay. She had always been *vivacious* and sparkling.

vi-vi-sec-tion \viv-ə-'sek-shən\ (*n*) act of dissecting living animals. The Society for the Prevention of Cruelty to Animals opposed *vivisection* and deplored the practice of using animals in scientific experiments.

vix-en \'vik-sən\ (*n*) female fox; ill-tempered woman. Furious at her nagging, he lost his temper and called her a shrew and a *vixen*.

vo-cif-er-ous \vō-'sif-(ə-)rəs\ (*adj*) clamorous; noisy. The crowd grew *vociferous* in its anger and threatened to take the law into its own hands.

vogue \'vōg\ (*n*) popular fashion. Body piercings became the *vogue* on many college campuses.

vol-a-tile \'väl-ət-ᵊl\ (*adj*) changeable; explosive; evaporating rapidly. The political climate today is extremely *volatile*: no one can predict what the electorate will do next. Maria Callas's temper was extremely *volatile*: the only thing you could predict was that she was sure to blow up. Acetone is an extremely *volatile* liquid: it evaporates instantly.

vo-li-tion \vō-'lish-ən\ (*n*) act of making a conscious choice. She selected this dress of her own *volition*.

vol-u-ble \'väl-yə-bəl\ (*adj*) fluent; glib; talkative. An excessively *voluble* speaker suffers from logorrhea: he runs off at the mouth a lot!

vo-lu-mi-nous \və-'lü-mə-nəs\ (*adj*) bulky; large. Despite her family burdens, she kept up a *voluminous* correspondence with her friends.

vo-lup-tu-ous \və-'ləp-chə-(-wə)s\ (*adj*) suggesting sensual delights; sensuously pleasing. Renoir's paintings of nude women accent his subjects' rosy-tinted flesh and full *voluptuous* figures.

vo-ra-cious \vȯ-'rā-shəs\ (*adj*) ravenous. The wolf is a *voracious* animal, its hunger never satisfied.

vo-ta-ry \'vōt-ə-rē\ (*n*) follower of a cult. He was a *votary* of every new movement in literature and art.

vouch-safe \vaùch-'sāf\ (*v*) grant; choose to give in reply; permit. Occasionally the rock star would drift out onto the balcony and *vouchsafe* the crowd below a glimpse of her celebrated features. The professor *vouchsafed* not a word to the students' questions about what would be covered on the test.

vul-ner-a-ble \'vəln-(ə-)rə-bəl\ (*adj*) susceptible to wounds. His opponents could not harm Achilles, who was *vulnerable* only in his heel.

vy-ing \'vī-iŋ\ (*v*) contending. Why are we *vying* with each other for his favors? vie \'vī\ (*v*)

W

waft \'wäft\ (*v*) move gently, as if impelled by wind or waves. Daydreaming, he gazed at the leaves that *wafted* past his window. also (*n*).

wag-gish \'wag-ish\ (*adj*) mischievous; humorous; tricky. He was a prankster who, unfortunately, often overlooked the damage he could cause with his *waggish* tricks.

waif \'wāf\ (*n*) homeless child or animal. Although he already had eight cats, he could not resist adopting yet another feline *waif*.

waive \'wāv\ (*v*) give up a claim or right voluntarily; refrain from enforcing; postpone considering. Although technically prospective students had to live in Piedmont to attend high school there, occasionally the school *waived* the residence requirement in order to enroll promising athletes.

wal-low \'wäl-₍ᵢ₎ō\ (*v*) roll in; indulge in; become helpless. The hippopotamus loves to *wallow* in pools of mud. The horror film addict loves to *wallow* in scenes of blood.

wan \'wän\ (*adj*) having a pale or sickly color; pallid. The convalescent looked frail and *wan*, her skin almost as white as the sheets on her sickbed.

wane \'wān\ (*v*) decrease in size or strength; draw gradually to an end. The verb *wax* or grow in size, is an antonym for *wane*. As it burns, does a wax candle *wane*?

wan-gle \'waŋ-gəl\ (*v*) bring about by manipulation or trickery. She tried to *wangle* an invitation to the party.

wan-ton \'wȯnt-ᵊn\ (*adj*) unrestrained; willfully malicious; unchaste. Pointing to the stack of bills, Sheldon criticized Sarah for her *wanton* expenditures. In response, Sarah accused Sheldon of making an unfounded, *wanton* attack. also (*n*).

---

war-ble \\'wȯr-bəl\\ (*v*) sing melodiously; trill. Every morning the birds *warbled* outside her window. also (*n*).

war-rant \\'wȯr-ənt\\ (*v*) justify; authorize. Before the judge issues the injunction, you must convince her this action is *warranted*.

war-ran-ty \\'wȯr-ənt-ē\\ (*n*) guarantee; assurance by seller. The purchaser of this automobile is protected by the manufacturer's *warranty* that he will replace any defective part for five years or 50,000 miles.

war-y \\'wa(ə)r-ē\\ (*adj*) very cautious. The spies grew *wary* as they approached the sentry.

wast-rel \\'wā-strəl\\ (*n*) profligate. He was denounced as a *wastrel* who had dissipated his inheritance.

wax \\'waks\\ (*v*) increase; grow. With proper handling, his fortunes *waxed* and he became rich.

way-lay \\'wā-ˌlā\\ (*v*) ambush; lie in wait. The muggers agreed to *waylay* their victim as he passed through the dark alley going home.

wean \\'wēn\\ (*v*) accustom a baby not to nurse; give up a cherished activity. He decided he would *wean* himself away from eating junk food and stick to fruits and vegetables.

weath-er \\'weth-ər\\ (*v*) endure the effects of weather or other forces. Would Governor Gray Davis *weather* this latest political challenge and remain in office, or would he be California's first governor to be recalled?

welt \\'welt\\ (*n*) mark from a beating or whipping. The evidence of child abuse was very clear; Jennifer's small body was covered with *welts* and bruises.

wel-ter \\'wel-tər\\ (*n*) turmoil; bewildering jumble. The existing *welter* of overlapping federal and state programs cries out for immediate reform. also (*v*).

whee-dle \\'hwēd-ᵊl\\ (*v*) cajole; coax; deceive by flattery. She knows she can *wheedle* almost anything she wants from her father.

\\ə\\ abut \\ᵊ\\ kitten, F table \\ər\\ further \\a\\ ash \\ā\\ ace \\ä\\ cot, cart
\\au̇\\ out \\ch\\ chin \\e\\ bet \\ē\\ easy \\g\\ go \\i\\ hit \\ī\\ ice \\j\\ job

whelp \'hwelp\ (*n*) young wolf, dog, tiger, etc. This collie *whelp* won't do for breeding, but he'd make a fine pet.

whet \'hwet\ (*v*) sharpen; stimulate. The odors from the kitchen are *whetting* my appetite; I will be ravenous by the time the meal is served.

whim-si-cal \'hwim-zi-kəl\ (*adj*) capricious; fanciful; quaint. The hero of *Mrs. Doubtfire* is a playful, *whimsical* man who takes a notion to dress up as a woman so that he can look after his children, who are in the custody of his ex-wife.

whin-ny \'hwin-ē\ (*v*) neigh like a horse. When he laughed through his nose, it sounded as if he *whinnied.* also (*n*).

whit \'hwit\ (*n*) smallest bit; iota. Unafraid of public opinion, Jennifer didn't give a *whit* what anyone said about her.

whorl \'hwȯr(ə)l\ (*n*) ring of leaves around stem; ring. Identification by fingerprints is based on the difference in shape and number of the *whorls* on the fingers.

wi-ly \'wī-lē\ (*adj*) cunning; artful. If coyotes are supposed to be such sneaky, *wily* creatures, how come Road Runner always manages to outwit Wile E. Coyote?

wince \'win(t)s\ (*v*) shrink back; flinch. The screech of the chalk on the blackboard made her *wince.*

wind-fall \'win(d)-ˌfȯl\ (*n*) unexpected lucky event. This huge tax refund is quite a *windfall.*

win-now \'win-₍ˌ₎ō\ (*v*) sift; separate good parts from bad. This test will *winnow* out the students who study from those who don't bother.

win-some \'win(t)-səm\ (*adj*) agreeable; gracious; engaging. By her *winsome* manner, she made herself liked by everyone who met her.

with-er \'wi<u>th</u>-ər\ (*v*) shrivel; decay. Cut flowers are beautiful for a day, but all too soon they *wither.*

wit-less \'wit-ləs\ (*adj*) foolish; idiotic. If Beavis is a half-wit, then Butthead is totally *witless.*

---

wit-ti-cism \'wit-ə-ˌsiz-əm\ (*n*) witty saying; wisecrack. I don't mean any criticism, but your latest *witticism* totally hurt my feelings.

wiz-ard-ry \'wiz-ə(r)-drē\ (*n*) sorcery; magic. Harry Potter amazed the whole school with his *wizardry.*

wiz-en \'wiz-ᵊn\ (*v*) wither; shrivel. The hot sun *wizened* all the trees and plants.

wont \'wȯnt\ (*n*) custom; habitual procedure. As was his *wont,* he jogged two miles every morning before going to work.

world-ly \'wər(-ə)l-dlē\ (*adj*) engrossed in matters of this earth; not spiritual. You must leave your *worldly* goods behind you when you go to meet your Maker.

wran-gle \'raŋ-gəl\ (*v*) quarrel; obtain through arguing; herd cattle. The quarrelsome siblings *wrangled* over their inheritance.

wrath \'rath\ (*n*) anger; fury. She turned to him, full of *wrath,* and said, "What makes you think I'll accept lower pay for this job than you get?"

wreak \'rēk\ (*v*) bring about or cause; inflict upon; vent. The brigands *wreaked* havoc in the town, breaking into stores and burning houses. Enraged, the town's mayor vowed to *wreak* vengeance upon them.

wrench \'rench\ (*v*) pull; strain; twist. She *wrenched* free of her attacker and landed a powerful kick to his kneecap.

wrest \'rest\ (*v*) pull away; take by violence. With only ten seconds left to play, our team *wrested* victory from their opponents' grasp.

writhe \'rīth\ (*v*) twist in coils; contort in pain. In *Dances with Snakes*, the snake dancer wriggled sinuously as her boa constrictor *writhed* around her torso.

wry \'rī\ (*adj*) twisted; with a humorous twist. We enjoy Dorothy Parker's verse for its *wry* wit.

\ə\ **abut** \ᵊ\ **kitten, F table** \ər\ **further** \a\ **ash** \ā\ **ace** \ä\ **cot, cart**
\au̇\ **out** \ch\ **chin** \e\ **bet** \ē\ **easy** \g\ **go** \i\ **hit** \ī\ **ice** \j\ **job**

XYZ

xe·no·phile \'zen-ə-ˌfīl\ (*n*) one attracted to foreign people, manners, and styles. A *xenophile,* she spent all her time exploring foreign cultures.

xe·no·pho·bi·a \ˌzen-ə-'fō-bē-ə\ (*n*) fear and hatred of anything foreign. *Xenophobia* is directed against foreign people, not necessarily against foreign goods: even *xenophobes* patronize Chinese restaurants and buy Japanese TVs.

yearn \'yərn\ (*v*) desire; long. After the long run I *yearned* to sit down and soak my throbbing feet.

yen \'yen\ (*n*) longing; urge. She had a *yen* to get away and live on her own for a while.

yeo·man \'yō-mən\ (*n*) farmer who cultivates his own land; freeholder ranking below gentry. Could Belle love a plain honest *yeoman,* or had her head been turned by her fine gentleman admirers?

yoke \'yōk\ (*v*) join together, unite. I don't wish to be *yoked* to him in marriage, as if we were cattle pulling a plow. also (*n*).

yo·kel \'yō-kəl\ (*n*) country bumpkin. Many of Abe Lincoln's contemporaries regarded him as a *yokel* and laughed at his rustic mannerisms.

za·ny \'zā-nē\ (*adj*) crazy; comic. I can watch the Marx brothers' *zany* antics for hours.

zeal·ot \'zel-ət\ (*n*) fanatic; person who shows excessive zeal. Though Glenn was devout, he was no *zealot*; he never tried to force his beliefs on his friends.

ze·nith \'zē-nəth\ (*n*) point directly overhead in the sky; summit. When the sun was at its *zenith,* the glare was not as strong as at sunrise and sunset.

zeph·yr \'zef-ər\ (*n*) gentle breeze; west wind. When these *zephyrs* blow, it is good to be in an open boat under a full sail.

Notes

Notes

Notes

Notes